I0893382

On Arrows

Essays in British Architecture and Its Environments

Laurent Stalder

The MIT Press

Cambridge, Massachusetts
London, England

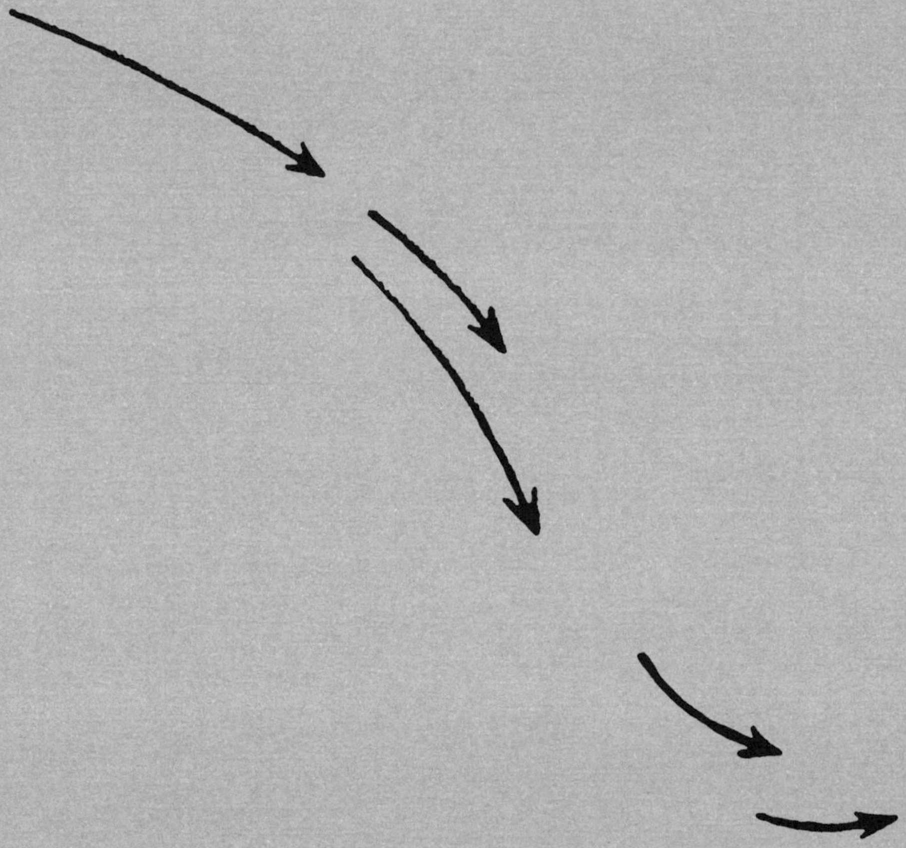

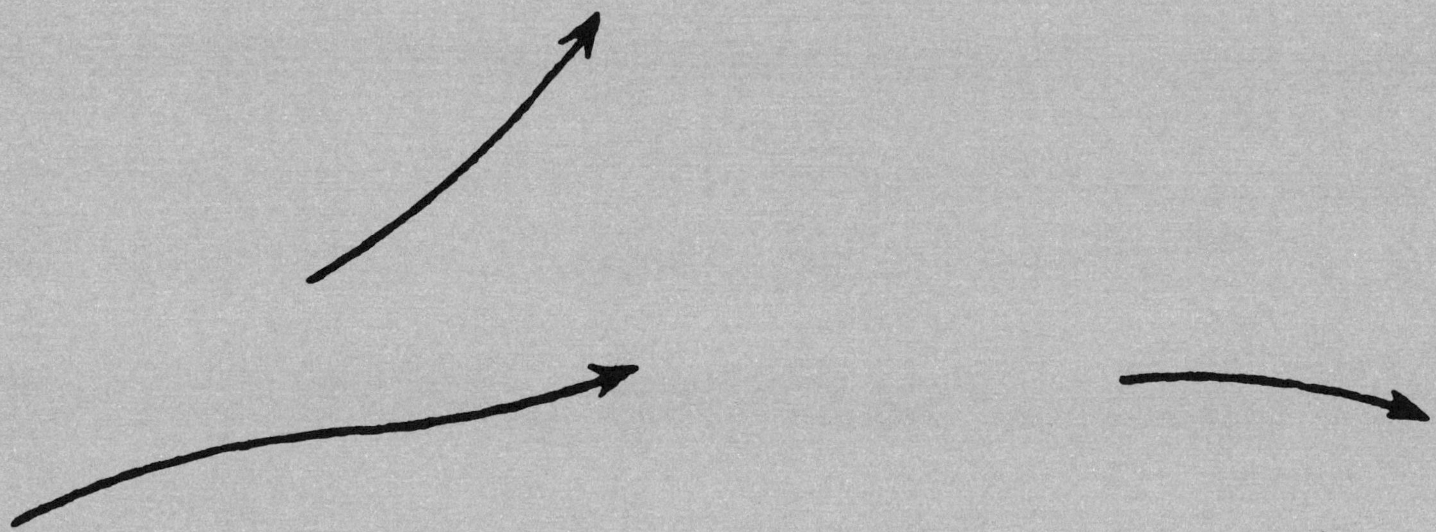

The essays that form this volume are either newly conceived or have been thoroughly rewritten, all deeply edited thanks to the help of Sarah Handelman. Parts of "Scientism" appeared in "'New Brutalism,' 'Topology' and 'Image': Some Remarks on the Architectural Debates in England around 1950," in the *Journal of Architecture* 13, no. 3 (2008). A previous version of "Arrows," limited to the work of one singular architect, was published as "Stirling's Arrows" in *AA Files* 72 (2016), with some sections co-authored with Moritz Gleich. An abridged version of "Milieu" was included in *A Companion to Architecture: The Nineteenth Century* (2017), edited by Martin Bressani and Christina Contandriopoulos. A shorter version of "Transparency" was published in German as "Glas. 1930–1970" in a volume edited by Susanne Hauser and Julia Weber, *Architektur in transdisziplinärer Perspektive* (2015) and translated for this publication by Jill Denton. "Interior" is a slightly rewritten version of "Interior Breakdown," first published in *Architecture through Drawing* (2019), edited by Desley Luscombe, Helen Thomas, and Niall Hobhouse. "Accidens" is an expanded version of a conference paper, "What Happens to Architecture" given at *Positions on Emancipation: Architecture between Aesthetics and Politics*, and published in 2017. The book's coda, "AS in DS," appeared in German in *Scholion* 6 (2010) and was translated for this publication by Jill Denton.

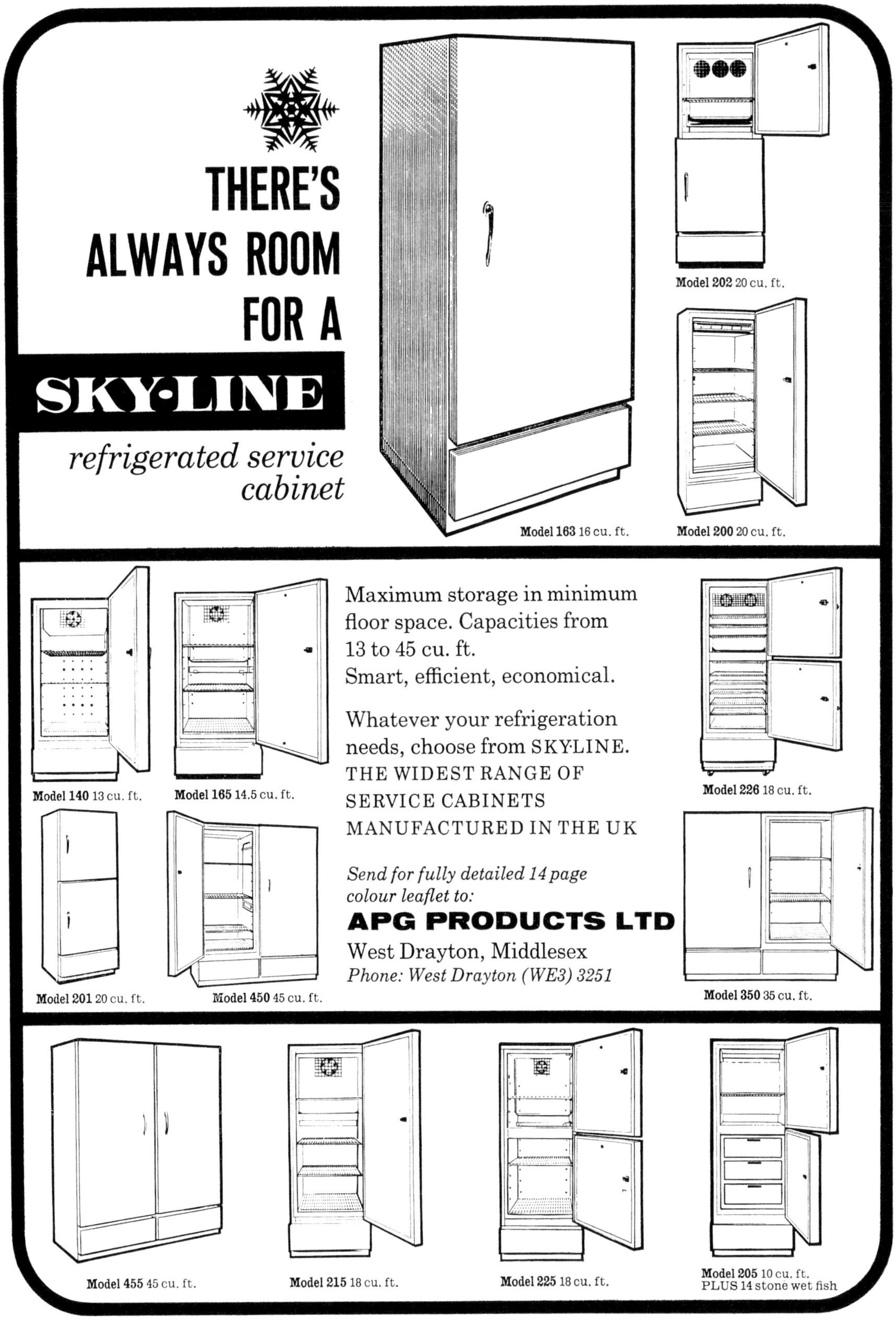
THERE'S
ALWAYS ROOM
FOR A
SKY·LINE
refrigerated service cabinet
Model 163 16 cu. ft.
Model 202 20 cu. ft.
Model 200 20 cu. ft.
Model 140 13 cu. ft.
Model 165 14.5 cu. ft.
Maximum storage in minimum floor space. Capacities from 13 to 45 cu. ft.
Smart, efficient, economical.
Whatever your refrigeration needs, choose from SKY·LINE.
THE WIDEST RANGE OF SERVICE CABINETS MANUFACTURED IN THE UK
Send for fully detailed 14 page colour leaflet to:
APG PRODUCTS LTD
West Drayton, Middlesex
Phone: West Drayton (WE3) 3251
Model 226 18 cu. ft.
Model 201 20 cu. ft.
Model 450 45 cu. ft.
Model 350 35 cu. ft.
Model 455 45 cu. ft.
Model 215 18 cu. ft.
Model 225 18 cu. ft.
Model 205 10 cu. ft.
PLUS 14 stone wet fish

← “There’s always room for a Skyline,” advertisement, *Architects’ Journal*, 1965

Prelude

→ Tall cupboard incorporating a refrigerator, designed for Hygena by George Fejér, *Architectural Design*, 1958

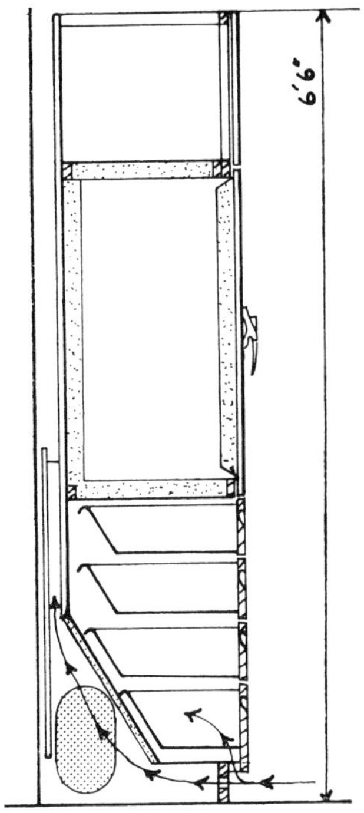

It is a small, rather inconspicuous drawing found in a 1958 issue of *Architectural Design*. A section, in black and white. Its graphical conventions could have been used in any other publication of the time to depict almost any other object: a radiator, light-fixture, or air-conditioner, or even a staircase, reading room, or city plan. In this particular drawing, however, the object is a refrigerator. As innocuous as the appliance may seem from today's perspective, looking back from a distance of almost two generations, the fridge was for a short moment pulled out of its anonymity to play a central part in postwar architectural design. It even became emblematic of a well-documented architectural debate spanning across Europe that involved the principal protagonists of the post-war years and their respective journals, as they fiercely disputed the heritage of what was claimed to have been a unified historic avant-garde.

It was in the June 1959 issue of *Casabella-continuità* that the fridge made its architectural debut (even if Nikita Khrushchev and Prince Philip had already been admiring the British model for some time). Writing as editor, the Milanese Ernesto Nathan Rogers labeled the English Reyner Banham, then literary editor of the *Architectural Review*, as "Custode dei Frigidaires" (Keeper of the Frigidaires), mocking his counterpart for what he perceived as a rather crude form of techno-philia. Just a few months earlier, Banham had accused the Italian postwar avant-garde of a "retreat from modern architecture," casting the Milanese

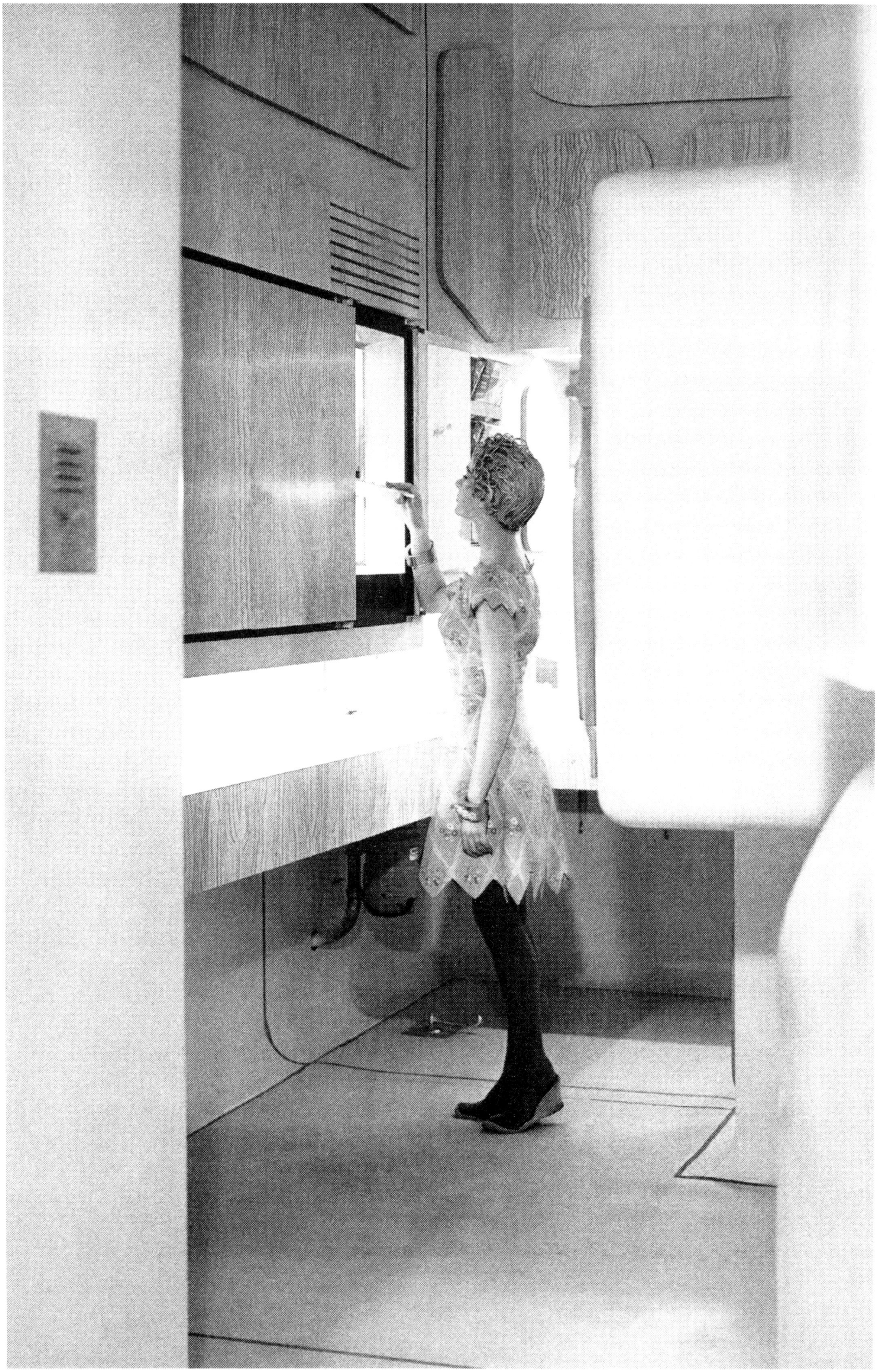

← Alison and Peter Smithson, House of the Future, Ideal Home Exhibition, 1956

especially as the worst offenders, guilty of a certain stylistic or historicist indulgence—that of the recently coined "Neoliberty." Depending on what side of the debate one was on, the fridge stood either for or against a commitment of the discipline to a second machine age.

The little drawing, however, points in another direction, beyond any stylistic preference, and stands out among the numerous representations of fridges of the time. It does not guarantee itself as a beacon of plenty, as seen in the American advertisements whose images Eduardo Paolozzi carefully transformed a few years earlier. Too large, too high, too new—and yet already part of a system of new things, like mixers, ovens, extractors, water- and waste-disposals, but also materials and furniture, all of which sought to seduce consumers with the promise of a living environment to come. Nor does the drawing depict an object of desire, with everything reduced to superficiality, as in *$he* (1958–1961) by Richard Hamilton, in which the wires of the freezer compete with the bottles of milk and Coca-Cola while the smooth surfaces echo the immaculate skin of a headless and legless bust. Neither does it represent a technological imaginary of any house of the future, as in the eponymous project by Alison and Peter Smithson, where the artificially lit open door of the fridge illuminated the surroundings. In such a representation, the refrigerator—already in use for more than thirty years by the late 1950s—merely stands in for the idea and potential of technology, since its own mechanics clearly belonged to the first machine age, not the second.

The black-and-white section drawing lacks any of this imagery. Instead, it stands out for its simplicity and scientific ambitions, aligning itself with another genealogy. If it appears somewhat conventional (a simple construction drawing in section showing the fridge and its wood encasing), its particularity lies in a chain of arrows that ascend from the kitchen floor along the back wall of a cupboard unit with the refrigerator and, below, a series of tall cupboards for storing food. These arrows describe the direction of the air, set into motion by a small compressor, as it removes the heat produced by cooling the fridge.

Similar drawings at a variety of scales can be found in many other publications from this period. In a scheme by the Building Research Station, the movement of food and utensils is depicted by meticulously drawn arrows of different sizes, each relating to the relative percentage of individual movements, from the sink to the worktop, table to larder—or the other way around, from the cooker or shelves back to the sink. In a different publication arrows are more schematically represented—as black rectangles with triangular heads, like to those found in communication diagrams, which unfold the sequences of activities throughout the space of the kitchen, as well as their feedback loops, from preparation to eating and washing up; from the "point of entry" up to that of "storage."

The frame can be widened further still. In *Homes for Today & Tomorrow*, a handbook published by the Ministry of Housing in 1961, rather than the object of the fridge or the space of the kitchen, it is now the whole apartment that is shot through by a series of soft arrows that adapt to the shape of the interiors and record various routes through the rooms. In a contemporaneous section from *Architectural Design*, drawn on an even larger scale, arrows made up of dotted lines map out the linear movement of waste, water, gas, and heat between a block of flats and a power station on the other side of the River Thames. The line of arrows finds its continuation, at least symbolically, at yet another scale and in another government report, *Traffic in Towns* (1963), which expands the reach of the arrow across the territory. At the same time, the motif is located at the opposite end of this ever-increasing scale. Returning to the refrigerator, as captured by another drawing, arrows fly across the section of an open unit as bows and loops of cold and warm air circulate inside. Even when depicting this level of detail, the drawing recalls the well-tempered workspaces illustrated in books of building physics.

› Eduardo Paolozzi, *It's a Psychological Fact Pleasure Helps Your Disposition*, 1948, part of *Ten Collages*, from *BUNK* 33

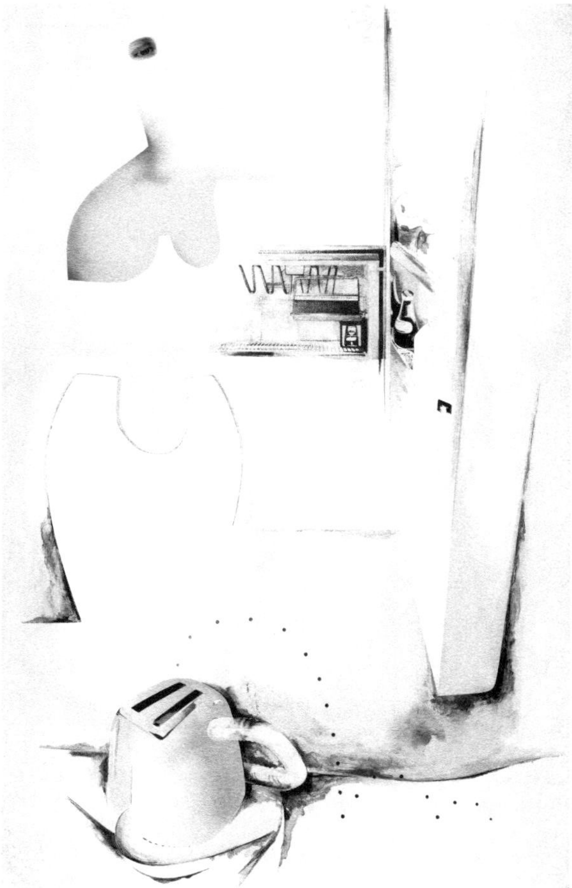

↘ Richard Hamilton, *$he*, 1958–1961

↓ Movement of food and utensils in the kitchen, experiment conducted by the Building Research Station, 1953

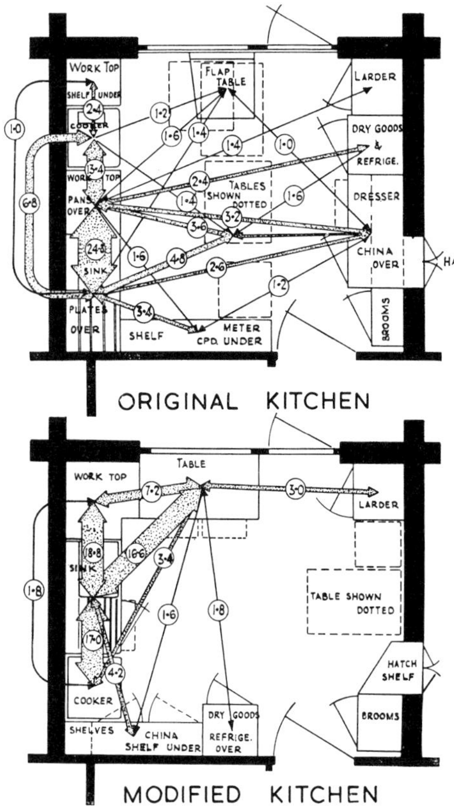

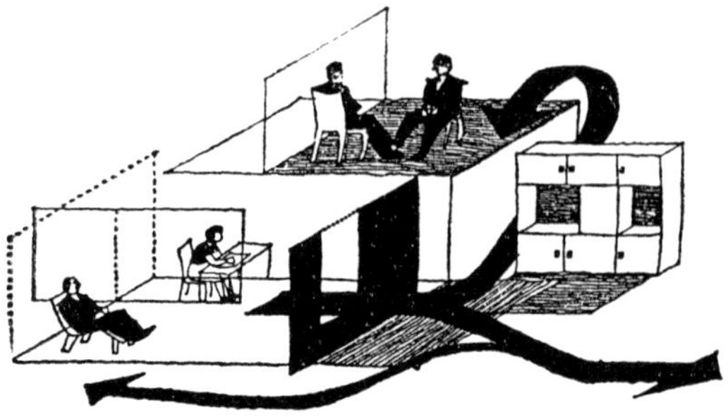

↑ "New Patterns of Living," *Homes for Today & Tomorrow*, 1961

↓ Powell and Moya, central heating and hot water system, Churchill Gardens, Pimlico, 1951

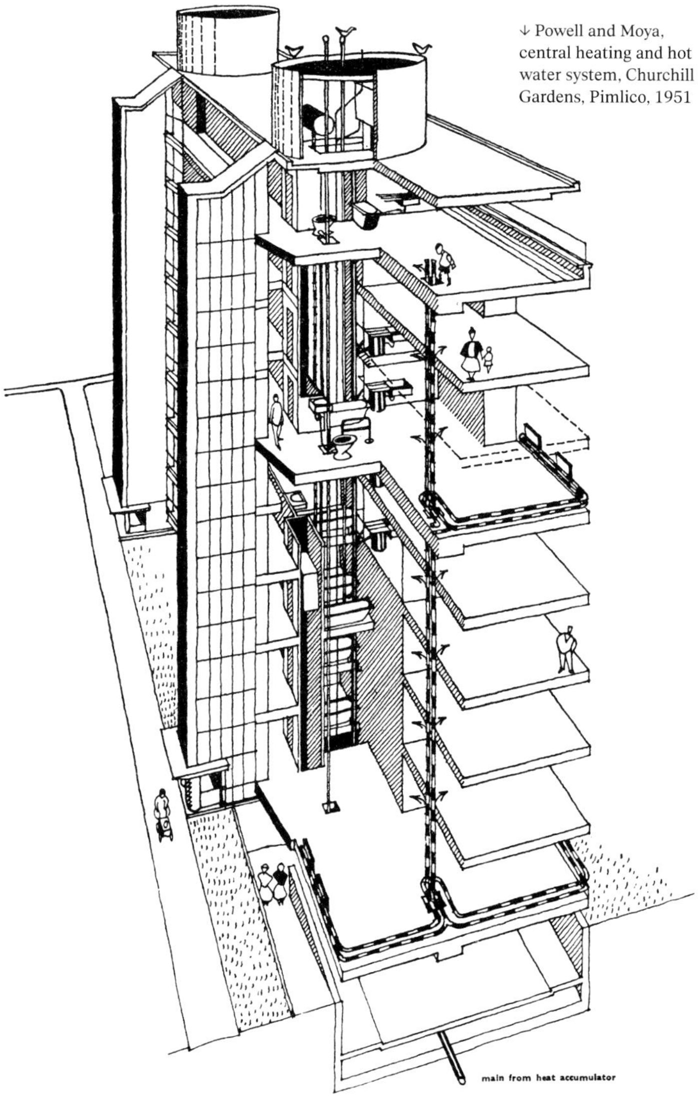

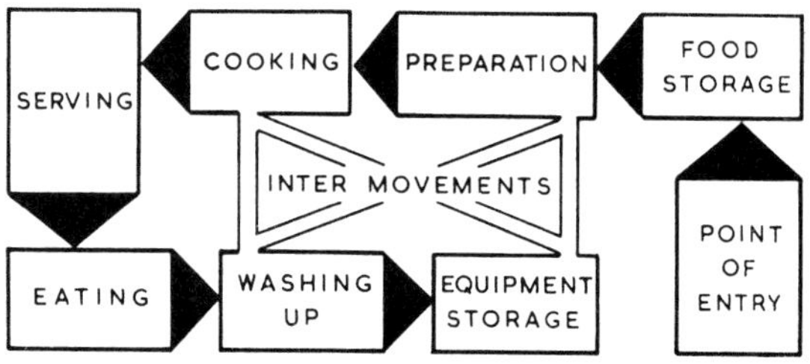

↑ Sequence diagram of movement in a domestic kitchen, *Architects' Journal*, 1959

↓ Powell and Moya, section showing district heating system, Churchill Gardens, Pimlico, 1951

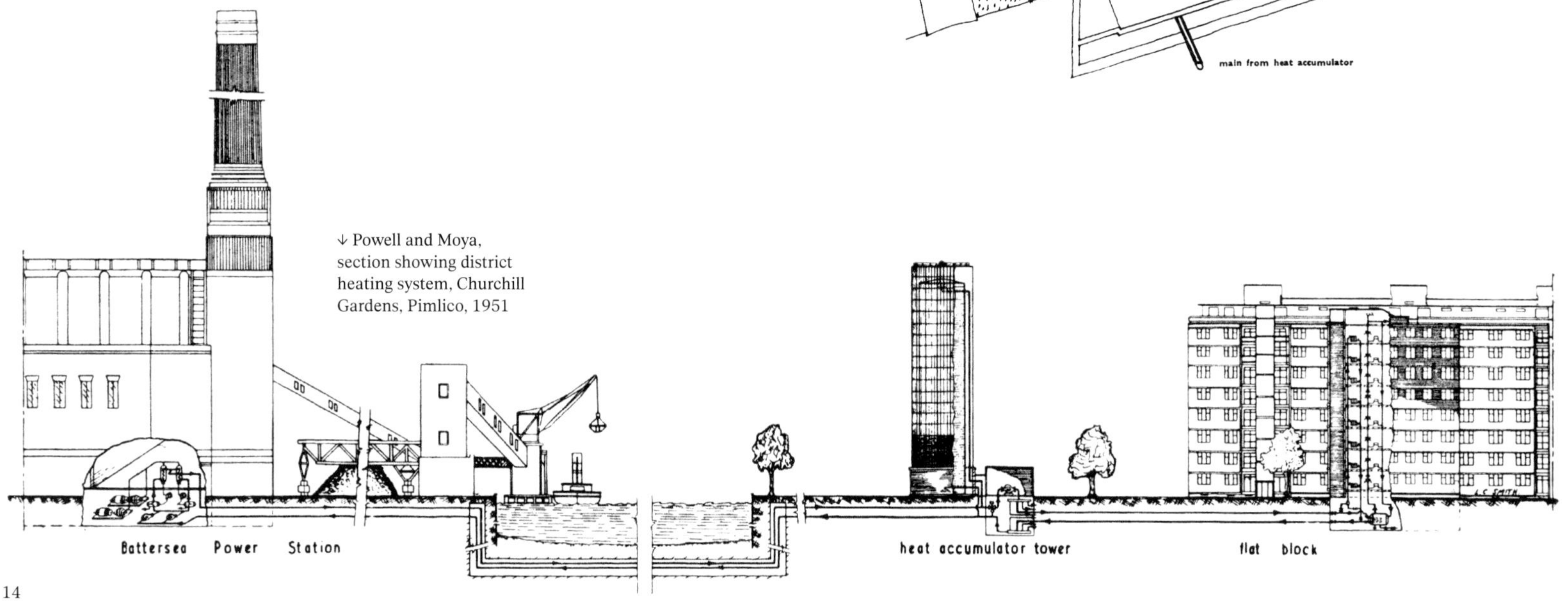

↓ Map of Britain, detail from advertisement for Colt Shingles All-Weather Roofing, *Architects' Journal*, 1954

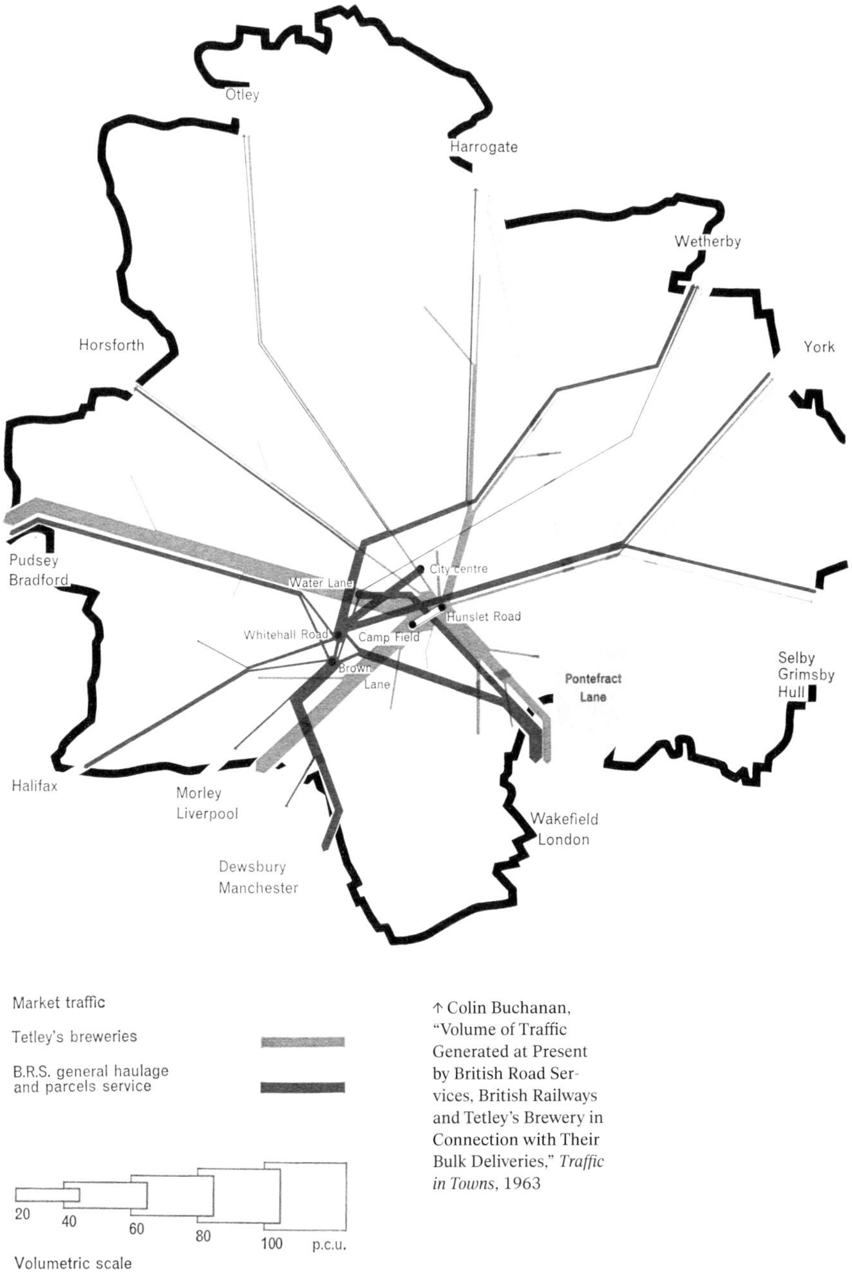

↑ Colin Buchanan, "Volume of Traffic Generated at Present by British Road Services, British Railways and Tetley's Brewery in Connection with Their Bulk Deliveries," *Traffic in Towns*, 1963

↓ "A Taximan's Solution to London's Traffic Problem," *Architects' Journal*, 1947

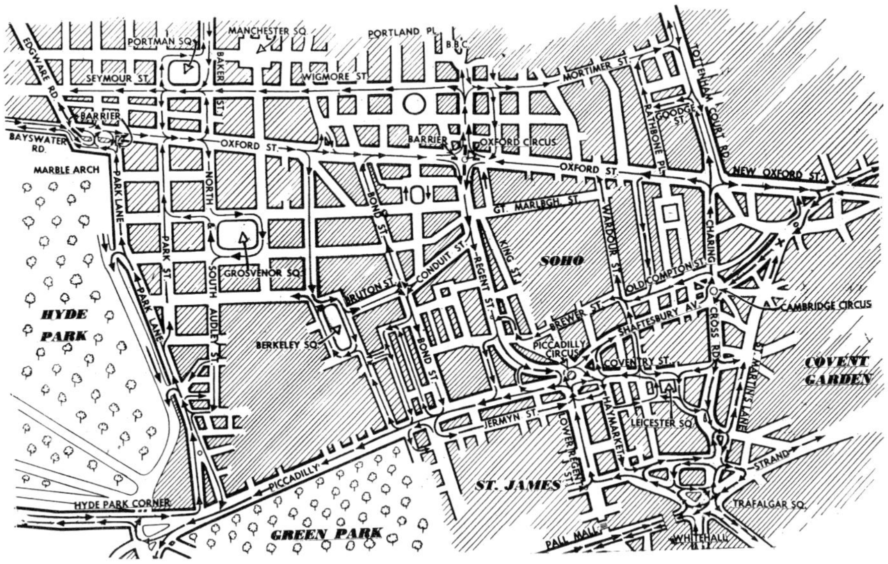

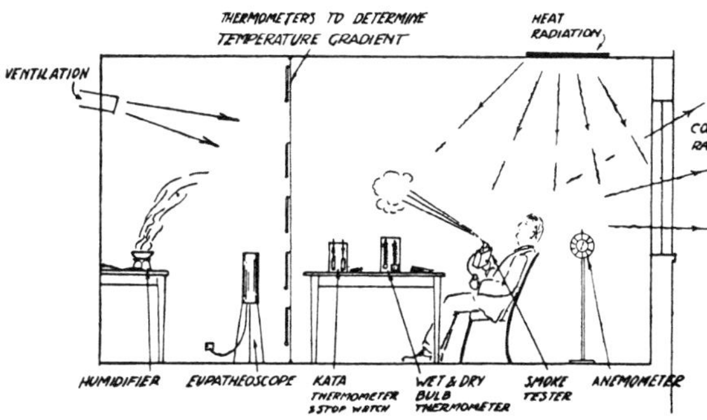

↑ "Means for Determining the State of Comfort," Oscar Faber and J. R. Kell, *Heating and Air-Conditioning*, 1958

→ Diagram of a refrigerated unit for storing perishable food, *Architectural Design*, 1954

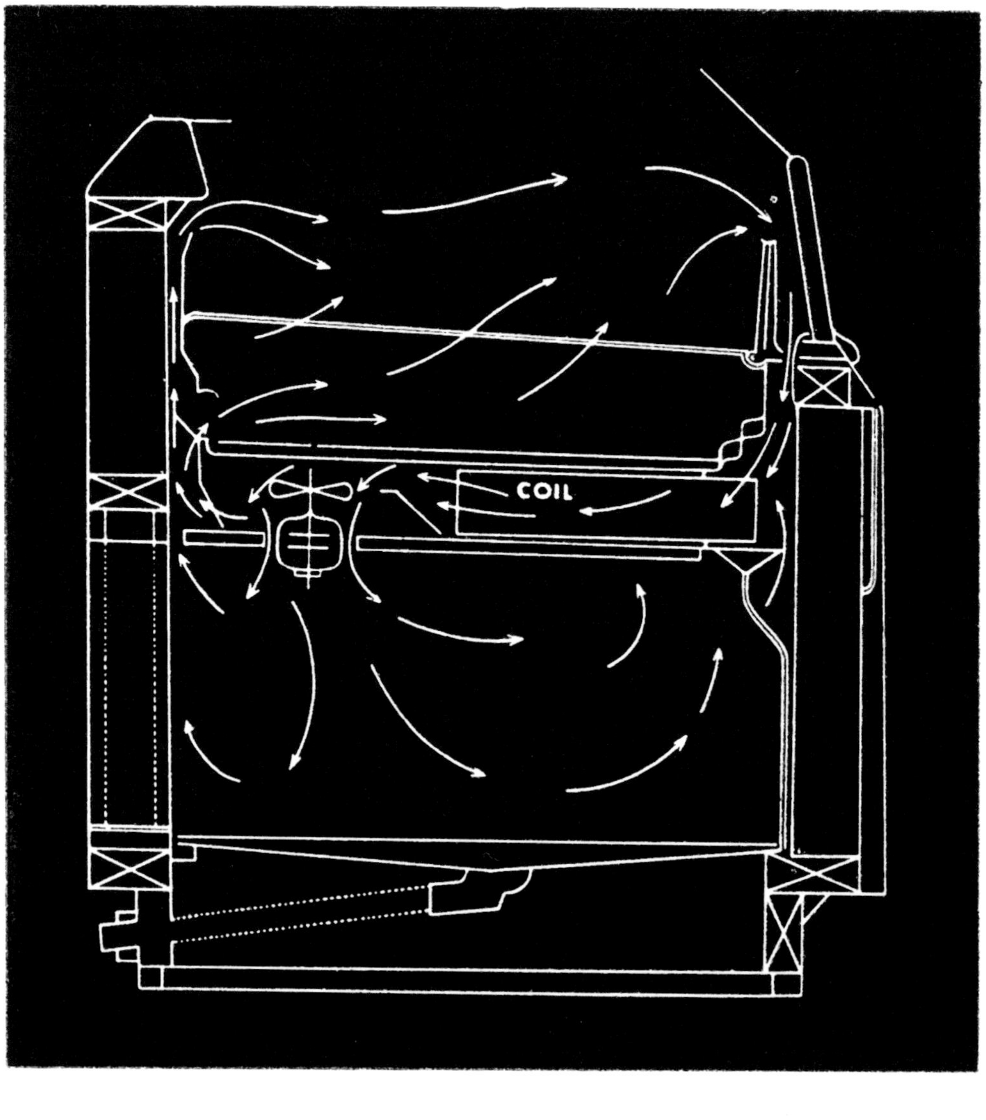

Despite the arrow's ubiquity in the 1950s, its presence in the field of architecture lasted for only a short period. Twenty-five years earlier one finds barely any at all within architectural publications, and fifteen years later they have all but disappeared. However, the figure existed long before it was adopted by architects, originating in classical studies of mechanics to illustrate the motion of bodies under the action of mechanical forces. From there it entered the fields of engineering and social sciences in the nineteenth century, where it was used to investigate movement within buildings, before finding its way into architectural design following the Second World War. The arrow therefore records the movements or actions in a specific environment while prefiguring them.

If the term performance is rare within architectural publications of the 1950s (on the few occasions that it does appear, it is understood from a technical perspective and not yet from one of pure economy), the widespread use of the arrow by architects and planners illustrates that the concept was well established, as were the techniques used to reflect and design it. While the modern concept of function allocates a particular task to a particular object, space, or building, performance deals with the way these tasks operate. It finds its expression at different levels: from that of materials, whose "physical functions" are analyzed in laboratories and regulated by standards; to the spatial articulations of new programs whose "activities" are precisely mapped; to the obsolescence of individual buildings and their parts whose lifespans can be accurately predicted; to the level of infrastructure, whose distribution can be assessed. Breaking the scale of the individual unit or typology, neither the singularity nor the autonomy of the individual parts (i.e., the fridge, the glass panel, or the road) come into focus, but that of the whole system: from the kitchen unit to the climate system, all the way up to the urban network, whose parts have to be coordinated, not because one is more important than another, but because they happen in simultaneity. This awareness of performance in architecture must therefore be understood not as reducible to a new form of calculable rationality, but as a new set of rules: topology (instead of geometry), patterns (instead of proportions), layers of transparency (instead of the open plan), environment (instead of space).

In its diagrammatic dimension, the arrow thus expresses and drives an increasing understanding of the discipline of architecture as both resulting from and impacting on its milieu—that is, the people, activities, orientation, programs, and other actors that make up any environment. Historically determined (often with nationalist undertones) in the nineteenth century and functionally legitimized via the interwar modernists, by the postwar period the correct management and control of natural and artificial factors provided the framework and point of reference for almost every design task.

The arrow in the postwar years points to this new environment, whose meaning and limits were however still being debated: understood from one extreme as a "well-tempered environment," both defined through and equipped by any available new technology; seen in another way as a historically legitimated *ambiente* determined by the preexisting factors of a site; or, alternatively, viewed as a socially informed "habitat" related to specific modes of living. Beyond these definitions, the concept of environment had already found its concrete manifestation in the architecture of the time. Within the art historical debates about the style to come the refrigerator may have served as the target to hit. However, the arrows twirling behind the appliance, as well as those separated by the perfectly insulated, flawless walls buzzing inside, point in another direction. Rather than encapsulating a style to come, it represented the very materialization of a new environmental understanding, opening the door to its precise mapping, conception, design, and realization.

Architects : Allison and Peter Smithson A/ARIBA. *Consultant Engineers : Ove Arup and Partners.*

Hunstanton Secondary Modern School — a completely welded structure

The steelwork to this fine modern building has interesting features. Allison and Peter Smithson have used the steel to support, define and ornament the whole. Ove Arup's design, based on the plastic theory evolved by Professor Baker of Cambridge University, necessitated all-welded construction of the highest standards at works and on the site.

A view of the Hall showing the clean lines of the stairs.

The slender lines of the lattice girders accentuate the spaciousness of the Assembly Hall and Gymnasium.

WHEN THE STRUCTURAL STEEL IS BY BOULTON AND PAUL IT'S A FIRST CLASS JOB

NORWICH · LONDON · BIRMINGHAM

CRC4CE

← "Hunstanton Secondary Modern School— a completely welded structure," advertisement for Boulton and Paul, *Architectural Review*, 1955

Scientism

The role of architectural media cannot be overstated in the emergence of a new generation of British architects and critics in the 1950s, all of whom seemed more concerned with placing themselves within a modern historiography than with determining their position in a longer genealogy of architecture and practice.[1] This self-designation made them the inheritors of a project that began at the turn of the century and reached its zenith with the pioneers of the interwar period. But unlike the work of their predecessors, the swiftness with which this latter-day rupture took hold was almost instantaneous. Where once the collusion of history and modern architecture had gradually made its way onto the international stage through the publication of books, the sheer rapidity and frequency of the postwar architectural press reversed this project, collapsing the space between the production of contemporary architecture and the writing of its history to get it all on the same page.

Exemplary of this mindset is the January 1955 issue of *Architectural Design*, whose technical editor, Theo Crosby, reports of an "overdue explosion" in architectural theory—one that had put an end, at least in Britain, to the dull imitations of Le Corbusier and misconstructions of traditionalism.[2] The first detonation was located in Alison

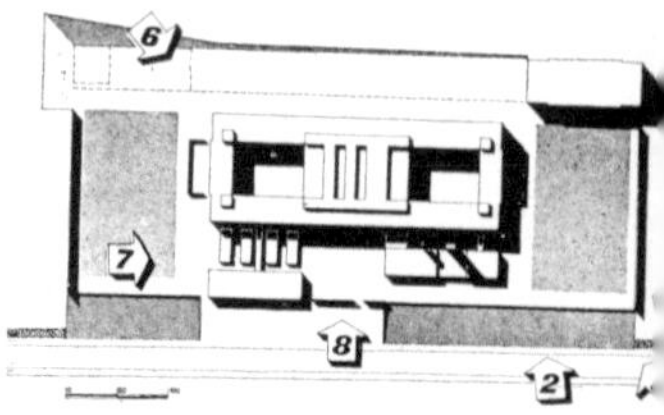

2 Looking toward gymnasium from the north-west.

SCHOOL AT HUNSTANTON

3 The western end of the main block.

4 Eastward view along the north side of the school.

5 The gymnasium from the south-west.

6 The entire complex of buildings seen from the south-east.

7 The eastern end of the main block.

and Peter Smithson's Hunstanton School, completed the year before and which he describes as a succinct "illustration of New Brutalism."[3] As the historian Reyner Banham would meticulously reconstruct just ten years later in his monograph *The New Brutalism: Ethic or Aesthetic?*, while also reinforcing the modern legacy, the term had been in use since the interwar period by Le Corbusier.[4] He had introduced it as early as 1923, when he defined architecture as the transformation of "matériaux bruts" into "rapports émouvants."[5] By 1946 the adjective had established itself as an attitude, in times of scarcity, towards construction, thanks to the Unité's *béton brut*, and by 1948 it was a distinct style, following Jean Dubuffet's founding of the Compagnie de l'Art Brut.

New Brutalism—or *nybrutalism*, as it was first called—found its first expression both architecturally and rhetorically in Hans Asplund's commentary on the Villa Göth before it was quickly co-opted in Britain.[6] The phrase was finally introduced to an audience beyond knowing practitioners in December 1953 when Alison Smithson, writing in *Architectural Design*, used it to describe a raw finish for a proposal for terraced housing on a bomb site in Soho.[7] According to Smithson, New Brutalism was based on the conditions of "a society that had nothing" and, nothing consisted of a "bare concrete brickwork and wood." Less than three years later, Crosby located the first true explosion of New Brutalism in the Smithsons' Hunstanton School. Before the dust had even settled, Reyner Banham had identified both the school and the unbuilt Soho house as the two "points of architectural reference by which the New Brutalism in architecture may be defined."[8] But like any number of iconoclasts, the movement was short-lived, a result of the incompatibilities between architectural practice and architectural discourse and their different temporalities. As quickly as it launched a formative debate, it also met its "sad end," as Robin Boyd would put it in 1967, in the title of his review of Banham's *The New Brutalism: Ethic or Aesthetic?*[9]

The initial blast called New Brutalism was quickly and widely recognized, both by its opponents who saw it as merely the latest stylistic trap, and by advocates such as Crosby, Banham, and Philip Johnson, who perceived it as both a radical turn in architectural thinking away from the historicizing of the discipline and a reaction against the search for a "new empiricism," or "new humanism," as coined by their slightly older contemporaries of the immediate postwar years.[10] However, a remark by the critic and historian Robin Middleton, almost fifteen years after the phrase was first introduced in print might well summarize the flattening of the ambitions first expressed. In his short history of the movement, he offered no further insight to the contemporary consensus on the term other than that it generally stood for, as he ironically put it, "exposed timber or rough brickwork" or, more often, "rough, in situ concrete."[11]

The very forums where these debates took place were far from coarse but rather the slick surfaces of avant-garde architecture magazines, where even the roughest of materials was reduced to a flat, publishable image for mass-consumption, so much celebrated by Richard Hamilton[12] and the Smithsons themselves.[13] To illustrate their Soho house in 1953 the Smithsons had relied on a set of simple drawings of orthogonal plans, sections, and elevations composed of black lines and white surfaces. Materiality was reduced here to hatchings. Similarly, the presentation of the school in Hunstanton in Banham's first historical assessment relied on a single small black-and-white photograph with a central view onto the gymnasium. But the flattening of New Brutalism (again, via Hunstanton) went beyond the writing of a new modern history: soon after the school was completed its images became an advertising device for the firm responsible for its construction.

The discussions on New Brutalism that followed continued along these lines, with the protagonists themselves contributing largely to this state of affairs. If the Smithsons had been the first to put a name (at least in English) to the movement, they were also one of the first to articulate the translation of architecture into advertising, and vice versa. In 1956 they ran a photo of Hunstanton's labs not to explain an aspect of New Brutalism but to illustrate their article "But Today We Collect Ads." Ads, they write, "are packed with information—data of a way of life and a standard of living which they are simultaneously inventing and documenting. ... The influence on mass standards and mass aspirations of advertising is now infinitely stronger than the pace-setting of avant-garde architects."[14] This was as true for prefabricated building elements as it was for the mass-produced appliances that featured in Hunstanton.

For those who had wished to avoid this short-circuiting between building and image there were still the technical reports written up on these very projects and published in the very same avant-garde journals.[15] One example worth noting is Dargan Bullivant's account of the construction of Hunstanton School. Published in September 1953, before the building's completion and two years before Crosby's article, the piece combines site photos with large-scale construction details, plans, and a thorough description of the structure. More than any other report of the time, it provides an in-depth look at the material conditions of a building that would become the cornerstone and de facto shorthand of New Brutalism. Bullivant reveals the technical ingenuity behind the rough visual expression that would attract the attention of architects, critics, and readers. "As found" was not a natural state.

According to the report, the framework of the school was "fabricated by welding the beams and stanchions of rolled steel section into frames on the site. ... The complete frame was then picked up by a caterpillar crane, carried to its position on the site slab and bolted down."

To the architects of the twenties 'Japan' was the Japanese house of prints and paintings, the house with its roof off, the plane bound together by thin black lines. (To quote Gropius 'the whole country looks like one gigantic basic design course'.) In the thirties Japan meant gardens, the garden entering the house, the tokonoma.

For us it would be the objects on the beaches, the piece of paper blowing about the street, the throw-away object and the pop-package.

For today we collect Ads.

↑ Alison and Peter Smithson, "But Today We Collect Ads," *Ark*, 1956

← "School in Hunstanton. Comment by Philip Johnson as an American Follower of Mies van der Rohe," *Architectural Review*, 1954

6, 7

8, 9

10, 11

12

6. *Beams and stanchions being laid in place, under lifting tackle.*

7. *Welding webs of beams to stanchion, before lifting into vertical position.*

8. *Whole frame held vertical by tackle, flanges and beams welded to stanchions.*

9. *Whole frame turned upside down and then lifted up by the feet so as to enable the underside of flanges to be welded down hand.*

10 *and* **11.** *Completed frames carried to their position on the site slab.*

12. *Detail of site welding between beam and stanchion; note stanchions strengthened by stiffeners.*

← ↘ Dargan Bullivant, "Hunstanton Secondary Modern School," *Architectural Design*, 1953

The facing frames of window size were mounted on this structural framework, serving as "lateral braying to the structural frames and at the same time as window frames and transoms and as a facing to the first floor and eaves." The solution for the corners proved more complicated: "where the structural frame changes direction, two stanchions are used at the internal corners. The two stanchions are joined together and sealed by an angle welded to both." Special attention was paid to the outer walls: "The facing frames welded to the main frames are glazed directly without sub-frames." The connection was correspondingly intricate since the glaziers required a certain tolerance between the frames. Brass dowels, aluminum fins (produced using the new cold-impact method), and various plastic seals enabled the glass to be fixed in a break-proof manner. The brick walls in turn were double leaf, attached to the steel profiles with metal wires. A water barrier of bitumen coating was inserted between them.[16] Yet, to properly fit into the frames, the corners of the bricks had to be cut away with a circular saw.

In addition to his construction analysis, Bullivant devotes a separate section of the report to the statics calculated on the base of plastic theory, adopted into British building law just five years earlier.[17] Its application at Hunstanton proved technically and economically advantageous as it allowed the architects to use smaller profiles for the roof of the main halls.[18] "An all-welded structure, such as the one designed for Hunstanton," writes Bullivant, "offers economies in the amount of steel used providing the method of design is made to take account of the fully rigid nature of the frame."[19]

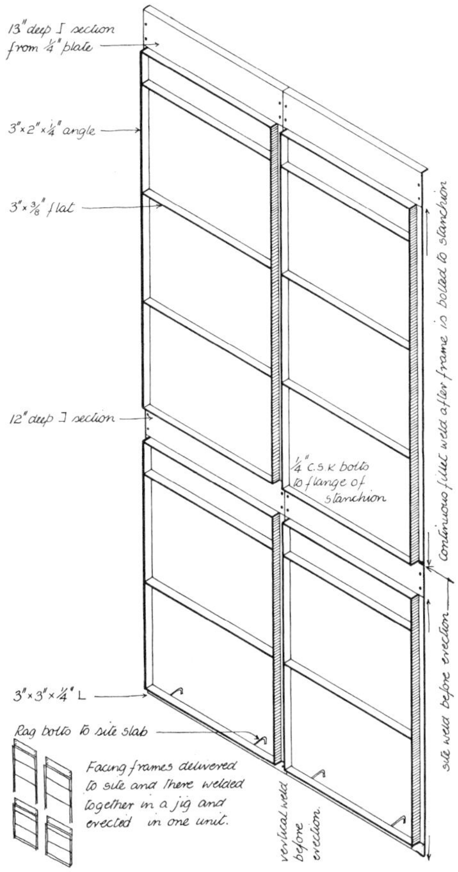

29. *An isometric of the facing frames as welded together for bolting to the structural frame prior to welding as shown in* **25** *and* **28.**

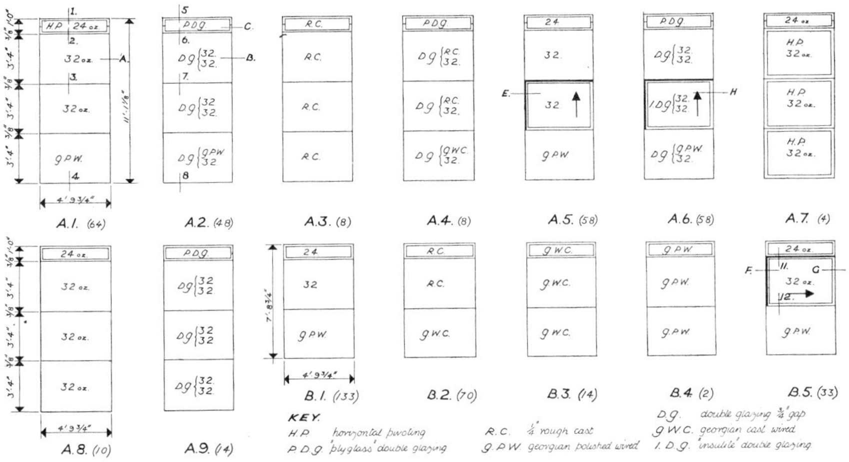

20. *The glazing assemblies used within the facing frames; the numbers in the brackets indicate the quantities used.*

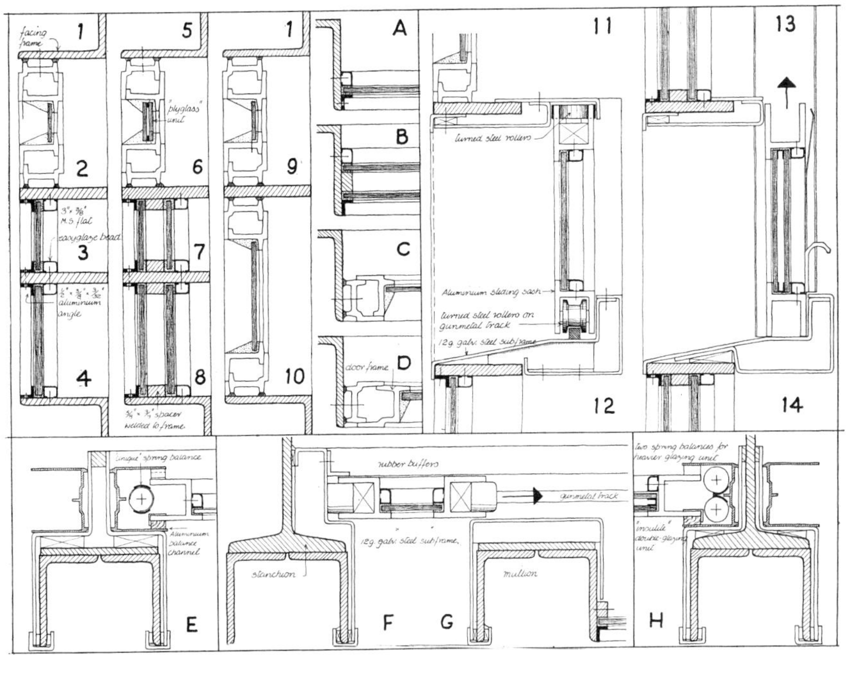

21. *Details of the facing frame glazing,* ¼ in. = 1 *in.*

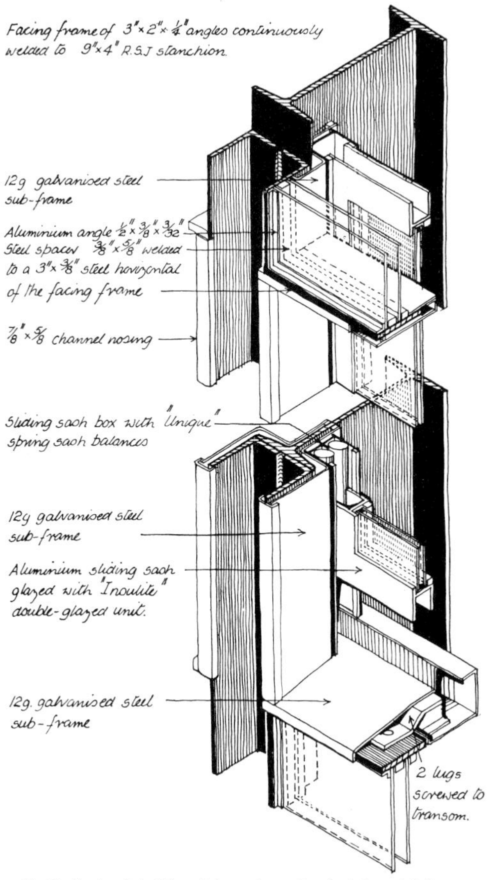

31. *Detail of vertical sliding window and pressed steel sub-frames bolted to facing frames. For details see* **21.**

The results of this advancement had prompted Philip Johnson to wonder in his own 1954 review of Hunstanton if in America "our steel is heavier." If Bullivant had offered a comprehensive account of how, technically, New Brutalism was realized, then Reyner Banham's own overview, "The New Brutalism," published two years later, would do the same for history—but by this time all of the details observed by Bullivant were almost entirely forgotten.

Hunstanton is a perfect example of the swift passage of images into buildings and back again. On the one hand, the "constructive and visual transparency between structure and appearance," as Claire Zimmerman has observed, made Hunstanton easy to transpose into a set of indexical images for the architectural press.[20] On the other hand, while the so-called image of Hunstanton became the poster child for New Brutalism, critics were also comparing it to references used by the Smithsons as they designed the project.[21] This would have included Mies van der Rohe's Metals and Minerals Buildings at the Illinois Institute of Technology, published in 1947 in the *Architects' Journal*. As Johnson would write, Hunstanton respected the Miesian "steel-glass-and-brick-filled-frame grammar," and its plan was "not only radical, but also very Mies-like in its nature."[22] In this process of building up and flattening down, the buildings themselves lose their materiality and specificity in favor of the indexicality of their expression. The transformation of a building into "data," as the Smithsons argued about advertising, may explain the success of the school and its worldwide diffusion.

To avoid being seen only as a "Mies-like" building, rather than as the benchmark for a new movement, other arguments were needed to support Hunstanton's revolutionary character. Reyner Banham would provide with his essay the methodological and analytical tools to elevate an avant-garde aspiration into an art-historical movement. Indeed, the argumentation through images, so important in the postwar years, had been central to art historical methodologies since at least the end of the nineteenth century—and in Henry Russell Hitchcock's and Philip Johnson's three-part codification of the International Style it found an appealing application within contemporary architecture. That relationship continued well into the twentieth century and can be equally found in Banham's much-cited, three-part reading of Hunstanton: a "clear exhibition of structure,' the "valuation of materials 'as found,'" and the building's "memorability as image."[23]

Initially the essay seems to follow the formalist trajectory by positioning Hunstanton, the house in Soho, and the 1953 Independent Group exhibition *Parallel of Life and Art*, edited by Alison and Peter Smithson, Nigel Henderson, and Ronald Jenkins, within a "cult of ugliness" that runs counter to the "photographic beauty" of its predecessors. But a few pages later, Banham expands this formalist reading by precisely referring to the notion of image: in the best Vitruvian tradition, he writes, good architecture emerges from the right interaction of structure, function, and form. Great architecture, however, has to be "conceptual" to become "image-making." Along with the school at Hunstanton, the examples used to make this distinction include Santa Maria in Todi, a painting by Jackson Pollock, the terrace of the Unité, the 1954 Cadillac Cabrio, the Lever Building in New York, and every photograph used in *Parallel of Life and Art*.[24]

These examples are striking since they refer neither to the modernist canon nor to buildings alone, but rather to a precise methodological framework, as laid out in contemporary art history. As a former student of the Warburg-affiliated Courtauld Institute, Banham seems to borrow from Erwin Panofsky's iconology and its definition of image as "secondary meaning" or "allegory" to establish connections between form and concept, thus situating any work of art inside a precise cultural framework.[25] Furthermore, in citing Santa Maria in Todi, Banham takes up one of the main examples given by Rudolf Wittkower in *Architectural Principles*. He had identified Santa Maria as the personification of the "symbolic values" of its time,[26] whose harmonic perfection reflected for the Renaissance man that of the universe. Banham continues this line by suggesting that Pollock's paintings, the 1954 Cadillac Cabrio and the Lever Building occupy a similar role—one that is deeply interlocked within the cultural framework of the "Second Machine Age" and its ordering principles.

Besides its status as a unique piece of architectural criticism in defense of the avant-garde, Banham's essay surpasses its contemporaries (and, one should add, its successors) through its fluent use of art-historical methodologies to locate a double-shift within contemporary British architectural writing. First is the move from an understanding of architectural history as a form of connoisseurship (perhaps best illustrated by Banister Fletcher's *A History of Architecture*) to an academic discipline firmly grounded in the methods of continental art and cultural history as introduced in the 1930s by émigrés in London, especially those from the Warburg Circle. The second shift, and also what makes the essay significant, is the transposition of these methods not only for the study of history, but for an outline of an architecture to come. Banham was fully aware of these transformations and situated his position on New Brutalism somewhere between a historical codification (like cubism) and a programmatic outcry (like futurism). Through this operative approach, Banham is able to define a new movement while grounding its rupture in the broader context of cultural history. Taking an admirable shortcut, he situates contemporary architecture both in relation to a formal chronology and to scientific progress, merging two independent discourses and blurring their differences.

A good example of this is Banham's description of Alison and Peter Smithsons' competition entry for Sheffield University with its "circulation routes" that flourish on the exterior and the "large blocks of topologically similar spaces." Banham writes: "now...the roles [between Platonic geometry and topology] are reversed, topology becomes the dominant and geometry becomes the subordinate discipline." Similar to his earlier use of image, this reference to the mathematical term of topology should not be understood simply as another counter-distinction, this time from the geometrical order (and proportional systems) of classical architecture (modernism included), since the mathematical term can only partially be applied to architectural discourse. Rather, the adoption of scientific language was an attempt to engage with the "symbolic values" (to invoke Wittkower) of postwar architecture.

Topology was, so to say, in the air. The topic had surfaced publicly in the 1950s with a special issue devoted to it in *Scientific American*.[27] Traditionally a subdivision of mathematics, it investigated the relationships between individual positions that themselves remain untouched by changes in dimension or form, such as the non-orientable surfaces of the Möbius strip or the Klein bottle, or reversible rubber tubing and the Königsberg bridge problem.[28] In the late 1930s the crystallographer John Desmond Bernal had introduced the concept into the field of urbanism and architecture. During a lecture at the RIBA in 1937 titled "Architecture and Science," which covered the potential of mathematics in form-finding, materials research, and sociological investigations, he described "topology" as a method for optimizing circulation in buildings.[29]

Banham seems to draw on this definition in his description of the topological organization at Sheffield that encompassed the "qualities of penetration, circulation and inside and out" and even collapses the domains of science and of architecture, when calling topology a "discipline of architecture."[30] But his deployment of the term is a matter of style, not science, at least at the level of the printed image. The Sheffield project is illustrated by a fairly conventional perspective drawing of the site entrance superposed with a plan in order to give the exact viewpoint. The focus is correspondingly placed (in the modernist tradition) more on the plasticity of the ramps and footbridges than

→ Reyner Banham, "The New Brutalism," *Architectural Review*, 1955

pollock

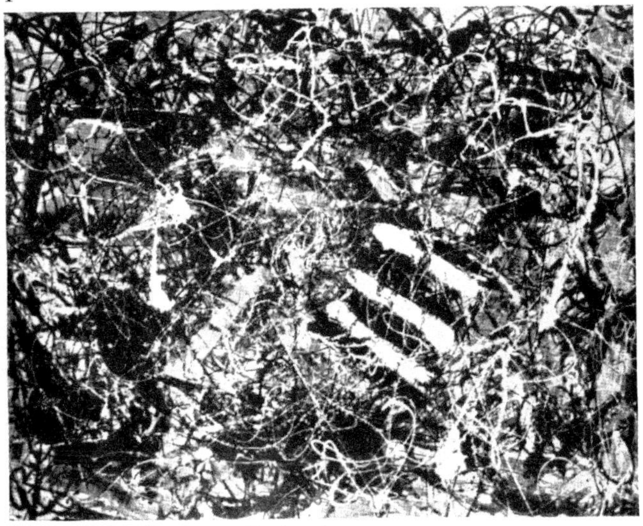

Painting, 1953—a-formal composition in action.

henderson

Sgraffiti on a Window (photograph)—image of human as well as formal value.

Parallel of Life and Art—exhibition of 100 Brutalist images.

burri

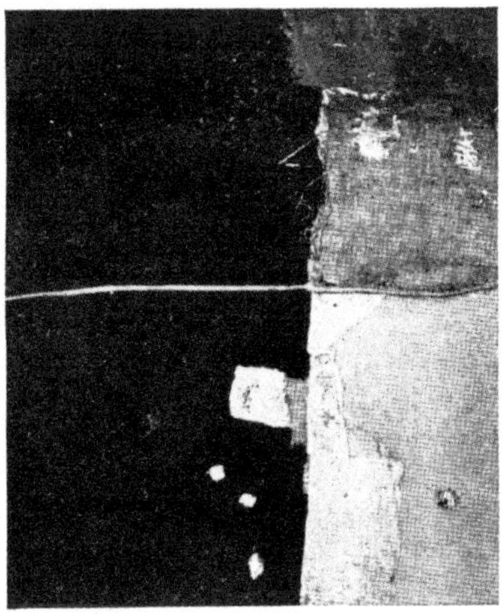

NEW BRUTALISM

Painting on burlap—typically Brutalist in his attitude to materials, Burri accords the burlap the same visual value as the paint it carries.

cordell

Figure, 1955—'anti-aesthetic' human image.

paolozzi

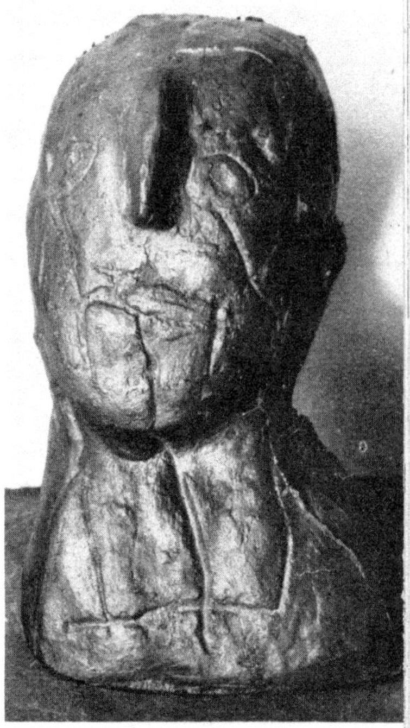

Head, 1953—'sophisticated primitivism.'

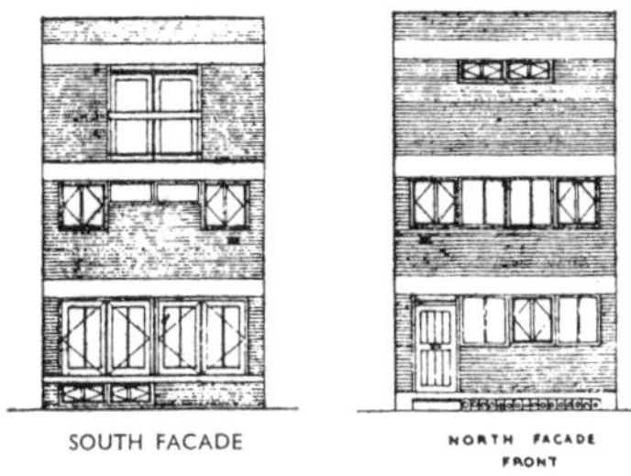

The first building to be categorized as Brutalist, this project for a house in Soho (A. & P. Smithson) exhibits not only the emphasis on materials and structure, but

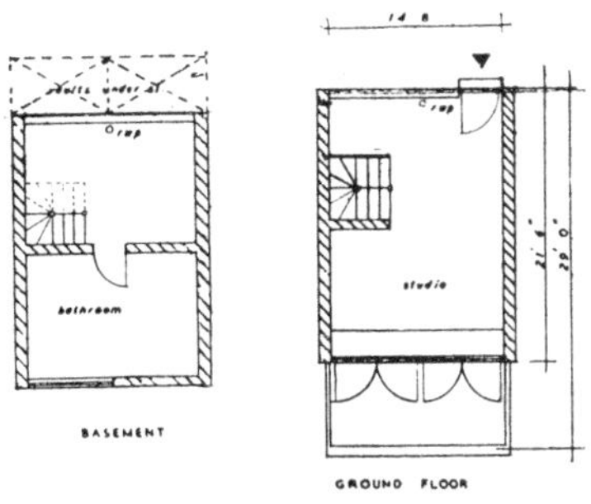

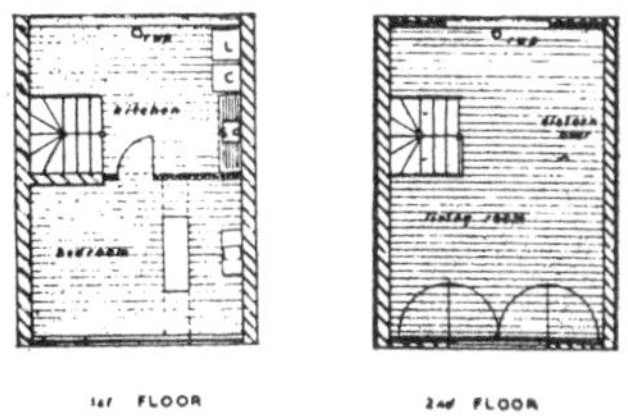

also the compositional formality of early Brutalism.

School at Hunstanton (A. & P. Smithson), first completed New Brutalist building, view toward gymnasium.

Coventry Cathedral competition entry (A. & P. Smithson) dramatic visual image created by spectacular structure, raised on a plan of Neo-Palladian symmetry—their last formal plan, 1951.

Yale Art Centre (architects: Kahn and Orr)—formality, expressed structure, exposed materials; the most truly Brutalist building in the New World.

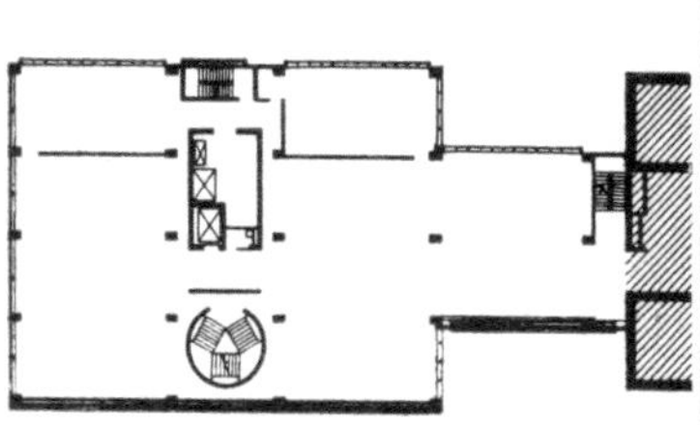

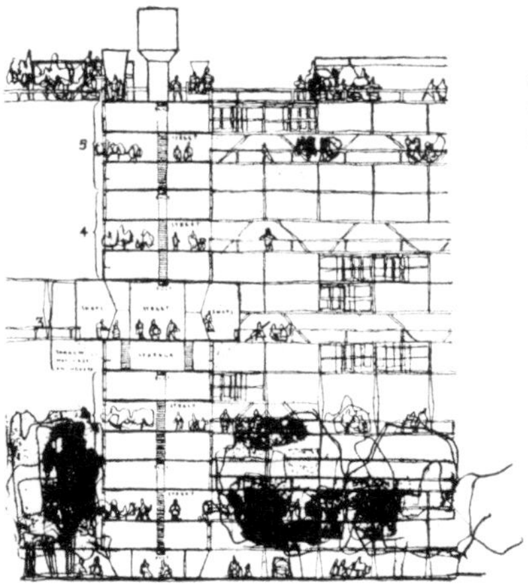

Golden Lane re-development project, shows Smithsons turn against geometry and formality, placing increased visual e phasis on site, circulation, habitation and human presen

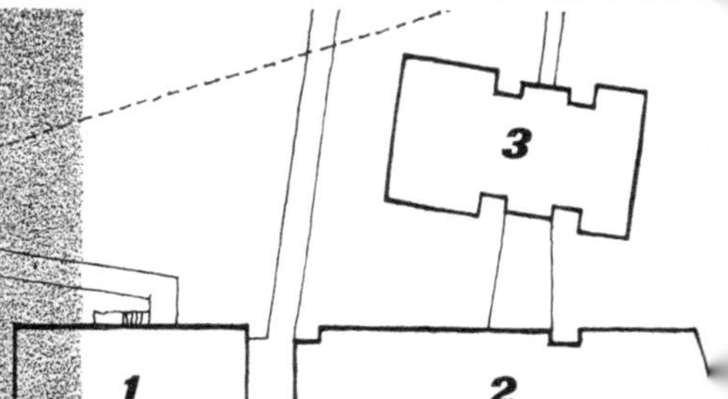

Sheffield University extensions (competition entry by A. & Smithson)—furthest development of New Brutalist architect toward the completely a-formal, anti-geometric, yet systema compositional methods exemplified in painting by Pollock a Burri. Raised walk-ways, one suspended beneath a box-duct services, connect the main entrance, under 1, with the A dept., 3, Senate House, 2, and other buildings on site.

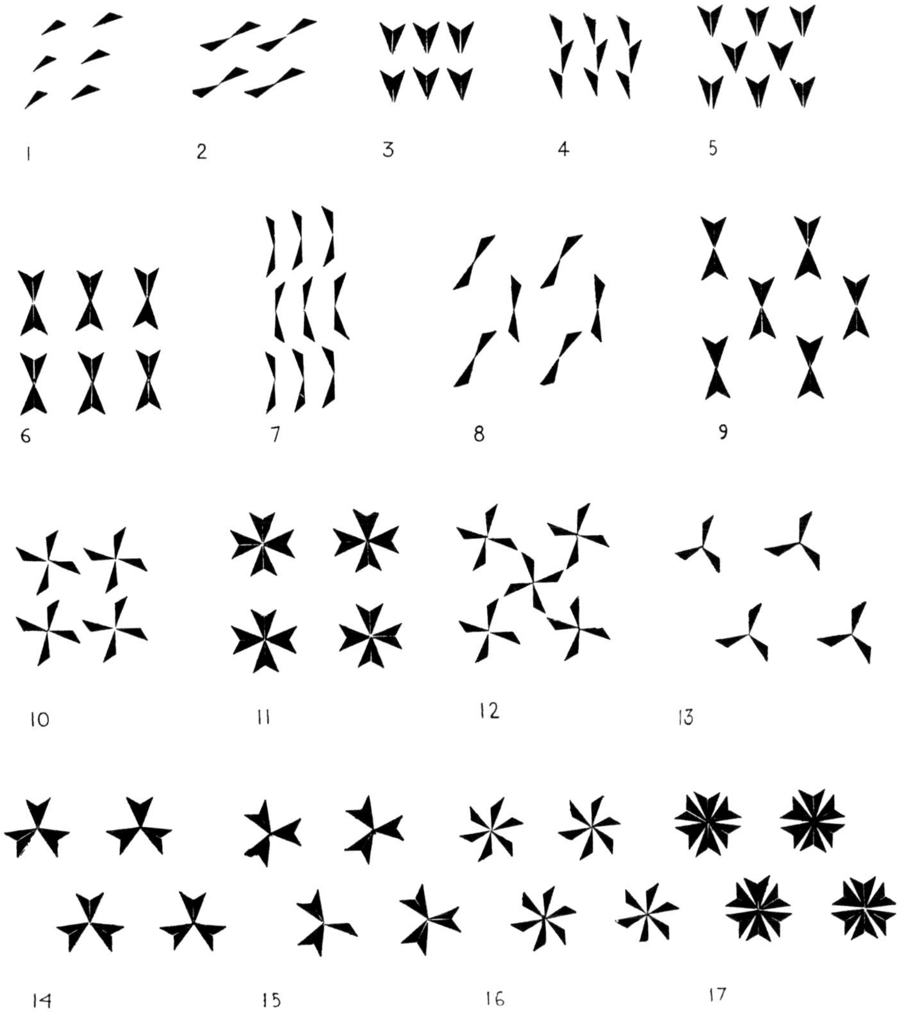

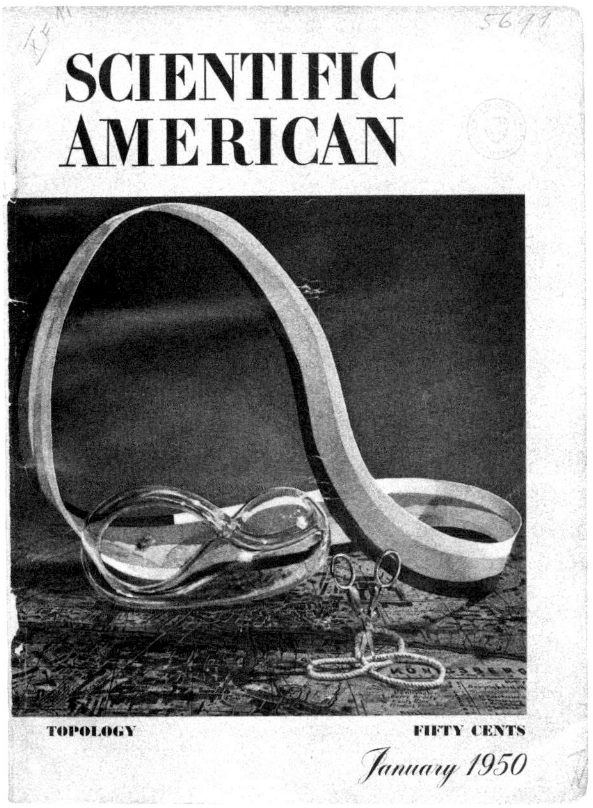

← Reyner Banham, "The New Brutalism," *Architectural Review*, 1955

↑ John Desmond Bernal, "Topology Studies from 'Architecture and Science,'" *Journal of the Royal Institute of British Architects*, 1937

↗ Cover of *Scientific American*, 1950, painting by Stanley Meltzoff

on the whole scheme of topologically organized buildings. Similarly, the use of "aspect" and "prospect" to describe the relationship between interior and exterior spaces, or "circulation" to apprehend movement or flows of movement in and around the building, is far from radical—the words had been used in British architectural theory and environmental design since the second half of the nineteenth century.[31] The analogy between mathematics and architecture served first to ascribe to the latter an allegedly overarching and contemporary, yet academic, foundation. To this end a single aspect was isolated from its complex reality and subjected to independent investigation, in a way analogous to scientific testing.[32] Topology was supposed to allow central design issues such as circulation or infrastructure to be explored under laboratory-like conditions and their effects on architectural form to be evaluated independently of the overall picture.

If, as John Summerson polemically put it in 1957, Banham's interest in topology might have been just an "attractive red herring" for architecture,[33] the relationship between science and the image was not. It was for some years a central topic for the members of the Independent Group, explored through the *Parallel of Life and Art* exhibition, but perhaps best seen in their interest in D'Arcy Wentworth Thompson's monumental and richly illustrated study on the physical and mathematical rules governing living organisms, *On Growth and Form*, first published in 1917 and re-released in 1942 and 1952.[34] Despite the weight it carried for the avant-garde, only one passage, on the division of surfaces, alludes to the potential of topology. Its presentation, however, is much more visual and evocative than other scientific reports of the time. A series of suggestive black line drawings of varying thicknesses accompanies a precise mathematical description of the physical rules pertaining to the formation of complex patterns, such as the wings of an insect or a butterfly.[35] These show the various forces acting on the wing as well as the size, distribution, and angle between the veins. This description of the forms and potential forms of organisms called deeply into question the widely upheld evolutionist perspective,[36] replacing a historical model of morphology by a mechanistic one.

In "Machine Aesthetic," published in the same year as "The New Brutalism," Banham takes a similar approach, using the 1953 Bertone racing car (or rather the full-size photograph published as an introduction to the essay), designed by Franco Scaglione and one of the first to be developed in a wind tunnel (significantly, not the more "high image" Cadillac Cabrio with its conspicuous stainless steel accessories) to demonstrate how its form had—literally—been streamlined by natural forces.[37] This provides the basis for his subsequent critique of the aesthetic positions adopted by Le Corbusier and Mies van der Rohe on modern architecture, and similarly Victor Pasmore and Piet Mondrian on modern painting. Banham admonishes the protagonists of the First Machine Age for upholding an "aesthetic *parti-pris*" in place of the form-function approach they had originally endorsed. Le Corbusier's comparison of the Parthenon and the modern automobile as respective expressions of the objective standards of their day was dishonest, he writes—first, because contrary to Le Corbusier's claim, the automobiles illustrated were not mass products and therefore not an expression of twentieth-century production methods; and second, Le Corbusier's automatic connection between a standardized product and a geometric shape, while a watertight claim for the modern architect, was for an engineer neither useful nor correct.[38]

As polemical as Banham's criticism of modern architecture and its aesthetic positions may have seemed, the issue at stake was not only about determining a mathematical formula to explain a causal relationship between force and form, but proposing an architectural genealogy beyond historical tradition—or (to return to D'Arcy Thompson) beyond its evolution.

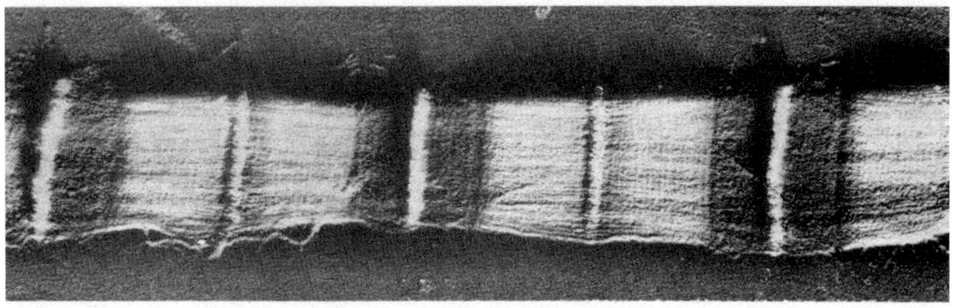

FIG. 4

FIG. 5

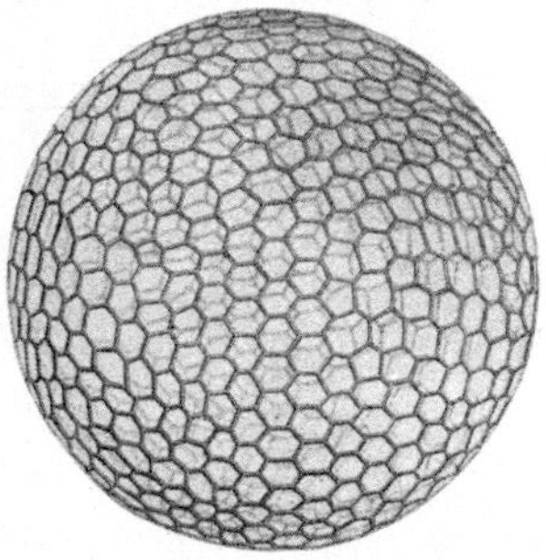

FIG. 1 The shell of the minute Radiolarian, *Aulonia Hexagona.*

FIG. 2 (*below*) Bone from a vulture's wing, to show internal structure.

FIG. 3 Native dyed textile from Nigeria.

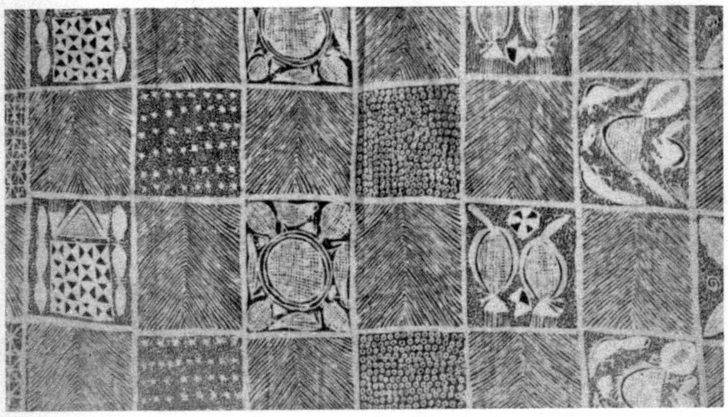

Contemporary interest in Thompson's work, at least among affiliates and future members of the Independent Group, went far beyond the plates in *Growth and Form.* Even for those unfamiliar with the book, its principal ideas were presented as powerful images in the eponymous exhibition initiated by Nigel Henderson and Richard Hamilton in 1951 at the Institute of Contemporary Arts. Conceived under the intellectual aegis of Thompson's research on morphology, the exhibition set out to represent the "physical laws of form"[39] through a presentation of the natural environment investigated by modern science at different scales. Ranging from the micro to macroscopic, installations included a sculptural molecular structure, a wall-size photographic print and a pair of films on the formation of crystals and the growth of a sea-urchin.[40] Crucial to this project was the formulation of a new visual language that could render visible the scientific landscape that until recently had been all but unseen.[41] This was the case not only for a general public overwhelmed by a landscape now suddenly visible in various exhibitions and magazines, but also for the scientists who had made their discoveries using new instruments and techniques.

While the ICA show provided a visual order to this scientific material, the "problem of form" and the principles of its developments and transformations made up the core of the scientific symposium that coincided with the exhibition. Acting as chair was the physicist Lancelot Law Whyte, whose work on the unitary principle sought to collapse the boundaries of specialization (an approach that would run anathema to an increasingly specialized post-war building society). As he emphasized in his introduction to the symposium publication, the goal, in the context of Thompson's theses, was to investigate and determine links between the complex processes involved in the emergence of spatial structures in the respective fields of physics, biology, psychology and art.[42] Among the participants there was a general consensus on the utility of the Thompson's approach. The physicist S. P. F. Humphreys-Owen, for instance, pointed out that objects on the smallest scale might now be described in terms only of their organization and not of their geometric characteristics.[43] The biochemist Joseph Needham, who in 1939 had published a substantial work on morphogenesis, demonstrated the limits of any analysis of a single form, emphasizing the necessity to think in terms of "groups" of enzymes or transfers of energy. The Belgian embryologist, Albert Dalcq, demanded that the process of morphogenesis no longer be investigated in terms of its appearance but from within, in terms of its functions.[44]

In the same way that Hamilton had distilled this obscure scientific language into an exhibition that captured the interest of both experts and non-specialists, the scientists relied on a few black and white photographs and sketches to precisely visualize their arguments. A significant example is by another embryologist, Conrad Waddington, who like his colleagues, had ascertained that the integrity of organic forms was best described in terms of their general structure and no longer in terms of individual elements.[45] He illustrated this point by grouping together a protozoon

↖ Joseph Needham, "Biochemical Aspect of Form and Growth," *Aspects of Form*, 1951

↑ Conrad H. Waddington, "The Character of Biological Form," *Aspects of Form*, 1951

→ D'Arcy Wentworth Thompson, "Of Topological Analysis," *On Growth and Form*, 1942

and a sample of hand-woven Nigerian textiles, thus proposing an analogy between the organizational patterns in nature and those in arts and craft.

While any single photograph illustrating the scientific essays in Whyte's collection could have appeared in the ICA exhibition, the reverse was not possible. In addition to scientific imagery, the show featured photographs, several drawings by Ernst Haeckel, two photograms by Nigel Henderson—one of a radish leaf and another of a spider—and a photograph from the twin series by the French filmmaker Jean Painlevé. Collectively these representations point to a crucial difference in the use of scientific imagery: in Whyte's book, images simply illustrate his argument, but to look at the exhibition imagery as mere illustration—this time of a new scientific landscape—means foregrounding the flatness of that representation at the expense of the materiality of the device or medium (i.e., the photograph itself). Although their use of photography differed, the two venues were linked by a shared interest in the role of science to better understand the becoming of things: however, in the first case, it was the patterns of growth and organization, whether in a sea urchin, a Nigerian textile or a bone; while in the second, it was the making of a photographic image through the placement of objects or organisms on a light sensitive paper. What was at stake was not only the illustration of a new visual environment and its metaphorical description, but perhaps more importantly the physical impact of science on new materials and technologies, capable of capturing it.[46]

Yet even if the aims of Banham and his contemporaries signaled the arrival of a new scientific attitude in architecture that attitude remained on the level of the textual and visual discourse. The duty to undertake a rational scientific investigation had been carried out since at least the early 1920s by others, only to be reinforced by the war efforts. The accounts are hard to trace in the architectural press but are all the more readily found in the dry research reports of institutions such as the Building Research Station in Britain (even if refuted by Banham[47]) or in the writings of numerous scientists, including the aforementioned Conrad Waddington and John Desmond Bernal. A member of the Architecture Science Group since 1941

→ Richard Hamilton, cover of *Growth and Form*, 1951

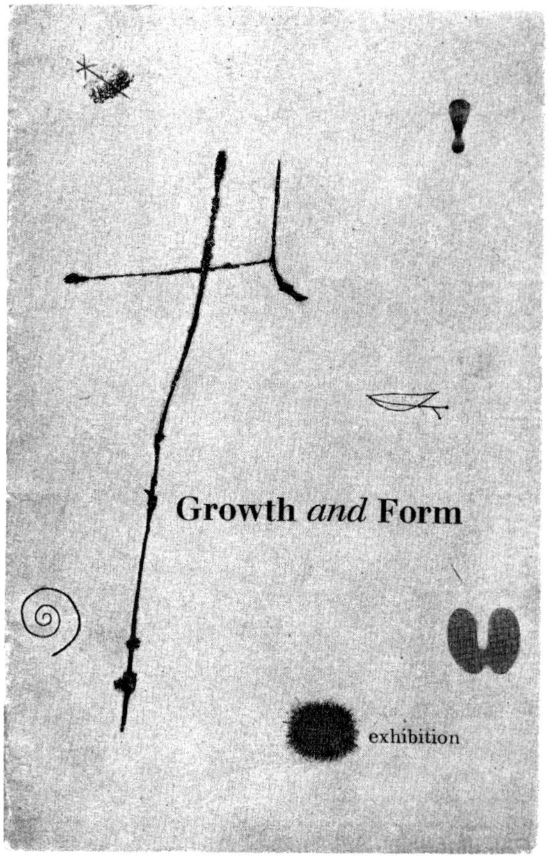

↓ D'Arcy Wentworth Thompson, "Of Topological Analysis," *On Growth and Form*, 1942

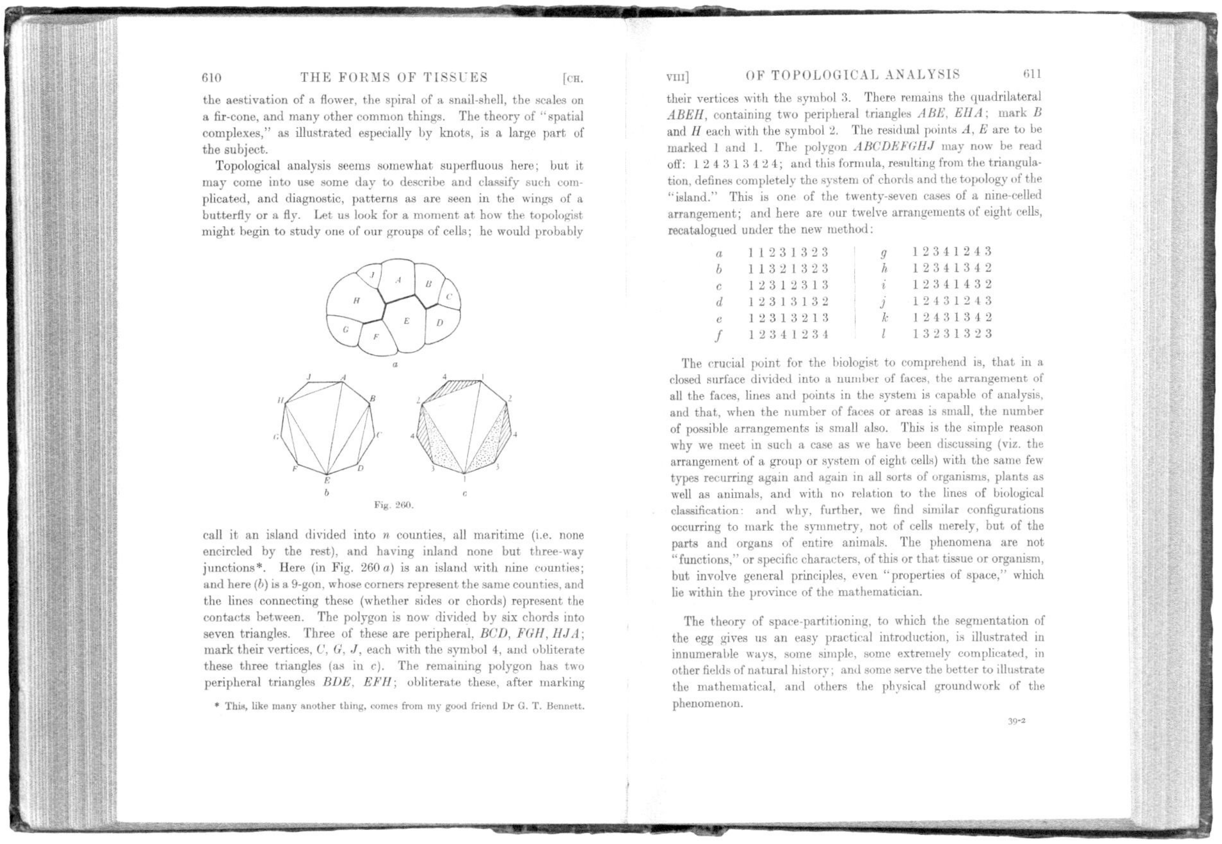

610 THE FORMS OF TISSUES [CH.

the aestivation of a flower, the spiral of a snail-shell, the scales on a fir-cone, and many other common things. The theory of "spatial complexes," as illustrated especially by knots, is a large part of the subject.

Topological analysis seems somewhat superfluous here; but it may come into use some day to describe and classify such complicated, and diagnostic, patterns as are seen in the wings of a butterfly or a fly. Let us look for a moment at how the topologist might begin to study one of our groups of cells; he would probably

Fig. 260.

call it an island divided into *n* counties, all maritime (i.e. none encircled by the rest), and having inland none but three-way junctions*. Here (in Fig. 260 *a*) is an island with nine counties; and here (*b*) is a 9-gon, whose corners represent the same counties, and the lines connecting these (whether sides or chords) represent the contacts between. The polygon is now divided by six chords into seven triangles. Three of these are peripheral, *BCD*, *FGH*, *HJA*; mark their vertices, *C*, *G*, *J*, each with the symbol 4, and obliterate these three triangles (as in *c*). The remaining polygon has two peripheral triangles *BDE*, *EFH*; obliterate these, after marking

* This, like many another thing, comes from my good friend Dr G. T. Bennett.

VIII] OF TOPOLOGICAL ANALYSIS 611

their vertices with the symbol 3. There remains the quadrilateral *ABEH*, containing two peripheral triangles *ABE*, *EHA*; mark *B* and *H* each with the symbol 2. The residual points *A*, *E* are to be marked 1 and 1. The polygon *ABCDEFGHJ* may now be read off: 1 2 4 3 1 3 4 2 4; and this formula, resulting from the triangulation, defines completely the system of chords and the topology of the "island." This is one of the twenty-seven cases of a nine-celled arrangement; and here are our twelve arrangements of eight cells, recatalogued under the new method:

a	1 1 2 3 1 3 2 3	*g*	1 2 3 4 1 2 4 3
b	1 1 3 2 1 3 2 3	*h*	1 2 3 4 1 3 4 2
c	1 2 3 1 2 3 1 3	*i*	1 2 3 4 1 4 3 2
d	1 2 3 1 3 1 3 2	*j*	1 2 4 3 1 2 4 3
e	1 2 3 1 3 2 1 3	*k*	1 2 4 3 1 3 4 2
f	1 2 3 4 1 2 3 4	*l*	1 3 2 3 1 3 2 3

The crucial point for the biologist to comprehend is, that in a closed surface divided into a number of faces, the arrangement of all the faces, lines and points in the system is capable of analysis, and that, when the number of faces or areas is small, the number of possible arrangements is small also. This is the simple reason why we meet in such a case as we have been discussing (viz. the arrangement of a group or system of eight cells) with the same few types recurring again and again in all sorts of organisms, plants as well as animals, and with no relation to the lines of biological classification: and why, further, we find similar configurations occurring to mark the symmetry, not of cells merely, but of the parts and organs of entire animals. The phenomena are not "functions," or specific characters, of this or that tissue or organism, but involve general principles, even "properties of space," which lie within the province of the mathematician.

The theory of space-partitioning, to which the segmentation of the egg gives us an easy practical introduction, is illustrated in innumerable ways, some simple, some extremely complicated, in other fields of natural history; and some serve the better to illustrate the mathematical, and others the physical groundwork of the phenomenon.

39-2

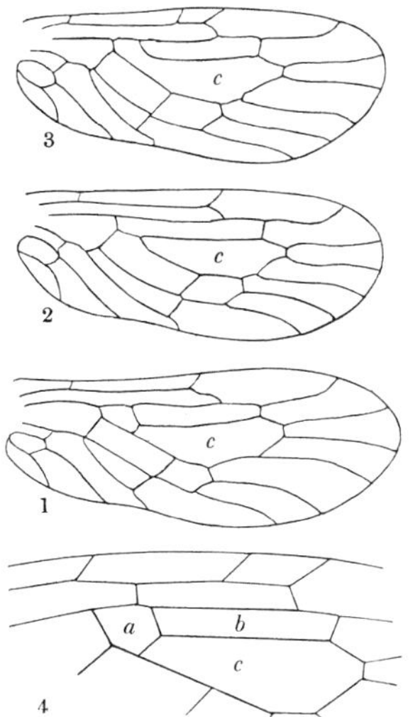

Fig. 263. Forewing of a stonefly, *Allocapnia* sp. 1–3 from A. Willey.

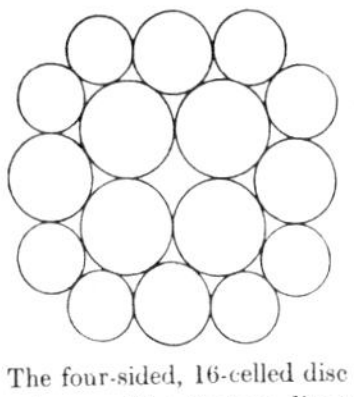

Fig. 264. The four-sided, 16-celled disc of *Gonium*, a minute algae. After Harper, diagrammatic.

12

12. a wall detail in one of the courtyards; the direct glazing shown here calls for very accurately made steel work. The aluminium angle bead is an extruded section produced by the new cold impact methods which are said to produce high physical properties due to work hardening and a better metal structure.

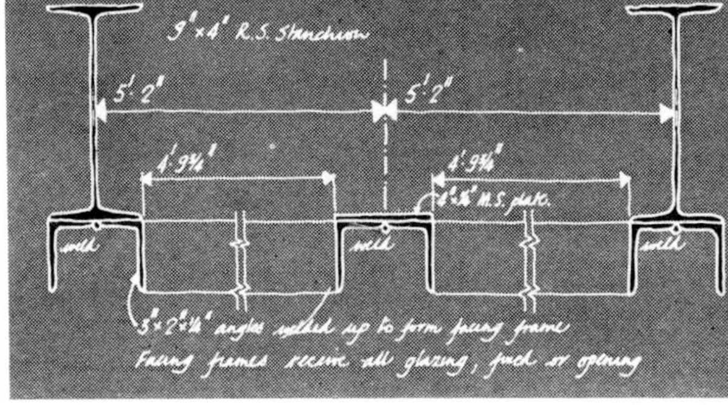

← ↗ "School in Hunstanton. Comment by Philip Johnson as an American Follower of Mies van der Rohe," *Architectural Review*, 1954

and Chairman of the Scientific Committee off the Ministry of Work (1945–1949), Bernal delivered two papers to the RIBA in 1946 that sketched out the scope of these investigations, from their social requirements, to their materials, construction, and structure, to the building industry.[48] More than other documents his papers testify to the significant efforts towards a scientifically planned society—one that finds its sources in the nineteenth century, whose importance is then reaffirmed in the interwar years by Marxist scientists, and whose impact on architecture becomes visible after 1945.[49] While this research did not explicitly articulate a role for architecture, it expanded the field of knowledge of the discipline and provided a solid foundation for future investigations, including Bernal's own wartime work on cement and, later, on housing, as well as John Baker's research into plastic theory, work by material scientist Harold E. Beckett on glass, and architect Richard Llewelyn-Davies study of building elements.[50] Scientific research, as Waddington had circumscribed it, comprised both the horizon as well as the conditions under which architecture had to perform.

Scientific research is equally inscribed in the seemingly Palladian plan and Miesian grammar of Hunstanton. Indeed, if the school was conceived with a structural transparency that could be easily translated in the architectural press, and if this was to be achieved with a specific set of readily available "families-of-components" or materials "as found"—a Brathwaite water tank, rolled steel profiles, Cambridge gault bricks, precast concrete decking units, industrial appliances and fixtures, aluminum fins and for the window plastic seals[51]—it was to do so under the calculable rationale of modern science. This approach applied both to the single object and to the system: the number of accessible classrooms per staircase, the reinforced window frames that are attached to the structure, and the optimization of the roof girders based on plastic theory. And while the idea of the performance in the number of staircases or the static structure of the girders is linked to a defined and measurable achievement, it is its qualitative and enigmatic aspect, which science enables, that formed the core of its design: the "terms of reference," according to the project's engineer, Ronald Jenkins, when describing the structure of the building, "were that the architects wanted to use steelwork 'architecturally.'" This meant that the roof beams had to contribute architecturally to the whole concept, which led to the "decision to use the plastic theory."[52] So the fineness of the steel frames that surprised the Mies-pupil Philip Johnson was intentional, since what was at stake was not so much the visual convention of structural solidity[53] than the expression of the formal potential of steel:[54] "a Piranesian trick" competing with "Miesian space," as another reviewer would put it.[55]

This approach applies not only to statics or access, but to other areas of Hunstanton, like in the wash basins of the school's toilet facilities. The models are obvious: on the one

↙ Dargan Bullivant, “Hunstanton Secondary School,” *Architectural Design*, 1953

THE PLASTIC THEORY OF BENDING

and its application to the design of the Hunstanton Steel Frames

DESCRIBED BY DARGAN BULLIVANT

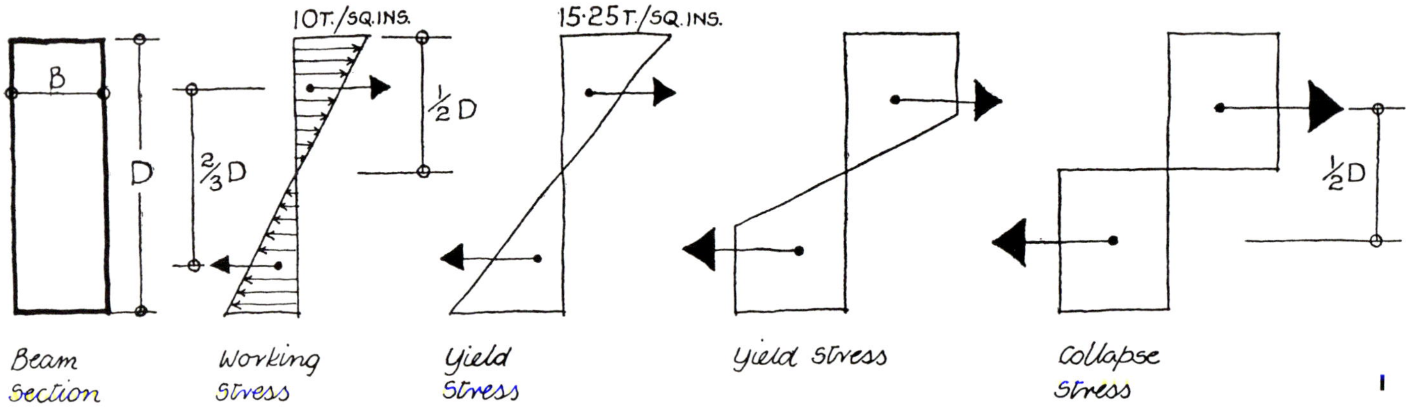

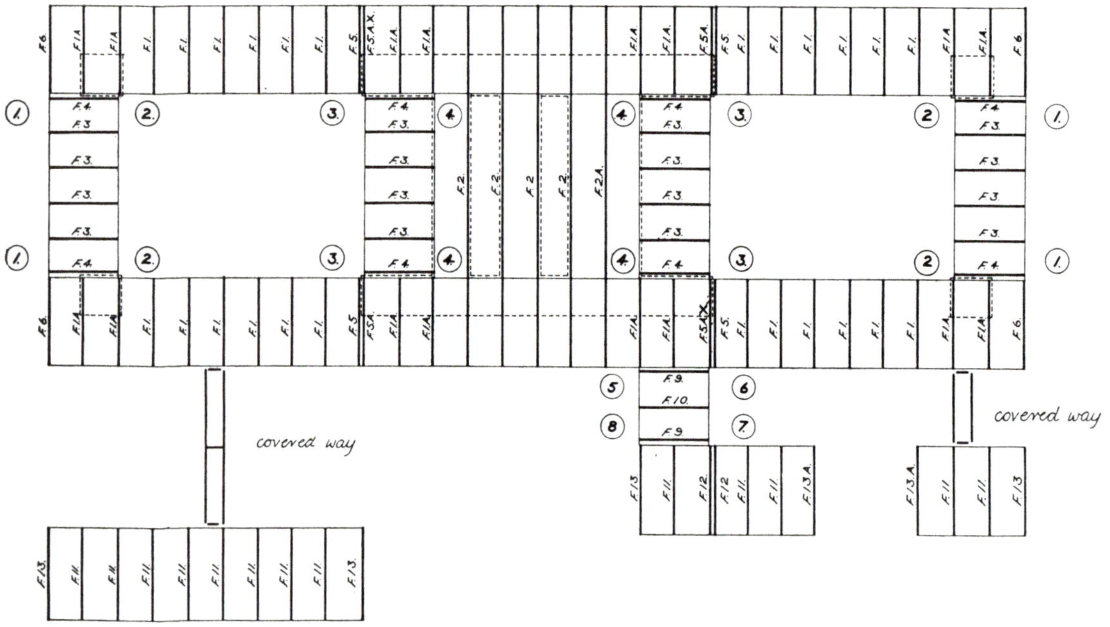

14. *Frame Plan. Ringed numbers refer to details in 15.*

15. *Details showing junctions of frames, and the use of site welded sealing angles.*

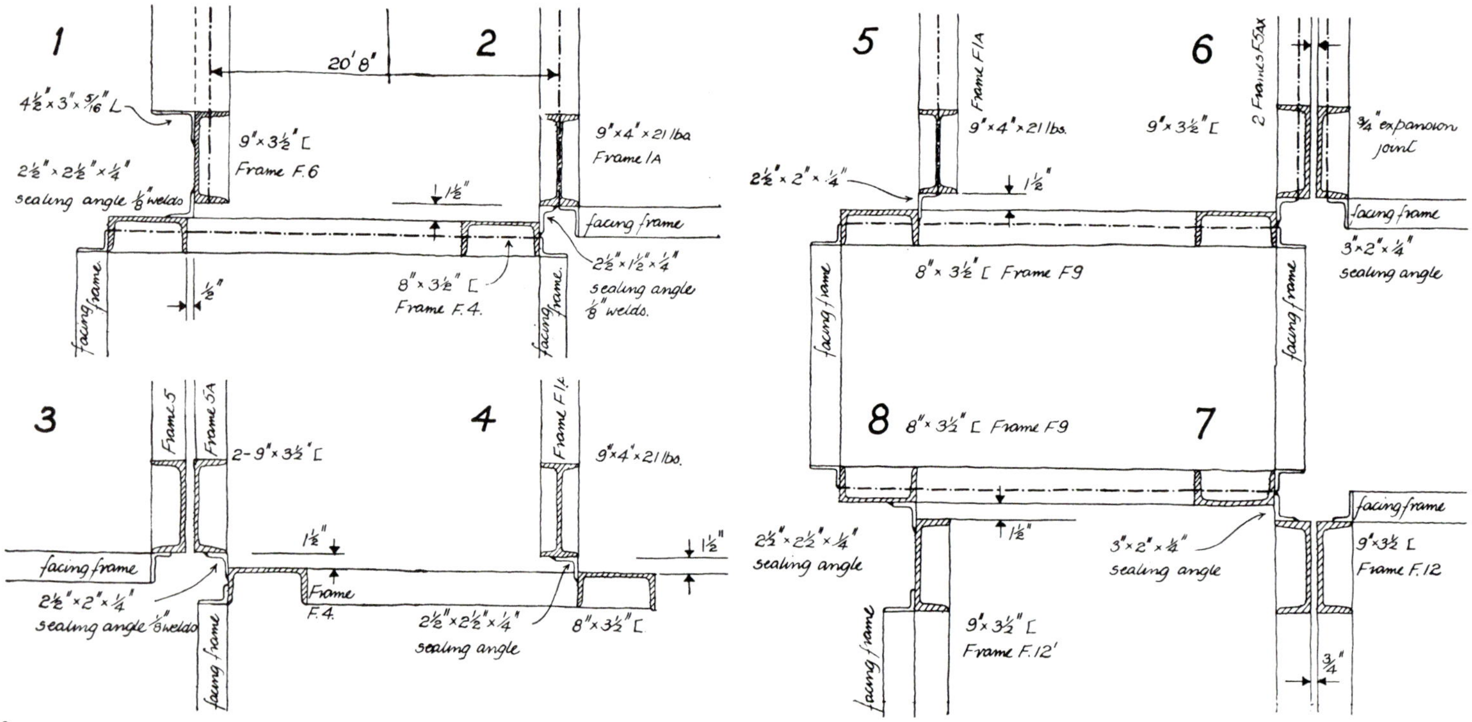

hand, the *objet-type* à la Corbusier, on the other hand, the Duchampian *objet-trouvé*.[56] In the school, however, it is not the form of the *objet* that dominates. It is instead its narrative dimension—the various moments of washing, which are explicated through single components: the main pipe with its connecting valve, the supply pipe, tap, wash basin, short drainage hose, and waste drain. Likewise, Hunstanton's facade structure is marked by the rawness of the details, whether in the tolerance of the window mounts, as revealed by the protruding rivets on the window frames, or in the visible welding seams of the steel profiles. Here, the modern canon of honesty in terms of materials and construction is confronted with the process of joining as an expression of the building process: the riveting, the welding, the brick-laying—in the words of the Smithsons, the "what's going on."[57] These various shifts distinguish Hunstanton from other possible models—at the time mention was made of buildings by Mies, Aalto, Le Corbusier or Loos, all projects concerned mainly with single constructive or technical aspects. In contrast, the Smithsons' project places these very aspects within a broad environment that goes beyond the individual element. This in turn affects the plan as much as the structure, the facade assembly, and the washing facilities. Science (not to be reduced to technology), in its performative ambition to lay out the various dimensions of things, had so altered the field of architecture (and its history) that it now offered a role-model for design (and its historiography).

→ James Maud Richards, "New Materials and Methods," *An Introduction to Modern Architecture*, 1944

↙ ↘ Conrad H. Waddington, "Art Looks to Science," *The Scientific Attitude*, 1941

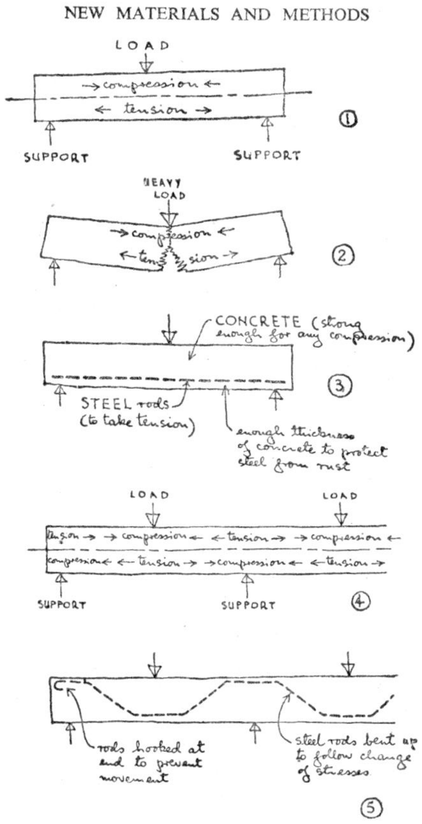

The Philips High Tension Generator for "atom-smashing" in the Cavendish Laboratory, Cambridge. Here is the modern æsthetic at its source. A modern sculptor like Brancusi would have been proud of this, but his version would not have produced 2,000,000 volts.

By permission of the Cavendish Laboratory, Cambridge.

A Surrealist picture by Paul Klee.

12. A Nazi aeroplane hangar. Notice the beautiful curve of the concrete shell, which is roof and wall together in one exactly calculated sweep. This is the sort of thing which persuades the German that he has got a step beyond the old imperial eagles of Potsdam.

9. The Surrealist Magritte looks, matter-of-factly enough, at his meal; and his meal looks, fixedly, at him.

1 This setting apart of the British avant-garde of the postwar, as Thomas Schregenberger, Richard J. Williams, and others argue, is not only artistic, but also social and political. See Claude Lichtenstein and Thomas Schregenberger, *As Found: the Discovery of the Ordinary* (Baden: Lars Müller, 2001); Richard J. Williams, "The New Brutalist," in *Reyner Banham Revisited* (London: Reaktion Books, 2021), 67–94.

2 Theo Crosby, "The New Brutalism," *Architectural Design* 25, no. 1 (January 1955): 1.

3 On New Brutalism in *AD*, see Steve Parnell, *Architectural Design 1954–72: The architectural magazines contribution to the writing of architectural history* (Diss. University of Sheffield, School of Architecture, 2011), 253–265. On the the Smithsons in *AD*, see: Stephen Parnell, "A Semi-social Magazine: Love, Life, and Architecture Design," *Histories of Postwar Architecture* 7, special issue "Committed, Politicized, or Operative: Figures of Engagement in Criticism from 1945 to Today" (2020): 75–103, here 91–92.

4 On the contested authorship on the history of "New Brutalism," see Dirk van den Heuvel, "Raw Brutalism: The Smithsons vs. Banham," in Anette Busse and Dorothea Deschermeier, *Brutalism: Contributions to the International Symposium in Berlin 2012* (Zurich: Park Books, 2017), 30–37. For a larger framework, see: Dirk van den Heuvel, *Alison and Peter Smithson. A brutalist story, involving the house, the city and the everyday (plus a couple of other things)* (Diss. TU Delft, 2013), here especially 161–180.

5 Le Corbusier, *Vers une architecture* (Paris: Éditions Crès, 1924 [1923]), 9, 121.

6 The literature on Brutalism and New Brutalism has been constantly growing and expanding its thematic and geographical scope in the last fifteen years and reaches from the most specialized studies to coffee table books: A first synthetic view on the movement with an anthology of texts was published as a special issue of *October* 136 (2011) edited by Alex Kitnick and Hal Foster. For an imbedding of the movement within a longer English history, see the monumental monograph by Elain Harwood, *Space, Hope, and Brutalism: English Architecture, 1945–1975* (New Haven: Yale University Press, 2015). An international perspective on the movement is given in the two-volume study edited by Oliver Elser and Anette Busse, *SOS Brutalism: A Global Survey* (Zurich: Park Books, 2017); Annette Busse and Dorothea Deschermeier, *Brutalism: Contributions to the International Symposium in Berlin 2012* (Zurich: Park Books, 2017). A careful study on the international carrier of the term "Brutalism" is to be found in Silvia Groaz, *The New Brutalism, invenzione di uno stile* (Diss. EPFL, 2021). A careful analysis of Brutalism as a cultural phenomenon deeply anchored in a specific "milieu or set of milieu," as he puts it, and their time, is offered by Ben Highmore, *The Art of Brutalism: Rescuing Hope from Catastrophe in 1950s Britain* (New Haven: Yale University Press, 2017).

7 P. D. S. [Alison Smithson], "House in Soho," *Architectural Design* 23, no. 12 (December 1953): 342; see also Alison and Peter Smithson, "Banham's Bumper Book on Brutalism," *Architects' Journal* 144, no. 26, (December 28, 1966): 1590. In this essay the Smithsons claim the term originated in an article in *The Times*, which reported that the French Society for Aesthetic Sensibilities had taken the Unité to court for being "brutal," symbolizing the decline of moral order, and affronting French style and aesthetics in general: Anonymous, "Radiant City Lawsuit. Complaint of Brutal Realism," *The Times*, December 3, 1952, [Folder G-059, Smithsons' Archive, Harvard University].

8 Reyner Banham, "The New Brutalism," *Architectural Review* 118, no. 708 (December 1955): 357.

9 Robin Boyd, "The Sad End of New Brutalism," *Architectural Review* 142, no. 845 (July 1967): 9–11.

10 Joan Ockman, "New Empiricism and the New Humanism," *Design Book Review* 41/42 (Winter/Spring 2000): 18–21.

11 Robin Middleton, "The New Brutalism or a Clean, Well-Lighted Place," *Architectural Design* 37, no. 1 (January 1967): 7.

12 Richard Hamilton, "Persuading Image," *Design* 134 (February 1960): 28–32. On the relation between New Brutalism and Pop, see Alex Potts, "Realism, Brutalism, Pop," *Art History* 35, no. 2, special issue "British Art and the Cultural Field, 1939–69" (2012): 288–313.

13 Alison and Peter Smithson, "But Today We Collect Ads," *ARK* 18 (1956): 49–50.

14 Smithson, "But Today We Collect Ads," 49.

15 "Secondary School at Hunstanton: A Discussion between the Architects (Alison and Peter Smithson), the Engineer (R. S. Jenkins of Ove Arup and Partners) and Editors of the Journal…," *Architects' Journal* 115, no. 3057 (September 10, 1953): 323–328; Dargan Bullivant, "Hunstanton Secondary School," *Architectural Design* 23, no. 9 (September 1953): 238–248; "School at Hunstanton," *Architectural Review* 116, no. 693 (September 1954): 152–162.

16 Dargan Bullivant, "Hunstanton Secondary School," 242; with almost identical wording: Dargan Bullivant, "Secondary School at Hunstanton, Norfolk," *Architects' Journal* 120, no. 3107 (September 16, 1954): 345; likewise: "School at Hunstanton Norfolk," *Architectural Review* 116, no. 693 (September 1954): 152–162.

17 Dargan Bullivant, "Hunstanton Secondary School," 242.

18 See Anthony Vidler, "Another Brick in the Wall," *October* 136 (Spring 2011): 117.

19 Dargan Bullivant, "Hunstanton Secondary School," 248.

20 Claire Zimmerman, "Photoghraphic Image from Chicago to Hunstanton," in *Neo-Avant-Garde and Postmodern : Postwar Architecture in Britain and Beyond*, ed. Claire Zimmerman and Mark Crinson (New Haven: Yale Center for British Art, 2010): 203–228, here 208.

21 For example, Banham, "The New Brutalism," 358.

22 Banham, "The New Brutalism," 358.

23 Banham, "The New Brutalism," 361.

24 Banham, "The New Brutalism," 358.

25 Nigel Whiteley, *Reyner Banham: Historian of the Immediate Future* (Cambridge, MA: The MIT Press, 2002), 27.

26 Rudolf Wittkower, *Architectural Principles in the Age of Humanism*, Studies of the Warburg Institute (London: The Warburg Institute, University of London, 1949), 18. Wittkower uses the expression "symbolic value" in his introduction to differentiate the singularity of the Renaissance from various "derivate styles."

27 Irénée Scalbert, "Towards a Formless Architecture: The House of the Future by A + P Smithson," *Archis* 9 (September 1999): 45; here is the first reference to this essay and its possible influence on Banham's definition.

28 Albert W. Tucker, Herbert S. Bailey, Jr., "Topology," *Scientific American* 182, no. 2 (January 1950): 18–24.

29 John Desmond Bernal, "Architecture and Science," *Journal of the Royal Institute of British Architects* 44, no. 16 (June 26, 1937): 807–809.

30 Banham, "The New Brutalism," 361.

31 Adrian Forty, "Spatial Mechanics: Scientific Metaphors in Architecture," in *The Architecture of Space*, ed. Peter Galison and Emily Thompson (Cambridge, MA: The MIT Press, 1999), 213–31.

32 Adrian Forty, "Language Metaphors," in *Words and Buildings: A Vocabulary of Modern Architecture* (London: Thames & Hudson, 2000), 62–85.

33 John Summerson, "The Case for a Theory of Modern Architecture," *RIBA Journal* 64, no. 7 (May 1957): 310.

34 Anne Massey, *The Independent Group: Modernism and Mass Culture in Britain, 1945–59* (Manchester: Manchester University Press, 1995), 42.

35 D'Arcy Wentworth Thompson, *On Growth and Form*, vol. 2 (Cambridge: Cambridge University Press, 1952 [1942]), 610–615.

36 For the plates, see D'Arcy Wentworth Thompson, *On Growth and Form*, 1026, in particular 1029; see also his introduction. Further: Stephen J. Gould, "D'Arcy Thomson and the Science of Form," in *Topics in the Philosophy of Biology*, ed. Marjorie Grene and Everett Mendelsohn (Boston: D. Reidel Publishing, 1976), 91; and Martin Kemp, *Seen/Unseen: Art, Science, and Intuition from Leonardo to the Hubble Telescope* (Oxford: Oxford University Press, 2006), 200.

37 Reyner Banham, "Machine Aesthetic," *Architectural Review* 118, no. 700 (April 1955): 224–228.

38 Banham, 226–227.

39 Isabelle Moffat, "'A Horror of Abstract Thought': Postwar Britain and Hamilton's 1951 *Growth and Form* Exhibition," *October* 94 (Autumn 2000): 99–100. Massey, *The Independent Group*, 42–45.

40 Victoria Walsh, "Reordering and Redistributing the Visual: The Expanded "Field" of Pattern-Paking in Parallel of Life and Art and Hammer Prints," *Journal of Visual Culture* 12, no. 2 (2013): 231.

41 Moffat, "'A Horror of Abstract Thought,'" 100–102.

42 Lancelot Law Whyte, "Introduction" in, *Aspects of Form*, ed. Lancelot Law Whyte (London: Lund Humphries, 1968 [1951]), 6.

43 S. P. F. Humphreys-Owen, in "Physical Principles Underlying Inorganic," in *Aspects of Form*, ed. Lancelot Law Whyte (London: Lund Humphries, 1968 [1951]), 8–9.

44 Albert Dalcq, "Form and Modern Embryology," in *Aspects of Form*, ed. Lancelot Law Whyte (London: Lund Humphries, 1968 [1951]), 93.

45 Conrad H. Waddington, "The Character of Biological Form," in *Aspects of Form*, ed. Lancelot Law Whyte (London: Lund Humphries, 1968 [1951]), 43.

46 On the role of the photographic reproduction technics in *Parallel of Life and Art*, see Hadas Steiner: "Brutalism Exposed: Photography and the Zoom Wave," *Journal of Architectural Education* 59, vol. 3 (February 2006): 15–27, here 16–18.

47 Reyner Banham, "The History of the Immediate Future," *RIBA Journal* 68, no. 7 (May 1961): 257. "The threat to any upswing of architecture based on human sciences could come, say, the Building Research Station quite as much as from irresponsible aesthetes."

48 John Desmond Bernal, "The Organization of Building Science Research," *Journal of the Royal Institute of British Architects* 53, no. 6 (April 1946): 236–240; see also: "Science in Architecture," *Journal of the Royal Institute of British Architects* 53, no. 5 (March 1946): 155–159.

49 Andrew Saint, *Towards a Social Architecture: The Role of School-Building in Post-War England* (New Haven and London: Yale University Press, 1987), 8.

50 Frederick Measham Lea, *Science and Building: A History of the Building Research Station* (London: HMSO, 1971), 78.

51 See Dargan Bullivant, "Hunstanton Secondary School," 238–248; Peter Smithson, "Reflections on Hunstanton," *Architectural Research Quarterly* 2, no. 8 (Summer 1997): 38.

52 Secondary School at Hunstanton, 324.

53 On this topic, see Alison and Peter Smithson, "The Stuff and Decoration of the Urban Scene," in *Ordinariness and Light: Urban Theories 1952–60 and Their Application in a Building Project 1963–70* (Cambridge, MA: The MIT Press, 1970), 92–94. This piece was written in 1952–1953, as the authors note in their introduction.

54 Secondary School at Hunstanton, 323.

55 "Three Approaches to Architecture," *Architectural Forum* 5, (May 1955): 142, 144.

56 See Jean-Pierre Keller, "Duchamp, ou l'objet comme symbole de lui-même," in *Pop art et évidence du quotidien: Pour une sociologie du regard esthétique* (Lausanne: Éditions de l'Âge d'Homme, 1979), 47–48.

57 Peter Smithson, Alison Smithson, Jane B. Drew, Edwin Maxwell Fry, "Conversation on Brutalism," *Zodiac* 4 (April 1959): 76.

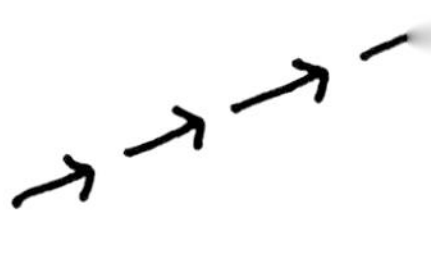

→ James Gowan and James Stirling, Detail from a diagram of vertical and horizontal circulation, Leicester University Engineering Building, 1959–1963

Arrows

→ Maxwell Fry, Sun House, 1935, from the title page of F. R. S. Yorke, *The Modern House in England*, 1937

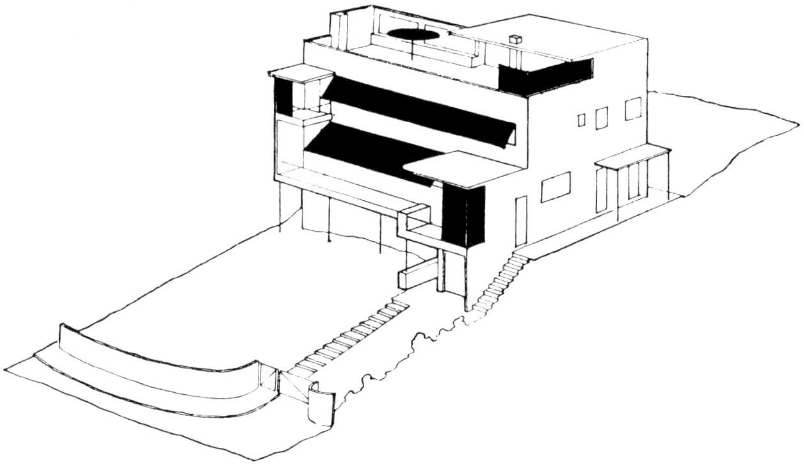

The small drawing that adorns the title page of F. R. S. Yorke's 1937 study, *The Modern House in England*, is typical for its time. It shows an aerial perspective, made in thin black lines, of a conventional modern house with all its attributes. Cubic in shape, the house is rendered in white with blacked-out ribbon windows spanning the whole facade. There are a pair of covered terraces and a roof garden, concrete slabs on pillars allowing a free plan of the main floor, and a carport at ground level. The house shown here, which seems to follow all the rules of international modernism as it spread from Europe is the Sun House, designed by Maxwell Fry and built in 1935 on sloping ground in Hampstead, North London. It is without doubt Fry's best-known house of the interwar period, and it marks his last in partnership with Thomas Adams and F. Longstreth Thompson before starting a new collaboration with Walter Gropius.[1] Yorke's use of the Sun House to open his survey, alongside Henry-Russell Hitchcock's laudatory appraisal published contemporaneously in *Modern British Architecture*, are proof of the allegiance of British architecture to the international modern movement of the mid-1930s, at least in terms of its formal vocabulary—since beneath their white render, around half of the examples published by Yorke were still brick or wooden structures.[2]

But where Yorke was using the exterior perspective to introduce the very language of modern architecture to an English audience, the origins of the drawing suggest it was produced to achieve precisely the opposite. In a 1935 article published in *Architects' Journal* titled "Analysis of a Building," Fry includes this drawing alongside several other diagrams, ground-plans, and construction sections of the Sun House. Rather than summarizing the building as a closed, impenetrable volume, the author uses this group of images to open it up and reveal its overall transparency towards its environment. A view oriented towards the London skyline fixes the position of the living room on the first floor. Vertical and horizontal circulation throughout the house and the main hall determines the placement of the service areas, living spaces, and terraces. Cross-distribution from facade to facade sets the northwest-oriented structural grid, while opening vents and slightly detached roller blinds allow hot air to circulate. The overall impact of the sun is also mapped, represented by three orbs that rotate around the parcel of land, clarifying not only the conditions of the site but also the inspiration for the project's name. Uniting these various drawings and in turn connecting the various conditions that shape the milieu of the house is one single, repeating motif: the arrow, which Fry uses to indicate everything from the orientation of the plot and the impact of the sun's rays, to the flow of people and the movement of wind. Placed within the text itself, arrows even direct the reader's eye. Whether straight or squiggly, fat, thin, short or long, the arrows are always black—and they are everywhere.

If Fry's house and its language are emblematic of this period, his use of arrows is rather exceptional. Unremarkable as such arrows may seem now, it is worth noting how rarely they appear among the published drawings by architects of the time. Le Corbusier, whose work provided the major references for the British avant-garde and who devoted a significant amount of attention to questions of light, ventilation, and circulation, mostly got by without any arrows at all, as seen in his plans and sections published in the first volumes of the *Oeuvre complète*, save for a few drawings of the Mundaneum (1929), and one or two for his Palace of the Soviets (1931).[3] While his competition entry for the Palais des Nations (1927) contains some arrows, more turn up in the sketches illustrating some of his theoretical arguments—in *Précisions* they are used on a board to chart the rapid thoughts of the speaker as he discusses the movements of cars, people, and air.

↓ Maxwell Fry, "Analysis of a Building: 2," *Architects' Journal*, 1935

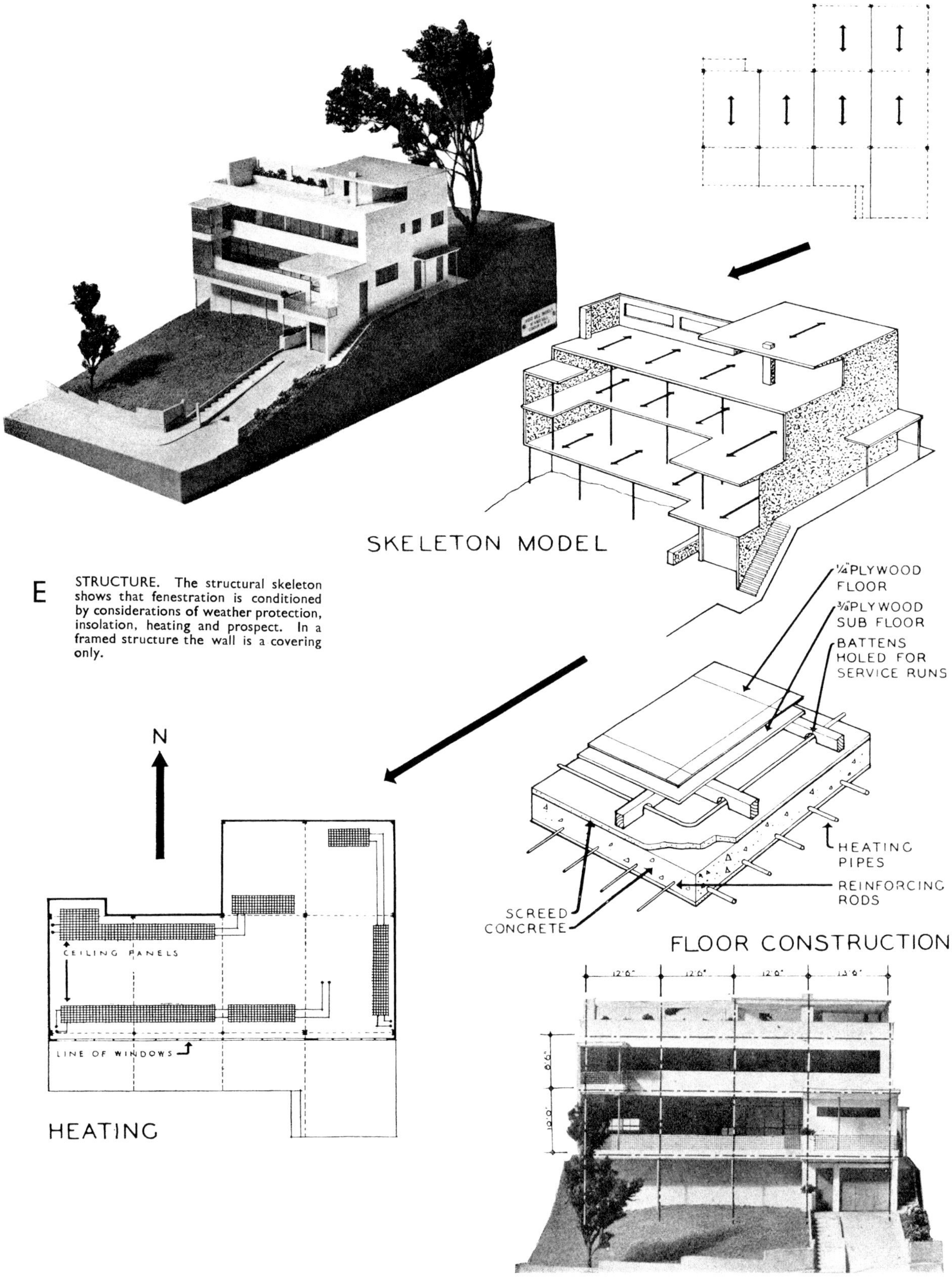

↓ Maxwell Fry, "Analysis of a Building: 2," *Architects' Journal*, 1935

HOUSE IN HAMPSTEAD BY E. MAXWELL FRY (OF ADAMS, THOMPSON AND FRY).

PROGRAMME

A SITE. A small and expensive piece of land sloping steeply to the south on to a quiet road, with a further fall beyond. There is a line of large elms across the top of the site.

REQUIREMENTS. A family of two, with housekeeper in charge of house by day, and no other service. There should be large spaces for the entertainment of friends, but provision should be made for one guest room only. The house must be planned for the maximum of usable space and light, but must be well warmed in cold weather. It should provide terraces for recreation and relaxation, which should neither overlook nor be overlooked by neighbours. Easily cleaned materials, built-in fitments and self-operating machinery should be used to reduce labour.

DETAILED REQUIREMENTS.

(*a*) Large living-room and dining space.
(*b*) Kitchen, servery, housekeeper's room.
(*c*) Own bedroom, dressing-room and bathroom en suite, with dressing-room as bedroom.
(*d*) Guest room and bathroom.
(*e*) Sewing room.
(*f*) Dark room.
(*g*) Cloakroom and lavatory.
(*h*) Garage.
(*k*) Roof terrace, tea terrace.

Note.—All living-rooms and principal bedrooms should face direct south.

SITE. The fall is diagonal to the length of the site, the road sloping steeply.

SUNLIGHT. The site commands a nearly unobstructed daily range of sunlight in winter and summer. Lines normal to the road frontage give a workable approximation to maximum sunlight penetration, and the enjoyment of varying conditions of sunlight.

SECTION. The flat portion above is occupied by large trees. The ground is clay with a safe bearing of $1\frac{1}{2}$ tons load per sq. foot, obtained from borings. Note the slight flattening of fall on the section, which is taken towards the eastern boundary. This suggests a garage entrance.

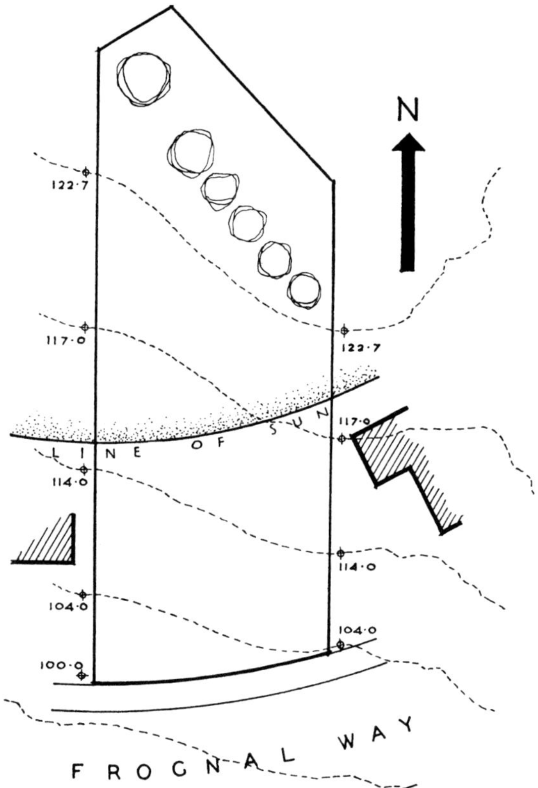

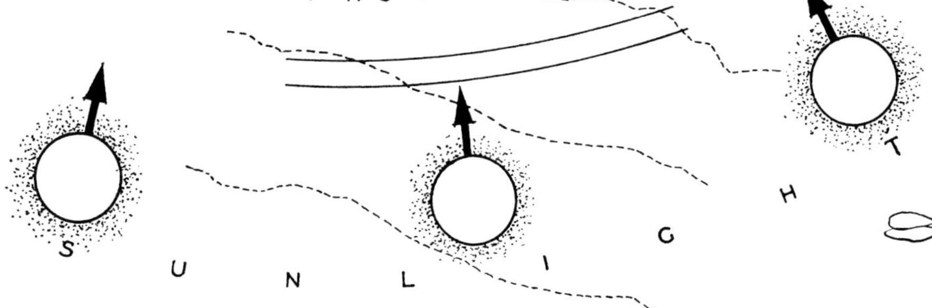

B ELEVATION AND VIEW. ¶ The view over London is important. The approach to the garage is no less important. The maximum rise for the car approach is 1 in 7, and there must be a level stretch in front of the garage doors. Between the sight line over the property on lower levels, and the mean line for car approach will be found the levels of ground floor and basement, and a possible frontage line for the house.

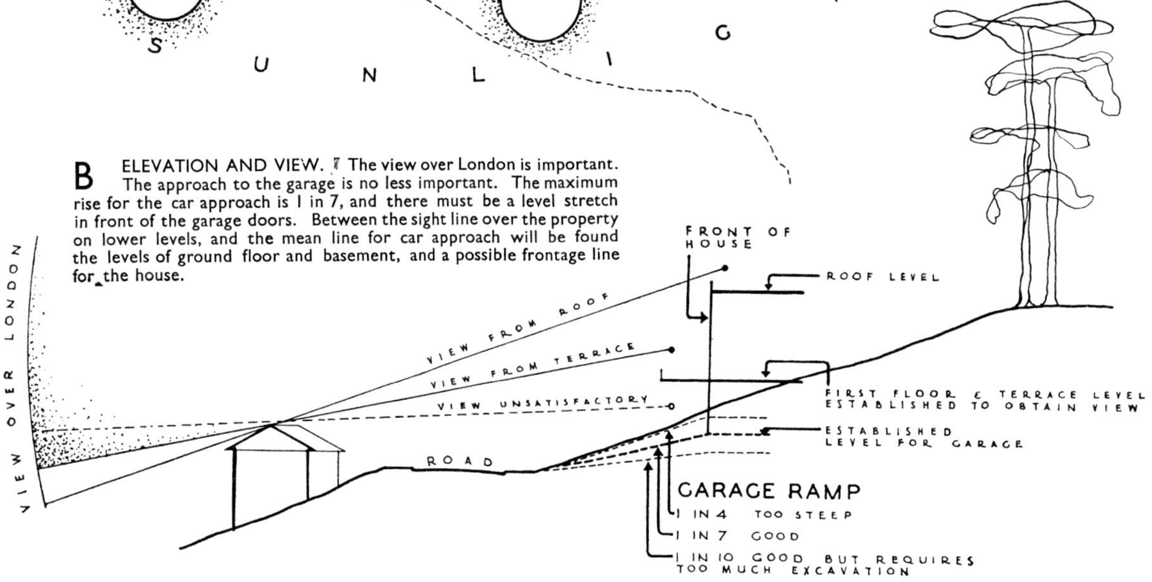

↓ Maxwell Fry, "Analysis of a Building: 2," *Architects' Journal*, 1935

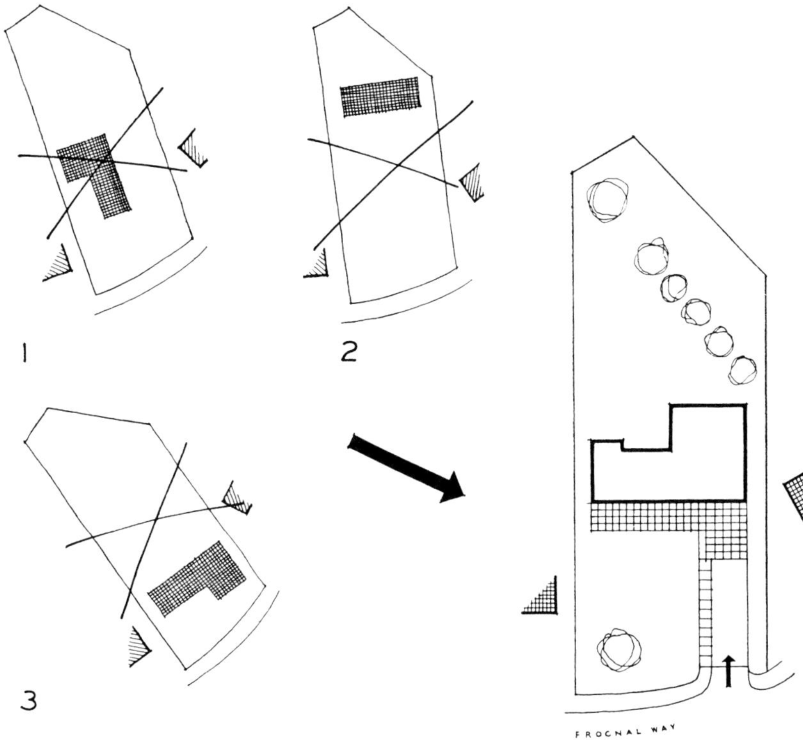

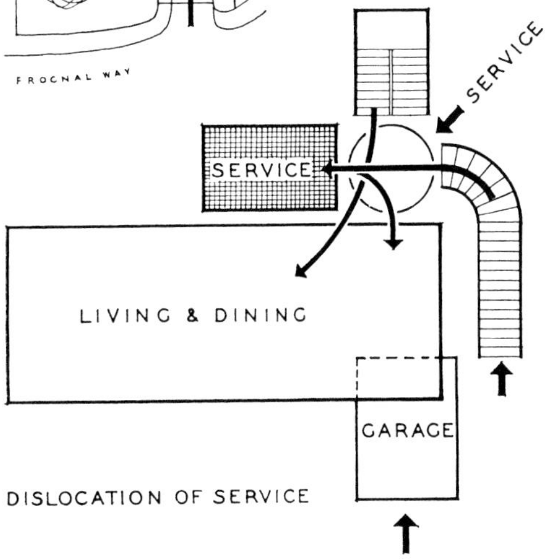

1 DISLOCATION OF SERVICE

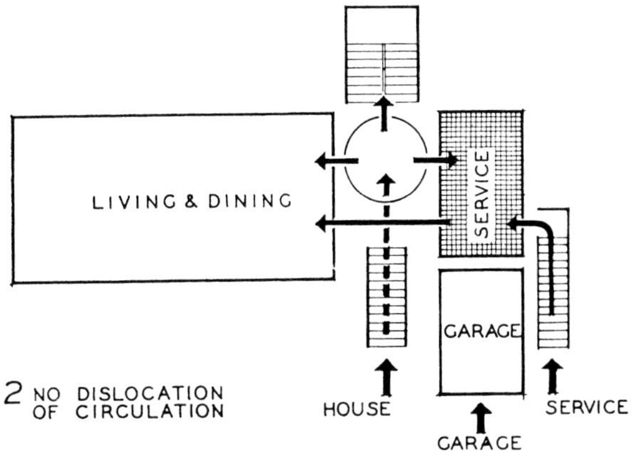

2 NO DISLOCATION OF CIRCULATION

THE PROBLEM RE-STATED.

C As arrived at by the foregoing consideration, we have a house of which the living-rooms and bedrooms above occupy most of the width of the site. The garage will be on the right, and will probably project to form a terrace. Entrance will be from a lower level and should not obtrude upon the living space. This *must* be entered from the side or from behind : practically and psychologically. From this a dilemma: how to avoid crossing the circulations of service and entrance to living space and bedroom space ? Entrance from outside, whether from the garage terrace or from the end, cannot reach living spaces without choking the circulations from service to living space. For easy running, service, entrance and stairs must be close together, but the service circulation must be short and unbroken. The two main alternatives are shown diagrammatically. They turn upon circulation, and Fig. 2, which is in effect an underground by-pass, leaves the service intact. See next page for details.

TRIAL AND ERROR. The scientific approach offers clear indications, but the goddess Chance still whispers : what about a house on the long axis ? (Fig. 1). Or on top of the site with all the goods in the window ? (Fig. 2). Or near the admittedly quiet road, with garden hidden away behind ? (Fig. 3). No, to all of them. Tested by sunlight, elevation, view, privacy, economy in foundations and ease of garage approach, chance has nothing better to offer.

↓ Alexander Klein, “Ganglinien,” *Zentralblatt der Bauverwaltung*, 1928

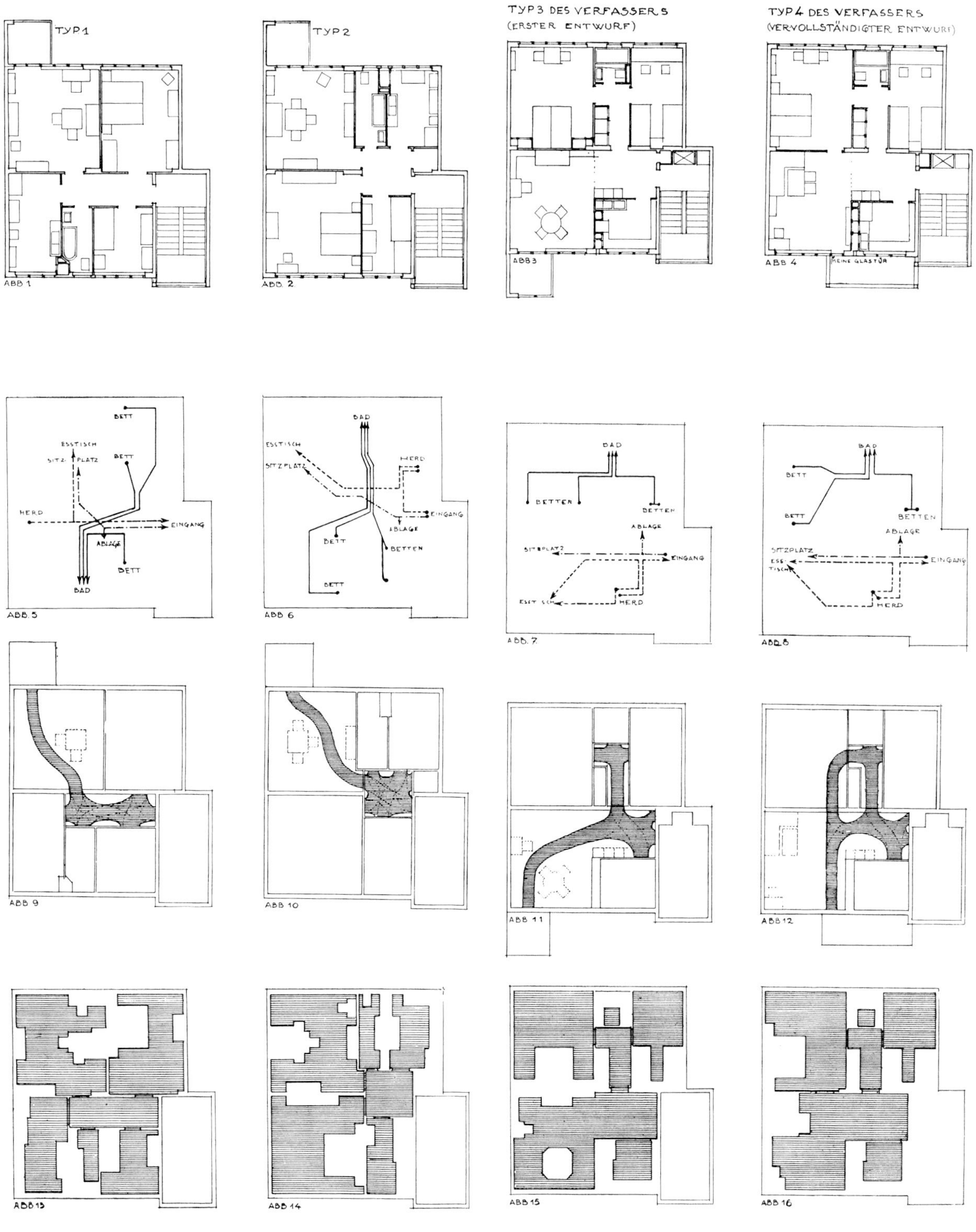

→ Bruno Taut, "'Ganglinien' between kitchen, scullery, corridor," *Ein Wohnhaus*, 1927

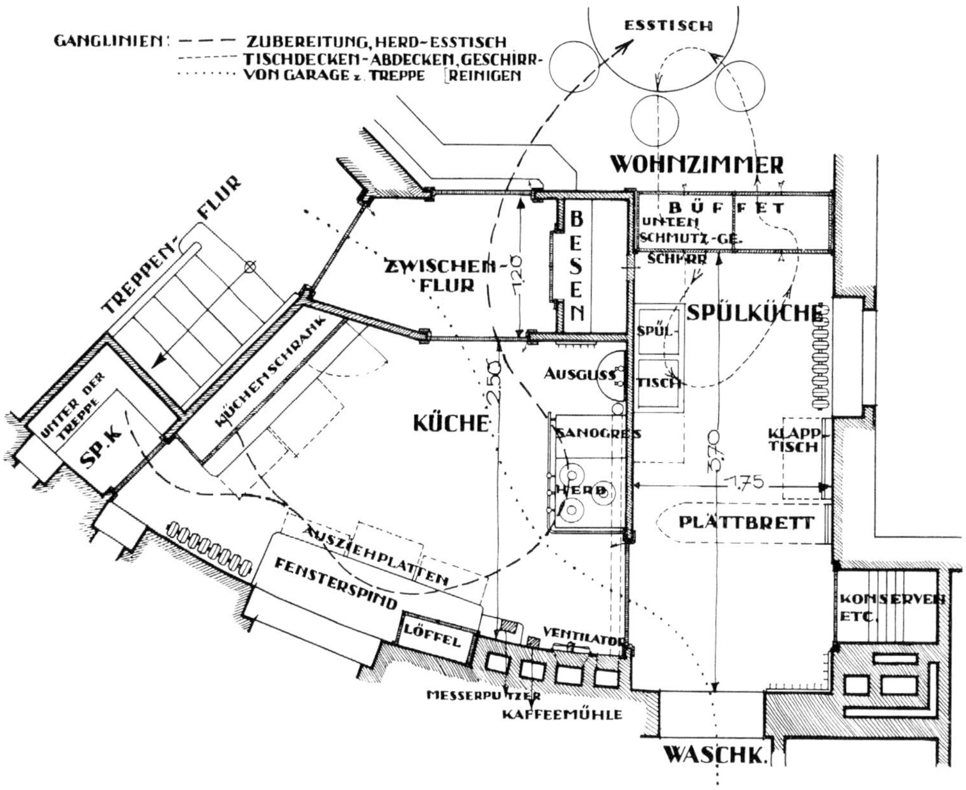

In Germany, Bruno Taut used arrows in a book about his own house in Berlin-Dahlewitz (1926) but only to illustrate the movement of servants, as did Alexander Klein in his famous movement studies for apartments of 1928, but again just to map the *Ganglinien* (literally, a line of movement that in the subsequent scheme becomes the line of a corridor).[4] Similarly in the work of a young Alvar Aalto, arrows make only a rare appearance, for instance in the ventilation system in the kitchen of the tuberculosis clinic in Paimio (1933).[5] Beyond these occasional moments, Louis Kahn stands as the outlier of his generation for his liberal use of the motif, notably in his traffic studies of Philadelphia (1952), highly acclaimed by the British avant-garde. But even here the arrows are restricted to large, urban-scale proposals, not buildings, and produced almost two decades after those of Fry.

Yet within a few years the figure is inexplicably ever-present in the work of postwar architects in Britain. A close inspection of plans and presentation drawings reveals its widespread use. Beyond the most common type—the north-pointing arrow that is found in almost every site plan—arrows both illustrate and represent multiple layers of information. In certain instances, they mark an entrance or point out the direction of a staircase, while in others they trace out a mechanical operation, such as the opening or closing of a window. Arrows are also used to represent the various technical stages of a construction process, from the laying of foundations to the tiling of a roof. They present the routes, both straight and circuitous, of pedestrians and leisurely visitors, vehicles, even the direction of passing ships. They indicate the angles of a boundary or the sun's rays, or the minimum water level in a tank. There are still more arrows to be found that do not seem to concern the building at all. Instead, they highlight intersecting perspectives (both critical and contemplative), or they illustrate a structural concept (pressure and resistance).

While it is impossible to pinpoint the moment postwar architects took notice of the unassuming arrow, it is equally difficult to explain its sudden ubiquity in historical terms. This is because allied to its scarcity among early twentieth-century modern masters, any precedents to the arrow in architecture are similarly patchy. Its history in architectural drawings is comparatively brief. Ever since the emergence of architecture as its own professional discipline, architectural and technical drawings have mainly been of an illustrative or figurative nature—their primary purpose has been to depict the structure of an object. This purpose remained predominant until well into the second half of the nineteenth century, rendering little need for arrows.[6]

↓ Louis Kahn, proposed movement pattern for midtown Philadelphia, 1953

↓ Le Corbusier and Pierre Jeanneret, Palace of the League of Nations, 1927

→ "Crittall—Anti-Noise Window," advertisement for The Crittall Manufacturing Company, *Architects' Journal*, 1938

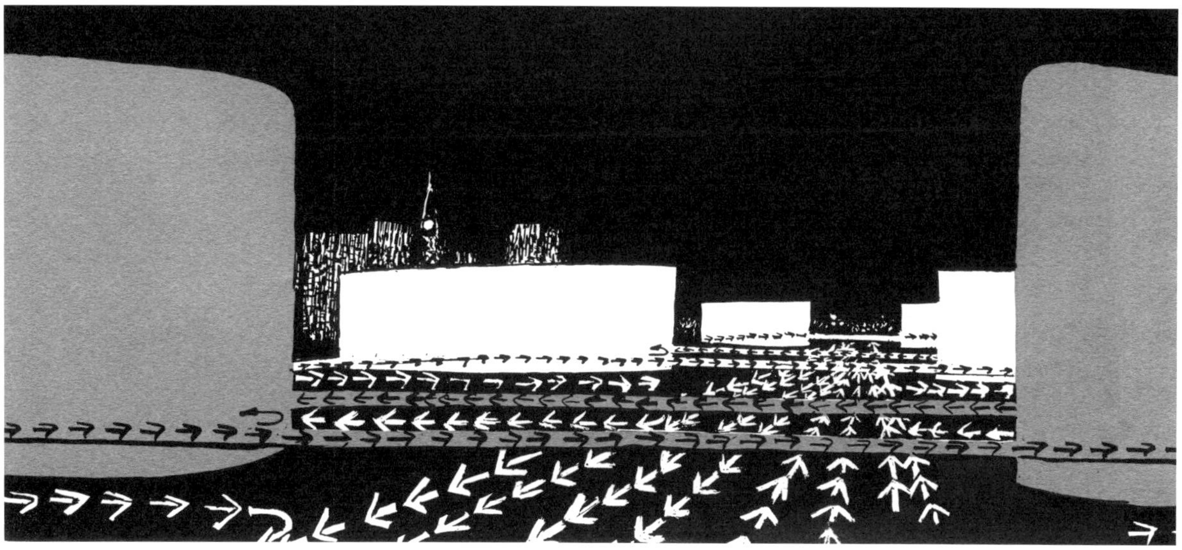

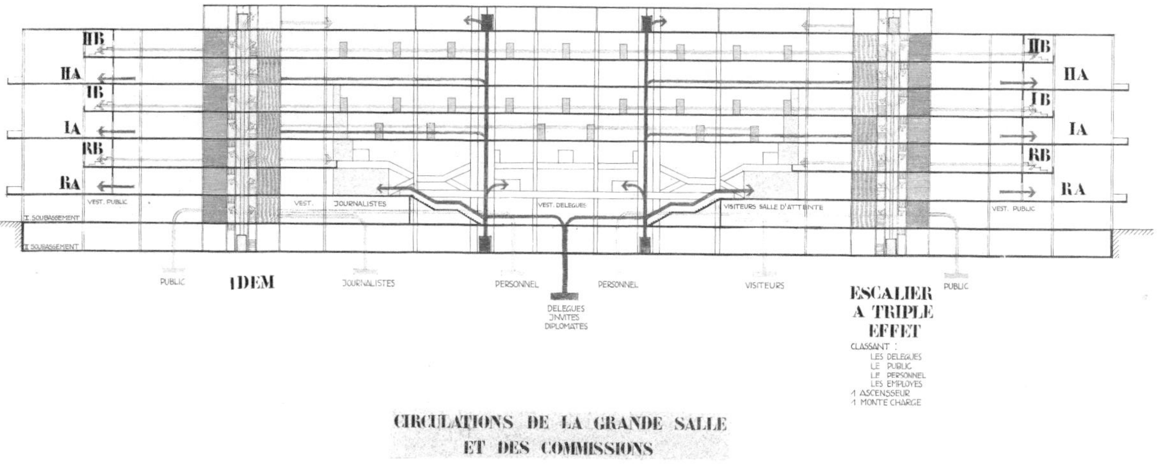

CRITTALL

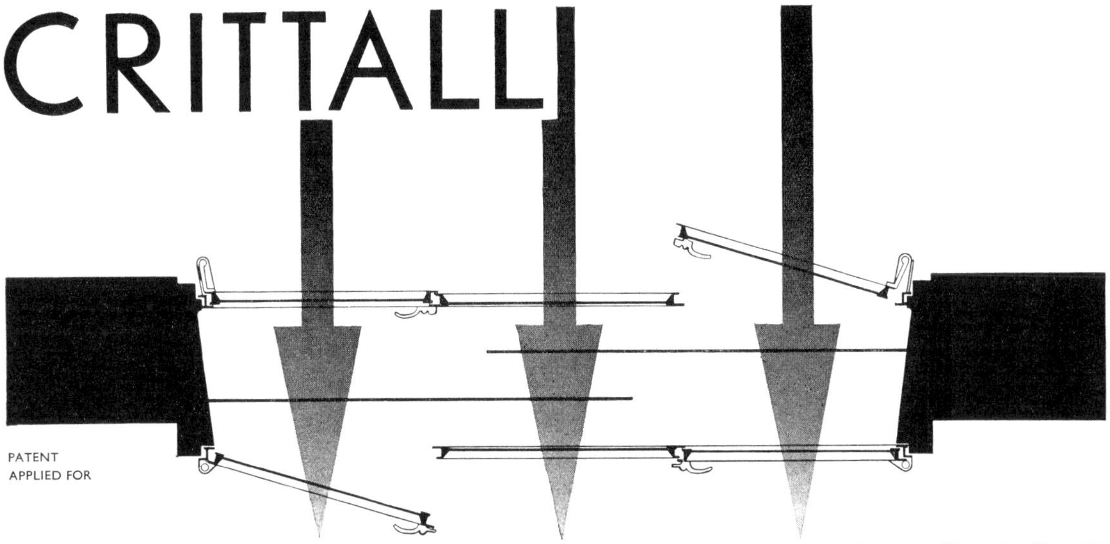

ANTI-NOISE WINDOW

A window which will give considerable protection against the ever - growing amount of street noise in towns and cities. It consists of an inner and an outer casement, between which are two sliding plate glass baffles, set in a reveal sloping inwards at 7°.

The purpose of a window of this design is to prevent direct entrance of any sound, and to deflect it on the planes of the baffles and the reveals, so that it is greatly reduced by the time it reaches the room, allowing ventilation through the window at the same time. The baffles are of ¼″ glass mounted on rollers, and make contact with a continuous rubber buffer at either jamb. Direct ventilation can be arranged by sliding both baffles to one side while the casements are open. All the glass faces of the baffles and the windows can be easily cleaned from the inside.

THE CRITTALL MANUFACTURING COMPANY LTD
HEAD OFFICE: 210 HIGH HOLBORN. W.C.1

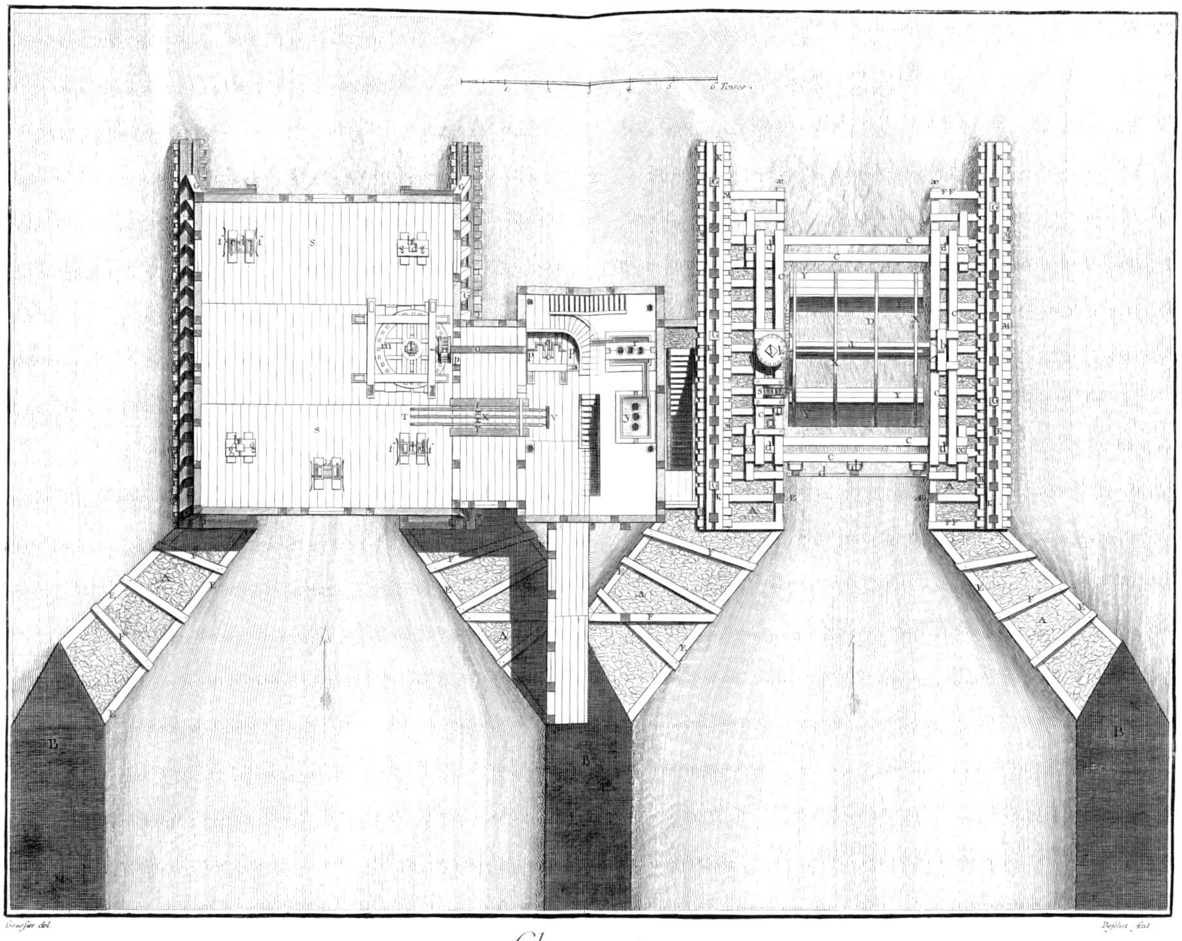

Charpente, Pompe du Pont Notre Dame.

It was only as scientific curiosity emerged during the Enlightenment that scientists began to investigate how things worked, that arrows appear in the realm of architecture.[7] In his study on smoking fireplaces, *La Mécanique du Feu* from 1713, the lawyer, naturalist, and physicist Nicolas Gauger used feathered arrows to illustrate the direction of air as it traveled up and down cavities behind the stove. In the next few decades, the arrow made several more appearances—in Bernard Forest de Bélidors' 1737 treaty on hydraulics to show the direction of water flow,[8] then in the 1743 *Description of Ventilators* by the physician Stephen Hales, illustrating the movement of processed air. In 1763 Denis Diderot and Jean le Rond D'Alembert conscripted the arrow for their *Encyclopédie* entry on the pump of the Notre Dame Bridge over the Seine in order to indicate the direction of the river.[9] What unites all these early instances is the authors' common understanding of the arrow's capacity to denote the movement of fluids by indicating direction. From Newton onward, fluids—that is, water or air (cold or warm) which is set in motion mechanically or otherwise—were seen to not simply surround bodies in space, but to determine their relation to one another. This original terminology evolved through eighteenth-century French studies of mechanics, as the philosopher Georges Canguilhem has shown, into the "milieu"—literally meaning the in-between.[10] The function of the arrow was therefore to precisely represent the movement carried within or between a supposedly static framework.

By the turn of the nineteenth century, through an interest of the natural sciences in architecture, arrows become more common, especially in French and English literature, where they typically help to convey the idea of direction and momentum in an otherwise static drawing.[11] The arrow itself was usually depicted as an archer's arrow, complete with head, shaft, and fletching, before being simplified into a more graphic register of direction—no longer a projectile but an abstract symbol.[12] Feathered or not, these arrows have since served to reveal a movement in time and space that could not be otherwise represented—initially the flow of water, then air, steam, or gas; later of people, goods, or vehicles; and, more recently, abstract entities such as energy or information.

← Denis Diderot and Jean le Rond d'Alembert, "Carpentry of the Pump at Notre Dame Bridge," *Encyclopédie*, 1763

→ John James Drysdale and John Williams Hayward, "Corniche [Inlet]," *Health and Comfort in House Building*, 1872

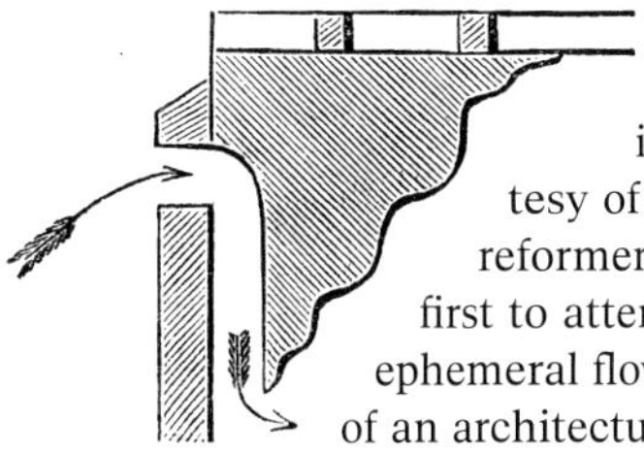

It is therefore no coincidence that the arrow found its way into architectural drawing courtesy of experts such as doctors, social reformers, and engineers, who were the first to attempt to map in their designs the ephemeral flow of fluids into, within, and out of an architectural object.[13] In connection with the numerous central heating and ventilation systems either developed or advocated by them in the early nineteenth century,[14] arrows were used to convey the proposed direction of flows, initially only in individual technical devices, subsequently in entire buildings. Exemplary in this regard are two houses built in Liverpool in around 1860 by the medical doctors John James Drysdale and John Williams Hayward. The plan, section, and eventual construction of these houses were designed to ensure good ventilation, from the intake of air in the basement and its technologically driven circulation through the individual rooms, to the thermal pull of the kitchen chimney, leading to its final disposal via the "foul air shaft."[15] Air circulation, not only in the pipes and chimneys, but also within the various rooms, was meticulously noted with an abundance of arrows, dissolving, at least from a technical point of view, any difference between infrastructural and architectural space.

Around the time of Drysdale and Hayward's houses, the arrow begins to be used in ground plans to map nonfluid entities. In drawings for Pentonville Model Prison, published in 1844, feathered arrows plot routes prescribed for inmates through the prison chapel and network of corridors.[16] This innovative practice of marking human movement in the architectural plan was to be eagerly adopted for other, non-penitentiary typologies, such as the townhouses of Eugène-Emmanuel Viollet-le-Duc,[17] as well as in the early ergonomic studies of the 1910s, in particular those

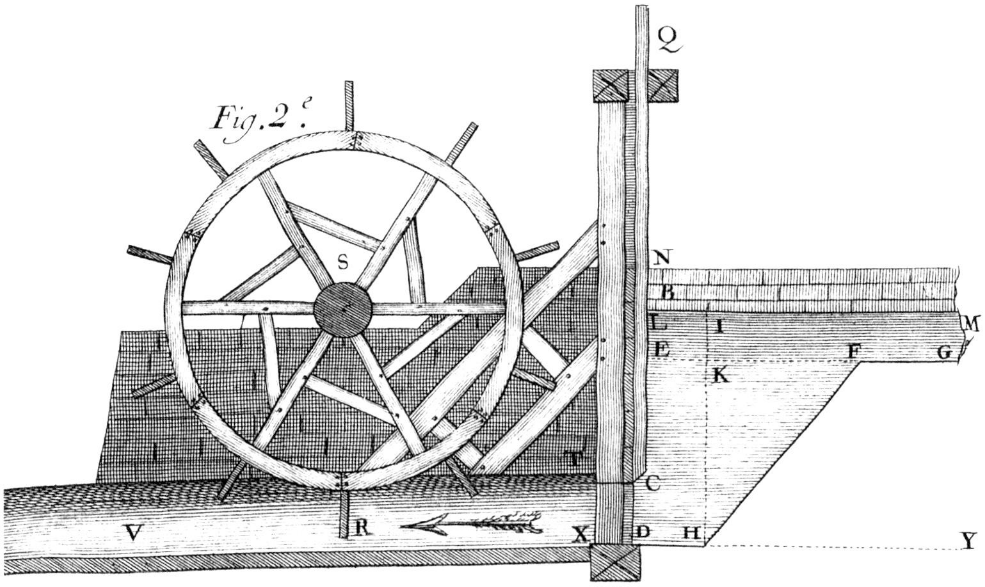

← Bernard Forest de Bélidor, "Different Ways to Set the Wheels of a Mill in Motion," *Architecture hydraulique*, 1737

↓ John James Drysdale and John Williams Hayward, "House No. 2," *Health and Comfort in House Building*, 1872

→ Thomas Pridgin Teale, "Window shut. Flame at the keyhole horizontal / Window open. Flame at the keyhole in repose," *Dangers to Health*, 1881 (1878)

↘ Thomas Pridgin Teale, "House with Every Sanitary Arrangement Fault," *Dangers to Health*, 1881 (1878)

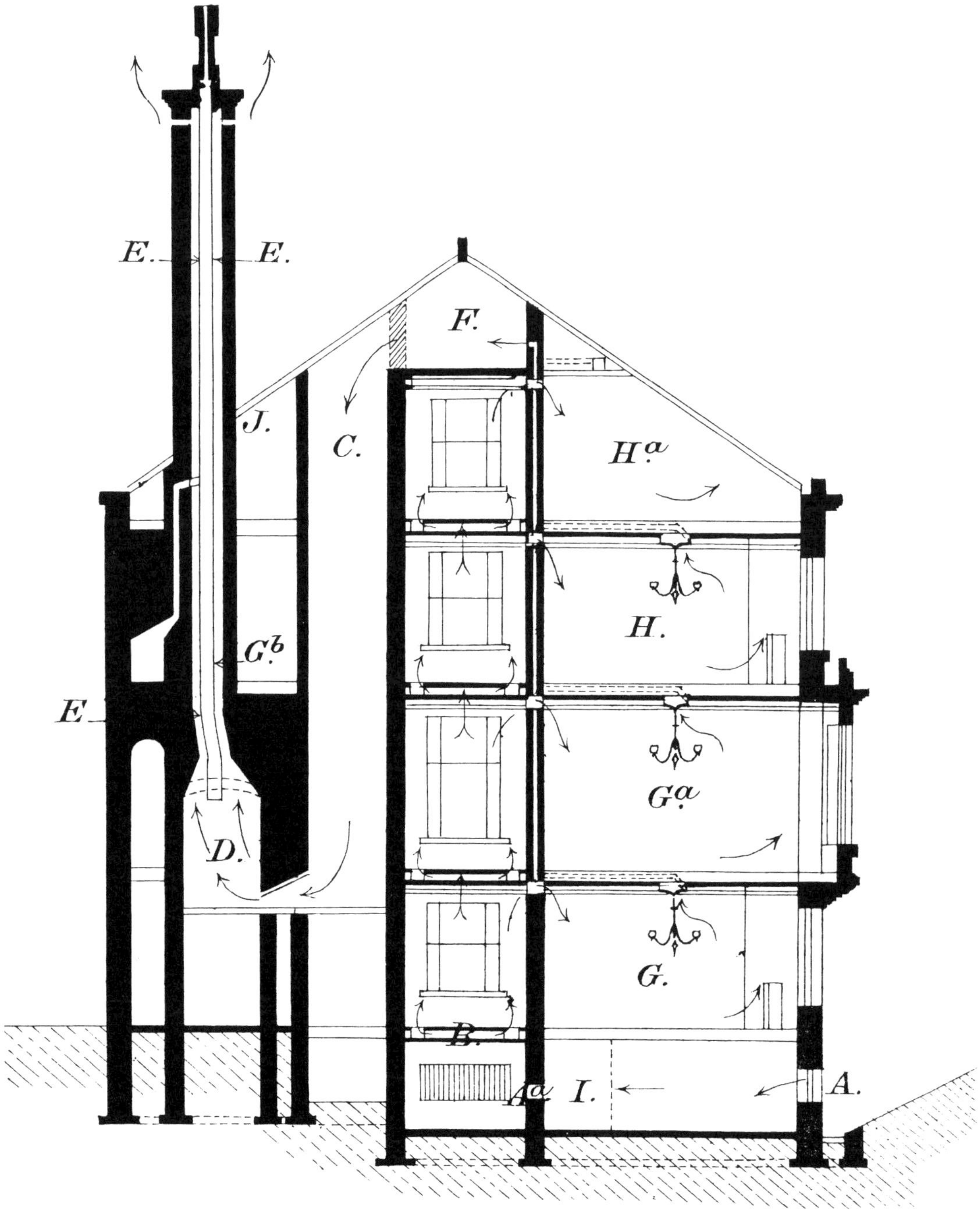

by Christine Frederick.[18] For both fluids and people, therefore, the arrow first served to map movements that were too volatile, ephemeral, or fragile to be otherwise visible or legible. They did this not just in terms of movement as an abstract condition, but in direct relation to the buildings that contained this movement. Moreover, besides being an effective tool for visualization, the arrow registered the possibility of investigating the potential operation of whatever was being represented on the drawing board.[19] In this sense, the arrow pointed the way for greater insights into flow and movement within pipes and shafts, as well as corridors and other spaces for the purpose of systematic planning, notably those demands at the end of the nineteenth century for better hygiene, and comfort. Nowhere is this more apparent than in the multiple editions of the successful "pictorial guide," *Dangers to Health*, first published by the British surgeon Thomas Pridgin Teale in 1878, and which highlighted the most common sanitary defects in building (and their remedy) in over fifty plates and a plethora of colored arrows, thus giving the arrow the leading role in the definition of better domestic design.[20]

By the 1930s arrows start to regularly appear in all the major journals of architecture—but mostly as a convention used in technical drawings. They depict situations as diverse as the direction of the flow in an air-conditioning pipe or warm air heating system, the ventilation in a school building, the movement of water in a swimming pool (from the inlets to the outlets, with or without wind), the loads in a facade, the artificial light sources inside libraries, the traffic flows of London, even the street-noise against a window. And yet despite this seemingly limitless variety of use, in drawings by architects they remain rare. This is not to say that the modern avant-garde was unconcerned with movement. On the contrary, in the projects of the Futurists, in the work of Ludwig Mies van der Rohe or Le Corbusier, and in the writings of *De Stijl*, movement is omnipresent. Absent, however, is the milieu in which it takes place. Significantly, very few arrows appear in Sigfried Giedion's *Mechanization Takes Command* (1948), the most comprehensive investigation of movement in the first half of the twentieth century.[21] The two most remarkable ones are taken from Paul Klee's *Pedagogical Sketchbook* (1925). The first, *Formation of the Black Arrow*, represents in the eyes of Giedion "the secret of projecting the psychological movement," while the second, *Spiral*, results from the shortening or lengthening of a radius. Movement in Giedion's survey is most memorably exhibited in the photographs of Jules Marey, Eadweard Muybridge, and Frank B. Gilbreth, or in the motion paintings of Marcel Duchamp. While these examples dissect the forms of subjects in different states of motion and time, they do not show the fluid in which this movement occurs.[22]

A parallel interest in arrows in both history and practice—or, more precisely, in historical and contemporary drawings—is possible to trace, but it happens at the very moment that arrows themselves start to disappear (an eventual absence that is perhaps the best proof of their general acceptance). One such example is to be found in the October 1968 issue of the *Architectural Review*. Here, Drysdale and Hayward's house in Liverpool with its arrow-mapped

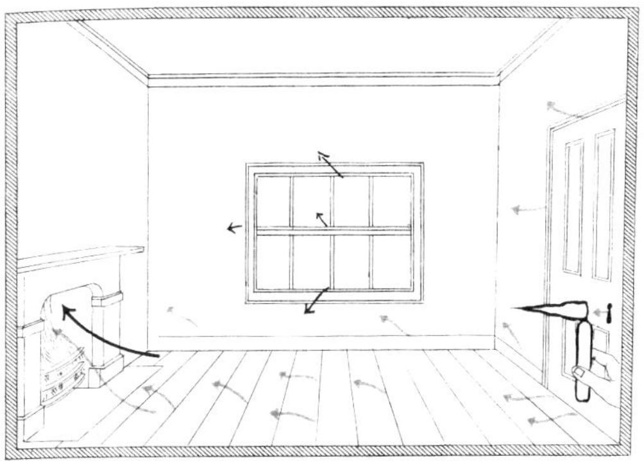

"A." Window shut. Flame at the keyhole horizontal.

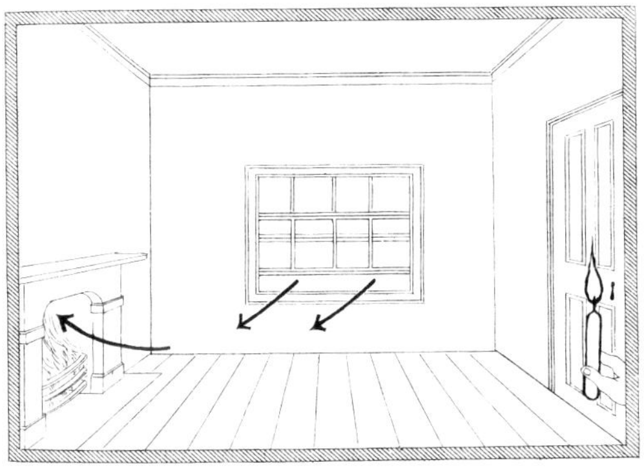

"B." Window open. Flame at the keyhole in repose.

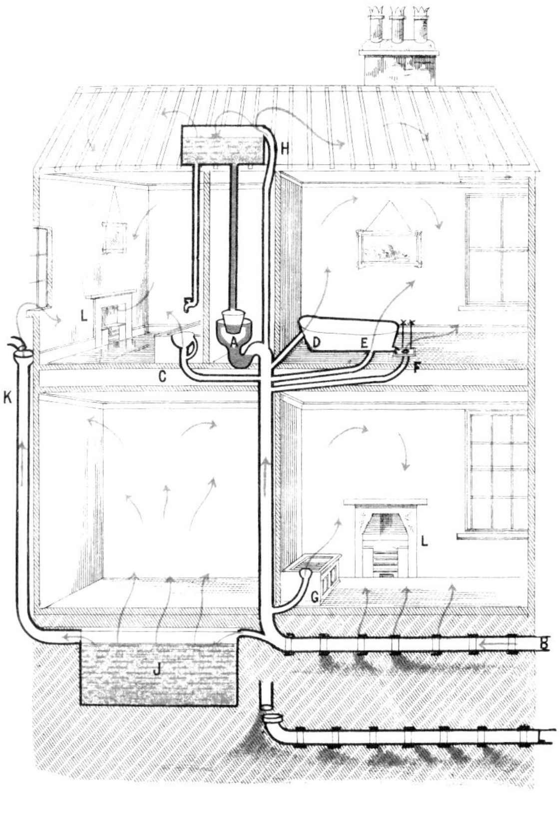

→ "Apparatus for Catching and Suspending Hogs," 1882, in Sigfried Giedion, *Mechanization Takes Command*, 1948

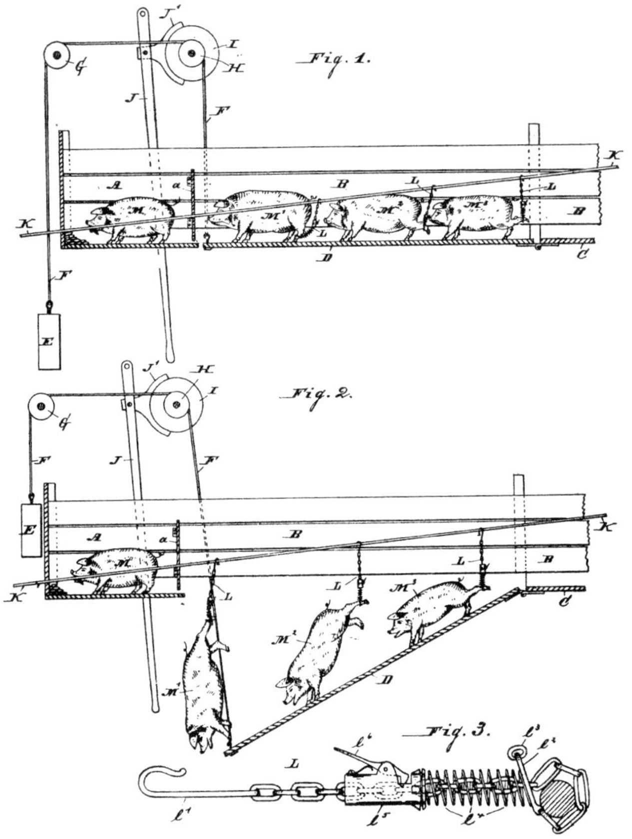

ventilation-system illustrates an article by Reyner Banham on the "Dark Satanic Century," an introduction to the history of artificial ventilation in interiors and a preview of the eponymous chapter of his broad-ranging study of the well-tempered environment of 1969. More than anywhere else, the full extent of Banham's future book, through his wink to the preludes and fugues of Johann Sebastian Bach's *Well-Tempered Clavier*, becomes evident as a plea to integrate all the technical mastery of all the major and minor keys at the turn of a new era.[23]

That this new era was already playing out was acknowledged by Banham just two months later in the same journal when discussing James Stirling's History Faculty library building in Cambridge (1968), whose "environmental mechanics" were amply illustrated by arrows across accompanying sections and plans.[24] While on paper Banham had been investigating past instances of attempts by Drysdale and Hayward to control the architectural climate, Stirling was busy attempting to control the same thing in red bricks and mortar, steel and glass, underfloor and ceiling heating, insulated double-glazing, and ventilation systems (both mechanical and natural), inducing the same well-tempered environment the critic was championing.[25] But however present the arrows are in these instances, they are never explicitly mentioned. Both Stirling and Banham evidently had more faith in their audience than Thomas Pridgin Teale, who eighty years earlier in *Sanitary Defects*, had been obliged to explain that "the course and escape of sewer gases are indicated by blue arrows."[26]

There is one small but meaningful difference between the arrows in Drysdale and Hayward's drawing and those that appear in Stirling's project. In addition to the curved arrows, which were the nineteenth-century convention for representing the circulation of fresh or foul air, the plans and sections for Cambridge introduce straight arrows. Following their trajectory reveals a concern that would have been overlooked by anyone who, like Banham, was obsessed with the climatically controlled environment. As Stirling's various arrows for Cambridge reveal, "environment" implied not merely technologically controlled climatic parameters (again, as represented in curved arrows) but, more ambitiously, architectural and spatial ones. This effect is succinctly represented in a sectional drawing that uses a pair of straight directional arrows to chart the gaze of the librarian overseeing the annular, slightly recessed complex of the reading room, stacks, and central lending desk. The visual arrangement enables the entire space to be monitored at a single glance, a feature evidently crucial to Stirling's success in the competition[27]—as in a prison, as one Cambridge don sniped.[28] Indeed, just like a panopticon, the assortment of shelves in the library are separated from each other by a corridor and are back-lit, allowing them to be viewed from the central desk, which again, true to Bentham's ideal prison, lies in the darkest area, its occupant seeing everything without ever being seen by the reader.[29]

↘ Paul Klee, *Formation of the Black Arrow*, 1925, and Frank B. Gilbreth, *Perfect Movement*, 1912, in Sigfried Giedion, *Mechanization Takes Command*, 1948

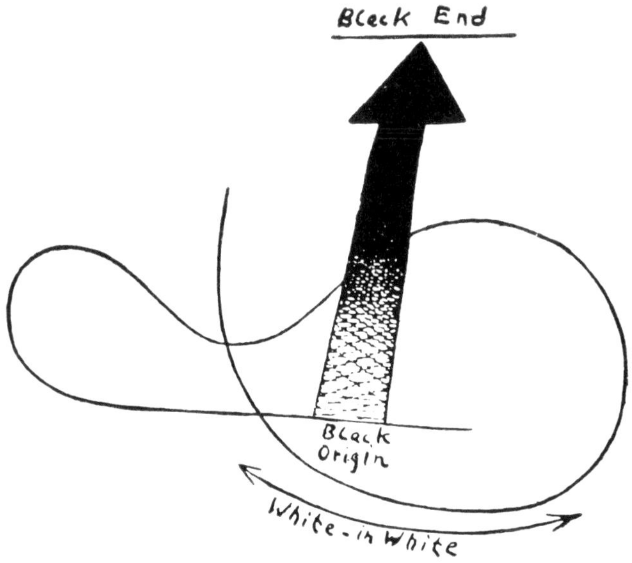

53. PAUL KLEE: 'Formation of the Black Arrow.' 1925. *Better perhaps than any other painter, Paul Klee has the secret of projecting psychological movement. In Klee's work the pointer arrow in the shape of a rectangle headed by a triangle first appeared — an artistic symbol before it became internationally familiar in ordinary use. 'The given white is accepted by the eye as customary, but the contrasting strangeness of action (black), sharpens vividness of vision for the climax, or end.' (Klee,* Pedagogical Sketchbook, *tr. Sybil Peech, Courtesy Nierendorf Gallery, New York)*

54. FRANK B. GILBRETH: Perfect Movement. Wire Model, *c.*1912. *(Courtesy Lillian M. Gilbreth)*

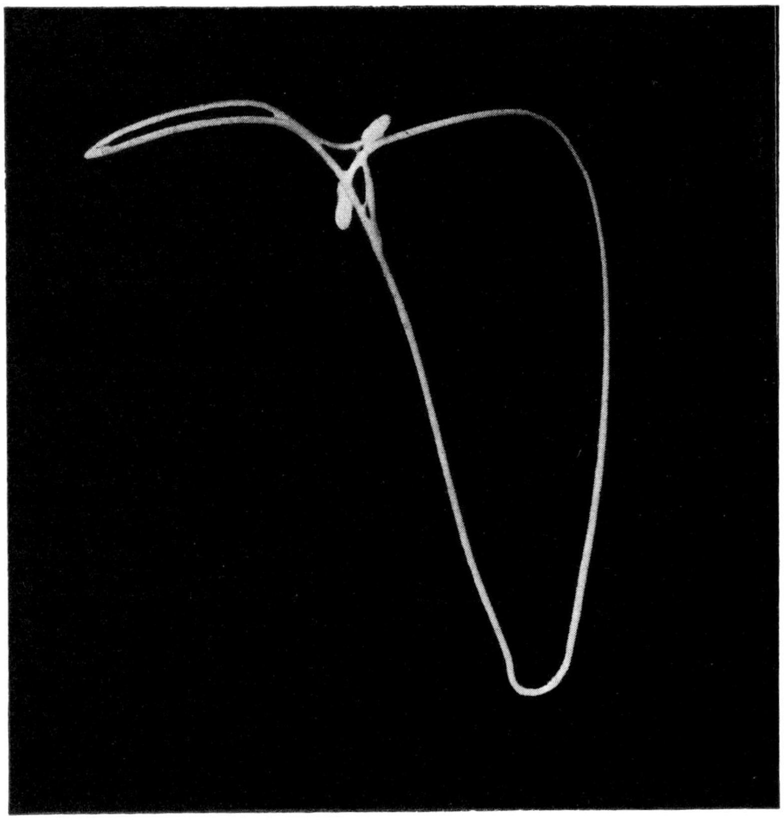

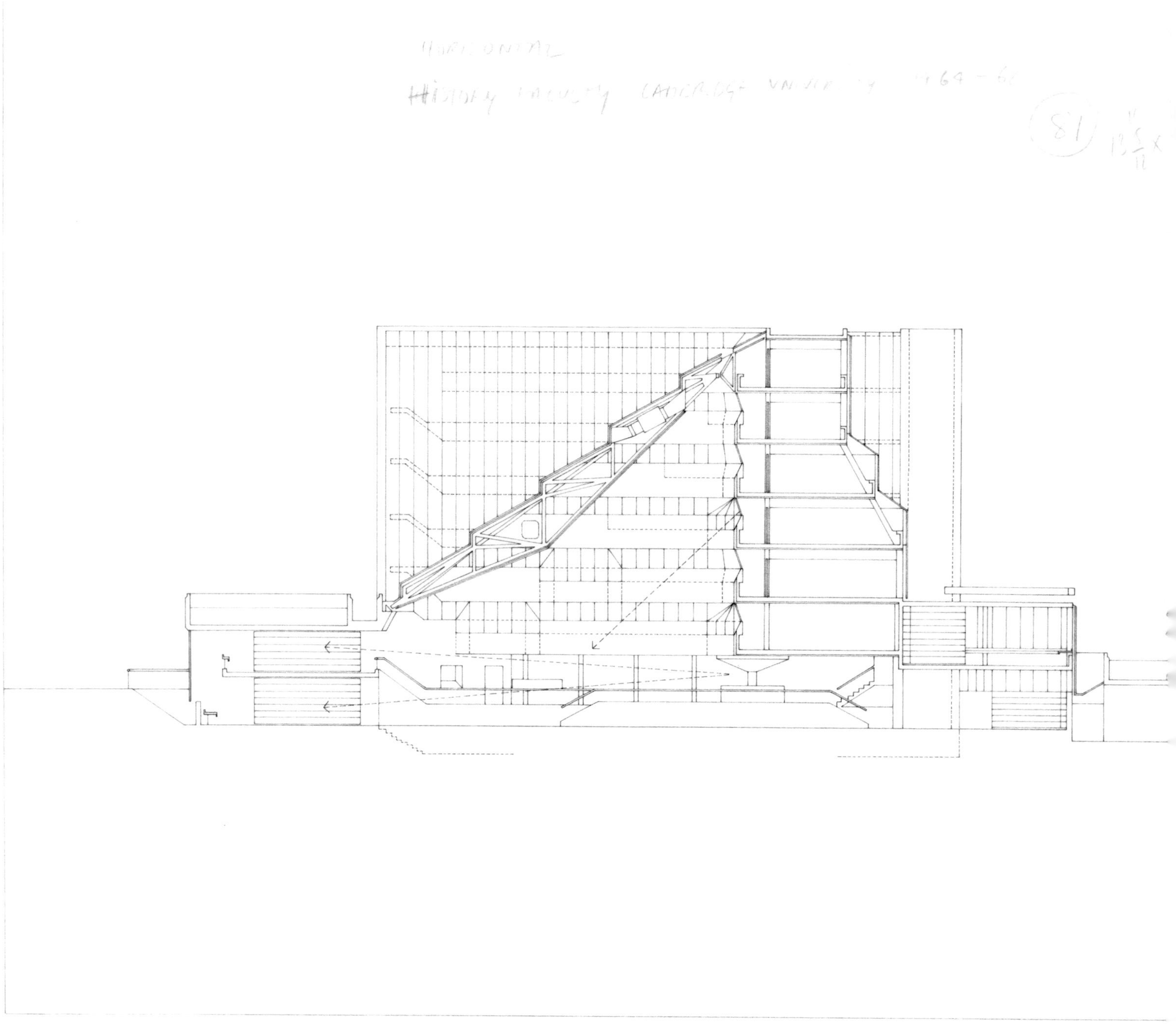
81

← James Stirling, section, Cambridge University History Faculty Building, Cambridge, 1964–1968

↓ James Stirling, solar diagram, Cambridge University History Faculty Building, Cambridge, 1964–1968

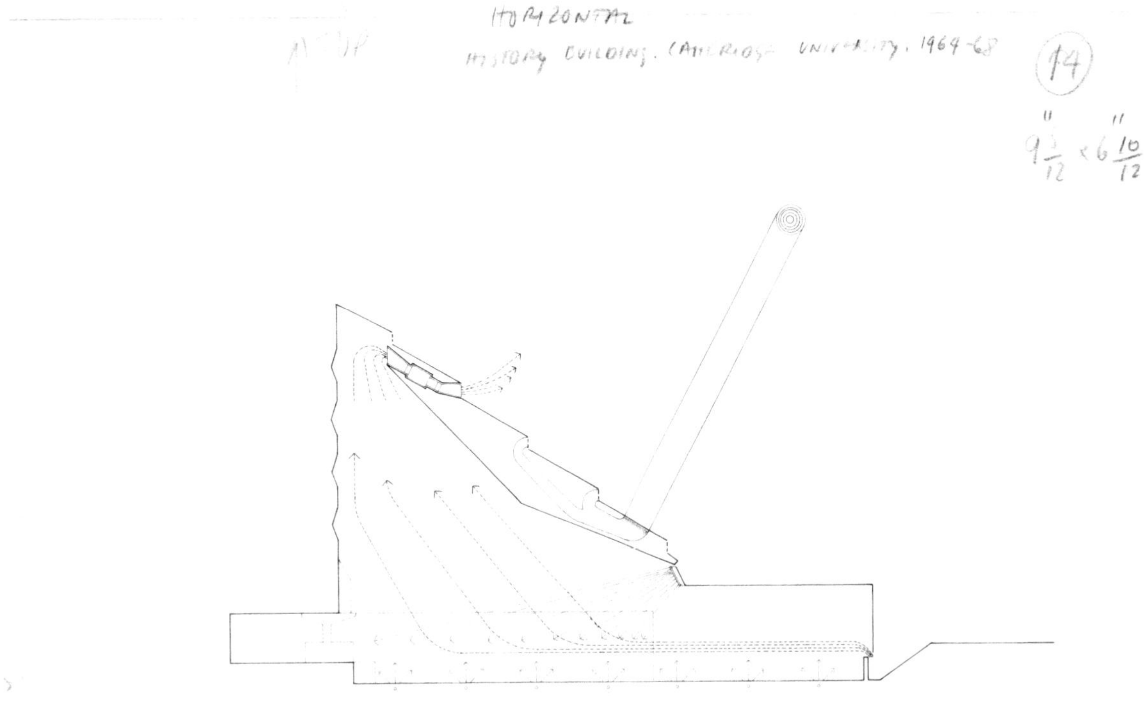

↓ James Stirling, ground floor plan, Cambridge University History Faculty Building, Cambridge,1964–1968

↘ James Stirling, first floor plan, Cambridge University History Faculty Building, Cambridge, 1964–1968

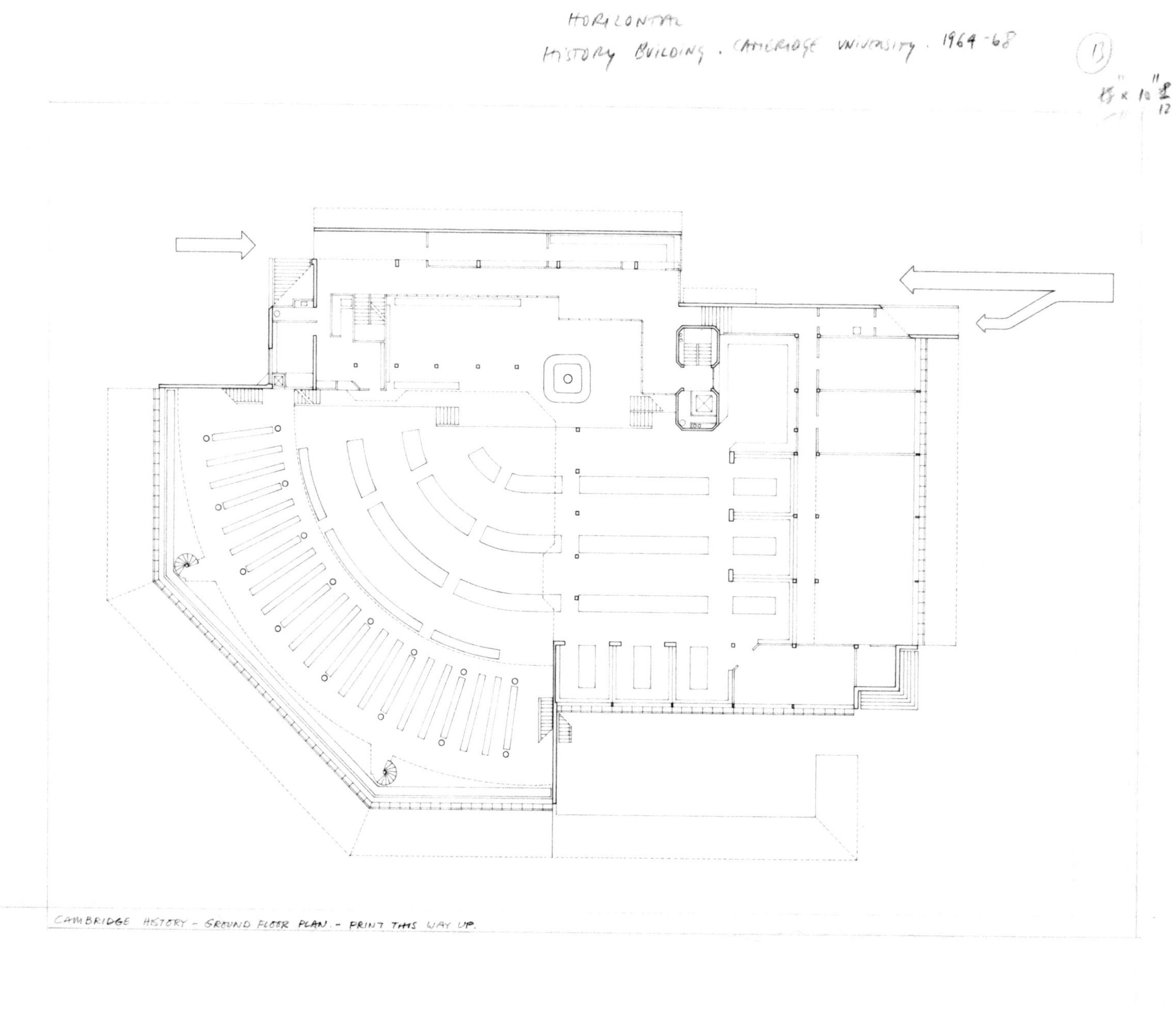

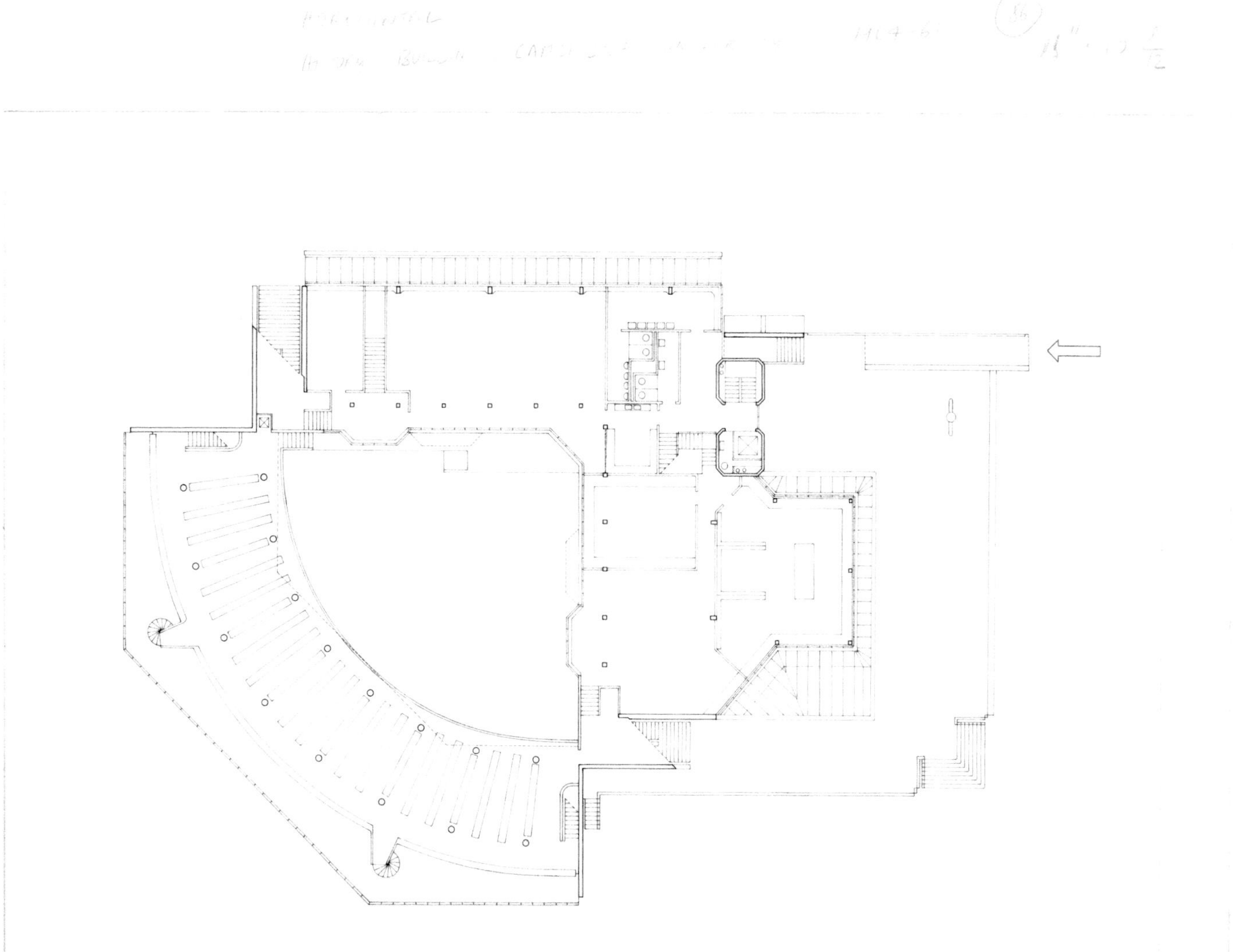
CAMBRIDGE HISTORY - FIRST FLOOR PLAN - PRINT THIS WAY UP

But if the library can be read as an apparatus, literally as well as metaphorically, which is determined by its concentrated disposition of figures, volumes, gazes, and light around a quarter-circle, it differs in a significant way from the disciplinary dimension of the prison. For the central lending desk not only is the preserve of the librarian but also houses the technical controls for the building's lighting, ventilation, and heating (as in the Staatsbibliothek, built in Berlin by Hans Scharoun that same year).[30] It organizes and guides the movement of users on the ground floor while supposedly controlling their wellbeing. In Cambridge what is at stake is less the even distribution of bodies in space than the control of a multi-layered visual, climatic, and spatial environment, whose borders are blurred by a combination of the white light of the ceiling, the atmospheric conditions of the reading room, and the open plan at the ground floor.

In the Cambridge project arrows reveal concerns by mapping out and controlling climatic conditions, social relations, or organizational matters. Their scope, to stay with Stirling's work, extends to picturesque dispositions in St. Andrews (1964–1967; where the rows of the student rooms open to the wider landscape), to structural information (as in his unbuilt Dorman-Long Headquarters in Middlesbrough of 1965, where the arrow uncovers forces otherwise not visible), to infrastructural provisions in the Leicester Engineering Building (1963; a building that could also be read as a circulation diagram) or to a notational device indicating the movement of people (those in a hurry at Leicester or those strolling through the galleries in Stuttgart; 1979–1984).

Stirling was not the only postwar architect to fall back on arrows in this way. Almost ten years earlier, as part of their London Road study of 1959, Alison and Peter Smithson used them to illustrate increased one-way traffic in Soho. In their entry to the 1957 Hauptstadt Berlin competition, arrows define the sightlines of users from viewing platforms, and in drawings for Robin Hood Gardens they map the "knowable area" of the neighborhood. In a group of 1956 studies on tropical architecture by Maxwell Fry and Jane Drew, arrows define the house as a response to the natural movement of air, and the incidence of sun or rainwater—as do the arrows trading wind and sun in Ralph Erskine's sketches for towns in hot climates.

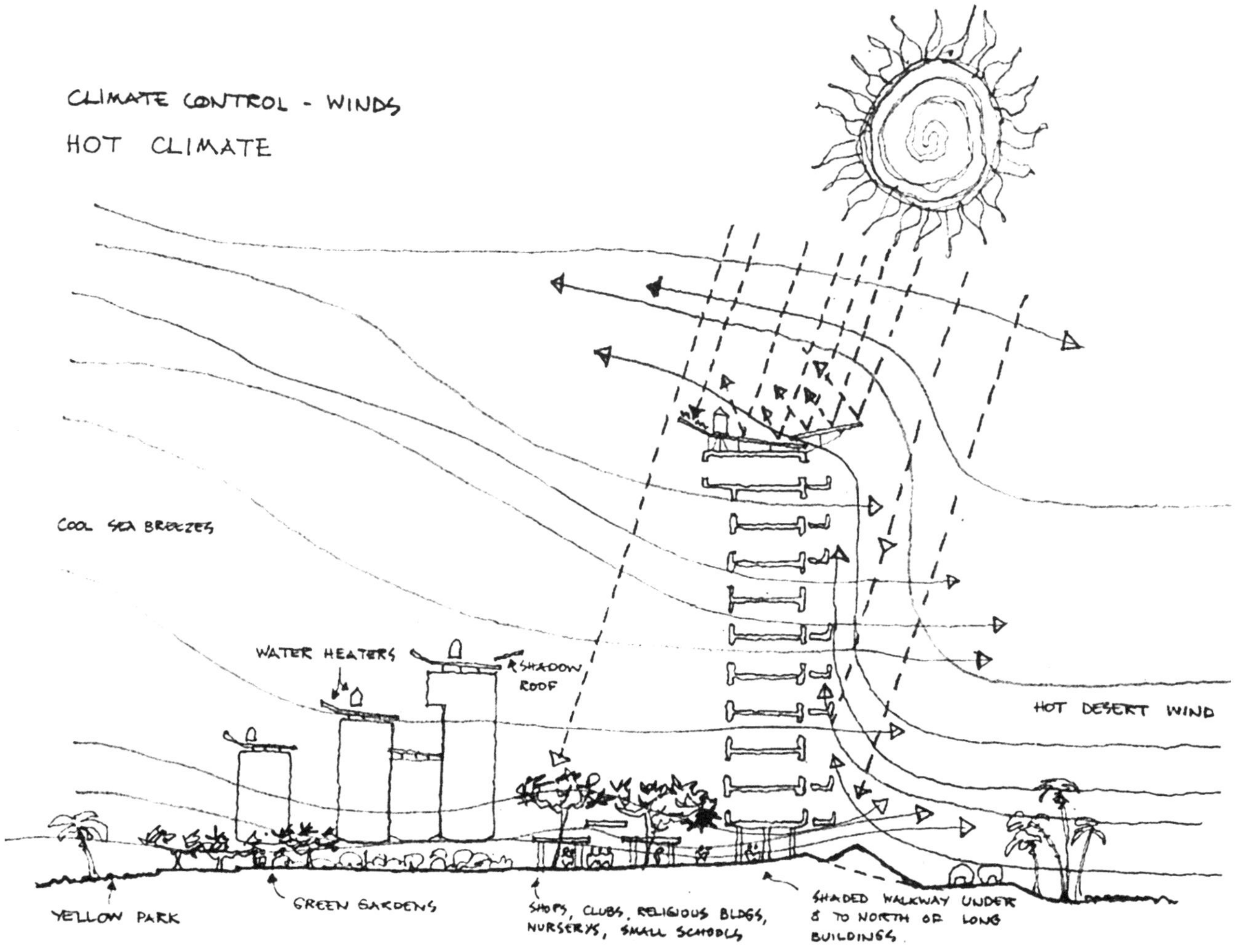

↙ Ralph Erskine, “Climate Control—Winds. Hot Climate,” 1966

→ Alison and Peter Smithson, “Knowable Areas,” Robin Hood Gardens, London, 1966–1972

↓ Alison and Peter Smithson, “Green Wedges,” from Street Somerset, 1975–1976

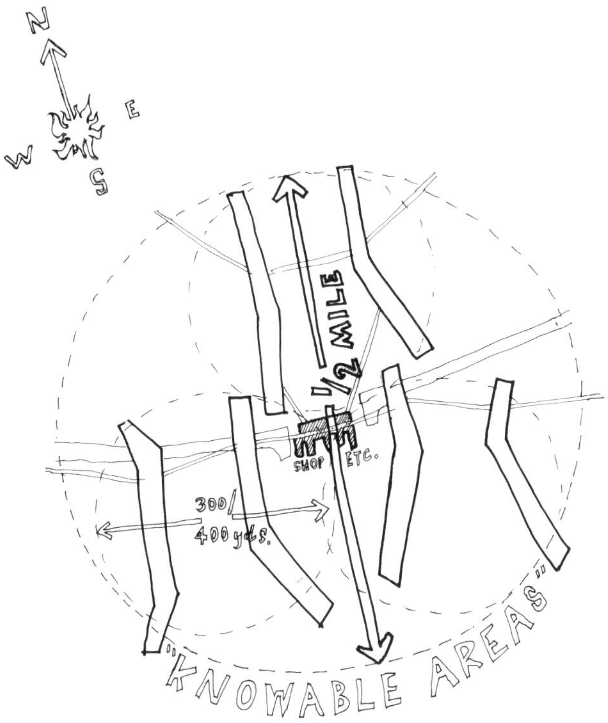

→ James Gowan and James Stirling, diagram of vertical and horizontal circulation, Leicester University Engineering Building, 1959–1963

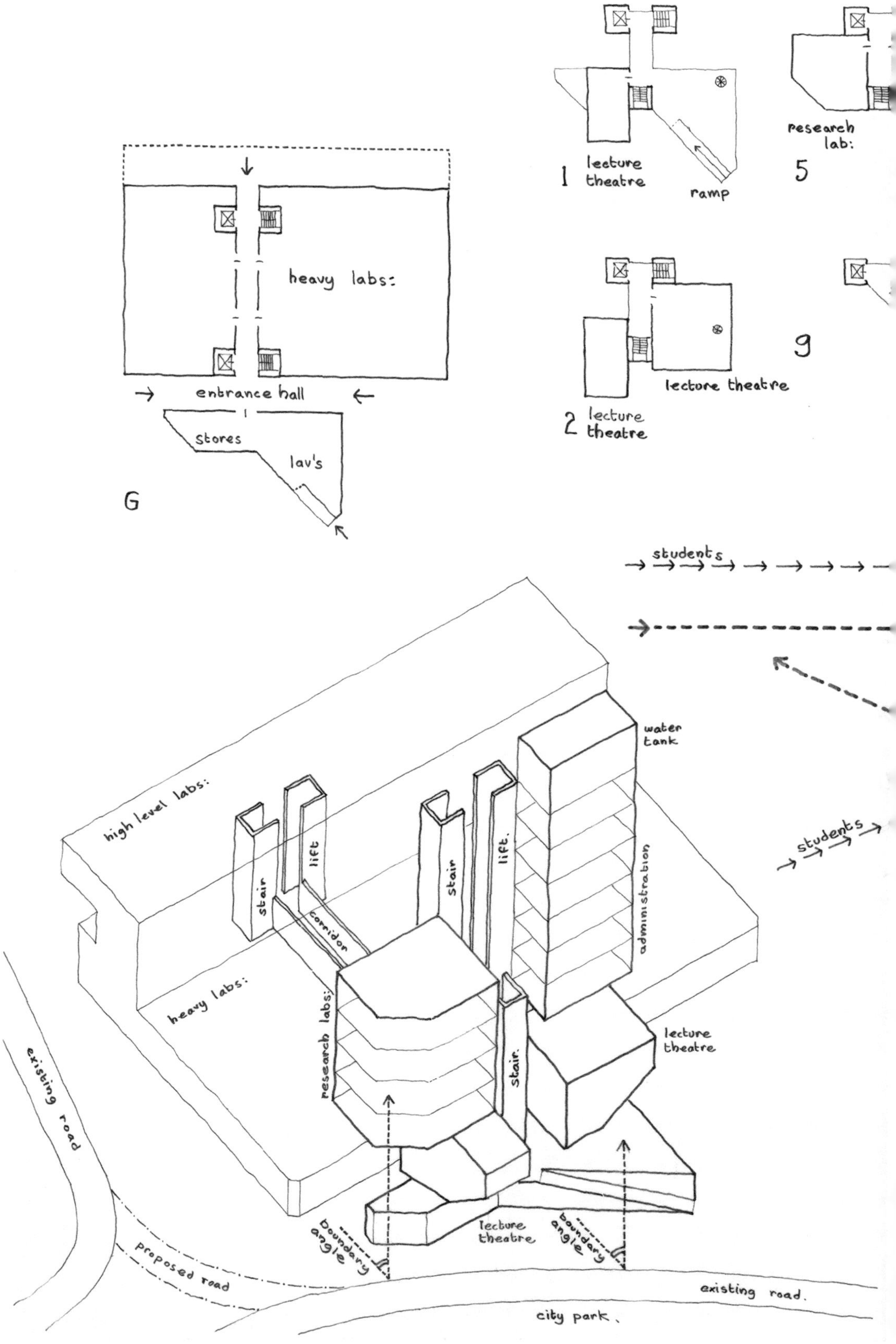

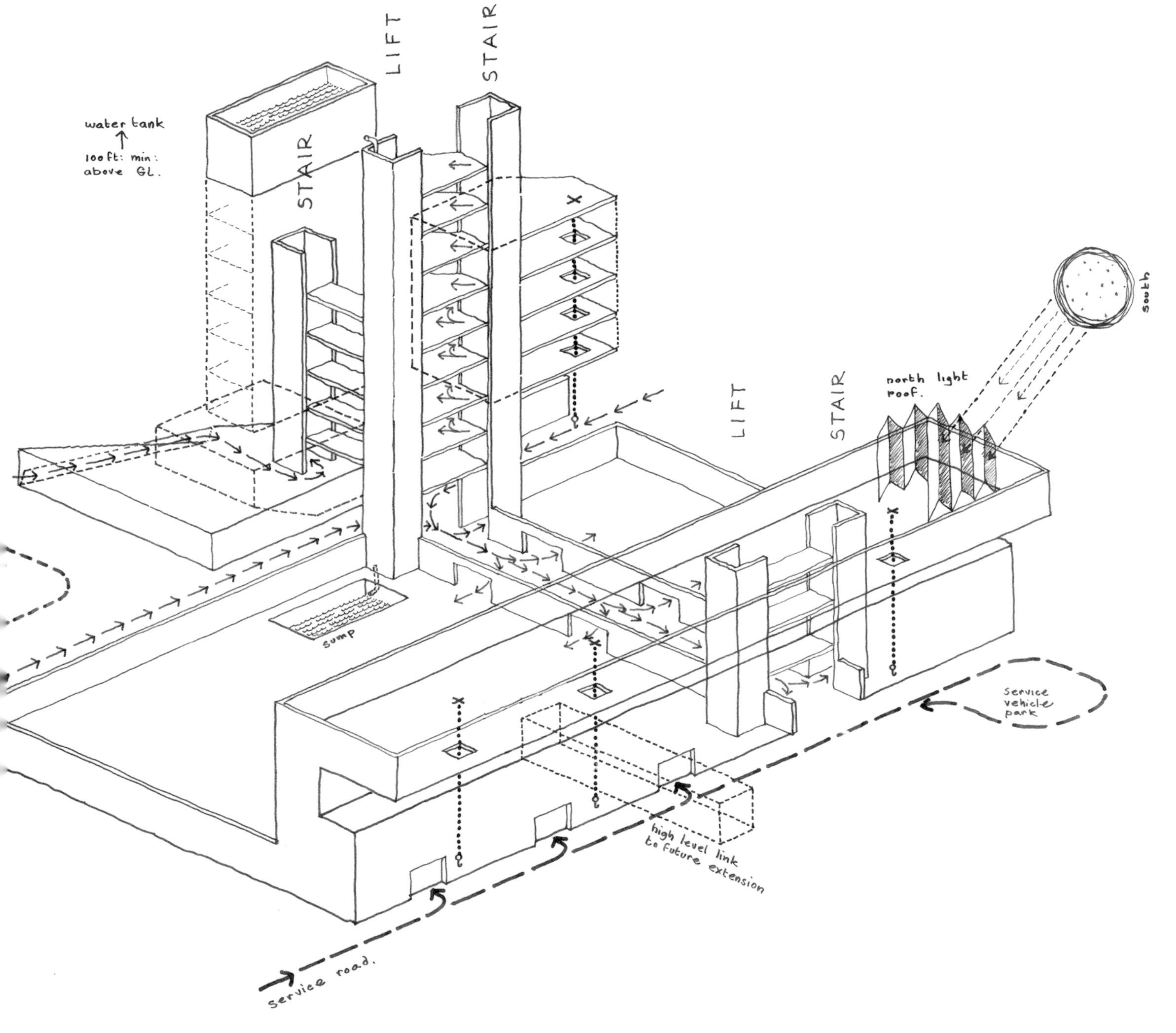

water tank
100 ft: min: above GL.
STAIR
LIFT
STAIR
north light roof.
south
LIFT
STAIR
sump
service vehicle park
high level link to future extension
service road.

Within all these drawings are curved or straight arrows. Yet, there are also other kinds of arrows that not only represent movement but also qualify it. This is achieved in one of two ways: arrows either stand in for the mass of movement and match its contours, or they convey the intensity or density of movement by replicating themselves. In Cambridge, for instance, arrows that map the ins and outs of the floor plans are shown at different widths, splitting into different smaller branches depending on the various user flows and sequences inside and outside the building. In the Drew and Fry studies on natural ventilation, the changing width of the arrow indicates the velocity of the wind, while in other drawings, the intensity of the sun is reflected in the compact arrangement of several arrows in parallel. Returning to the Smithsons' London Road study, the precision of the movement to be achieved in the planning of the inner-city traffic is represented by the high density of arrows that map out the equally dense net of one-way streets.[31] Arrows in these projects not only mimic movement but, more importantly, quantify performance—in the case of the London Road study, it was the provision for a three hundred percent increase in traffic over the next thirty years.

In this sense, the arrow moves beyond architecture towards the realm of the social sciences, appearing across charts, graphs, and reports, recording data in real time. A particularly striking example involves no arrows at all, but a "trail of cotton" used in 1955 by Richard Llewelyn-Davies while leading a team of architects, historians, physicians, nurses, statisticians, and accountants as part of the Nuffield Foundation's first systematic investigation of postwar hospital environments. The resulting publication, *Studies in the Functions and Design of Hospitals*, recorded the trajectories of nurses in different ward units, not unlike earlier studies by Christine Fredericks, which focused on the movements of housewives in kitchens, or Alexander Klein's research into the habitation of flats. For the Nuffield project, the research group methodically charted the movement patterns and frequencies of every nurse at different stages of education. These routes were individually recorded on hospital plans using trails of stretched cotton wool. Inasmuch that arrows had been used by architects to animate the otherwise invisible or hidden infrastructure of static objects, this method enabled an even greater—and literal—degree of transparency: opaque crossings, created by overlapping routes, allowed researchers to identify the principal movements and the critical circulation points inside the ward.[32] Even if the transformation of the arrow back into its geometrical progenitor, the line, might appear as a return to a more conventional art-historical lineage (in which the line demarcates a wall), it is not. Instead, it follows a trajectory in which the line delineates the movement between the walls, connecting two points on a plan, as seen in the single strokes darkening the hospital floor where the movements were most frequent, and grinding around every corner of the contorted geometry of the wards.

The use of arrows (or a trail of cotton) as both a design tool and medium of representation differs from earlier incarnations, such as those seen in the planning of heating systems, say of the Houses of Parliament by the chemist David Boswell Reid in the mid-nineteenth century up to those used by Maxwell Fry in his analysis of the Sun House in the 1930s. During this period, with the exception of the heating or ventilating infrastructure, questions of disposition and composition dominated the architect's intentions. As Fry writes of his Hampstead project: "All architects know that 'design' is ... the inherent result of the proper planning of a building and the arrangement of its parts."[33] In line with his argument, the house follows the latest recommendations in terms of its orientation while answering certain economic considerations regarding circulation. And yet its formal expression still corresponds to the purist canon. In the built environment of the postwar years, however, this attitude changes as the good management of "fluids" and their thorough control begin to dominate the whole building and its spaces. Evidence of this is not merely limited to the imposing images of the avant-garde, as epitomized by the shafts of Warren Chalk's capsule towers (1964) or Michael Webb's furniture factory (1957–1958), whose rhetorically inflated forms later transpired in the heroic projects of Richard Rogers and Renzo Piano. The careful, even visionary, design of infrastructure comes through in the numerous less emphatic proposals and built works that defined architecture throughout Britain in the 1950s and 1960s.

↓ Maxwell Fry and Jane Drew, "Air Heated by the Sun," *Tropical Architecture*, 1964

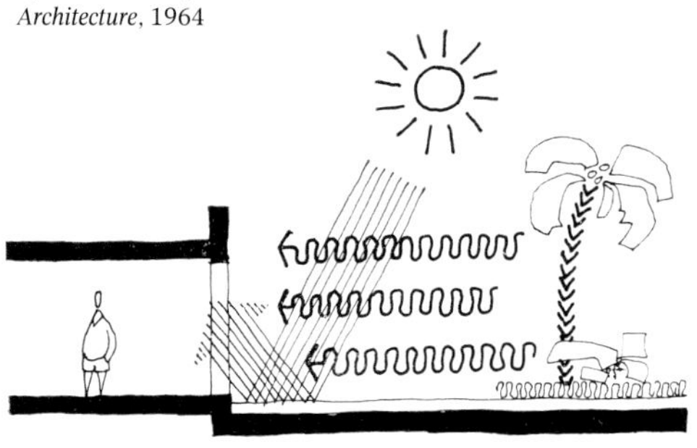

↓ Maxwell Fry and Jane Drew, "Air Movement," *Tropical Architecture*, 1964

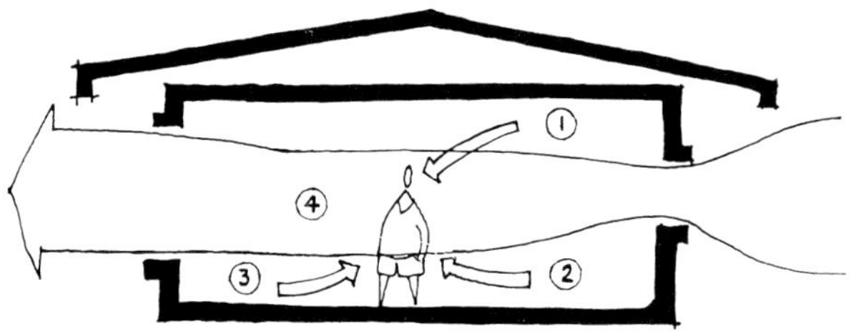

↓ University of Bristol, “Pattern of Movement in Ward Units,” *Studies in the Functions and Design of Hospitals*, 1955

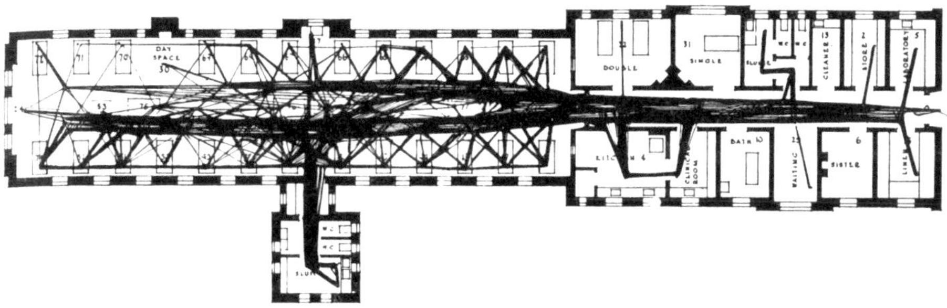

Fig. 3. The pattern of movement of a first-year student nurse during a complete tour of duty in a ward unit in the Bradford Royal Infirmary

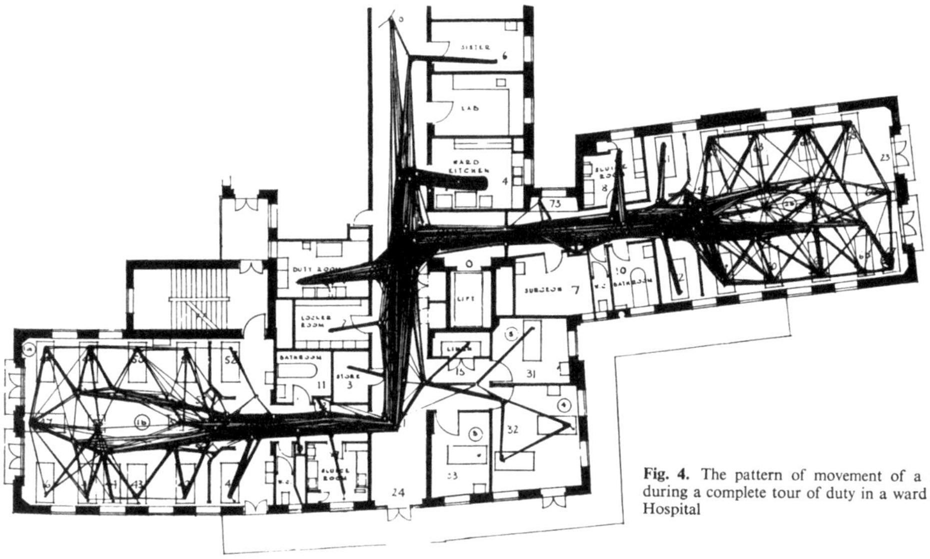

Fig. 4. The pattern of movement of a first-year student nurse during a complete tour of duty in a ward unit in the Westminster Hospital

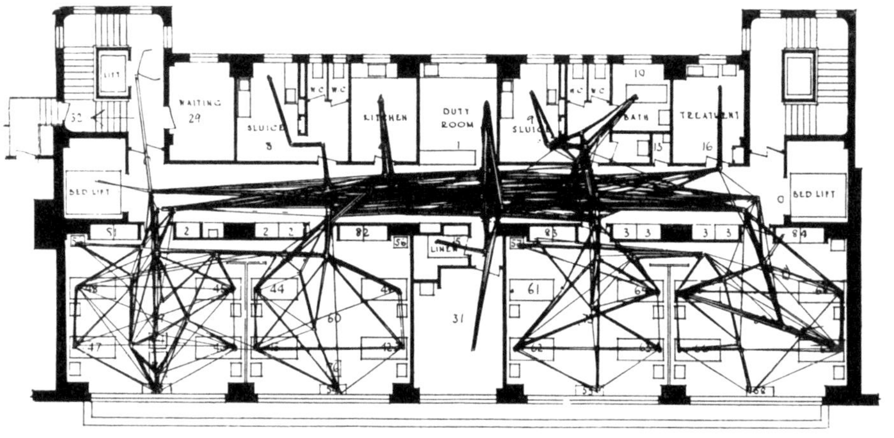

Fig. 5. The pattern of movement of a nurse in training, during a complete tour of duty in a ward unit in the National Hospital, Queen Square

HOLBORN MET B & PH
SOUTH BLOOMSBURY WARD
LINCOLN'S INN WARD
CENTRAL ST GILES WARD
ST ANNE WARD
COVENT GARDEN WARD
REGENT WARD
PALL MALL WARD
CHARING CROSS WARD
STRAND
RIVER THAMES
NEW WAYS FOR LONDO
PLAN TQ 3080
MOTORWAY.
60 STREET – ONE WAY DISTRIBUTION TO & FROM
MECHANICAL PARK FOR ... CARS
SELF PARK UNIT FOR COMMUTORS, ADJACENT TO TAKE-OFF
3-TIER PARKING BENEATH MOT
MOTORWAY LEVEL.

← Alison and Peter Smithson, "New Ways for London," from the London Road Study, 1959

↓ Denys Lasdun, axonometric of typical structural bay showing services, University of East Anglia, Norwich, 1962–1968

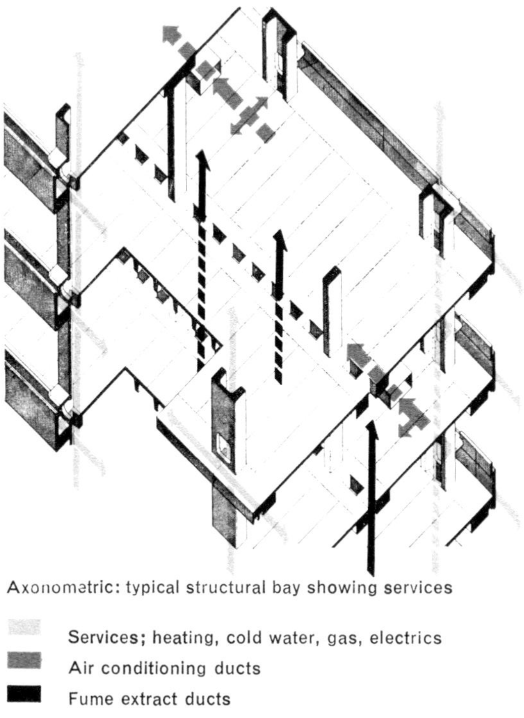

If asked to identify a single element that could have served as the built equivalent of the arrow and which illustrated this approach, one might suggest the triangular elevated decks with central staircase that first appeared in the competition entry for the Berlin Hauptstadt, made by the Smithsons with Peter Sigmonde. These would resurface in the London County Council's South Bank Center (1962–1965) and in Denys Lasdun's University of East Anglia (1964–1968). Similarly prominent are the towers that appear in Lasdun's major university buildings from the mid-1960s and his Cluster Block in Bethnal Green (1952–1955), George Finch's Lambeth Tower (1965–1967), or Ernö Goldfinger's Balfron Tower (1965–1967), all of which showcase their freestanding lifts or vertically arranged service tracts, while rhythmically articulating their plans.

Even where the preoccupation with infrastructure is not immediately apparent—presumably because we have now grown accustomed to this type of organization—the logic of infrastructure decisively shaped the ground plan. A good example is Lasdun's University of East Anglia, where the relationship between infrastructure and architecture is blurred (if not reversed). Looking at the published presentation drawings, arrows appear parsimoniously, and when deployed they follow in the tradition of technical drawings.[34] Such restraint, whether as a reaction against a certain form of avant-gardist exaltation or as general acceptance of the ideas they convey, reveals that the operative dimension is still present in Lasdun's hand. Thus in the axonometric of the teaching and research wing in Norwich, arrows are only used to map the obvious movements of heating, water, and energy supplies in the service ducts.[35] More important, however, is the impact of these movements on the whole structure of the building. Encased in lateral U-shaped pillars of precast concrete, the supply services along with the middle pillars supporting the precast ceiling elements, determine the seventy centimeter module of the laboratory building. While these concrete elements are designed to meet the static requirements, their rhythm and size is dictated by the infrastructural and organizational demands of the individual laboratories. In this sense the once dominant, prescriptive structural logic of the Dom-ino system, as described by Le Corbusier thirty years earlier, is replaced by that of infrastructure from which all other elements are derived. This includes the various built-in fittings and furnishings, such as the specially designed lamps installed between the T-girders and the windows whose various functions (lateral ventilation through aluminum vents and in-built rainwater gutters) constitute an integrated facade system.[36] On a larger scale, a design based on an infrastructural model simultaneously guaranteed the optimal serial production of construction elements while ensuring maximum flexibility for users to come. The same organizational logic of the natural sciences block could therefore be applied to the humanities wing, allowing for future transformations of the classrooms into laboratories.

At East Anglia, the various dimensions—structural, constructive, infrastructural, circulatory, or otherwise—are entangled. Contrary to the typically modernist endeavor to separate and specify the different functional elements, the most distinct strands are also the most mutually dependent

↓ Alvin Boyarsky, Vitruvian man overlaid onto a plan of the Royal College of Physicians, *Architectural Design*, 1965

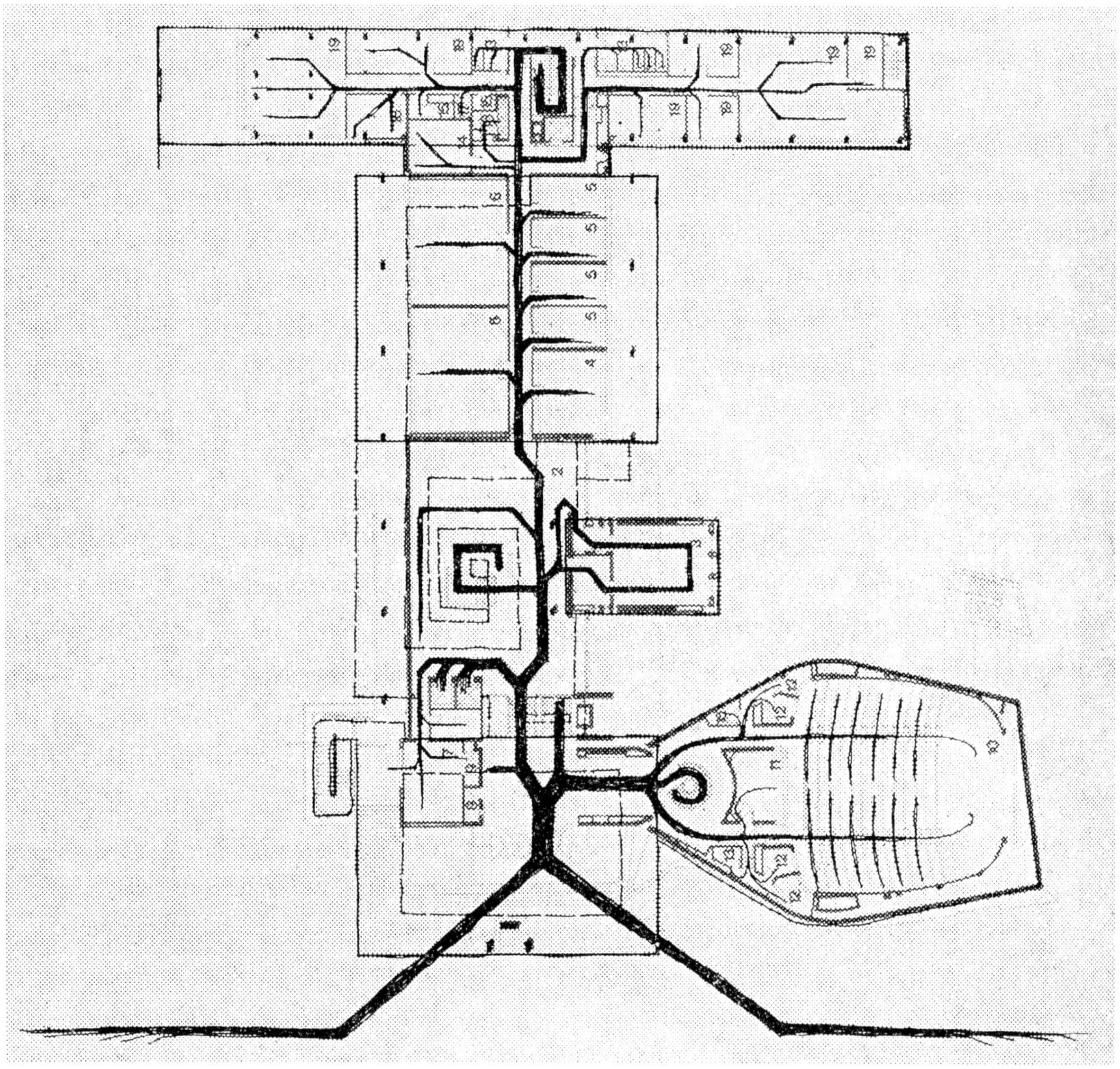

on the common performance to be fulfilled: the statics and the organization of the laboratories; the composition of the facades and the ventilation and heating; prefabrication and use. This entangling is in fact integral to the logic of infrastructure and its attendant issues of performance. Not limited to specialized buildings, such as laboratories or office complexes, it featured much more generally across postwar modernism and its corresponding spatial concepts.

The theoretical and spatial implications of Lasdun's approach at East Anglia were to be addressed in another of his buildings, the Royal College of Physicians, built in London from 1959 to 1964. While redolent of his more formally ambitious projects, a variety of innovative technologies allowed it to correspond fully to what was then expected for a building of its standard. Heating panels located in the floor and ceiling, for instance, served public areas and offices located at the rear, while individual air-conditioning units were installed in the assembly rooms, library, conference room, and canteen. A radio system in the main auditorium was designed for simultaneous translation, and complementing the more conventional networks conveying energy or water was a TV system interlinking the various theaters.

None of this, however, is mentioned by Alvin Boyarsky in his elaborate review of the completed project for *Architectural Design*, which dissects the architect's *parti pris* by looking, literally, under the skin. Perhaps more important than the text is an illustration of a Vitruvian Man—not the typical *homo ad quadratum*, rather his *circulatio sanguingis* overlaid as a diagram onto the plan of the building.[37] The vascular analogy was precisely Boyarsky's argument when comparing the layout of the building with a group of four seventeenth-century wooden panels that displayed the arterial system. The English physician William Harvey had used these when presenting his discovery of the continuous circulation of blood before the very same College of Physicians. As Boyarsky writes speaking about the building (not the panels): "there are the major arteries, the bifurcations for the limbs, with their secondary and tertiary tributaries; there are the overlapping spirals connecting the organs to each other and to the central spine."[38]

Again (as in Nuffield) the arrow cedes to circulation routes (this time organic ones). The main path starts at the portico (with its central pillar aligned on this major axis), continues through the foyer to the main auditorium and the spiral staircase that leads to the split-level library. Or, after a further turn, it flows to the assembly room. Alternatively, it moves down from the foyer to the below-ground theaters. Drawn with a thick black stroke that tapers in a point at the end, the movement throughout the building is conceived as a flow modulated by stairs, ceilings, stairs, doors, and windows into a sequence of spatial layers with their own atmoswphere: "formal, informal, warm, cold, public or private, high or low status," as Lasdun would put it years later, when describing the different spatial effects achieved throughout the building by altering the light, proportion, material, and climate.[39]

The Vitruvian Man is notable for establishing the obvious biological analogy between the building and organism, or routes and the circulation system, or an enclosing fabric and cellular membranes (Boyarsky, pushing the comparison further, would underline all these points in his article).[40] What is perhaps more interesting, is when the biological analogy confronted with the "environmental mechanics"—not only those highlighted in other buildings of the time, like Stirling's Cambridge Library, but also those which are equally present in the Royal College of Physicians and yet ignored in the comments of both the architect and the critic. It would, however, be wrong to read this distinction as a simple move away from a mechanistic understanding towards an organistic conception of architecture. These two perspectives—one mechanical, the other biological or vital—do not contradict each another but represent two sides of the same coin. They point towards the extent to which the technical became rooted in a new understanding of the living.[41] The arrows that therefore direct the gaze of a librarian, or distinguish a "knowable area," or chart the path of a pedestrian or a ship, or even map the acoustic reflection inside a building—and not just these but also the arrow-less strokes that illustrate the movements of people—are for sure precise ways of depicting the operational demands put on postwar architecture, but perhaps more importantly they are expressions of a new infrastructurally informed organization of the human environment.

At this point it might be tempting to draw connections between the arrows in architectural plans and others that emerged in the 1950s: the innumerable ones that appeared on roads and on signage along the streets that Gordon Cullen and members of the Townscape movement had critiqued as an outrage (the most improbably yet widespread arrows being those indicating how to circumnavigate a roundabout); the arrows in the psychogeographic map of Guy Debord illustrating the different field of attractions between neighborhoods in Paris and collaged in the overall installation of Archigram's 1961 *Living City* exhibition at the Institute of Contemporary Arts;[42] or the arrows in scientific and, especially, communication studies, which would find their way into the catalogue entry by Richard Hamilton, John Voelcker, and John McHale for the *This Is Tomorrow* exhibition of 1956. In their collage *See, Hear, Smell, Touch*, different arrows—long and fat, curved and small with dwindling tails or forming a zig-zag pattern—point to the different organs of environmental perception: the eye, nose, mouth as well as the skin. Beyond their variety, what unites them all is the intrinsic semiotic link between the arrow-sign and the action it signifies.

Therein lies the difference between these arrows and those found in the architectural plans (say, of Fry and Drew drawn in the same years) whose particularity lies less in their semiotic than diagrammatic dimension.[43] What makes architecture's arrows so fundamentally different is that they not only anticipate an action that is yet to happen—that is, they not only signify a signified *to come*—but, more importantly, they transgress the realm of semiotics altogether. They bring together signs with other materials: diagrams of movement with bricks and mortar, glass and steel, enabling a reality to transform into another state.[44] After all, these arrows not only represent movement in architecture; like the archer's arrows they were first modeled on, they create it.

↑ Richard Hamilton, *See, Hear, Smell, Touch*, 1956

→ Gordon Cullen, "Outrage," *Architectural Review*, 1955

KEEP
LEFT

1 Iain Jackson and Jessica Holland, *The Architecture of Edwin Maxwell Fry and Jane Drew: Twentieth Century Architecture, Pioneer Modernism and the Tropics* (Farnham: Ashgate, 2014), 69.

2 Ironically, it was Fry's work preceding his association with Gropius that Hitchcock had been deemed superior. See: Henry-Russell Hitchcock, *Modern Architecture in England* (New York: The Museum of Modern Art, 1937), 30.

3 Willy Boesiger and Oscar Stonorov, eds., *Le Corbusier et Pierre Jeanneret: Oeuvre complète 1910–1929*, vol. 1 (Zurich: Girsberger, 1937 [1929]), 208.

4 Alexander Klein, "Grundrissbildung und Raumgestaltung von Kleinwohnungen und neue Auswertungsmethoden," *Zentralblatt der Bauverwaltung* 48 (1928): 541–49; 35 (1928): 561–568; here 562–563.

5 Alvar Aalto, *Alvar Aalto: 1922–1962*, vol. 1 (Zurich: Les éditions de l'architecture Artemis, 1963), 40.

6 André Lavarde, "La flèche, le signe qui anime les schémas," *Communication et Languages* 109, vol. 3 (1996): 51.

7 Moritz Gleich, "Bewegung entwerfen. Eine kurze Geschichte des Pfeils im architektonischen Plan," *Horizonte: Zeitschrift für Architekturdiskurs* 12 (2018): 155–169.

8 Ernst Gombrich, "Pictorial instructions," in *Images and Understanding*, ed. Horace Barlow, Colin Blakemore, and Miranda Weston-Smith (Cambridge: Cambridge University Press, 1991), 26–45. See also: G. D. Schott: "Illustrating Cerebral Function: The Iconography of Arrows," *Philosophical Transactions: Biological Sciences* 355, 1404 (2000): 1789.

9 Denis Diderot and Jean le Rond d'Alembert, eds., "Charpente: Pompe du Pont Notre Dame," in *Encyclopédie, ou dictionnaire raisonné des sciences, des arts et des métiers, etc.*, vol. 2 (Paris, 1763), plate 36.

10 Georges Canguilhelm, "Le vivant et son milieu," in *La connaissance de la vie* (Paris: Hachette, 1952), 160.

11 Lavarde, "La flèche, le signe qui anime les schémas," 51.

12 Rebekka Ladewig, "Über die Geschicke des Pfeils," in *Im Zauber der Zeichen: Beiträge zur Kulturgeschichte des Mediums*, ed. Jörn Ahrens and Stephan Braese (Berlin: Vorwerk, 2007), 17–30.

13 Gleich, "Bewegung entwerfen," 164. See also Paul Emmons, "Intimate Circulations: Representing Flow in House and City," *AA Files* 51 (Winter 2005): 48–57.

14 See Neville S. Billington, "A Historical Review of the Art of Heating and Ventilating," *Architectural Science Review* 2 (1959): 118–130.

15 John James Drysdale and John Williams Hayward, *Health and Comfort in House Building or Ventilation with Warm Air by Self-Acting Suction Power : with Review of the Mode of Calculating the Draught in Hot-Air Flues and with Some Actual Experiments* (London: E. & F. N. Spon, 1872): 58, [plate] House No 2.

16 See Joshua Jebb, *Modern Prisons: Their Construction and Ventilation* (London: John Weale, 1844), plate 3.

17 Eugène-Emmanuel Viollet-le-Duc, *Entretiens sur l'architecture*, vol. 2 (Paris: Morel, 1872), 823.

18 On kitchen plans and home economics, see Lisa M. Tucker, "The Labor-saving Kitchen: Sources for Designs of the Architects' Small Home Service Bureau," *Enquiry. The ARCC Journal* 11, no. 1 (2014): 52–63. Also, Emmons, "Intimate Circulations."

19 See Sybille Krämer, "The Mind's Eye: Visualizing the Non-Visual and the Epistemology of the Line," in *Image and Imaging in Philosophy, Science and the Arts*, ed. Richard Heinrich et al., vol. 2 (Frankfurt: De Gruyter, 2011), 275–287.

20 T. Pridgin Teale, *Dangers to Health: A Pictorial Guide* (London: J. & A. Churchill, 1881 [1878]), xii.

21 See Sigfried Giedion, *Mechanization Takes Command: A Contribution to Anonymous History* (New York: Oxford University Press, 1948).

22 Laurin Schwarz proposes an elaborated cultural history of the arrow in the interwar period, ranging from art to film, up to traffic engineering: Laurin Schwarz, *Pfeilzeichen und Moderne. Visuelle Ordnungen des Transits von den Avantgarden zur Massenkultur* (Master Thesis, Humboldt University, 2022).

23 The connection to J. S. Bach (now seemingly obvious) was suggested to me by Virginia Zaretskie in a second-year seminar at the ETH Zurich.

24 Reyner Banham: "History Faculty, Cambridge," *Architectural Review* 144, vol. 861 (1968): 328–332.

25 Banham: "History Faculty, Cambridge."

26 Teale, *Dangers to Health*, 8.

27 F. E. Heppenstall, "Some Notes on the Services," *Architectural Review* 144, no. 861 (1968): 338.

28 See Hugh Brogan, "Cambridge Diary," *Cambridge Review* (October 1968): 15.

29 See Michel Foucault, *Discipline and Punish: The Birth of the Prison* (New York: Vintage Books, 1995), 195–228.

30 Information given to the author by Matthias Schirren, TU Kaiserslautern.

31 See Alison and Peter Smithson, *CIAM 59, Otterlo, October 7–15*, 1959, 72–79. Also: Colin D. Buchanan, *London Road Plans 1900–1970* (London: Greater London Council, 1971) 39.

32 Nuffield Trust and University of Bristol, *Studies in the Function and Design of Hospitals* (London: Oxford University Press, 1955), 8–10.

33 Maxwell Fry, "Analysis of a building," *Architects' Journal* 81, 2108 (1935): 909.

34 "University of East Anglia: Denys Lasdun and Partners," *Architectural Design* 39, 5 (1969), 252.

35 "University of East Anglia," 252.

36 "University of East Anglia," 253.

37 Alvin Boyarsky, "The Architecture of Etcetera," *Architectural Design* 35, 6 (1965): 269–270.

38 Boyarsky, "The Architecture of Etcetera," 269–270.

39 Stephen Greenberg, "Lasdun Extends Lasdun: The Royal College of Physicians," *Architects' Journal* (1994): 17–18.

40 Boyarsky, "The Architecture of Etcetera," 269.

41 See also: Georges Canguilhem, "Machine et Organisme," *La connaissance de la vie* (Paris: Hachette, 1952), 159.

42 See Simon Sadler, *The Situationist City* (Cambridge, MA: The MIT Press, 1998), 132–133.

43 In his study of architectural modernism in the US, Hyungmin Pai describes the diagram (in a chapter using drawings with arrows from Alexander Klein and others) in a similar way, clarifying its role as an intermediary between object and mind: Hyungmin Pai, *The Portfolio and the Diagram: Architecture, Discourse, and Modernity in America* (Cambridge, MA: The MIT Press, 2002): 162–197.

44 Building on Felix Guattari's idea of "a-signifying semiotics," Moritz Gleich developed this argument in our essay, "Stirling's Arrows," *AA Files* 72 (2016): 67. See also Félix Guattari, *Molecular Revolution: Psychiatry and Politics* (London: Penguin, 1984).

→ "The Habitat," *Report of CIAM* 10, Dubrovnik, August 1956

B. THE HABITAT

What means HABITAT?

"HABITAT": Terme de Botanique, lieu spécialement habité par une espèce végètale, on l'applique aussi aux animaux et à l'homme. L'habitat le mieux approprié à leurs aptitudes natives et à leurs besoins futurs.

Dictionnaire de la langue francaise, Paris 1882, Vol. III, p. 1967.

"HABITAT": The locality in which an animal naturally grows and lives.

Oxford Dictionary, Vol.V.

"HABITAT": As Gropius writes us, you will find a similar explanation for the same term in Webster's American Dictionary.

"HABITAT": "L' Habitat" représente les conditions de vie dans le milieu total (implique par conséquent les grandes modifications qui s'annoncent sur l'occupation du territoire par le travail de l'homme de la civilisation machiniste. C'est l'état de confusion et de déchirement actuel).

Le Corbusier à Emery, le 9 mai 1955.

All these "definitions" are concerned with an atmosphere properous to "grow and live". To create this atmosphere for the human being is the principle aim of CIAM.

Milieu

1486

siderable saving in building is effected. The door to the screen at *g*, in fig. 1481, and at the head of the stairs, in the same figure, will effectually exclude all sounds and smells. It is proposed to have cellars only under the hall and library; but these may be extended if thought necessary. The kitchen-court and stable offices for this villa have not been sent by Mr. Fowler; but they may be formed on the plan of some of those already given, or to be given, in this department of our work.

Design IX. — *The Villa of Hannayfield, the Residence of —— Hannay, Esq., in the Neighbourhood of Dumfries.*

1768. *The Situation* of this house is on the face of a bank, sloping to the west, at the bottom of which is the vale of Nith, and at the top an extensive tract of table land. The approach ascends from the public road, along one side of the grounds, through a plantation which conceals the house: when it arrives, by a winding course, at the top of the bank, it turns to the right, so as to enter from what may be called the back front. The area before the entrance floor is raised nearly to a level with the principal floor on that side; while, on the other side, the kitchen floor appears entirely above ground. Fig. 1489 will give a general idea of the situation of the house, *a*; relatively to the approach, *b*; the public road, *c*; the sloping bank from the west front, *d*; and the level platform on the entrance front, *e*. The stable offices are shown at *f*; *g* is a path, partly under ground, between them and the house; *h* is the walk to the kitchen-garden; and *i*, the back way to the stable offices. Fig. 1487 shows the general appearance of the building, independently of the surrounding scenery, as seen on coming up to the entrance front.

1487

1769. *Accommodation.* The ground floor, fig. 1488, shows a servants' entrance, *a*, with two large closets on each side; a laundry, *b*; two water-closets, *c*; two linen-closets, *d*; housekeeper's bed-room, *e*; stairs to the principal floor, *f*; housekeeper's sitting-room, *g*; bath-room, *h*; the bath being placed in the scullery, for the convenience of supplying hot water, and the opening to it being into the bath-room; kitchen, *i*; scullery, with cistern and sink, *k*; pantry, *l*. From the area, *m*, under the made ground, there are coal, wine, beer, and other cellars, a water-cistern, and a man-servant's water-closet. Fig. 1490 is a plan of the principal floor, showing the main entrance, *m*; vestibule in the centre, lighted from the roof, *n*; bed-room, *o*; dining-room, *p*; library, *q*; evening-room, *r*; bed-room, *s*. There are two large closets on each side of the entrance, one of which is a water-closet, and the other a place for keeping hats, sticks, and shoes; both being lighted from the vestibule: there is another closet under the stairs. Fig. 1491 is a plan of the upper part of the roof, in which are shown four small bed-rooms, *t*; and a lumber-room, *u*. The roof over these rooms is flat, and covered with lead; and there is a staircase to it with a trap-door. The flat part of this roof is surrounded by a

1488

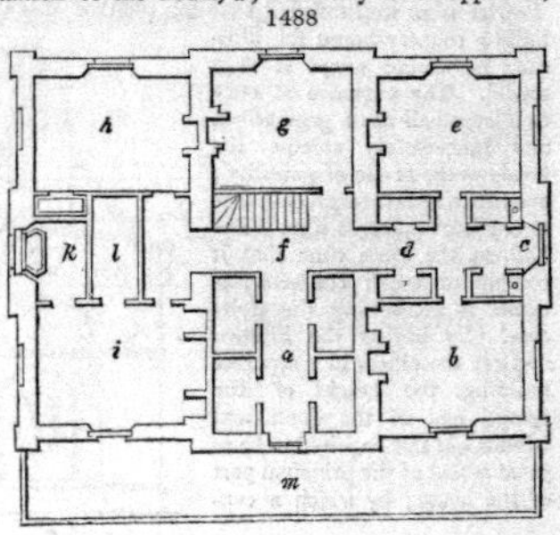

1489

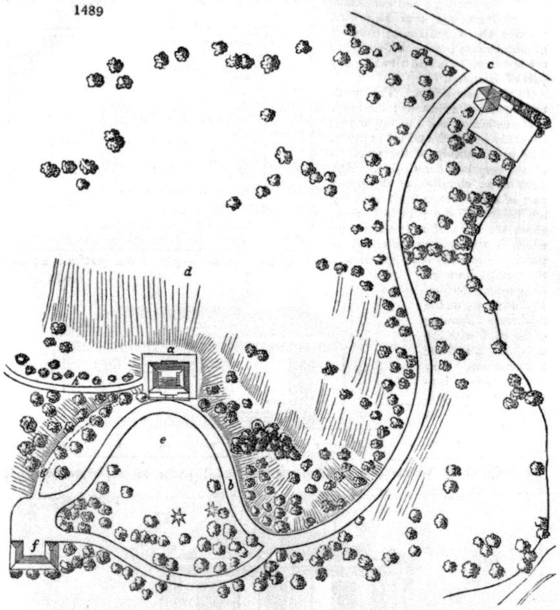

1490

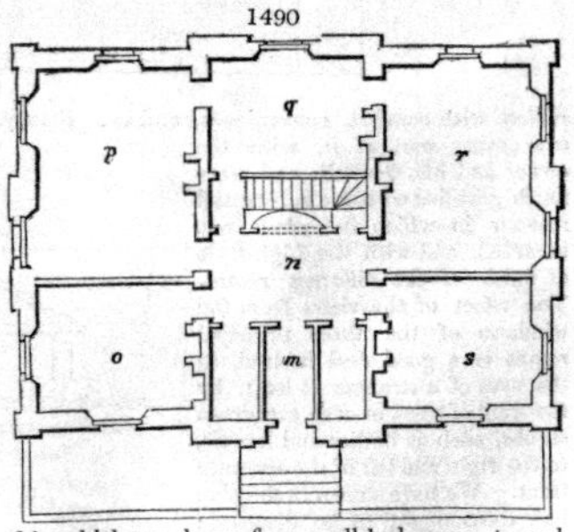

← John Claudius Loudon, "Villas in Various Styles," *An Encyclopaedia of Cottage, Farm, and Villa Architecture and Furniture*, 1833

Read any number of articles in the architectural press of the 1950s and 60s, and the word "environment" is everywhere. Not yet a subject of debates around sustainability (this would come later), it encompassed a more general notion, exchanged freely and synonymously with terms such as context, *ambiente*, ecology, or habitat. The use of these words was not merely illustrative, or even metaphorical, but integral to discussions and efforts to articulate through built projects a new relationship between society and its surroundings. This interest seems, at least initially, to take the form of a rhetorical instrument wielded by certain protagonists who placed themselves in opposition to the architectural modernism of the interwar years. For instance, at the Congrès Internationaux d'Architecture Moderne (CIAM) of the 1950s, the concept of "habitat" was offered as an alternative to the "habitation" examined in the "minimum subsistence dwelling" that members had proposed three decades earlier in 1929.[1] The urban historian Erwin Anton Gutkind, who covered the subject throughout the late 1940s and early 50s, repeatedly called for a holistic "Social Ecology" to mitigate the fragmentation of contemporaneous knowledge.[2] Ernesto Nathan Rogers, writing in an article in a 1955 issue of *Casabella*, favored *preesistenze ambientali* (environmental circumstances) as a response to the autonomy propounded by modernism.[3] And even as late as 1969, Reyner Banham saw his research into the well-tempered environment as a response to the new realities of postwar building technology.[4] These catchwords, to name but a few, came to dominate postwar discourse, blurring the walls of architecture in such diverse dimensions as its relation to the territory, to history, to society, or to natural and artificial climates in an attempt to redefine its boundaries.

Certainly, this new interest in the environment can be put down in part to postwar social and technological change. Yet isolating it to this single period overlooks a much longer trajectory, whose modern origins can be traced through the term "milieu" to eighteenth-century physics. From there the idea evolved, manifesting in the biological sciences, and influencing fields as diverse as literature, ethnology, and geography. In terms of architecture, one searches in vain for the word in the writing of nineteenth-century practitioners, but even in its absence from the discourse (at least until the first decade of the twentieth century), the leading voices of postwar architecture were unanimous in connecting the origins of the concept to this longer historical tradition, albeit in quite general terms. While Gutkind, along with the secretary general of CIAM, the indefatigable architectural historian Sigfried Giedion, identified the early nineteenth-century studies of "habitat" within biology as the root of the theoretical debate, Banham traced the technological control of the environment to the large glasshouses of the same period.

These historical references point to two different genealogies that would meet in the second half of the nineteenth century and deeply transform the understanding of architecture: the first was obsessed with the regulated distribution of light, air, people, and liquids (of which the various devices, ducts, and machines are a single expression and not its prerequisite); the second was concerned with the precise programming of spaces, from different rooms to the thoroughfares and services that efficiently connect them.[5] Both would find their expression in the organization of the plan and a new understanding of its design: from a question of composition, or wise arrangement of rooms, to that of circulation, which would enable the efficient flow around and through the domestic interior. It was therefore in the plan that the nineteenth-century architects found a relevant technical aid. As both a mode of representation and a design tool, it acquired a privileged role in residential architecture from the mid-nineteenth century, especially in the context of large country estates, gradually superseding other techniques including the cross section, elevation, or perspective.[6]

By the interwar period, the plan (along with photography) was the universally favored approach of modern architects, if not the most innovative (this accolade was reserved for axonometry).[7] Le Corbusier hailed it as the "generator" of architecture;[8] and, although never completed, Walter Gropius vowed to follow up his richly illustrated *Internationale Architektur* of 1925 with a second volume devoted exclusively to plans.[9] The exhibition accompanying the second CIAM, held in Frankfurt in 1929, was illustrated almost exclusively by plans, all drawn to the same scale and selected on account of their "rational use of space ... and high accommodation capacity."[10] It was then only a small step from a normative mode of representation towards a claim for a scientific approach to architecture, which Hannes Meyer accomplished when he proclaimed that the plans for housing and urban development—among other "things of this world"—were a product of the formula "function times cost."[11] By the 1930s, the plan ruled supreme.

But however self-evident the importance of the plan seemed around 1930, it was far from that a century earlier. For instance, in one of the most comprehensive works on nineteenth-century residential architecture, John Claudius Loudon's highly successful *Encyclopaedia of Cottage, Farm, and Villa Architecture and Furniture*, published first in 1833 and in no fewer than fourteen editions, plans feature as merely one of several representational methods including site plans, elevations, section drawings, and technical details. The most predominant drawing type are exterior perspectives that show "Various Styles" of houses in their respective settings, which Loudon used to strengthen the analogy between the "Style" of architecture and "Certain Characters of Ground and Scenery."[12] A landscape architect, Loudon had studied the relationship between the natural and built environment, combining the two in advocating for the "gardenesque." He identified the associative aesthetic characteristics in individual elements such as windows or chimneys in relation to their background, or in individual fixtures like doors, cornices, or fireplaces in interiors, which acted like a canvas and for which he required a degree of authenticity on moral and functional grounds. His approach allowed him to both distance himself from the picturesque tradition of the eighteenth century and to chalk out a theme later pursued by John Ruskin and Augustus W. N. Pugin. It was, significantly, Ruskin, whose essays on cottage and villa architecture in Great Britain, Switzerland, and Italy were published by Loudon in his *Architectural Magazine* and later compiled under the title *The Poetry of Architecture*, who saw in these external characteristics the basis for a "science of architecture." The exterior silhouettes and diverse motifs he identified were not only expressions of respective situations, climates, and movements, but also, in psychological terms, reflective of individual nations' "turn of mind."[13]

This associative tradition continued well into the second half of the nineteenth century. Writing from a historicist perspective in a chapter titled "Notes on Architectural Style" of his 1864 reference work *The Gentleman's House*, Robert Kerr, the architect and co-founder of the Architectural Association School of Architecture, emphasized the importance of style in defining the character of a building. "Classical" and "picturesque" were not seen as diametric opposites, but rather distinct traits with their own aesthetic impact, and informed by the architectural aspirations of the building at hand. Yet these "Notes on Style" were not Kerr's principle aim. While Ruskin had regarded the picturesque character of architecture as the foundation of its science, Kerr set out to systematically classify the various factors he believed to be decisive for the arrangement of a gentleman's house.[14] These were not found, as Loudon or Ruskin suggested, in aesthetic qualities or materials, but were instead located in the plan and could indeed be considered, as he wrote elsewhere, as the basis of a "science of plan:"[15] "Let it be again remarked that the character of a gentleman-like residence is not a matter of magnitude or of costliness, but of design—and chiefly of plan," he writes in relation to the establishment of the program, "and that, as a very modest establishment may possess this character without a fault, all unadorned; so also the stately seat of a millionaire's may perchance have so little of it that the most lavish expenditure shall but magnify its defects." To demonstrate their importance, plans alone illustrate Kerr's book, with the exception of two section drawings, one diagram of the aspect-compass, and a handful of the aforementioned perspectives, which showed how the same plan could absorb myriad external variants. Thus, a gentleman's house was plan first, then style.

The scope of the "science of the plan" is indeed impressive. Kerr distinguishes between more than one hundred different rooms: rooms for the family, rooms for servants, rooms for larger residences and state rooms, as well as rooms in stables, outbuildings, and structures related to agricultural production. Each room is then subdivided into further spatial sequences or entities, in accordance with program, time of day, season, or the class, social standing, or gender of the inhabitant. Kerr presents this principle of division as the key to the entire history and efficient running of the English house. Within this parallelism of space and everyday activities, the plan becomes the vehicle for expressing the ever-more specialized social relationships that shaped human dwelling from the late eighteenth century. Ambitions to raise standards of comfort and convenience sparked successive refinement of the house plan throughout the nineteenth century. Early pioneers of these aspirations towards differentiated living included the Scottish architect Robert Adam, whose

↓ William Burn, main floor, Camperdown House, 1821

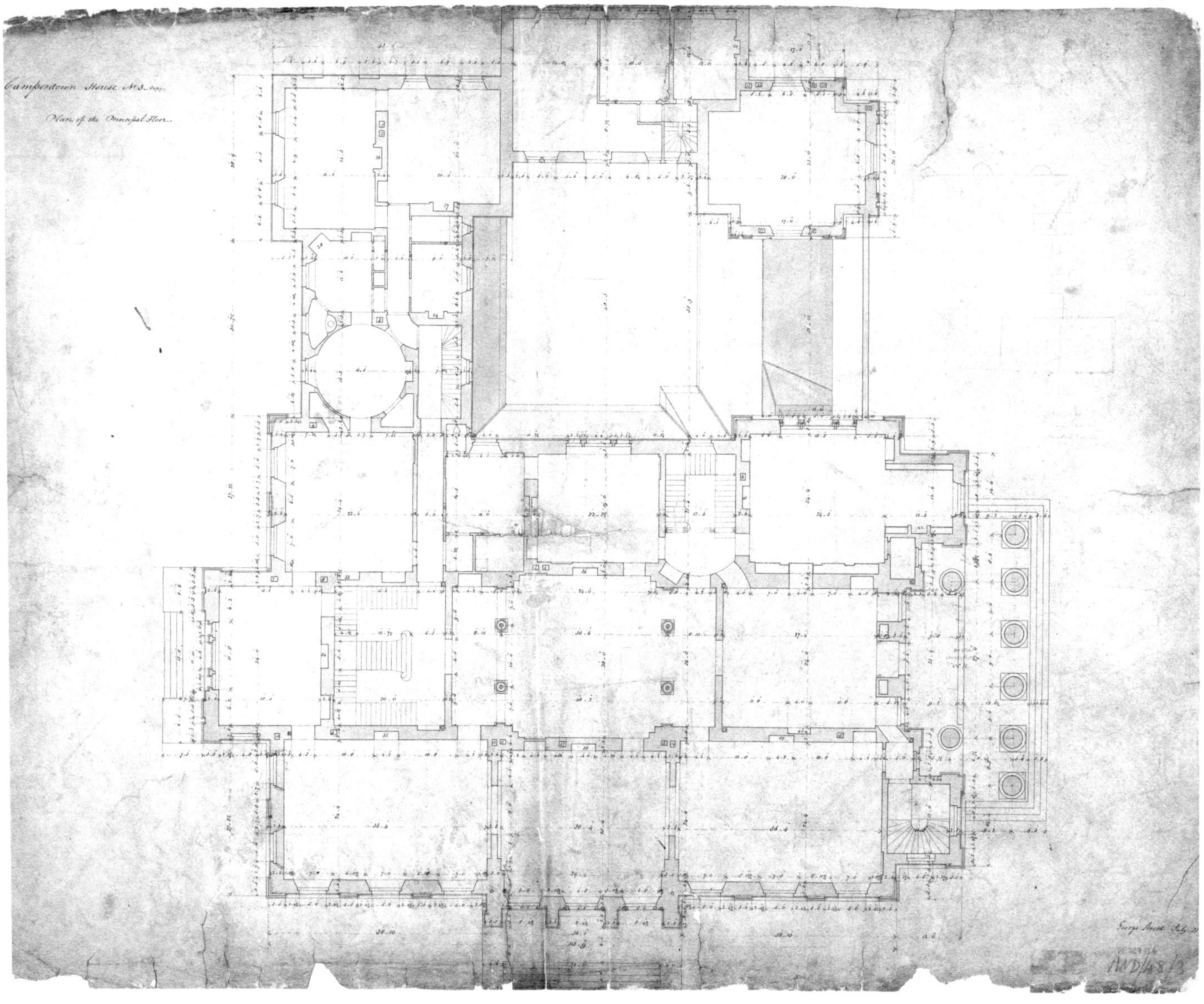

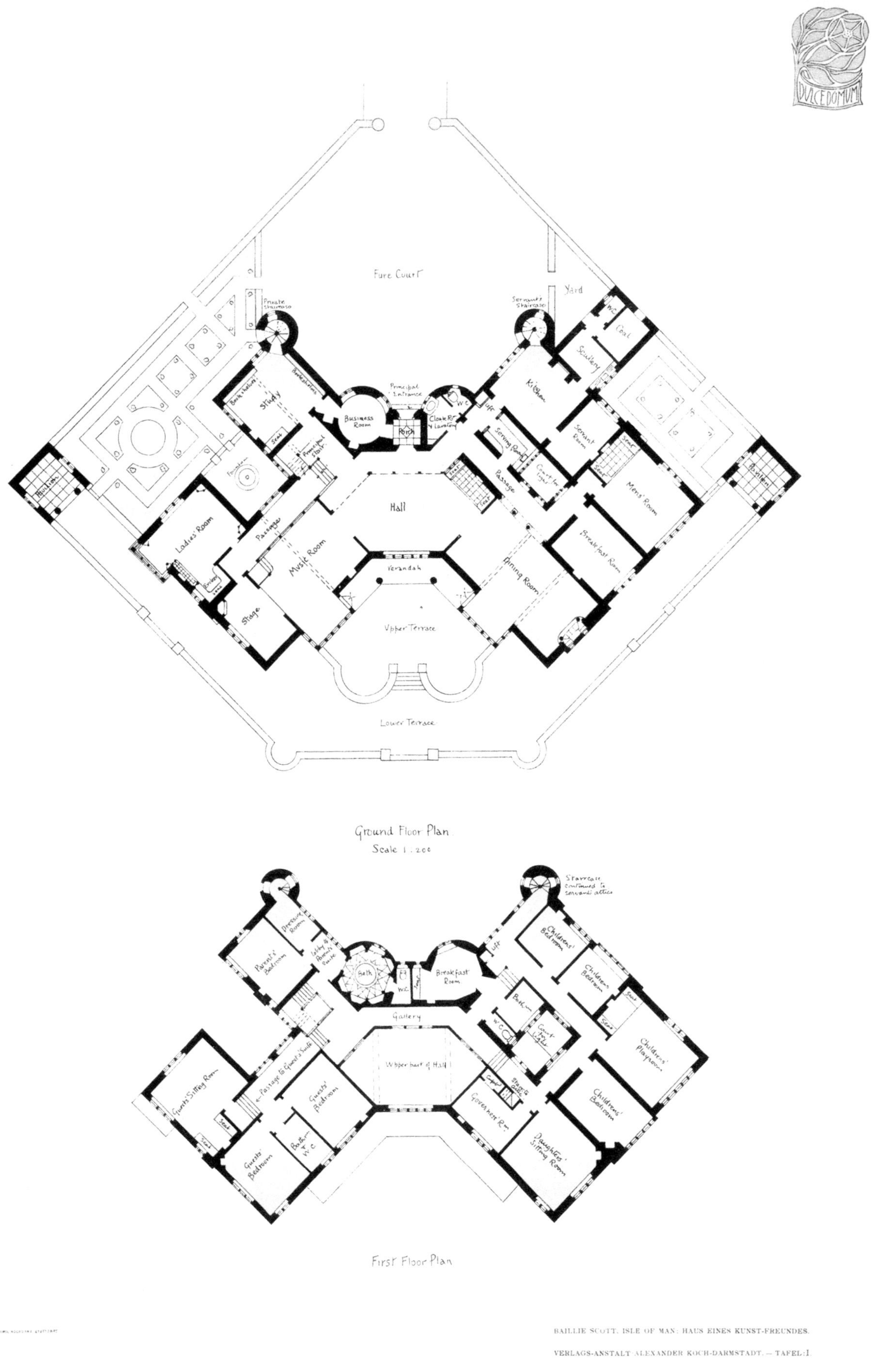

↑ Mackay Hugh Baillie Scott, ground and first floor plans, House for an Art Lover, competition entry, 1901–1902

← Robert Adam, main floor, Mellerstain House, 1768–1970

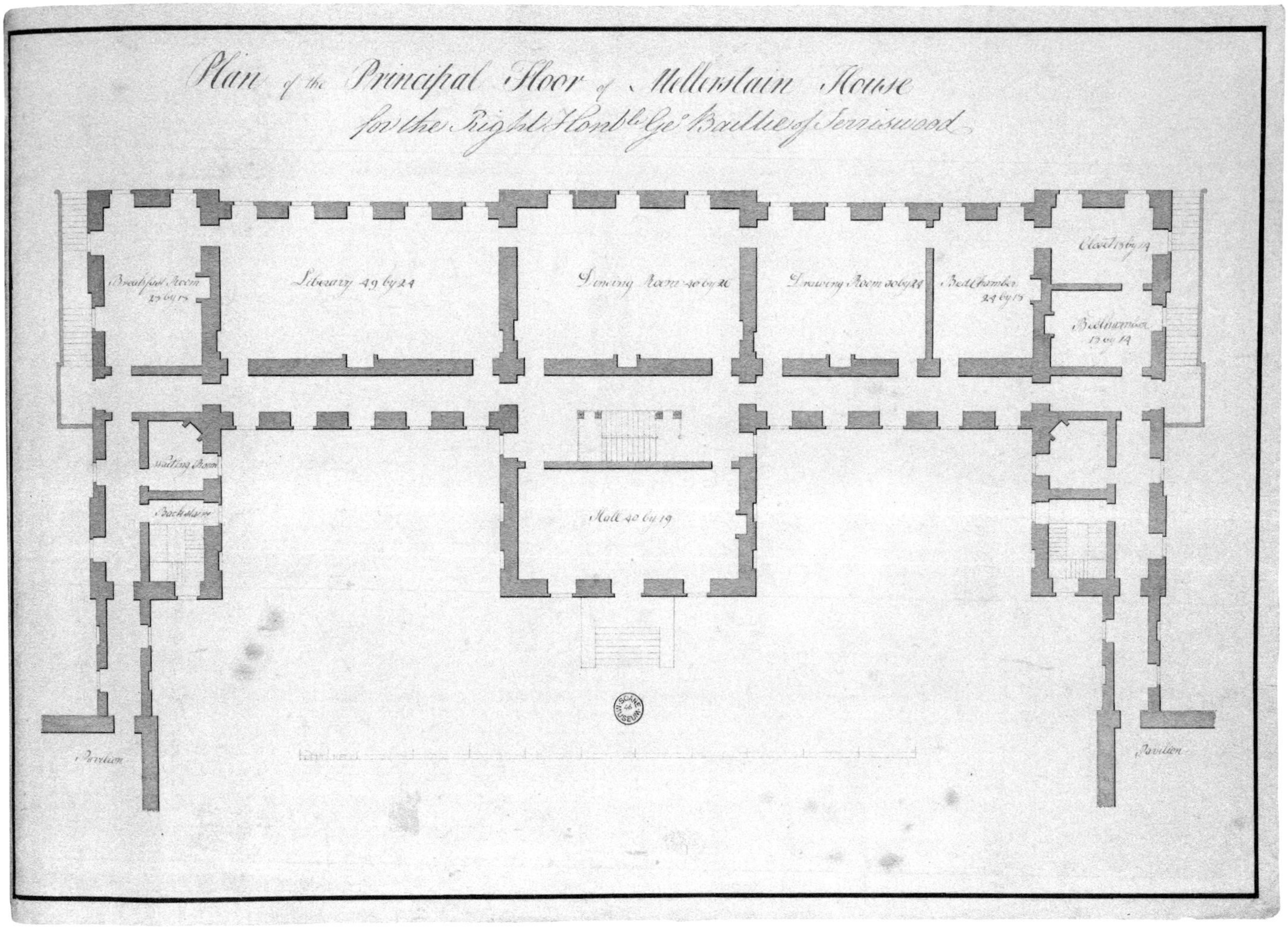

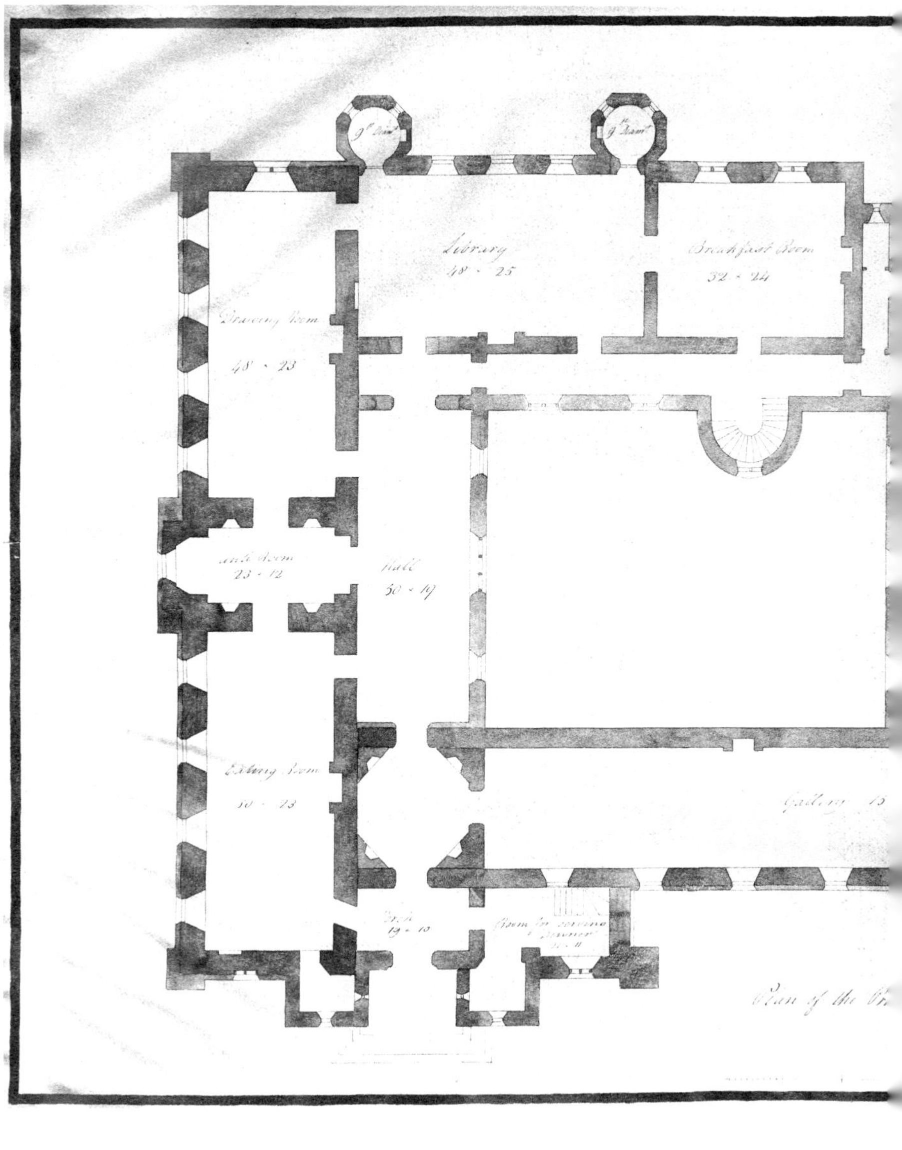

designs for Mellerstain (ca. 1770) introduced a succession of private rooms linked by a lateral corridor; William Atkinson, who in Scone in 1803 packed private quarters into a self-contained wing; and William Burn, who arranged private quarters and reception rooms at Camperdown (1828) in the sequence in which the lady of the house tended to use them. It is in Burn's elongated plans, which Kerr strongly admired,[16] that such strict division begins to establish itself: between the lords' and ladies' quarters and those of the servants; between the main house and the wings; between stables and kitchens, which articulate a protected entrance area. These projects anticipate a growing appreciation of an architecture characterized by the demands of not only privacy, comfort, and convenience,[17] but other principles—"Light and Air," "Salubrity," "Aspect and Prospect," "Cheerfulness," "Elegance," "Importance," and "Ornament"[18]—while presuming all possible divisions of the house. However often the interiors of the bourgeois middle-class of the nineteenth century were described as "worlds unto themselves," or "anti-worlds"[19] turned away from public life, and above all, the realm of industry and labor, the new science of planning showed that in reality they were organized, developed, and inhabited with the same efficiency as the modern world on their doorsteps.

Loudon in his encyclopedia had examined individual dwellings—villas, cottages, or estates—and the detailed arrangement of individual rooms in plans drawn exactly to scale. Kerr on the other hand was concerned less with concrete buildings or the materiality of specific rooms. Instead, his objectives were to control the different movements of people and things in and around the house by precisely organizing—and segregating—the "lines of traffic" of residents, guests and staff;[20] to exclude "such evils and draughts, smoky chimneys, kitchen smells, damp, vermin, noise and dust;"[21] and to orientate a house on its lot to a certain view, thereby taking into account the effects of sun, wind and rain.[22] At the same time, he aimed to program such rooms on the basis of first maintaining their differing functions (dining, dwelling, entertaining, sleeping, cooking, administration, cultivation, smoking, and circulating), which vary from household to household; and second, provisioning for either an "amplitude of space" or "concretion of rooms." All of these various factors comprise a number of givens—natural ones, such as air and light, and man-made ones, such as customs, technology, and economics—which, according to Kerr, must be respected to maintain a harmony of design, yet whose variability could decisively influence the design of a house and individualize its arrangement.[23] While, for example, an "amplitude of space ought never to be grudged,"[24] an architect tasked with designing a large and sprawling country estate must also consider the "exquisite quality of compactness."[25] In other words, "the more we have the harder is the task of keeping it well together—the greater the aggregate the more difficult the preservation of its unity."[26] What Kerr is therefore proposing are not so much strict formal rules for the organization of a house and its rooms, whether regarding their proportion or composition, but a series of changing constellations, which influences the plan of the house and individualizes it.

Of particular importance and exemplary of his approach was the "whole system of thoroughfares"—a "backbone" or "skeleton" as he called them—that enabled any number and class of inhabitant to easily and independently move through a series of spaces.[27] Their necessity is demonstrated in the final plate of the book. Printed across a double-page spread, the ground plans of six different houses all previously investigated and illustrated, are drawn to the same scale and set at the same orientation. Yet in this exercise Kerr subverts his representational technique, darkening the room sequences to instead highlight how each unique system of thoroughfares connects the rooms. The aim was to foster future designers' anticipation of "the operations which have to go on throughout the system."[28] A house that gave sufficient attention to these activities, such as where doors stand in relation to each other and the ease of "transit" between rooms, would achieve "practical harmony."[29] Consequently, the plan as a

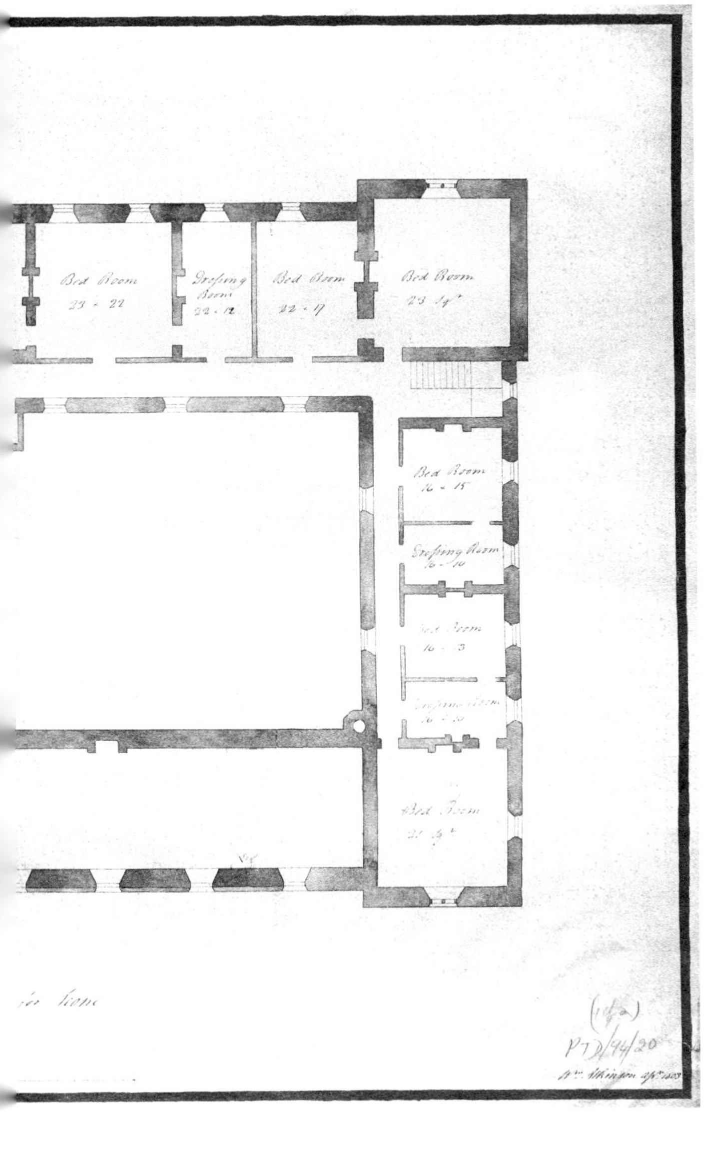

← William Atkinson, main floor, Scone Palace, 1803

representation technique—as "a horizontal section through the wall'—gained legitimacy because it not only facilitated the comparison of different arrangements but, moreover, allowed a clearer reading of the spatial interrelation of "windows, doors, and fireplaces."[30]

Although Kerr never used the word "environment" in the pages of *The Gentleman's House*, he appears to have been the first architect to so clearly address and establish the plan of a house as exactly that. The concept is implicit throughout, in its systematic compilation of the sum of external circumstances and factors that influence the plan, the range of events it can (or must) anticipate, and the solutions it provides for the regulation and control of their consequences.[31] Only a few years later, Edmund Beckett in his *Book on Building* from 1876, or John James Stevenson in *House Architecture* of 1880, were propounding similar ideas, with the latter emphasizing the "multifariousness" of the modern plan before systematically listing its individual categories that were almost identical to Kerr's.[32] Beckett, meanwhile, underscored the "variety of circumstances" which make nonsense of the insistence on a specific plan.[33] In 1899, when asked to write the entry on the plan for the multi-volume manual *The Principles and Practice of Modern Building*, except for a few clarifications, Kerr simply reiterated what he had formulated four decades earlier.[34] By the turn of the century, the "science of plan" had not only gained general acceptance, it had also anticipated a counter-current that would mark the design of residential architecture in the second half of

→ Robert Kerr, "The Tudor Period," *The Gentleman's House*, 1865 (1864)

↓ Robert Kerr, "The Anglo-Norman Castle," *The Gentleman's House*, 1865 (1864)

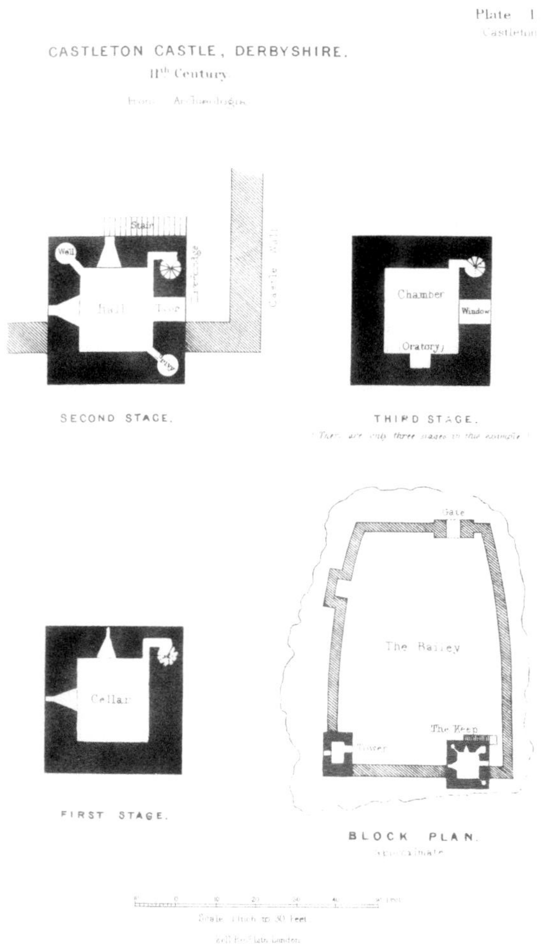

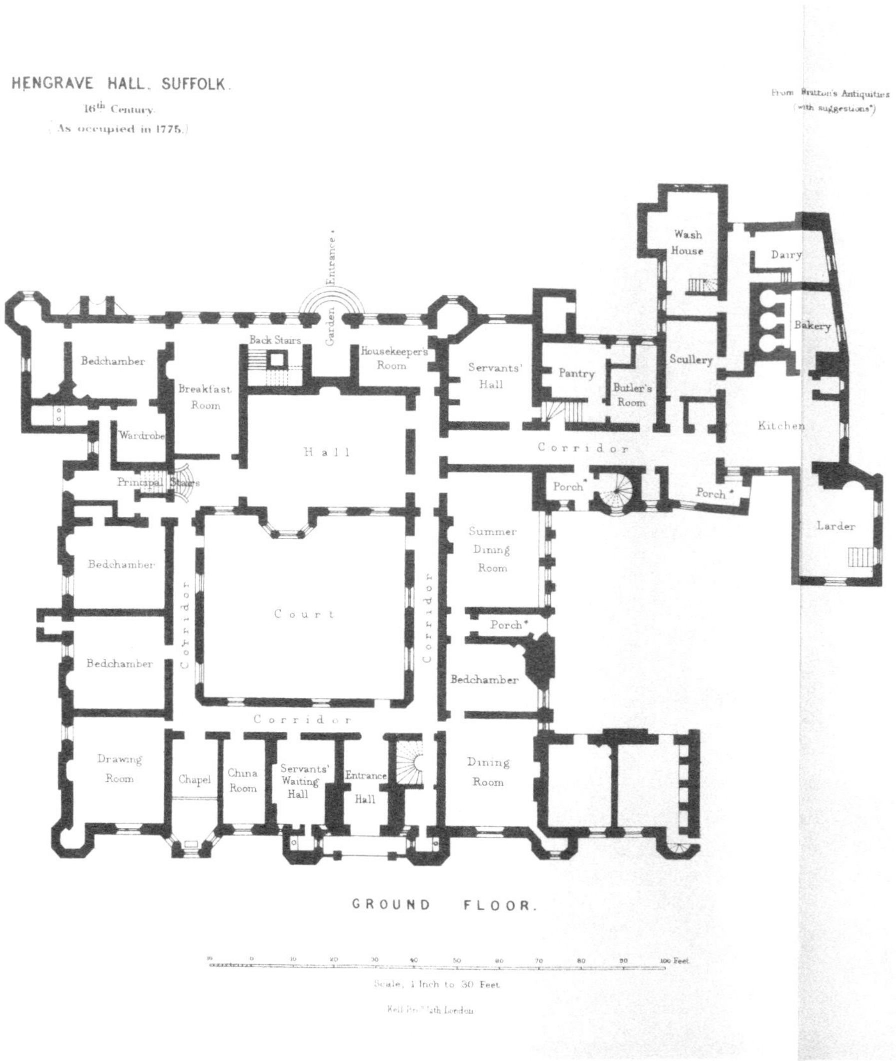

the nineteenth century, reversing its dynamics in the following few years. On the one hand, the demand for more closely differentiated and individualized rooms and the need to program them in the most efficient way possible sparked a shift that would gradually come to challenge the closed, self-contained character of domestic spaces. On the other hand, and somewhat ironically, as a result of their efficient planning, the thoroughfares of Kerr's era were slowly replaced throughout the twentieth century by a highly efficient infrastructure of services. This evolution ultimately led to concepts such as the free plan, or the open plan and their counterparts, such as the centralized services spaces and "cores" of the postwar years.[35]

But Kerr's "science of plan" was only the second part of *The Gentleman's House*. The first sixty-three pages are rather more quaintly devoted to a potted history of the English house from the eleventh century to the present. The goal of this excursus, large sections of which closely echo T. Hudson Turner's *Some Account of Domestic Architecture* from 1851, was to explain under which circumstances the principles for the modern English house were first formulated.[36] These, reasoned Kerr, were unique to those of other nations because their "occupiers differ in the habits of life." Correspondingly, the historical development of the house could be described as a line running from the "Hall of the Saxon Thane to the Mansion of the Modern Gentleman," with a few classical influences of the Renaissance sprinkled throughout. This line was not arbitrarily drawn, but—at least metaphorically—naturally given: "The germ of the Gothic plan," writes Kerr, at the outset of this historical account, "coming from the less hospitable North, is essentially different [from the Roman house]."

This argument would be taken a step further not by another Englishman, but by Hermann Muthesius, a German architect, former technical attaché at the embassy in London, later founder of the Deutsche Werkbund, and author of *Das englische Haus* of 1904–1905. Of the numerous works published in England in the late nineteenth century on the subject of the contemporary English house, it is only *The Gentleman's House* that Muthesius references in his monumental study. Indeed, for Muthesius the major cultural achievement of the nineteenth century were not the reforms propounded by the Arts and Crafts movement as later historiography would suggest, but the "scientific work on the ground plan of the private house." Kerr, he claimed, "had not only been the first to fix the requisite attributes of an elegant English house, but had done so with acuity and in what might be called a classic manner."[37] Correspondingly the crux of the matter, he states at the start of his historical survey was to identify "the original cell from the division of which this organism [the late nineteenth-century English house] had ensued."[38] In combining the biological metaphor with a geographical setting Muthesius assumes a relationship between the environment, or the milieu, and the evolution of architecture. The concept as formulated in this passage suggests the house is not only defined by its environment, but also that the relationship between both is historically determined.[39] In this latter point Muthesius

← Robert Kerr, "Nineteenth Century," *The Gentleman's House*, 1865 (1864)

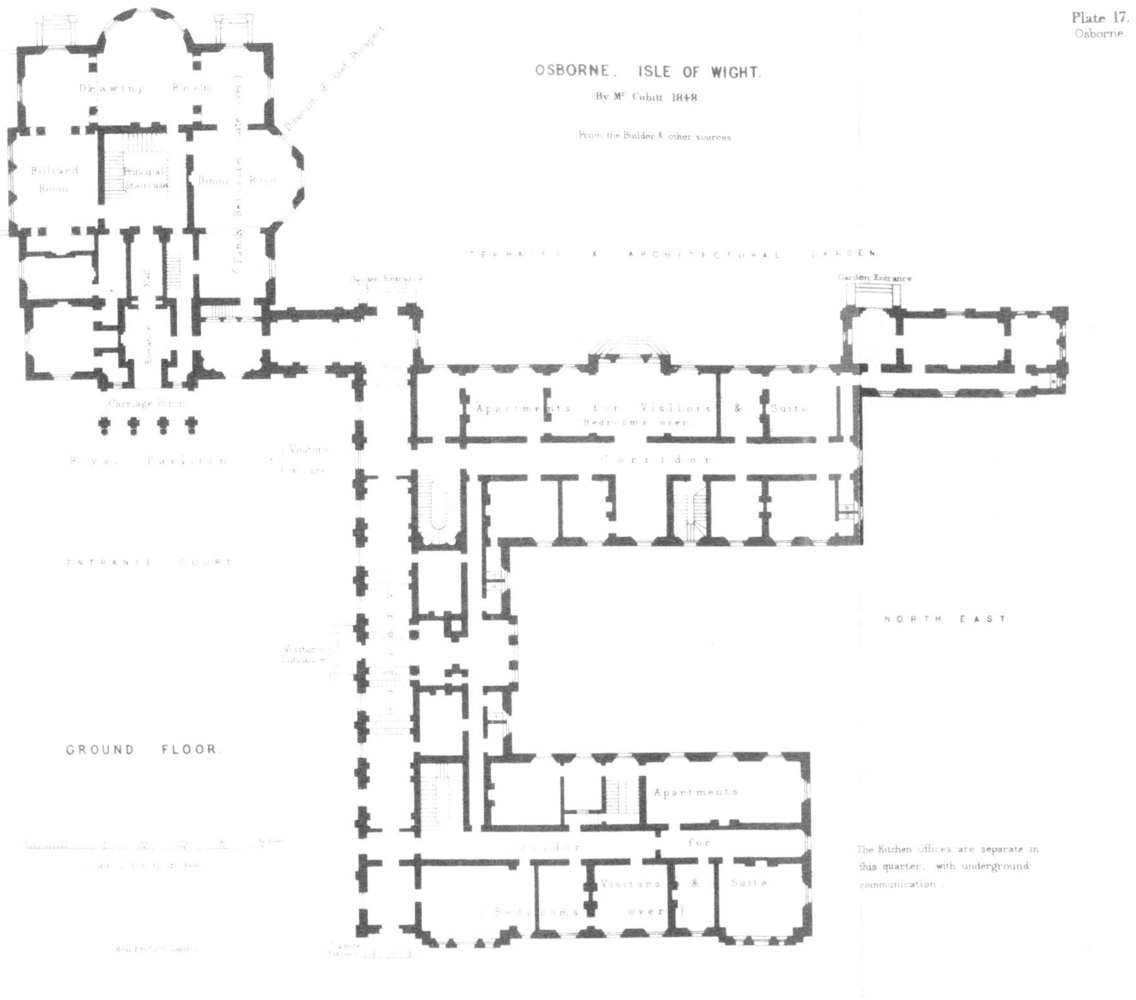

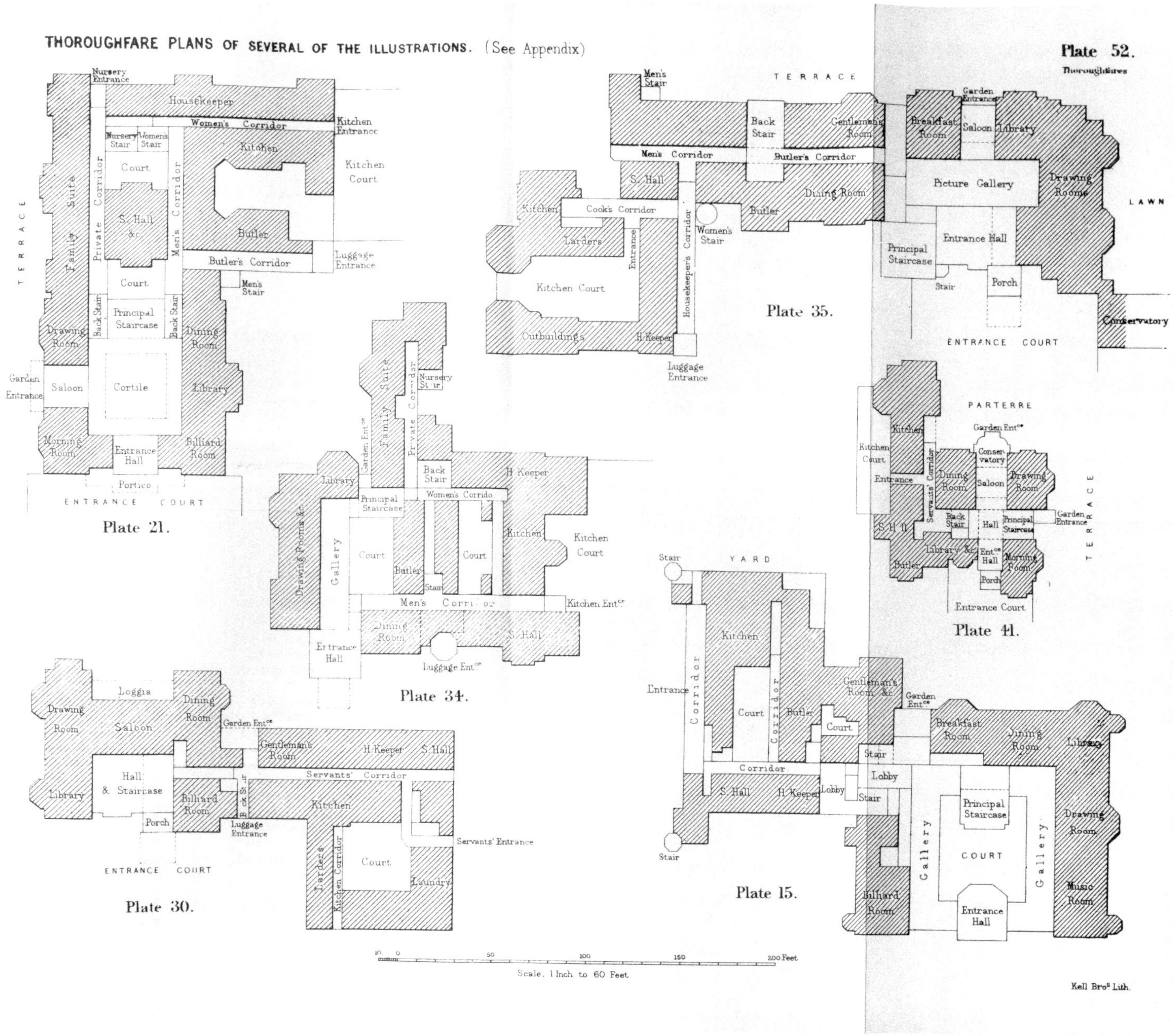

↑ Robert Kerr, "Thoroughfare Plans," *The Gentleman's House*, 1865 (1864)

↗ August Meitzen, *Das deutsche Haus in seinen volksthümlichen Formen* [*Popular Forms of the German House*], 1882

diverges from Kerr's hypothesis, whose "science of plan" was founded in social differentiation. Instead, for *Das englische Haus*, as well as numerous volumes published contemporaneously, the "science" of a plan expands to both unlock a spatial logic and locate, or assert, a national identity. Indeed, what distinguished Muthesius' study from Kerr's book (and those that succeeded it) was that it was one in a proposed series of publications on the architecture of various "cultivated countries," preceding F. Rudolf Vogel's *Das amerikanische Haus* (1914) and Paul Ehmig's *Das deutsche Haus* (1922).[40]

These new national histories of the house were part of larger research into ethnography and architecture that was proliferating across Europe in the second half of the nineteenth century. *Das englische Haus* for instance relied on several English studies providing both the necessary arguments for and the methodology to follow: Henry Thomas Buckle's *History of Civilization in England* from 1857, had not only searched "to ascertain the whole of the laws which regulate the progress of civilization," but similarly proposed a parallelism between the insularity of Great Britain and the stability of its political system, while Thomas Babington Macaulay's *History of England* from 1849, which traced contemporary English culture back to the Magna Carta, would provide Muthesius the necessary social model for his own *bürgerliche* architecture. And the other way around, *The Evolution of the English House*, a study on the origins of the house in Great Britain by the antiquarian and savant Sidney Oldall Addy, first published in 1898 and reissued in 1933, would rely primarily on German references, straight from the opening pages. These included Robert Lange's historical study on the basilica-type *Haus und Halle*; works by the linguist Theodor Siebs' on English and Frisian language; and most importantly a short study published in 1882 on the German house by statistician August Meitzen, *Das deutsche Haus in seinen volkstümlichen Formen* (Popular Forms of the German House) alongside *Das deutsche Haus in seiner historischen Entwicklung* (Historical Development of the German House) by philologist Rudolf Henning, which, released in the same year, can be considered the first attempt at a monographic survey of the German farmhouse. By exploring the origins of individual regional models the authors trace the history of the house from its "original basic form" through to "modern types."[41] The following year, Carl Schäfer, a gothic revivalist and monuments conservator with whom Muthesius had studied (alongside Friedrich Ostendorf, Hans Poelzig, Fritz Schumacher and Paul Schmitthenner), took up the same theme in *Ueber das deutsche Haus* (On the German House).[42]

While the farmhouse research sketched out essential lines of inquiry into house development, its comparative assessment of ground plan typologies and their subsequent classification amounted to a scientific methodology on which architects could rely. Meitzen, for example, traced the preeminence of the polynomial house typology in the German state of Franken to its viability,[43] even going so far as to suggest that it accounted for more than half of the housing in France.[44] Schäfer, too, in his lectures on the topic, classed the Frankish typology as the most progressive of all German farmhouses.[45] By tracing the one-room house to the modern polynomial house with its supposedly typical "free plan development," later demonstrated by Muthesius with reference to the "organic" growth of the English model, the contemporary demands on the house plan were thoroughly substantiated in both historical and cultural terms.[46]

Beyond any insights into ground plan typologies, a defining feature of research into the German house, by now the built emblem of the ideal traditional family, was its significance in the history of *das Volk*, the German people. There was no greater champion of the traditional home's ability to restore homogeneity to a perceived degenerating society than the ethnographer and journalist Wilhelm Heinrich Riehl. In *On the Natural History of the German People as the Foundation of German Social Policy*, published serially from 1851 to 1869, Riehl presents German society as an ideal organic entity that had thrived for centuries. But the threat of industrialization, he claimed, was splitting households

⇲ Banister Fletcher, "The Tree of Architecture," *A History of Architecture on the Comparative Method*, 1905

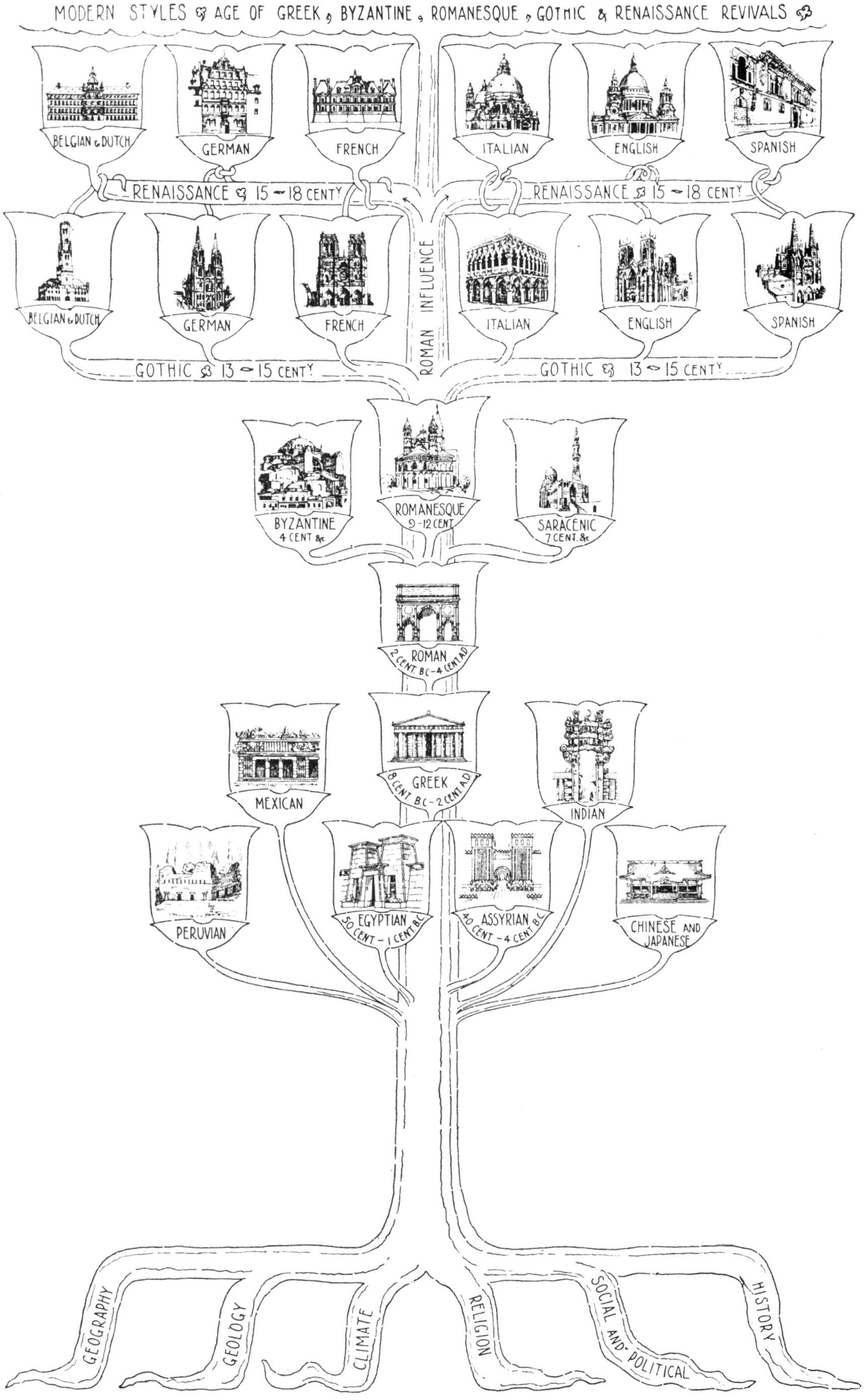

THE TREE OF ARCHITECTURE,

Showing the main growth or evolution of the various styles.

The Tree must be taken as suggestive only, for minor influences cannot be indicated in a diagram of this kind.

and luring workers away from more wholesome agrarian occupations.[47] In the wake of this rapid modernization, Riehl sought to reassert the German home in the lives of *das Volk*, extending the idea of the "family" beyond the house's immediate residents to incorporate the distant relatives and numerous domestic workers and staff who lived on its grounds. The house therefore became the embodiment of traditional German values and maintaining it a moral duty. The historical, cultural, and often exclusionary reading of this pretense to unity continued well into the twentieth century, from Meitzen, for whom the Frankish typology was an expression of a "functional bourgeois arrangement" that could promote "a more civilized family life" and afford "cleanliness and moderation,"[48] through to Muthesius, who described the English house as the "epitome of English habits" and the answer to "local climatic and geographical conditions."[49]

The common reference for nineteenth-century German scholars and architects in search of the origins of their homeland architecture was the work of architect and theorist Gottfried Semper. Muthesius, in *Das englische Haus*, names Semper's *Style in the Technical and Tectonic Arts; or Practical Aesthetics* (1860–63) alongside Eugène-Emmanuel Viollet-Le-Duc's *History of Human Habitation* (1875) ahead of any English publications.[50] In *The Four Elements of Architecture* of 1851, Semper transposes the hearth, roof, enclosure, and mound (or terrace) onto local architectural forms—regional variants that have, he writes, evolved from "the most diverse effects of the climate, the characteristics of each respective country and their relation to each other, and variations in the dispositions of the races." He then identifies "two predominant elements," namely terrace construction and the roof, as characteristics of the "old Nordic construction style."[51] In *The Style*, which he published a decade later, the question of the causality of architecture and environment—its material, use, time, place—becomes more sophisticated, and the examples more specific. For instance, in his chapter on tectonics, the "Scandinavian gentry's estate" is an expression of "Old Germanic circumstances" and the aristocratic social order. Its peculiarity is found in the so-called "isolation principle" evinced by the clear separation of the various functions in the ground plan as well as by the form of its roof.[52] In Semper's study the supposed objectivity of the "science of the plan" had found a well-argued cultural and historical legitimacy.

Comparable explanatory models proliferated in the second half of the nineteenth century. Viollet-le-Duc, better known than Semper in the English context, makes explicit reference to the importance of "milieu," the environment, in his popular book, *History of Human Habitation*.[53] Like Semper, he had by this time identified the distinguishing features of various world architectures, emphasizing that *agglomeration*, or the cluster, was an enduring characteristic of the Nordic construction style, notably the architecture of Scandinavian estates.[54] One of the most sweeping applications of the theory of natural evolution to architecture and its relation to specific people, and on which Kerr and Muthesius both drew, was that made by the Scottish architectural historian James Fergusson, who in 1862 published "Ethnology from an Architectural Point of View" as an appendix to his *History of Modern Styles*. Architectural history, he claimed, began with the "history of the world...where it [was] left by its elder sister Geology."[55] The goal of ethnology was to trace the forms of art back to their origins to gain an understanding of their different cultural trajectories. In addition to prevailing technical and material considerations, implicit in this aim were the customs and character traits of the various "races of mankind." While Semper describes the roof and terrace as characteristic of Nordic art, Fergusson (like Viollet-le-Duc) goes a step further, turning the spotlight on the character of the architecture of "Aryans," among whom he ranks "the Saxons" as "thoroughbreds," correlating their "practical common sense" with "convenience," and the "immaterial nature of their

↓ Herman Sörgel, family tree of the German house, *Wohnhäuser*, 1927

Abb. 1.

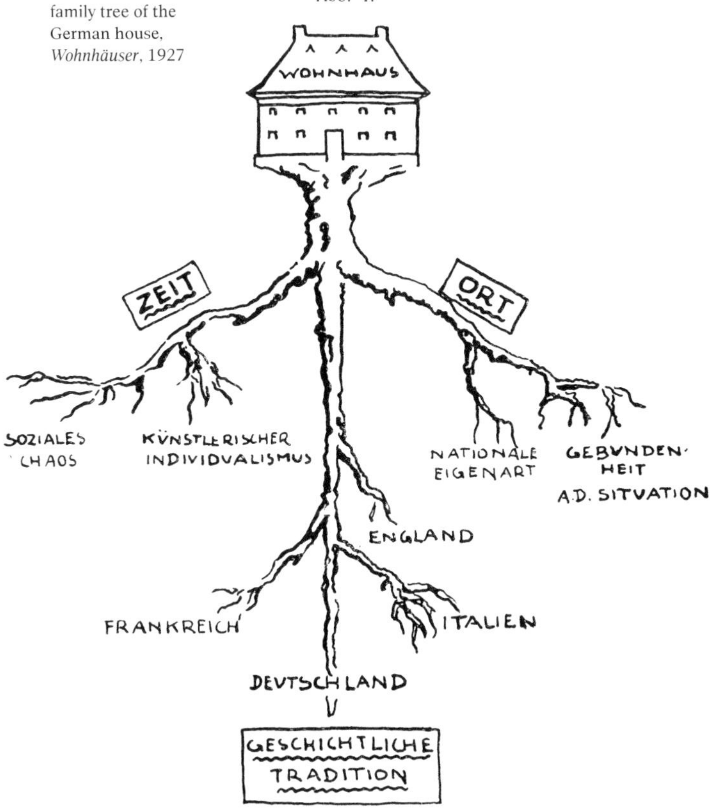

Stammbaum des deutſchen Hauſes.

ANATOMY OF A DWELLING

With very little exaggeration, this baroque ensemble of domestic gadgetry epitomizes the intestinal complexity of gracious living—in other words, this is the junk that keeps the pad swinging. The house itself has been omitted from the drawing, but if mechanical services continue to accumulate at this rate it may be possible to omit the house in fact.

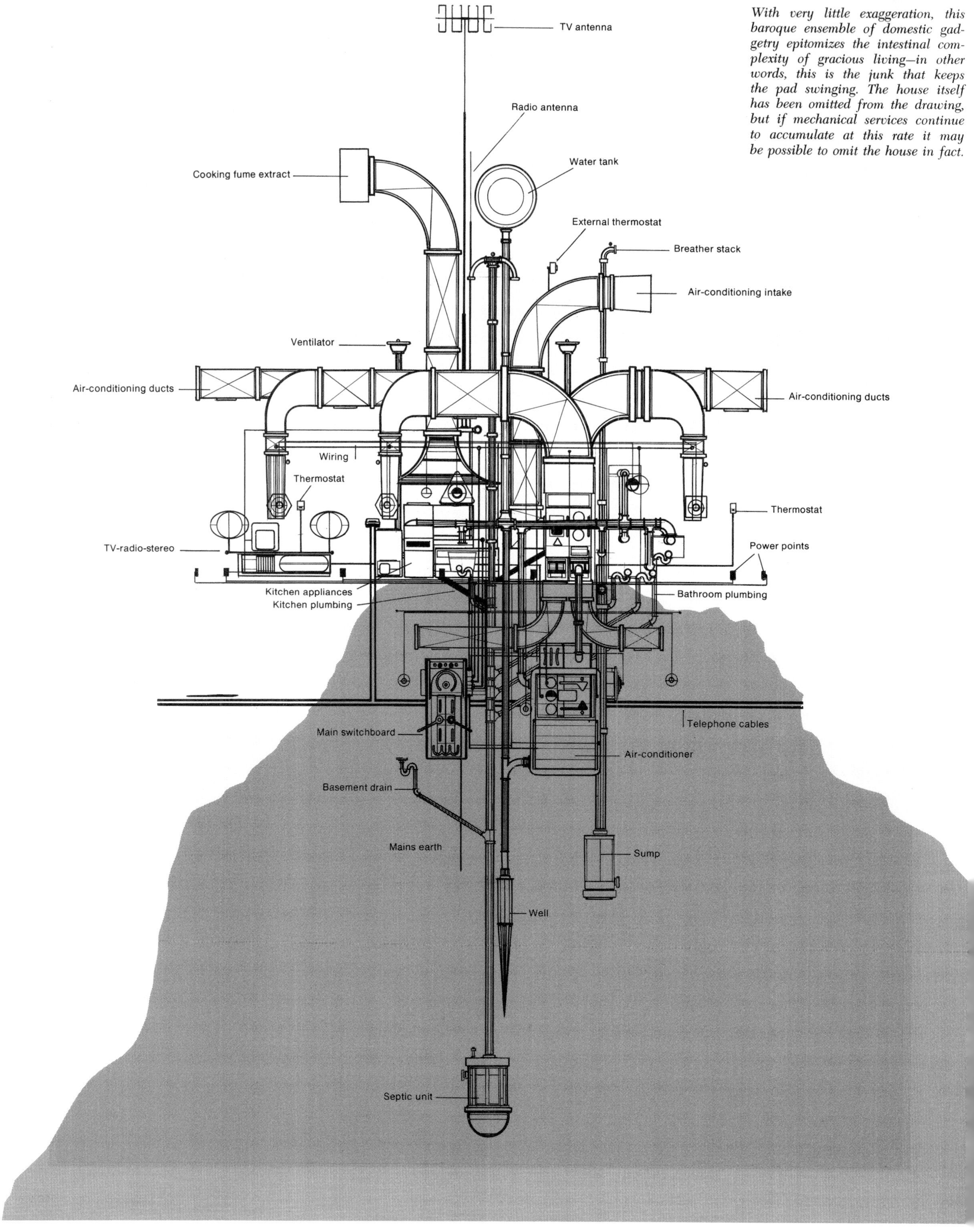

← Reyner Banham and François Dallegret, *Anatomy of a Dwelling*, 1965

faith" to their rejection of "architectural magnificence." It was a short step from an ethnographically informed history of architecture to a normative nationalist one.

While regionally specific artifacts of world architecture—farmhouses, roofs, terraces and estates—constituted the analytical context for the writings of Semper, Viollet-Le-Duc and Fergusson, in 1905 it was Banister Fletcher who in the fourth edition of *A History of Architecture on the Comparative Method*, doubtless the most successful twentieth-century history of architecture, imposed a synthetic order.[56] This took the form of a "family tree" of world architecture, which sprang forth from five roots—geography, geology, climate, religion and social history—and graphically brought to life the history of the discipline in relation to its environment while also showing that certain branches (the Europeans) would proliferate as the growth of others (Byzantine, Mexican or Indian, for instance) had been permanently stunted.

The tree metaphor was wide open to reinterpretation, as Herman Sörgel demonstrated in "The House" in 1927, one of the volumes of the *Handbuch der Architektur*, the most extensive encyclopedia of architecture in the German-speaking world. Not one to shy away from imposing a nationalist-inspired order onto vast swathes of the world, as illustrated by his Atlantropa project of the same period, he transformed Fletcher's tree into a German root system.[57] Up from the center rises "Deutschland," bypassing the weaker roots of France, Italy, and England. As the root breaks through the ground, instead of growing into a tree it is capped by a "German" house (interestingly enough, a French-inspired neo-Biedermeier—"Um 1800"—model). Its neat windows and roof project a calm, clear order compared to the shriveled roots on its left (labeled "social chaos," "artistic freedom'). It seems to draw strength from the more robust system to its right, comprising "national character" and "moral commitment." Looking at Sörgel's elevation drawing, which recalls the milieu theories from one century earlier, it is almost possible to forget that the same year this handbook was published, the science of plan, which draws on similar sources, was becoming a truism in international architecture. The plans published on the occasion of the CIAM congress of 1929 meet very few of Sörgel's criteria: all aim to efficiently program individual apartments whose sizes are understood as a function of volumes, surface, "light-giving facade" area, and number of beds. Furthermore, the surface area in most plans is clearly divided into various functional spaces that are rigorously distinguished from one another.

While Kerr and Muthesius saw the relationship between architecture and the environment as one that evolved historically, from the 1930s this same relationship was seen as functional, determined by the inhabitant's "periodic sequence of precise activities" (the typical laborer with his quantifiable needs)[58] and the "system of circulation," as Le Corbusier and Pierre Jeanneret noted in their CIAM paper. They went onto demand (and consequently break the unity of the floor plan) a distinction between the load-bearing architectural structure of the "static event" and the rational arrangement and furnishing of the home, or "biological event."[59] The design focus was therefore no longer the building in its materiality but the individual inhabitant and his needs, no longer a milieu permanently prescribed on the inhabitant's behalf but one that had to be recurrently redefined; for as CIAM's 1953 Charter of Habitat states, the cells "are born, live, and die."[60] No longer the origin of an evolution, they comprised the sphere of inhabitation.

A further step was proposed at the finale CIAM congress of 1959. There, the architects Candilis, Josic and Woods defined "habitat" as the interplay of "determined elements" (isolation and infrastructure) and "non-determined elements" (spatial organizations, functions, etc.) that fostered the organization of living around a core infrastructure. Similarly, Alison and Peter Smithson would articulate a model in their Appliance House of 1956, where the core is at the center of an ever-evolving residence, while Reyner Banham and François Dallegret would lay out in 1965 a dwelling determined by its treelike service-infrastructure. And here, then, is where the science of the plan, that building block of architecture, divides, where the milieu theory becomes its inverse, where the services that once flowed around the space are now centralized to let the individual spaces move around them.

What distinguishes this notion of the individual habitat is the fact that the various circumstances of the milieu can in these projects be reviewed, modified, improved, and discarded accordingly. They can also be designed. Such a distinction reveals better than anything the growing scope of architecture in two contrary directions throughout the latter half of the twentieth century: one is focused on the interior, the other on the exterior sphere, one concerns the well-tempered environment, the other the environment, both natural and artificial, in its entirety. And yet, this turn should be read not merely as opposition but juxtaposition, for life in a completely well-tempered environment or perhaps simply a socially determined one is not only economically, socially, and environmentally unsustainable; it is not even possible.

1 This text is an expanded version of my essay "The Science of Plan," in Harry Francis Mallgrave et al., *The Companions to the History of Architecture: Nineteenth-Century Architecture*, vol. 3 (London: Wiley, 2017), 285–305. Sigfried Giedion, *Raum, Zeit, Architektur: Die Entstehung einer neuen Tradition* (Ravensburg: Maier 1965), 422. See also Eric Mumford, *The CIAM Discourse on Urbanism, 1928–1960* (Cambridge, MA: The MIT Press, 2002), 201, 215.

2 Erwin Anton Gutkind, *Community and Environment: A Discourse on Social Ecology* (London: Watts, 1953), xi. See also Gutkind's comprehensive definition of environment, encompassing everything from a suit to the universe (46), and his call for a study of human communities "as a *whole* and in their *total* relationship to their physical and social environment" (50), emphasis in original.

3 Ernesto Nathan Rogers, "Le preesistenze ambientali e i temi pratici contemporanei," *Casabella-Continuità* 204 (February–March, 1955): 3–6. See also: Adrian Forty, *Words and Buildings: A Vocabulary of Modern Architecture* (London: Thames & Hudson, 2000), 132–135.

4 Reyner Banham, *The Architecture of the Well-tempered Environment* (London: Architectural Press, 1969), particularly "Machines à habiter," 143–170.

5 Georges Teyssot, *Die Krankheit des Domizils: Wohnen und Wohnbau 1800–1930* (Braunschweig: Friedr. Vieweg, 1989), 50.

6 Robin Evans's classical text on the "history of the house in relation to human affairs" can be considered today both as a study and a source: Robin Evans, "Figures, Doors and Passages," *Architectural Design* 38, no. 4 (April 1978): 267–278.

7 On the role of axonometry in modernism, see Yve-Alain Bois, "Metamorphosen der Axonometrie/Metamorphosis of Axonometry," in *Daidalos* 1 (1981): 40–58; Bruno Reichlin, "L'assonometria come progetto. Uno studio su Alberto Sartoris," *Lotus International* 22 (1979): 82–93.

8 Le Corbusier, *Vers une architecture* (Paris: Crès, 1923 [1924]), 33.

9 Walter Gropius, *Internationale Architektur* (Munich: Albert Lange, 1925) 5.

10 Internationale Kongresse für Neues Bauen und Städtisches Hochbauamt Frankfurt am Main, eds., *Die Wohnung für das Existenzminimum: auf Grund der Ergebnisse des 2. Internationalen Kongresses für Neues Bauen sowie der vom Städtischen Hochbauamt in Frankfurt a.M. veranstalteten Wander-Ausstellung* (Frankfurt am Main: Englert & Schlosser, 1930), 45.

11 Hannes Meyer, "Bauen," *Bauhaus* 4 (1928): 12.

12 John Claudius Loudon, "Principles for Designing Villas," in *An Encyclopaedia of Cottage, Farm and Villa Architecture and Furniture* (London: Longman, Rees, Orme, Brown, Green & Longman, 1833), 772.

13 Kata Pushin [John Ruskin], "The Poetry of Architecture, or, the Architecture of the Nations of Europe Considered in Its Association with Natural Scenery and National Character," in *The Works of John Ruskin*, vol. 1, ed. E. T. Cook and Alexander Wedderburn, (London: George Allen, 1903–1912), 5.

14 Robert Kerr, *The Gentleman's House or, How to Plan English Residences, from the Parsonage to the Palace* (London: John Murray, 1865 [1864]).

15 Kerr, *The Gentleman's House*, 31, see also 37, 61.

16 See Thomas Leverton Donaldson, "Memoir of the late William Burn, Fellow," *Transactions of the Royal Institute of British Architects*, 1st series, 20 (March 28, 1870): 121–129, particularly the short entry by Robert Kerr (129); Hermann Muthesius, *Das englische Haus*, vol. 1 (Berlin: Ernst Wasmuth Verlag, 1904), 93.

17 On the history of comfort, see Renzo Dubbini, "Birth of the Idea of Comfort," in *History of Industrial Design, 1750–1850: The Age of Industrial Revolution*, vol. 1, ed. Alessandra Ponte (Milan: Electa, 1990), 86–107.

18 Kerr, *The Gentleman's House*, 66–90.

19 Thomas Nipperdey, *Deutsche Geschichte 1866–1918*, vol. 1: *Arbeitswelt und Bürgergeist* (Munich: Beck, 1994), 138.

20 Kerr, *The Gentleman's House*, 68.

21 Kerr, *The Gentleman's House*, 70.

22 Kerr, *The Gentleman's House*, 81–83.

23 See Georges Teyssot, *Die Krankheit des Domizils*, 50.

24 Kerr, *The Gentleman's House*, 74.

25 Kerr, *The Gentleman's House*, 75.

26 Kerr, *The Gentleman's House*, 75.

27 On the history of the corridor, from the "courier" in the fourteenth century to the most differentiated corridor system of the Houses of Parliament, up to its dissolution in the Bürolandschaft of the 1960s, see Mark Jarzombek: "Corridor Spaces," *Critical Inquiry* 36, no. 4 (Summer 2010): 728–770. And also Stephan Trüby, *Geschichte des Korridors*, (Paderborn: Brill, 2018). Trüby in his cultural history of the corridor, dedicates one chapter to ninteenth century.

28 Kerr, *The Gentleman's House*, 462.

29 Kerr, *The Gentleman's House*, 155.

30 Kerr, *The Gentleman's House*, xii.

31 On the term environment in urban planning, see Michel Foucault, "January 11, 1978," in *Security, Territory, Population. Lectures at the Collège de France 1977–78* (New York: Palgrave Macmillan, 2007), 16–38; 35–36.

32 John James Stevenson, *House Architecture*, vol. 2 (London: Macmillan and Co., 1880), 47–52.

33 Edmund Beckett, *Book on Building, Civil and Ecclesiastical; With the Theory of Domes, and of the Great Pyramid; and a Catalogue of Sizes of Churches and Other Large Buildings* (London: Crosby Lockwood & Co., 1876), 116.

34 Robert Kerr, "The Plan," in *The Principles and Practice of Modern House Construction*, ed. G. Lister Sutcliffe, vol. 1 (London: Blackie & Sons, 1899), 29–52; 31–36.

35 See also, for example, Josef Frank, "Das Haus als Weg und Platz," in *Der Baumeister* 29, no. 8 (1931): 316–323; Le Corbusier and Pierre Jeanneret, "Fünf Punkte zu einer neuen Architektur," in *Bau und Wohnung*, ed. Deutschen Werkbund (Stuttgart: Akad. Verlag Dr. Fritz Wedekind & Co, 1927), 27–28.

36 Kerr, *The Gentleman's House*, 1.

37 Hermann Muthesius, *Das englische Haus*, 94.

38 Muthesius, *Das englische Haus*, 13–14.

39 On this, see Paul Rabinow, *French Modern: Norms and Forms of the Social Environment* (Cambridge, MA: The MIT Press, 1989), 128.

40 On the history of house research in Germany, see Konrad Bedal, *Historische Hausforschung: eine Einführung in Arbeitsweise, Begriffe und Literatur* (Münster: Coppenrath, 1978), 12–16.

41 Rudolf Henning, *Das deutsche Haus in seiner historischen Entwickelung* (Strasbourg: Karl J. Trübner, 1882), 172.

42 Carl Schäfer, "Ueber das deutsche Haus. Vortrag gehalten zum Schinkelfest im Berliner Architektenverein am 13. Maerz 1883," *Zeitschrift für Bauwesen* 33, no. 4–6 (1883): 209–222, published also as a special issue: *Ueber das deutsche Haus* (Berlin: Ernst & Korn Verlag, 1883); on the lecture series, see the preface of Carl Schäfer, *Deutsche Holzbaukunst: die Grundlagen der deutschen Holzbauweisen in ihrer konstruktiven und formalen Folge*, ed. Paul Kanold (Dresden: Wolfgang Jess Verlag, 1937). On Schäfer, see Jutta Schuchard, *Carl Schäfer: 1844–1908: Leben und Werk des Architekten der Neugotik. Materialien zur Kunst des neunzehnten Jahrhunderts* (Munich: Prestel, 1979).

43 August Meitzen, *Das deutsche Haus in seinen volkstümlichen Formen. Behufs Ermittlungen über die geographische und geschichtliche Verbreitung, besprochen auf dem Geographen-Tage zu Berlin am 7.–9. Juli 1881* (Berlin: Verlag Dietrich Reimer, 1882), 16.

44 Georges Teyssot, *A Topology of Everyday Constellations* (Cambridge, MA: The MIT Press, 2013), 57.

45 Schäfer, "Ueber das deutsche Haus," 213–214.

46 On the reasoning behind the pre-eminence of the Franks in German myth creation of the nineteenth century, see Léon Poliakov, *Der arische Mythos: zu den Quellen von Rassismus und Nationalismus* (Vienna: Europaverlag, 1977), 98–134. What Poliakov offers as a basis for the definition of German unity in the field of linguistic research applies equally to the field of architectural research.

47 Teyssot, *A Topology of Everyday Constellations*, 53–58.

48 Meitzen, *Das deutsche Haus*, 16.

49 Muthesius, *Das englische Haus*, 10.

50 See Heidrun Laudel, *Gottfried Semper: Architektur und Stil* (Dresden: Verlag der Kunst, 1991), 37–57; otherwise, on Semper and Cuvier: Andreas Hauser, "Der "Cuvier der Kunstwissenschaft.' Klassifikationsprobleme in Gottfried Sempers "Vergleichende Baulehre,'" in *Grenzbereiche der Architektur: Festschrift Adolf Reinle zum 65. Geburtstag*, ed. Thomas Bolt et al. (Basel: Birkhäuser, 1985), 97–111; and Michael Gnehm, *Stumme Poesie: Architektur und Sprache bei Gottfried Semper* (Zurich: gta Verlag, 2004), 43–54.

51 Gottfried Semper, *Die vier Elemente der Baukunst. Ein Beitrag zur vergleichenden Baukunde* (Braunschweig: Vieweg & Sohn Verlag, 1851), 55.

52 Gottfried Semper, *Der Stil in den technischen und tektonischen Künsten oder praktische Ästhetik* vol. 2 (Munich: Friedrich Bruckmann Verlag, 1863), 290–293.

53 On the racial stereotypes in the work of Gottfried Semper and Eugène-Emmanuel Viollet-le-Duc, see Charles Davies II, *Building Character: the Racial Politics of Modern Architectural Style* (Pittsburgh: University of Pittsburgh Press, 2019). While the embedment of Viollet-Le-Duc's and Gottfried Semper's writing inside a larger discourse on race sheds new light on their work, underlining especially, their evolutionary models centered around a European, often national ideal, it does not take into account the highly differentiated (yet also exclusionary) environmental discourse present in their work (and that of others), which similarly addressed questions of topography, climate, craft, material, and construction, to better understand the particularities of the specific architectures under scrutiny.

54 Eugène-Emmanuel Viollet-le-Duc, *Histoire de l'habitation humaine* (Paris: Bibliothèque d'Education et de Récréation J. Hetzel, 1875), 357; see also Martin Bressani, "Notes on Viollet-le-Duc's Philosophy of History: Dialectics and Technology," *Journal of the Society of Architectural Historians* 48, no. 4 (1989): 327–350.

55 James Fergusson, *History of the Modern Styles of Architecture: Being a Sequel to the Handbook of Architecture* (London: John Murray Press, 1862), appendix, 493.

56 Banister Fletcher, *A History of Architecture on the Comparative Method for the Student, Craftsman, and Amateur* (London: B. T. Batsford, 1905 [1896]), iii. The "family tree" appeared in the *History* until the sixteenth edition (1954). In his definition of "historical" and "non-historical styles" Fletcher falls back on a distinction proposed by Charles Garnier and A. Ammann in their history of world architectures. See also Charles Garnier and A. Ammann, *L'habitation humaine* (Paris: Hachette, 1892). I thank David Theodore for the information on Fletcher.

57 Herman Sörgel, "Wohnhäuser," in *Handbuch der Architektur* 1 (Leipzig: J. M. Gebhardts Verlag, 1927), fig. 1. In 1928 Herman Sörgel copied Fletcher's family tree and used it to illustrate his essay, "Baukunst. Über Ihr Wesen, ihre Geschichte und ihre Stile," which appears in the second volume of *Wissen ist Macht. Ein Handbuch des Wissens unserer Zeit und der Kulturfortschritte der Menschheit*, ed. Arthur Krause (Nordhausen am Harz: Volkshochschul-Verlag, 1928), chart 11. I thank Rainer Schützeichel for this information.

58 See Teyssot, *A Topology of Everyday Constellations*, 68–82.

59 Le Corbusier and Pierre Jeanneret, "Analyse des éléments fondamentaux du problème 'Maison Minimum'," in *Die Wohnung für das Existenzminimum: auf Grund der Ergebnisse des 2. Internationalen Kongresses für Neues Bauen sowie der vom Städtischen Hochbauamt in Frankfurt a. M. veranstalteten Wander-Ausstellung*, eds. Internationale Kongresse für Neues Bauen und Städtisches Hochbauamt Frankfurt am Main (Frankfurt am Main: Englert & Schlosser, 1930), 24–33, here 24–25.

60 Congrès Internationaux d'Architecture Moderne, eds., *Contribution à la charte de l'habitat: CIAM 9, Aix-en-Provence, 19–25 juillet 1953* (Boulogne-sur-Seine, 1953).

→ Norman Foster, Detail of Façade Willis Faber Office, Ipswich, 1971–1975

Transparency

↑ Norman Foster, Willis Faber Office, Ipswich, 1971–1975

At the very same moment the British architectural press was devoting page after page to the debate on New Brutalism, seemingly in an effort to make what was actually a rather complicated concept even more transparent, the British architectural historian Colin Rowe and the American painter and critic Robert Slutzky were penning an essay on the subject of transparency itself. Written between 1955 and 1956, "Transparency: Literal and Phenomenal" offered a theoretical reappraisal of sorts on modernism through this single-defining architectural element. Ironically, the text was rejected by the *Architectural Review* for what Nikolaus Pevsner took to be its anti-Gropius bias,[1] and it was not until eight years later, in 1963, that the first part of the essay was finally published in the Yale University journal *Perspecta*. Another eight years passed before *Perspecta*'s rolling cohort of student editors published the second half of the essay in 1971, meaning by the time it was released in full, "Transparency" (that is the phenomenal and the literal) was absorbed into a moment and milieu quite distinct from where it had originated. Its significance cannot be underestimated within the architectural debates of the US (and also in Switzerland, thanks to Bernhard Hoesli, a colleague of both Rowe and Slutzky and fellow Texas-Ranger), but when viewed from an English perspective, its publication was badly timed.

Just as Rowe and Slutzky were finally able to demonstrate in the second part of the essay that the concept of transparency was not limited to the present, but a way of analyzing centuries of classical buildings, their subject was being challenged by the very material that had initiated their investigation all those years ago. Because also in 1971, Norman Foster was putting the finishing touches on his design of the Willis Faber & Dumas offices in Ipswich. As soon it was completed in 1975, the building stood as a challenge to conventional wisdom about glass and transparency. Neither literally see-through nor spatially revealing, its mirrored-glass envelope gave nothing away. Instead, the shining, undulating, black form rose up over the medieval street, reflecting "every era of East English architecture"[2] across a surface that, as Christopher Woodward observed in the *Architectural Review*, had been reimagined from "something you look through, a mere facility, to something you look at, a high-class surface material such as would have made the Ancients green with envy."[3] While the Willis Faber & Dumas building marked the first major office project for the recently formed Foster Associates, it already foreshadowed what would become a career-spanning investigation into glass and its obfuscating (rather than transparent) qualities, marking a shift in the accepted wisdom on glass architecture, moving from the transparency of modernism to something much more opaque.[4] In this facade—slick as a "big black piano" or "Rolls Royce"—Charles Jencks detected the central motif of a visually endowed, postmodern architecture. Its tinted glass was not only a signal of "cool office work" but would become in critiques of this time a more universal expression of 1970s cultural policy:[5] the expression of a self-referential mirror economy, a corporate culture disengaged from the public realm, its flat surface posing a challenge to both phenomenal and literal transparency.

Without doubt the Willis Faber & Dumas building belongs to the post-industrial economic order that so defined western society from the 1970s. But as tempting as it may be to draw, in the vein of Jencks, metaphorical links between material and conceptual orders, doing so reverses cause and effect: the image the building conjures arrives before the building itself, reducing the architecture to perception rather than grounding it in the reality of its built materials.

As Rowe and Slutzky write in the opening lines of their essay, "we are familiar with [the] use" of words like transparency but "rarely seek to analyze their application." If "Transparency: Literal and Phenomenal" can be understood as a parsing of the word and a close examination into the images and references that construct its meaning, Foster's Ipswich project is more forthright. But where the authors treat images and references as the material of their investigation, the architect focuses on the physical matter of transparency: the "glassiness of glass," as Woodward suggested. And where Rowe and Slutzky are, in their own words, "pedantic" in their analysis of something so "familiar," the Ipswich office is straightforward in its approach, revealing the meaning of glass and its material potential. It takes any assumptions about glass and inverts them, revealing the meaning of transparency through its negation, so that one sees not only glass but its material potential—and exactly how glass is used is what defines the facade of the Willis Faber & Dumas building.[6] Bronze-tinted glazing panels, each 2m square and 12mm thick, are connected by corner patch fittings and joined with a silicone sealant, forming an uninterrupted three-story sheath that is suspended from roof level and protects from the elements.[7] The application of such innovative technologies—the float glass manufacturing process, the Total Vision System produced with silicone sealants, the complete absence of any frame to hold the windows (a modern vision finally come true) or the vast scale of the suspended glazing[8]—is less a rupture with the logic of modernity than the continuation of its operative dimension. From this perspective, the comments on transparency or opacity are not unrelated, as both illustrate an increasing divide between architectural criticism's tendency towards metaphor and the material logic of production, a separation that has shaped modern and postmodern architectural historiography alike.

But if in the context of modernism the metaphor of transparency had become all-too familiar and undisputed, the word was not always so readily available. Critics in the second half of the nineteenth century initially struggled to explain the new effects of glass on modern architecture. In his analysis of the Crystal Palace, Gottfried Semper described walls and ceilings that were "invisible to the eye" and compared the interiors to a "glass-covered vacuum,"[9] while Richard Lucae, examining its successor at Sydenham some years later, wrote of the "unsubstantial" boundaries between inside and outside.[10] And in the early twentieth century Alfred Gotthold Meyer depicted the shadowless "space of light" caused by glass in his influential study on iron buildings.[11] By the late 1920s, however, a more defined conceptual understanding of transparency had emerged via Sigfried Giedion. Writing in *Bauen in Frankreich*, he located within the "endlessly open" houses of Le Corbusier a "floating transparency" not unlike what he had seen in Cubist painting.[12] Later, in the "dematerialization of the corner of the [workshop] building" at the Bauhaus he identified a "sort of crystalline transparency,"[13] thus launching the modern use of the word, and establishing the precedent to which Rowe and Slutzky would later turn.

If in transparency modernism created its most potent images, it was through glass that they materialized, and by the mid-1920s clear window glass was ubiquitous in both practice and theory.[14] Its ability to connect the interior and exterior realms was unanimously proclaimed by

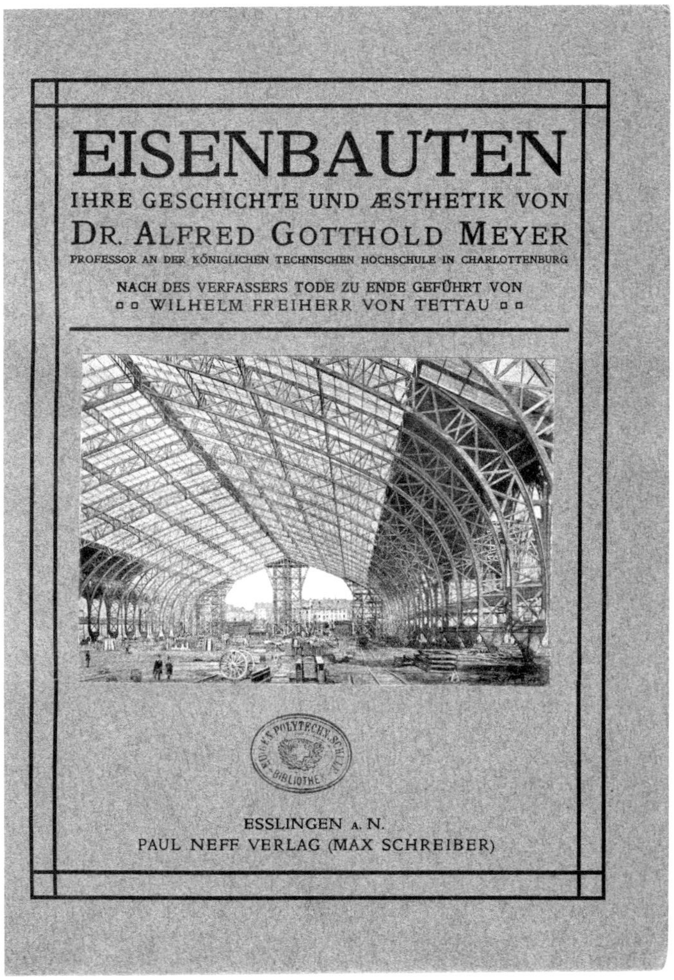

↑ Cover of Alfred Gotthold Meyer, *Eisenbauten, ihre Geschichte und Aesthetik* [*Iron Buildings: Their History and Their Aesthetic*]. 1907

key figures who emphasized the "new sense of space" that connected the indoors with "outer space" (Gropius); the advantages of ample access to daylight (Le Corbusier); the potential of "weightlessness and transparency" (Ludwig Hilberseimer); and the novel and formal possibilities it offered (Ludwig Mies van der Rohe).[15] Whether as layers that seemingly collapsed in the corner of the Bauhaus workshop, or the streamlined curtain skimming the surface of Mies van der Rohe's Friedrichstrasse skyscraper, or the "glass palace" of Rotterdam's Van Nelle factory, or the Centrosoyus in Moscow, an "orgy of glass and concrete" to quote Hannes Meyer,[16] or more generally across commercial and retail buildings, schools, transport hubs, tenements, private villas, exhibition venues, and even churches, but also tableware or test tubes, glass was the material of choice.

Glass is noticeable, wrote the architect Arthur Korn in 1929 in his extensive monograph on the material, "yet not quite visible. It is the great membrane, full of mystery, delicate yet tough." On observing the whole range of possibilities that the material now offered, Korn adds, "Its peculiar advantage is in the diversity of the impression it creates." [17] Glass could both dissolve interior and exterior worlds and create a sense of depth akin to that of the Bauhaus workshop corner, but it could also reflect and mirror environments or shield as a "medium against the weather"—as demonstrated by Korn's own shop design for Kopp & Joseph (1922–1930), in which display shelving completely encased by glass protruded onto the pavement.[18]

Despite the more radical experiments with the material and the claims of its defenders, the inumerous photographs and drawings depicting these glass buildings largely question their transparency. With the exception of some interior views, the buildings that appear in architectural journals rarely stand out on account of the characteristics cited by Giedion and his followers. Instead of transparent surfaces, reflective, illuminated, or opaque facades tend to be the rule. Accompanying Gropius's article, "Glasbau," for example, is a charcoal drawing that shows the workshop wing of the Bauhaus as an opaque, vertically articulated volume. Similarly, in line drawings for other projects, the windows of largely glazed buildings such as those by Alberto Sartoris, Ilja Golosov, and Eduard and Otto Fucker's are shown as solid black or white surfaces. Even in photographs the houses of the Weissenhof Estate, for example, are distinguished by their white volumes and bands of windows, always presented in an impenetrable black, while the rounded edges of Erich Mendelsohn's commercial buildings reflect the sky and surrounding city—only in the famous night-time shots do we see into their illuminated interiors. In these different buildings one finds neither "the visible depth behind the thin skin of glass [as] the exciting factor" (as Korn observed), nor the "extensive transparency that permits interior and exterior to be seen simultaneously" revealing a new "conception of space-time" (as Giedion described), but an array of qualities, ranging from opacity to the complete absence of any effect.[19]

By the late 1920s, as the metaphorical link between glass and transparency was becoming common parlance in architectural discourse, it was already being challenged by the tangible effects and properties of the material's "enclosing," "sheltering," and "insulating" qualities. In 1929, the same year that Korn released his monograph, Konrad Werner Schulze published his own survey on glass. Like his contemporaries Schulze acknowledges architecture's new "spatial aspiration," which he writes is rooted in the need for "insight and outlook and spatial clarity." But this is where his thesis diverges, for it is the technical potential of glass that serves as his main interest (hardly surprising given his previous publications—one on brick and another on steel frame construction in commercial and high-rise buildings).[20] Turning to his latest subject, Schulze meticulously outlines the consequences of building: modern architecture,

Ludwig Mies van der Rohe: Hochhaus

122

↓ Mies van der Rohe, “Office Buildings,” *Frühlicht*, 1922

→ Sigfried Giedion, *Space, Time and Architecture*, 1941, with Picasso, *L’Arlésienne*, 1911–1912, and Walter Gropius, Bauhaus Dessau, 1926

↘ Walter Gropius, “Glassbuilding,” *Deutsche Bauzeitung*, 1926

229. PICASSO, “L’Arlésienne,” 1911–12. *Oil. “In the head may be seen the cubist device of simultaneity — showing two aspects of a single object at the same time, in this case the profile and the full face. The transparency of overlapping planes is also characteristic” (Catalogue of the Picasso Exhibition, Museum of Modern Art, New York, 1939, p. 77).*

402

230. WALTER GROPIUS, The Bauhaus, Dessau, 1926. *Corner of the workshop wing. In this case it is the interior and the exterior of a building which are presented simultaneously. The extensive transparent areas, by dematerializing the corners, permit the hovering relations of planes and the kind of “overlapping” which appears in contemporary painting.*

403

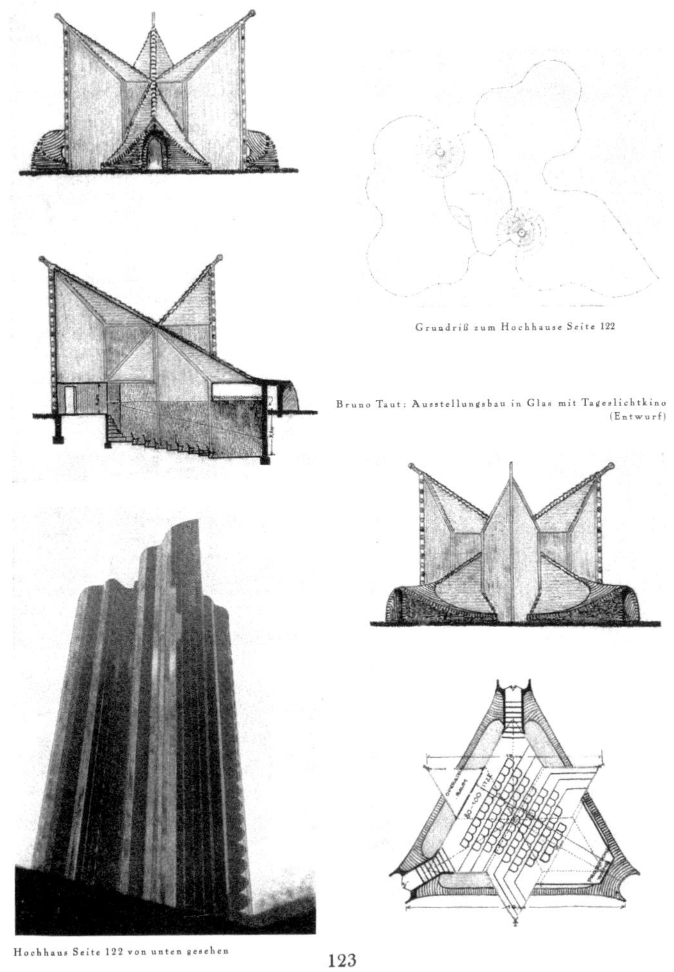

Grundriß zum Hochhause Seite 122

Bruno Taut: Ausstellungsbau in Glas mit Tageslichtkino (Entwurf)

Hochhaus Seite 122 von unten gesehen

123

DIE BAUZEITUNG

VEREINIGT MIT

„SÜDDEUTSCHE BAUZEITUNG“ MÜNCHEN

Hauptschriftleiter: Regierungsbaumeister H. P. ECKART, Dipl. Ing., Stuttgart, Sedanstraße 16
Schriftleitung für bayer. Angelegenheiten: Dr. ing. G. STEINLEIN, Arch., München, Paul Heysestr. 29/31

XXIII. Jahrgang. Nr. 20. *Stuttgart, den 25. Mai 1926.*

Zur 5. Glastechnischen Tagung in Köln.

Am 27. und 28. Mai findet in Köln, einberufen von der Deutschen Glastechnischen Gesellschaft, die 5. Glastechnische Tagung statt. Ueber die Einzelheiten dieser Veranstaltung ist am Schluß dieser Nummer (Seite XVII) des nähern berichtet.

arch.: walter gropius mit adolf meyer
bauhausneubau dessau. ansicht von der friedrichsallee

Unsere Zeit strebt nach Helle, Licht, Sauberkeit und Reinlichkeit. Das drückt sich auch darin aus, daß in der Architektur in weit stärkerem Maße als früher das Glas Verwendung findet. Nicht nur im Fabrik- und Geschäftsbau haben sich die Wände in dünne Stützen aufgelöst, die mit Glasfenstern ausgefüllt werden, sondern auch im Wohnhausbau macht sich seit Jahren eine ausgesprochene Strömung bemerkbar, die den Wohnräumen mehr Licht und mehr Sonne zuführen will. Wir haben uns daher veranlaßt gesehen, in dem vorliegenden Heft auf die glastechnischen Probleme in der Architektur in einigen Artikeln etwas näher einzugehen, um die Architekten und Baugewerbetreibenden auf die Verwendungsmöglichkeiten des Glases vor allem als Baustoff aufmerksam zu machen. Das Glas hat in technischer Hinsicht gegenüber früher eine gewaltige Entwicklung erfahren und es ist daher anzunehmen, daß es vielleicht doch noch eine größere Rolle in der Baukunst spielen wird.

Wir wünschen nun der Glastechnischen Tagung in Köln die besten Erfolge. Möge sie in technischer Hinsicht Fortschritte zeitigen, die eine vermehrte Verwendung des Glases in der Baukunst ermöglichen und so „mehr Licht“ in unsere in vielfacher Hinsicht trübe Zeit gebracht werden kann.

glasbau **von walter gropius, dessau, bauhaus.**

Architekt Walter Gropius, Direktor des Bauhauses in Dessau, hat uns nachstehende Abhandlung zur Verfügung gestellt. Um die Eigenart dieses Künstlers voll zum Ausdruck zu bringen, veröffentlichen wir den Aufsatz in der uns zugegangenen Originalabfassung. Die Hauptschriftleitung.

die entwicklungsgeschichte der baukunst zeigt, daß die veränderungen der bauformen an die entwicklung ihrer technischen mittel gebunden sind. die freude des gotischen baukünstlers, hohe spitzbögen einwölben zu können an stelle der bisherigen schwereren rundbögen muß seine phantasie in gleichem maße angeregt haben, wie die neuen technischen konstruktionsmöglichkeiten der gegenwart den gestaltungsbetrieb unserer baukünstler befruchten.

die technische entwicklung der letzten generationen hat ein so gewaltiges tempo angenommen, daß man eine spanne von tausend jahren der vergangenheit als vergleichsmaß heranziehen muß. die umwälzungen infolge der neuen mechanischen kräfte kamen so schnell über nacht, daß die zivilisierte menschheit erst in den anfängen der entwicklung ihrer technischen weltordnung steht, vorläufig sklave und noch nicht herr der neuen gewalten ist, die sie doch erdachte, um

159

he concludes, is no longer an optical phenomenon that must satisfy aesthetic requirements alone but serves, in a very physical and immediate sense, as a "tool" in and of itself—and as a tool its design must be as practical and economic as possible; a glance at its form should reveal the purposes it serves, individually or in combination.[21] A building must bow throughout the design process to the demand for "maximal performance," and glass, he continues, is thereby "an essential component of [its] spatial function."

But achieving maximal performance required a thorough knowledge of the material and its properties. From the late nineteenth century, the scientific community had been studying the physical and chemical makeup of glass as it sought to establish industrial norms across Europe.[22] Yet even in light of this short but prolific thirty-year history, and even after repeated mention of the latest "findings of modern physics and chemistry," Schulze abandons any description of their application to glass architecture. He almost certainly would have known of a few pioneering projects: glass that was permeable to ultra-violet rays, for example, appeared in 1915 as the Uviol Glass of sanatoriums such as the German House in Agra, near Lugano;[23] then ten years later in the Vitaglass of the monkey house at London Zoo; and again, in 1928, in Robert Mallet-Stevens' design for the Villa Cavroix in Croix.[24] In his Palace of the League of Nations (1927),[25] Le Corbusier not only introduced his first-ever *mur neutralisant* as an active thermal system, tested in the Saint Gobain Glass company under the supervision of Gustave Lyon,[26] but also designed a double-acoustic shell for the ceiling of the main hall, composed of glass panes to ensure better sound transmission.[27]

One of the more fruitful collaborations of glass in architecture during this period took place in Cambridge,

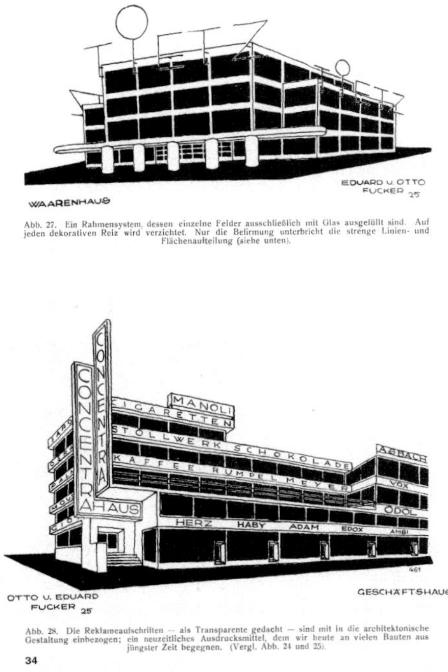
WAARENHAUS

EDUARD U. OTTO FUCKER 25

Abb. 27. Ein Rahmensystem, dessen einzelne Felder ausschließlich mit Glas ausgefüllt sind. Auf jeden dekorativen Reiz wird verzichtet. Nur die Befirmung unterbricht die strenge Linien- und Flächenaufteilung (siehe unten).

HERZ

HABY

ADAM

EDOX

AMBI

ÖDOL

VOX

OTTO U. EDUARD FUCKER 25

GESCHÄFTSHAUS

Abb. 28. Die Reklameaufschriften — als Transparente gedacht — sind mit in die architektonische Gestaltung einbezogen; ein neuzeitliches Ausdrucksmittel, dem wir heute an vielen Bauten aus jüngster Zeit begegnen. (Vergl. Abb. 24 und 25).

34

↖ Erich Mendelsohn, Herpich House, Berlin, 1924–1928, in Konrad Werner Schulze, Glas in der *Architektur der Gegenwart [Glass in Contemporary Architecture]*, 1929

↑ Eduard and Otto Fucker, office building, in Konrad Werner Schulze, *Glas in der Architektur der Gegenwart [Glass in Contemporary Architecture]*, 1929

← ↑ Walter Gropius and Carl Fieger, Bauhaus building, Dessau, 1925–1926, in Konrad Werner Schulze, *Glas in der Architektur der Gegenwart* [*Glass in Contemporary Architecture*], 1929

in the form of a house called Finella, designed by Raymond McGrath. A pioneer of modern British architecture and ranked by the industrial designer George Nelson among the most important modern architects in Europe,[28] McGrath is best known for St. Anne's Court (1936) in Surrey. Nicknamed the Round House, its curved and flush-mounted *fenêtre en longeur* wraps around the south facade. But it was ten years earlier in 1927 at Finella where McGrath engaged most thoroughly with his what would become a career-spanning obsession with glass. The client, an enchanting eccentric Cambridge don named Mansfield "Manny" Forbes,[29] commissioned the architect to reimagine the dusty Georgian villa he was renting as an "exhibition-piece-cum-arts-center"[30] for hosting the artists, writers, scientists and other intellectuals he kept as company.[31] McGrath answered by transforming the house into an homage to its titular Scottish noblewoman who, according to legend, was the inventor of glass, lived in a glazed castle and died by throwing herself over a waterfall while fleeing her assailants. As Albert Frost wrote in a particularly florid article for the *Architectural Review*, Finella—both heroine and house—was "before her time."[32] If the Scottish queen was half "Lady Macbeth and half Saint Bride ... anticipating the modern woman twice as much as either," then McGrath's incarnation was a cross of its own. On the outside it was an elegant yet unassuming villa; inside it embodied a phantasmagorical world made possible through technical wizardry and, above all, glass. The Georgian wired plate-glass of the front door contrasted with the forty-foot-long hall where artificial light was reflected and refracted onto myriad "atlantean" surfaces: a semi-octagonal ceiling arch covered in silvered fluted glass, walls of silverleaf licked in aquamarine lacquer and mirror-glazed pilasters that marked the passage to either the staircase or the illuminated glass threshold of the living room. Beyond its entrance, Finella held more delights: copper-clad doors, aluminum-lined bathroom walls, rubber floors, and in the dining room a shallow, translucent, and silvered glass dome.[33]

← Le Corbusier and Pierre Jeanneret, house at Weissenhof Siedlung, Stuttgart, 1927, in Konrad Werner Schulze, *Glas in der Architektur der Gegenwart* [*Glass in Contemporary Architecture*], 1929

← Raymond McGrath, entrance hall, Finella, Cambridge, 1929

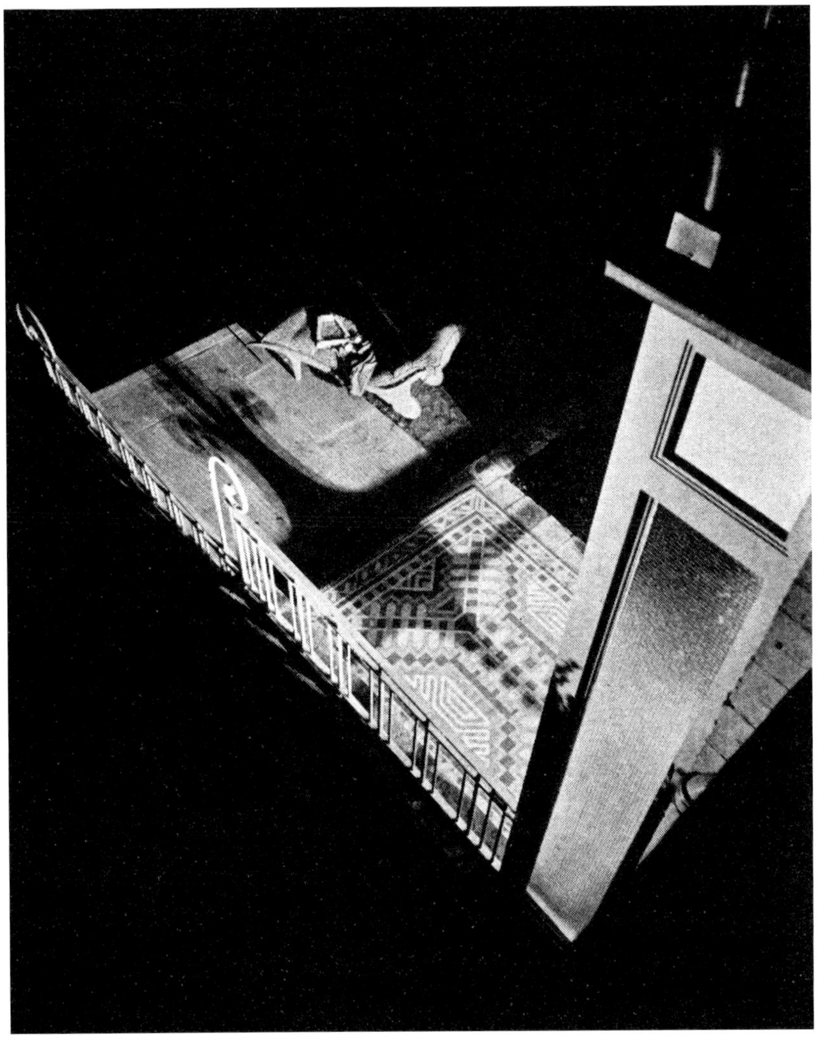

← Raymond McGrath, entrance, Finella, Cambridge, 1929

↓ Raymond McGrath, dining room ceiling viewed from below the glass dining table, Finella, Cambridge, 1929

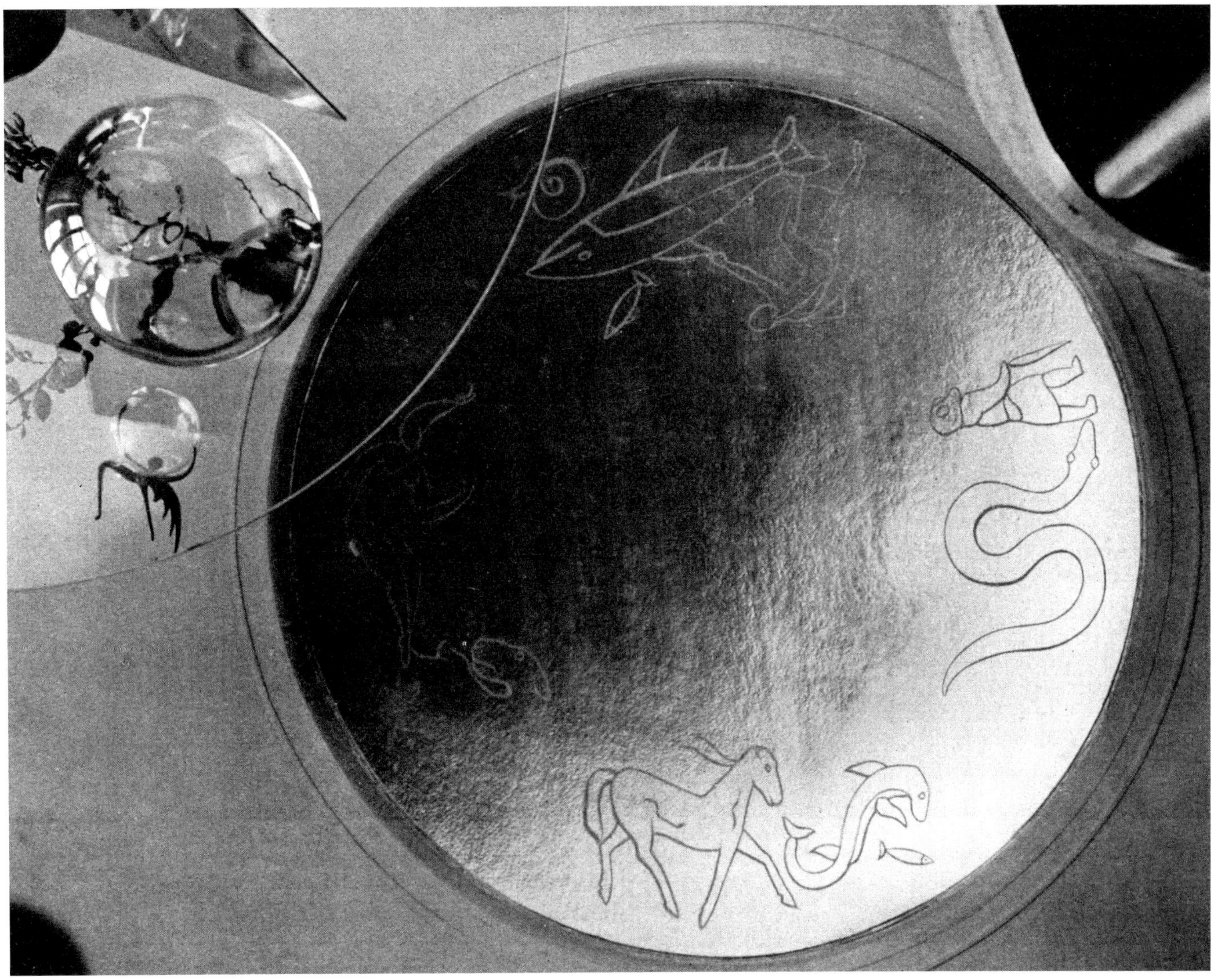

← Ellis and Clark with Owen Williams, Daily Express Building, London, 1932, in Raymond McGrath, *Glass in Architecture and Decoration*, 1937

→ H. E. Beckett, "Microphotographs Showing Structure of Opal Glass," in Raymond McGrath, *Glass in Architecture and Decoration*, 1937

This sumptuous house became a showroom for McGrath and Forbes to display the aesthetic potential of glass. The pictures taken by Dell & Wainwright, the young photographers hired to shoot the house, lived up to the ethereal qualities of its physical spaces as they pursued the "shadows over the floors and furniture," using their arc lamps at night to create "elusive phenomena" that seemed to rise like the moon. More than anyone else in Britain until now, Dell & Wainwright (who in 1929 would become official photographers of the *Architectural Review* on the back of these images[34]) were able to translate into images what McGrath had described as the metaphysical qualities of glass, its ability to recreate the "psychological effects" of architectural space through its reflective and refracting qualities.[35] A glass environment that flickered with distortions and illusions, both revealing and obscuring depth: this was a new layered atmosphere—transparent only in its affinity for the material—that served as a laboratory for Forbes and his Cambridge milieu of scientists, artists, Marxists, writers, and architects. Among Finella's regulars were Aldous Huxley and his brother Julian, the book designer and editor Noel Carrington, the sculptor Jacob Epstein and Serge Chermayeff and Wells Coates, both McGrath's future colleagues in the design of the BBC's Broadcasting House. Finella also provided the backdrop to meetings of the 20th Century Group, a predecessor of the MARS Group.[36]

It was not until 1937 that McGrath gave his material of choice its long-overdue and cross-disciplinary investigation in *Glass in Architecture and Decoration*. Part historical survey, part investigation into the techniques of production, the study's fusion of scientific data and buildings is rare for the period, as architectural writing was gradually splintering into ever more specialized fields, and technology and design increasingly parted ways. Alongside the main text, written with Albert Frost, is a separate section titled "The Nature and Property of Glass," by Harold E. Beckett, a scientist of the Building Research Station, which details the countless environmental conditions and material characteristics that glass can be used to address: depending on the issue (sunbeams, UV-rays, warmth, sound, light or the view) and type of glass (whether flat, ribbed, sandblasted, blocked or opalescent), the material can reveal itself to be insulating, permeable, reflective, refracting, diffusive or even tinted.[37] In the foreground of this decidedly "scientified" approach to glass are its material properties, which Beckett examines through a series of photographs illustrating the concealing power of different glass surfaces and X-ray photographs that show the crystalline structure of the material. These technical insights would in turn inform McGrath's thesis and choice of illustrations throughout the book, which included the Vitrolite-clad Daily Express Building in London (1930–1932), designed by Ellis and Clark and the engineer Owen Williams, who supposedly determined the thickness of the facade by the "insulation value of its material;" the "insulating wall" of the William Lescaze House in New York (1933–1934), built out of "partially evacuated hollow glass bricks;" and the glass screens of the bandstand at the Hamburg Horticultural Show (1935) that acted as an acoustic "reflector." "The point to stress," McGrath had written a few years earlier,

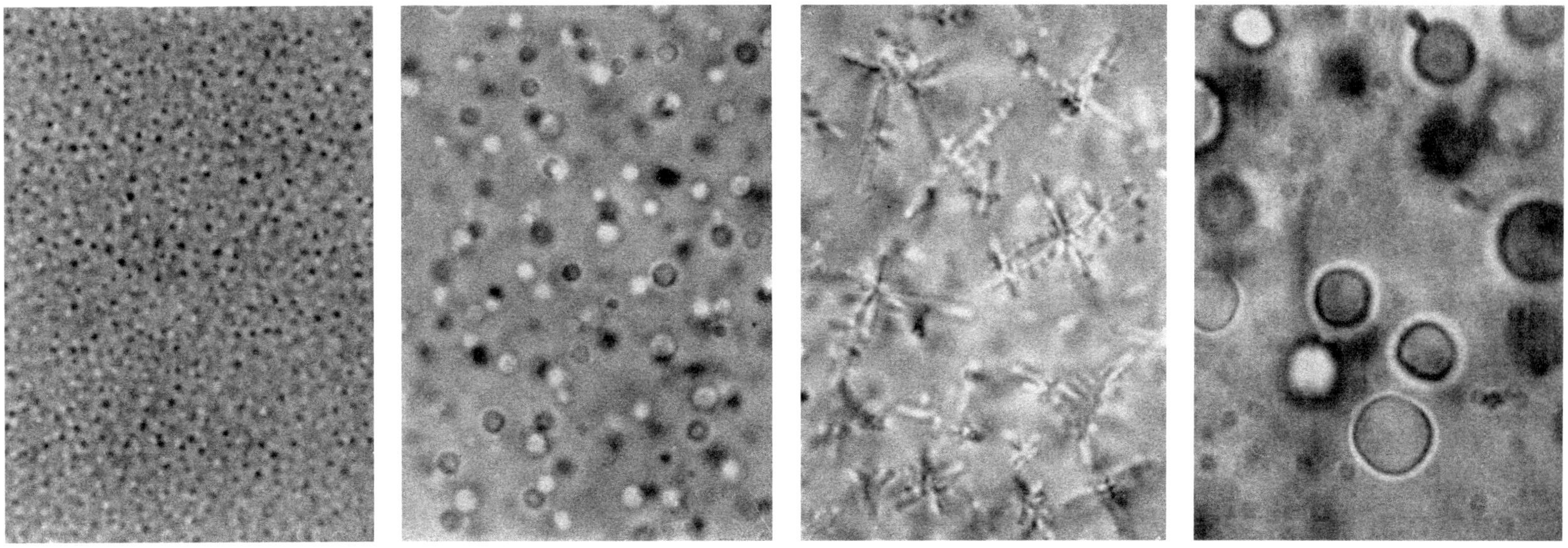

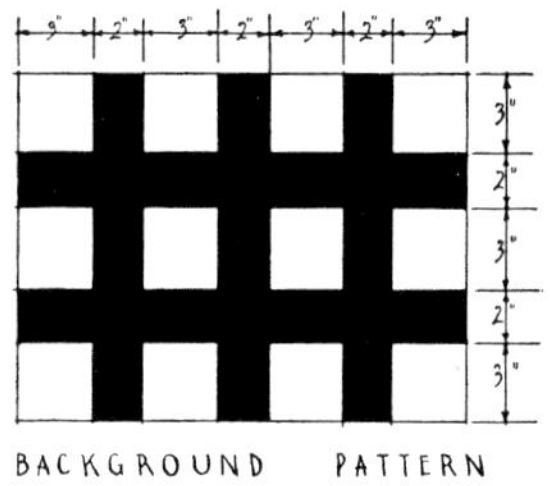

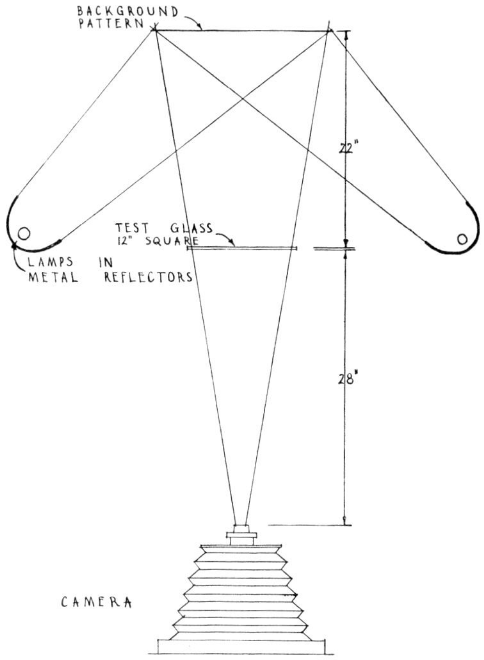

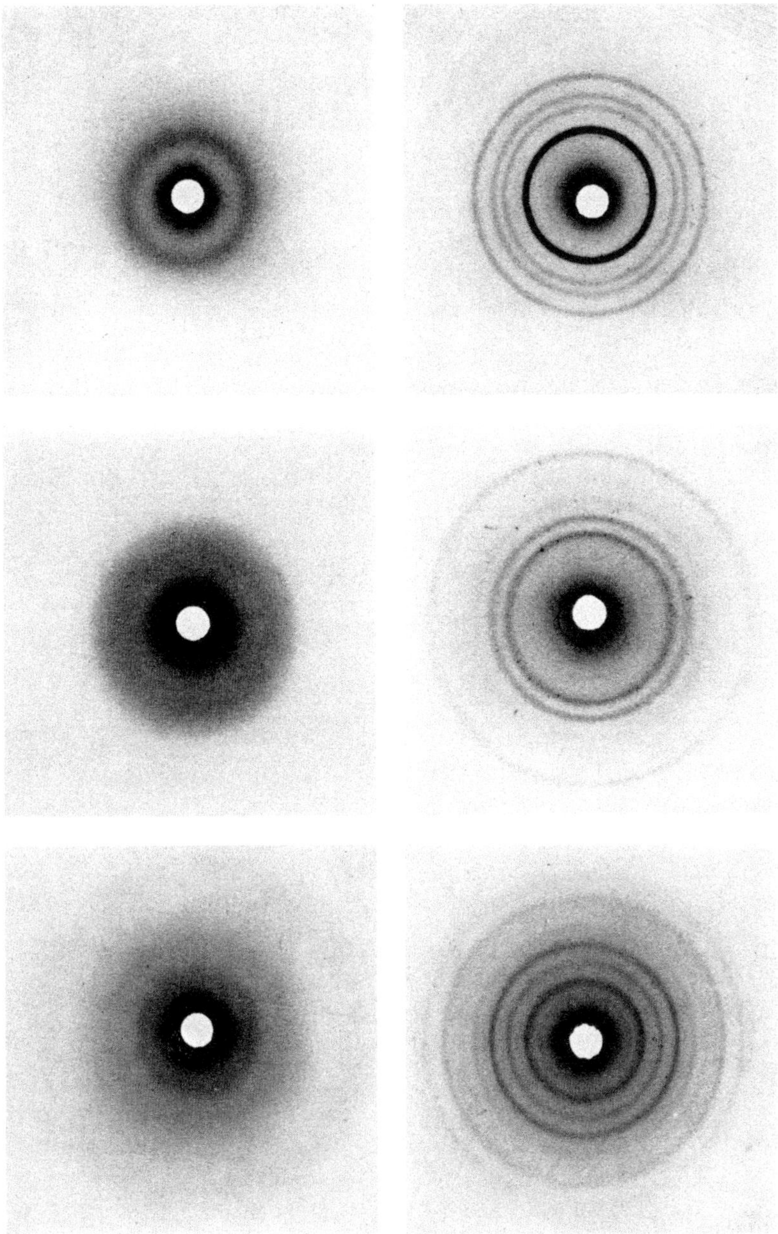

↑ H. E. Beckett, "Method Adopted to Illustrate Concealing Power of Glass," in Raymond McGrath, *Glass in Architecture and Decoration*, 1937

← H. E. Beckett, "X-Ray Defraction Photographs," in Raymond McGrath, *Glass in Architecture and Decoration*, 1937

← H. E. Beckett, "The Concealing Power of Typical Obscuring Finishes," in Raymond McGrath, *Glass in Architecture and Decoration*, 1937

was the "pre-eminent structural quality of modern glass." The issue was therefore not a matter of looking through but literally "*into* glass."[38]

Techniques like X-ray photography, which were being developed inside scientific laboratories and found their way into McGrath's study, were rapidly adopted in the postwar years, either to represent the new visual environment produced through scientific investigation, as in the exhibition and publications of the Independent Group, or literally as part of interior design, as in the Festival of Britain in 1951. For the latter, the crystallographer Helen Megaw with Max Perutz, John Kendrew and Dorothy Hodgkin (future joint recipients of the Nobel Prize for chemistry), established the so-called Festival Pattern Group that furnished the festival spaces with wallpapers, curtains and carpets whose patterns were created by abstracting and enlarging various molecules and proteins such as hemoglobin, myoglobin, or insulin from X-ray photographs.[39] While the endlessly repeatable makeup of the atoms was to become an ideal subject for a decorative yet abstract geometry of wall papers, the patterns themselves can be considered the best illustration of the materiality of the particles then under investigation in laboratories.

Besides this direct transposition of subatomic particles to a building's interiors, another path between science and architecture had been sketched out by the former Bauhaus teacher László Moholy-Nagy a few years earlier. Since the early 1920s Moholy-Nagy had been investigating the visual potential of glass and plastic through his "'transparent' pictures" and "light display machines." The photographs and photograms of his studies were first published in *Von Material zu Architektur* the same year as Korn's and Schulze's respective research on glass.[40] Like them, Moholy-Nagy had observed the simultaneous effects of glass and equally used a photograph of the Bauhaus workshop facade to illustrate the capacity of glass to unify inside and outside. More than the clarity of glass alone, it was the mirroring and refracting effects of the window that blurred the interior and exterior into the single plane of the fully glazed facade.

Glass was perhaps the first step in Moholy-Nagy's larger investigation of "space-time" problems, which he would trace out almost two decades later in *Vision in Motion*. Published posthumously in 1947, almost contemporaneous with Giedion's *Mechanization Takes Command*, the book would become influential among the postwar avant-garde for its author's affinity for technology.[41] To introduce the idea of "space-time," Moholy-Nagy turns to X-ray pictures—"among the outstanding space-time renderings on the static plane"—reproducing in a paragraph titled "transparency and light" a photograph of a man shaving.[42]

→ ↘ "Photograph and Its Distortion behind Corrugated Glass," in László Moholy-Nagy, *Vision in Motion*, 1947

The image clearly exposes the trappings of modern life (electric razor in motion, shirt sleeve, watch buckle, ring, spectacles) against the fuzzier, organic substance of the man's bony fingers and skull. X-rays, like this one, according to Moholy-Nagy not only signaled transparency—an ability to "see through" skin, whether physiologically or metaphorically (as Mies' X-ray-style photograph of his model for the 1922 Berlin Skyscraper attests),[43] but also represented materiality; "the view of an opaque solid, its outline, but also its inner structure." In this sense they do not stand for the metaphor of transparency but are instead proof that "structure becomes transparency and transparency manifests structure." Hence the importance of this medium for Moholy-Nagy and Beckett when dealing with glass itself.[44]

But the passage on transparency is just one part of a longer argument that leads from questions of motion, transparency and light in the visual arts and photography, to architecture, display, theater, and dance. The coalescing of space and time on a static plane, which Moholy-Nagy had discovered in X-ray imagery, is taken to the next logical place: the "space-time reality" of mobile architecture. For this, he relies on yet another crystallographer, Helen Megaw's thesis adviser in Cambridge, John Desmond Bernal. Moholy-Nagy must have come to know Bernal, a molecular biologist and pioneering X-ray crystallographer, or at least his work, during his years in London. Both moved in the same social circle (and drank at the same Breuer-designed bar at the Isokon Building, a kind of north London inheritor of Finella, where European émigrés including Walter and Ise Gropius and Arthur Korn would stay for some time). However, in his excursus on spatiotemporal aspects of architecture and art in *Vision in Motion*, Moholy-Nagy cites neither Bernal's scientific research on crystallography nor his use of radiographic photography as an analytical technique (nor the role of those resulting images as a metaphor for new scientific discoveries). Instead he draws on a chapter from a 1939 book titled *The Social Function of Science*, in which Bernal used science to answer a far more existential problem of his specific space and time: that of reuniting a society that had been splintered as a result of a tendency towards the specialization of disciplines.[45] Bernal's thesis supported what he saw to be a centrally planned society where scientists no longer kept their distance from the public but were directly and holistically involved in its activities—and this included architecture.[46]

What set Bernal's study apart from others of his time, whether historical or theoretical writings on architecture, building projects, or even the studies on glass strength conducted by the Building Research Station,[47] was his sweeping ambition to reinterpret a discipline based on its "physical functions." Regarding architecture, "physical functions" meant the two principal components of contemporary construction: that which serves to support a building and that which insulates it: "Of the new materials," he wrote, "some, such as the light metals, can be used exclusively for support, others, as yet but imperfectly developed, for insulation... What we require at the moment is a material as light as, if not lighter than, cork, strong enough to withstand wind-pressure, fireproof, and offering good insulation against heat and sound."[48] If such a material existed, he continued, it would be possible to break with architectural conventions, in particular, with the tradition, "of putting stone on stone or brick on brick unchanged since the time of the Pharaohs, and move in the direction of rational fabrication."[49]

For Moholy-Nagy it was this very merging of science and architecture that could inform the "space-time reality" of mobile architecture in order to move it beyond the present condition of automobiles and trains "still largely designed with the traditional principles of static architecture, a more or less obsolete superstructure erected upon a new type, the mobilized base." He lists the various houses that epitomize his thesis on these new spatiotemporal

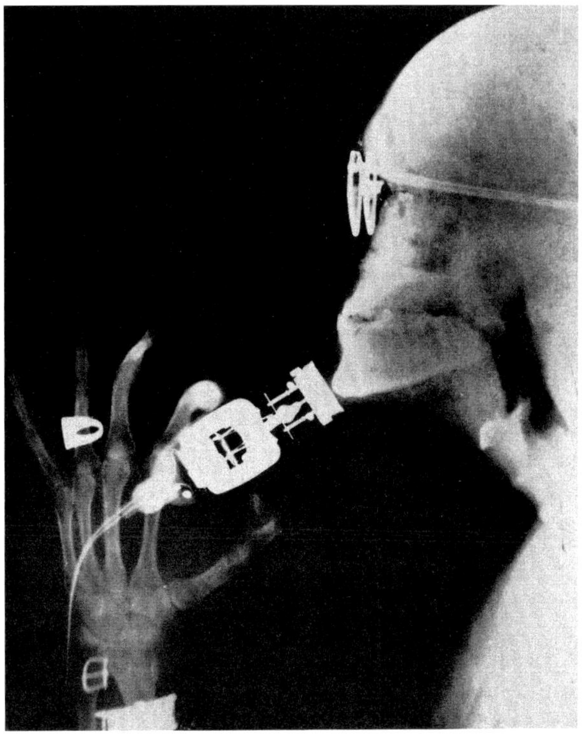

→ "Man Shaving (X-Ray Photograph)," in László Moholy-Nagy, *Vision in Motion*, 1947

dimensions—from humble trailers ("which must influence all architecture") to the more enigmatic growing house of Walter Gropius or Martin Wagner, even to Frank Lloyd-Wright's Fallingwater whose cantilevering and proximity to nature inspired the experience of plane travel. "Such buildings may be disturbing," he writes, "to a few unimaginative people, who probably would be even more aghast at the plan of Professor J D Bernal of Cambridge, England, to construct houses whose walls are produced by compressed air, by rotating air streams or opaque gases. Yet these walls guarantee perfect insulation."[50]

The issue therefore was not that of literal transparency, but the substance and performance of the materials that resulted in any transparent surface. It is this shift in perspective that enables Moholy-Nagy to challenge, as he shows in another passage the by now canonical trajectory of modern architecture propounded by Gropius, Pevsner, and Giedion—from Paxton's Crystal Palace to the Bauhaus workshop. The "transformation of solid architecture into transparency," he explains, was made possible by the plate glass window, which laid the foundations for an architecture that shifts away from "the heavy solid mass of the Pantheon," to a process that is "built not from bodies but from slabs, from planes of different substances such as concrete, glass, sheet metal, plywood"[51]—and, one would have to add, air.

The implication of reading materials as substances is considerable: to interpret the wall no longer as a window or glass panel but through its performance, no longer as a component but in terms of its physical functions, is to propose an operative answer to the aesthetic perception

← Emslie A. Morgan, view of solar wall, Wallasey School, Merseyside, 1961

↙ Marcel Breuer, Van Leer building, Amstelveen, 1957–1958, in Raymond McGrath, *Glass in Architecture and Decoration*, 1961

↓ "Visual Control Tower of the RAF Aerodrome, Boscombe Down," in Raymond McGrath, *Glass in Architecture and Decoration*, 1961

of the open and transparent house. This is precisely the conclusion Bernal had drawn in the paragraph quoted by Moholy-Nagy and underlined by several built examples, such as the air-curtain, designed in 1930 to contain unpleasant odors at Arthur Korn's Berlin rubber factory, and a gas curtain onto which advertising films could be projected, a device Moholy-Nagy had proposed to Swiss architects Moser and Steiger in 1927. The question, then, for both scientists and architects, as Moholy-Nagy himself succinctly articulated, was "why should one live between stone walls when one could live under the blue sky between green trees with all the advantages of perfect insulation?"

Not surprisingly, the practical consequences of such proposals were limited. As Raymond McGrath would write in 1961, in the second edition of *Glass in Architecture and Decoration*, with the exception of new fashions, players, and a handful of technological refinements, such as colored glass or insulating fiberglass, little had changed in two decades.[52] Beyond the use of ultra-violet glass, pioneered as early as 1903, the most important inventions dated from the 1920s—first as heat-absorbent glasses (1923) and security glass (1928).[53] In the early 1950s, improved thermal insulation reduced condensation on the windows of the control tower at the Boscombe Down RAF base, while in Marcel Breuer's Van Leer Building (1957–59) heat-absorbent security glazing suspended in front of the actual facade optimized insulation. At the Hunstanton School by Alison and Peter Smithson (1949–53) the thermal insulation was assured through the double-glazing of the north and east elevations (although the protection from the sun limited to natural linen curtains),[54] and famously at the Cité Refuge (1929–33), a *brise-soleil* was added after the Second World War to compensate for the original lack of sunshade.[55]

The examples McGrath parades before us represent the first attempts to combine the advantages of the glass facade with those of the classic wall, given that the scientific approach to architecture hones the discipline's capacity to distinguish the traditional functions of the wall (load-bearing, sheltering or protective, and insulating) as well as opportunities to delegate these functions to individual components. The task of architecture, then, was to resolve and optimize, in the words of Bernal, the various physical functions which over time had become more nuanced and individuated but also more adaptable in terms of their design. While production techniques of the late nineteenth and early twentieth centuries transformed glass from a medium of light to a medium of the gaze,[56] it can be said that from the 1930s, the comprehensive scientific investigation of glass transformed it into a medium of precise environmental design.

This concept of architecture as a space no longer delimited by a solid, opaque wall but as an environment capable of being modified by means of a permeable membrane, was harnessed in the postwar years by the British architectural avant-garde and vanguard alike, whose radical proposals and realized works sought to test the conceptual and material limits of a controlled and controllable environment.

... not so! Pimlico Comprehensive features Heywood Williams' traditional patent glazing in an exciting new way.

The intriguing facetted glass form of the new Pimlico School allows plentiful light into its many deep rooms. It also successfully complements the older adjoining buildings. The glazing structure — so fundamental to the whole design concept — testifies to the sound principles and flexibility of the patent glazing methods for which Heywood Williams have long been renowned.

Aluminium patent glazing bars form the basis of the construction, the roof being double-glazed with expanded PVC sheet in the interspace. The sidewalls are single glazed with galvanised steel opening lights. Horizontal and vertical fabric blinds are installed.

All glazing work including erection was carried out by Heywood Williams. The architect for the Inner London Education Authority was Sir Hubert Bennett, F.R.I.B.A., F.S.I.A.; group leader and job architect was John Bancroft, A.R.I.B.A., Dip.Arch. (Nottm). W. J. Simms, Sons and Cooke Ltd. was the general contractor.

Heywood Williams also offer a comprehensive range of doors and windows, in aluminium and steel, for all commercial applications. Literature will gladly be sent.

Heywood Williams Ltd

Bayhall Works, Huddersfield. Telephone: 0484 26594

Associate Company in Scotland:
Heywood Maclean Ltd., 3/5 Napier Place, North Wardpark, Cumbernauld, Dumbarton. Telephone: Cumbernauld 25007.

← Pimlico Comprehensive School, London, advertisement for Heywood Williams Ltd, *Architectural Review*, 1971

→ James Stirling, Cambridge University History Faculty Building, Cambridge, 1964–1968

In the Wallasey School (1961) by Emslie Morgan, for example, individual and patented components are assembled one-by-one to create a veritable climatic machine: transparent exterior facades, a sixty-centimeter curtain of air, an interior facade of cathedral glass with pivoting or retractable wings that absorb or reflect as required, lockable ventilation shutters, heat-emitting tungsten light tubes, solid walls, and a polystyrene-insulated concrete roof. In glass walls of the Wallasey type, the issue is no longer about dissolving the borders between interior and exterior space but, rather, as Banham remarked, to create a "complete man/structure/lighting/ventilating system" that must be calibrated according to the seasonal requirements.[57]

But in Wallasey, the glass wall is merely a part of the building's thermal system, and by the late 1960s more comprehensive demands on the material were turning up in projects such as the History Faculty Building (1964–68) designed by James Stirling for the University of Cambridge. Here, glass facilitates the complete interpenetration of inside and out, above and below, private and public, as well as the simultaneous separation of dedicated spaces. The building is lit by its glazed roof, the surface of which is lined with vinyl to reduce glare. Heating is made possible by the ventilator-equipped double membrane of the steeply pitched roof, and the upper circulation routes around the reading room are acoustically closed off by glass.[58] Or in John Bancroft's now demolished Pimlico School in London (1965–1970), the double glazing of the ceiling panels (each lined by clear insulating PVC sheets) functioned solely in combination with the sunshade, the low-pressure radiators of the central heating system, and the automatic ventilation, thanks to warm air convectors, air-conditioning in the south-facing spaces, and warm and cold air circulation between the south- and north-facing classrooms[59] (what was worth noting, an advertisement for Pimlico stated, was not the "method of glazing" but the "exciting new way" it featured).[60] By the late 1960s the fully operative scope that Schulze had called for in 1929 had been realized: architecture now comprised a kit of tools—if not always practical and economic, then still in service of achieving the maximal performance of the material it used.

During this time architects continued to rely on terms such as wall, slab, skin, membrane, plane or surface to alternatively define the different layers of the exterior shell.[61] Scientists, however, including those in the laboratories of the Building Research Station,[62] were defining that shell by its different physical functions: the "exclusion of rain," "heat isolation," "fire resistance," "sound isolation," even the changing volume of the wall under the influence of "temperature and moisture."[63] Thanks to this work the "reliance upon the teachings of experience"[64] was replaced by a "technique of scientific testing," through which the wall could be apprehended as a permeable membrane (i.e., one that is simultaneously transparent and insulating),[65] allowing, or at least promising, the design and regulation of distinct environments. This ambition is particularly evident in publications on building physics, as for instance in Faber and Kells' classic *Heating and Air-Conditioning Buildings*, which both describes the conductivity of the walls and identifies the right quality of the air, its movement, its temperature, and its humidity as the constituent elements of comfort. Liberated from their shells, houses had become the living, breathing cubes of air that Giedion had foreseen in the spatial layout of Le Corbusier's private residences, albeit, one has to add for the 1960s, climatically controlled.

If these visions were being realized through the concerted efforts of scientists and practitioners, architectural theory had its own version of events—one that was more concerned with the metaphor of transparency than with the matter of glass. But even in the late 1920s as architectural theory was just beginning to outline a definition of

NO
RIGHT
TURN

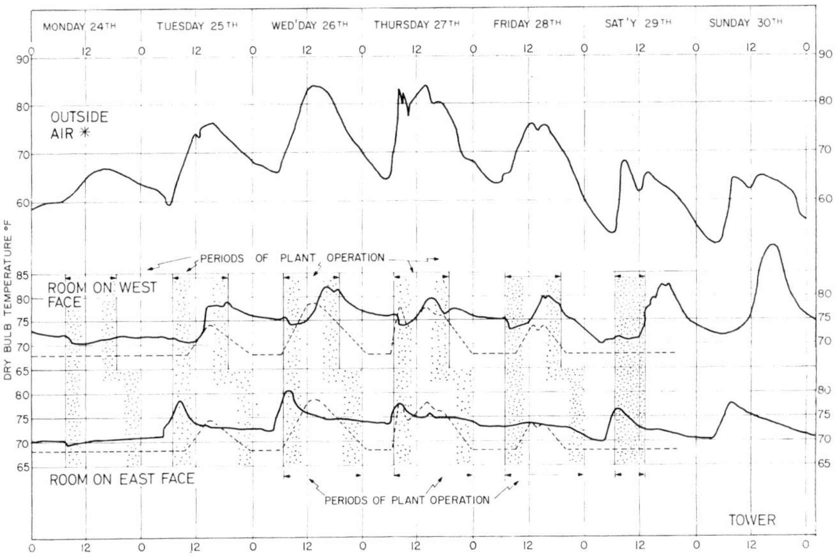

↑ "The Mechanical Services at New Zealand House: Temperature of Record Tower," *Journal of the Institution of Heating and Ventilating Engineers*, 1965

← Robert Matthew, Johnson Marshall & Partners (RMJM), New Zealand House, London, 1959–1963

→ László Moholy-Nagy, special effects for *Things to Come*, 1936

transparency and thus prepare the ground for the debate of the postwar years, Bernal was exploring and articulating some of the most radical answers to the physical understanding of transparency not only for glass, but more broadly for human inhabitation. In 1929 Bernal published his book-length essay "The World, the Flesh and the Devil: An Enquiry into the Future of the Three Enemies of the Rational Soul." The essay belongs to an interwar genre based on scientific progress that encompassed both literature and scientific writings of the time (even if Bernal himself was critical of any form of prospective idealism).[66] Distinct from his later writings and papers, the essay came much closer to contemporary science fiction, allowing Bernal to demonstrate how a rigorous theory of techno-science could inform a speculative vision of the future. Here Bernal recast the three temptations of the human soul (or to be more precise the Christian soul) as the three forces that humanity had to rationally master in order to successfully inhabit outer space.

The result of this was a fundamental rethinking of human existence in terms of physics, energy production and resources, technology, interiors, and supply chains, setting out the model of a space habitat, or "celestial station," that could accommodate a growing population of up to 30,000 long-term residents. The sphere of the station comprised a thin and regenerative transparent shell hard enough to give rigidity to the structure while preventing gases from escaping and protecting against meteorites (large ones could be navigated around, but smaller ones would be "impossible to avoid"). Inside—or "below the epidermis"—was a device that imported radiant energy and another that regulated the interior climate. "Even with our present primitive knowledge," Bernal writes, "we can plan out such a celestial station in considerable detail."[67] This approach, not least his predictions about space travel (the so-called Bernal Sphere would be resurrected in the mid-1970s in the American physicist Gerard O'Neill's proposed space colony) were already far-reaching for their time, but when compared to the "radical" and by comparison quite technocratic proposals of Britain's avant-garde made four decades later (from Archigram's drawings of bubbles and capsules to François Dallegret's "Power-Membrane House, all more expressive of a moment than a plausible future), Bernal's vision, in its methodical extrapolation of what was scientifically possible at present, seems both outrageous and yet somehow more persuasive.

Along this path towards a celestial future, the traditional distinction between natural and artificial environments, organisms, and machines, would be challenged. As Bernal writes, "In the alteration of himself, man has a great deal further to go than in the alteration of his inorganic environment."[68] Through the lens of his physical functions, the human would become organs without a body, his brain artificially fed and permanently active, with visual devices, like periscopes and microscopes extending the eyes, microphones amplifying the ears, chemical-tasting organs prolonging taste, and so on, until "finally, consciousness itself may end or vanish in a humanity that has become completely etherealized, losing the close-knit organism, becoming masses of atoms in space communicating by radiation, and ultimately perhaps resolving itself entirely into light."[69] What Bernal is describing is a completely transparent environment where man, machine, and space constitute a new living machine organized and regulated through the performance of physical functions. Where the skin becomes the first and final membrane, the development sketched by Bernal in the pre-war period reaches its end—at least provisionally. Hardly any building, either in the interwar or postwar years, could ever match a vision so radical. Yet the materialist perspective propounded by the crystallographer and the transparency implied are an expression of a profound shift in the discipline, one that would not stop at the skin of the building and would profoundly alter its spatial configuration.

1 Joan Ockman, "Form without Utopia: Contextualizing Rowe," *Journal of the Society of Architectural Historians* 57, no. 4 (December 1998): 448.

2 Charles Jencks, *The Language of Post-Modern Architecture* (New York: Rizzoli, 1977), 80–81.

3 Christopher Woodward, "Head Office, Ipswich, Suffolk," *Architectural Review* 158, no. 943 (September 1975): 131.

4 On opacity as a category of post-modernism, see Gianni Vattimo, "The Postmodern: A Transparent Society?" in *The Transparent Society*, trans. David Webb (Cambridge: Polity, 1992), 1–11.

5 A persuasive survey and critique of this issue can be found in Reinhold Martin, "Spiegelglass," *Archplus* 191/192 (March 2009): 106–109.

6 Woodward, "Head Office, Ipswich, Suffolk," 131.

7 Martin Francis, "Glass Wall Assembly Notes," *Architectural Review* 158, no. 943 (September 1975): 144.

8 Ian Lambot, "Willis Faber & Dumas: The Glass Wall," in *Norman Foster, Foster Associates: Buildings and Projects: 1971–1978*, vol. 2 (Haslemere: Watermark, 1989), 34–35.

9 Anonymous [Gottfried Semper], "A Foreign Architect's View on the Building," *Edinburgh Review* 94, no. 192 (October 1851): 576.

10 Richard Lucae, "Ueber die Macht des Raumes in der Baukunst," *Zeitschrift für Bauwesen* 19 (1869): 303.

11 Alfred Gotthold Meyer, *Eisenbauten. Ihre Geschichte und Ästhetik* (Esslingen am Neckar: Paul Neff Verlag, 1907), 66.

12 Sigfried Giedion, *Bauen in Frankreich: Eisen, Eisenbeton* (Leipzig: Klinkhardt & Biermann, 1928), 85.

13 Sigfried Giedion, *Raum, Zeit, Architektur: Die Entstehung einer neuen Tradition*, (Ravensburg: Otto Maier Verlag, 1965 [1941]), 311.

14 Raymond McGrath et al., *Glass in Architecture and Decoration* (London: Architectural Press, 1937), 30–34; Otto Völckers, *Bauen mit Glas: Glas als Werkstoff—Glasarten und Glassorten—Glas in Bautechnik und Baukunst*, Die Baubücher, vol. 17 (Stuttgart: Hoffmann, 1948), 16–17.

15 See Walter Gropius, "Glasbau," *Die Bauzeitung* 23, no. 20 (May 1926): 159–162; Ludwig Hilberseimer, "Glasarchitektur," *Die Form* 4, no. 19 (October 1, 1929): 521–522; Le Corbusier, "5 points d'une architecture nouvelle," in *Le Corbusier et Pierre Jeanneret: Oeuvre complète 1910–1929*, ed. Willy Boesiger and Oscar Stonorov, vol. 1 (Zurich: Girsberger, 1967 [1929]), 129; Ludwig Mies van der Rohe: "Hochhausprojekt für Bahnhof Friedrichstrasse in Berlin," *Frühlicht* 1, no. 4 (Summer 1922): 122–124.

16 Hannes Meyer, "Hannes Meyer über Sowjetrußland," *Die Baugilde* 11, no. 30 (1931): 1602, quoted in Jean-Louis Cohen, "Le Corbusier's Centrosoyuz in Moscow," *Future Anterior* 5, no. 1 (Summer 2008): 54.

17 Arthur Korn, *Glas im Bau und als Gebrauchsgegenstand* (Berlin: Pollak, 1929), 5-6.

18 Korn, *Glas im Bau*, 6.

19 Sigfried Giedion, *Space, Time and Architecture: The Growth of a New Tradition* (Cambridge, MA: Harvard University Press, 1941), 489.

20 Konrad Werner Schulze, *Der Stahlskelettbau: Geschäfts- und Hochhäuser* (Stuttgart: Zaug, 1928); *Der Ziegelbau*, Architektur der Gegenwart, vol. 4 (Stuttgart: Akademischer Verlag Der, Fritz Wedekind & Co.) 1927.

21 Konrad Werner Schulze, *Glas in der Architektur der Gegenwart* (Wissenschaftlicher Verlag Dr. Zaugg & Co: Stuttgart, 1929), 91.

22 See Kijan Malte Espahangizi, "Wissenschaft im Glas. Eine historische Ökologie moderner Laborforschung," PhD diss. (ETH Zurich, 2010), 247–271.

23 E. Wipf, "Die Heilstätte 'Deutsches Haus' Agra bei Lugano," *Schweizerische Bauzeitung* 66, no. 16 (October 16, 1915): 185–187; E. Wipf, "Die Heilstätte 'Deutsches Haus' Agra bei Lugano," *Schweizerische Bauzeitung* 66, no. 17 (October 23, 1915), 195. McGrath refers to this example: McGrath, *Glass in Architecture and Decoration*, 167.

24 "Les idées novatrices de M. Mallet-Stevens. Entretien de Robert Mallet-Stevens," *Le Rez-de-Chaussée* 4 (1928): 75–77, cited in Katrin Eberhard, *Maschinen zuhause: Die Technisierung des Wohnens in der Moderne* (Zurich: gta Verlag, 2011), 95. On Vita-Glass, see John Sadar, "The Healthful Ambience of Vitaglass: Light, Glass and the Curative Environment," *Architectural Research Quarterly* 12, no. 3–4 (December 2008): 269–281.

25 Le Corbusier, *Précisions sur un état présent de l'architecture et de l'urbanisme* (Paris: Crès, 1930), 164–65; and see also *Une maison—un palais: "à la recherche d'une unité architecturale"* (Paris: Crès, 1928), 129.

26 Reyner Banham, *The Architecture of the Well-Tempered Environment*, (London: The Architectural Press, 1969), 160.

27 McGrath et al., *Glass in Architecture and Decoration*, 181.

28 Nelson's series of articles for *Pencil Points* on modern architecture in Europe features McGrath as well as Gropius, Mies, Le Corbusier and the Luckhardt brothers. See Kurt W. Forster, ed., *Building a new Europe: Portraits of Modern Architects: Essays by George Nelson, 1935–36* (New Haven and London: Yale University Press, 2007), especially 125–135.

29 See Elizabeth Darling, "Finella, Mansfield Forbes, Raymond McGrath, and Modernist architecture in Britain," *Journal of British Studies* 50, no. 1 (January 2011): 125–145.

30 Raymond McGrath, "Recalling the 20s and 30s," typescript of a lecture to the Architectural Association of Ireland, 1972 quoted in Darling, 'Finella', 141.

31 Donald O'Donovan, *God's Architect: A life of Raymond McGrath* (Bray: Kilbride Books, 1995), 89.

32 A. C. Frost: "Finella. A House for Mansfield D. Forbes, esq. Raymond McGrath Architect," *Architectural Review* 66, no. 397 (December 1929): 265.

33 Frost, "Finella," 265.

34 Valeria Carullo, "The Robert Elwall Photographs Collection at the RIBA British Architectural Library," 2015, http://www.historyphotography.org/doc/CARULLO_The_Robert_Elwall_Photographs_Collection.pdf.

35 Raymond McGrath, "Looking into Glass," *Architectural Review* 71, no. 422 (January 1932): 29–30.

36 Elizabeth Darling, "Institutionalizing English Modernism: from the Vers Group to MARS," *Architectural History* 55 (2012): 302.

37 H. E. Beckett, "The Nature and Properties of Glass," in McGrath et al., *Glass in Architecture and Decoration* (London: Architectural Press, 1937), 462.

38 McGrath, "Looking into Glass," 29.

39 Lesley Jackson, *From Atoms to Patterns: Crystal Structure Designs from the 1951 Festival of Britain: The Story of the Festival Pattern Group* (Shepton Beauchamp: Richard Dennis, 2008), 5–14.

40 László Moholy-Nagy, *Von Material zu Architektur* (Munich: Albert Langen Verlag, 1929).

41 Laurence Alloway, "The Development of British Pop," in *Pop Art*, ed. Lucy R. Lippard (New York: Praeger, 1966), 32–33, quoted by David Robbins, "Modernist Sources," in *The Independent Group: Postwar Britain and the Aesthetics of Plenty*, ed. David Robbins (Cambridge, MA: The MIT Press, 1990), 55.

42 László Moholy-Nagy, *Vision in Motion* (Chicago: Theobald, 1947), 253.

43 Beatriz Colomina, *X-Ray Architecture* (Zurich: Lars Müller Publishers, 2019), 138–139.

44 Colomina, *X-Ray Architecture*., 252.

45 On radiographic photography, see Peter Trent, "The Scientist," in *J. D. Bernal: A Life in Science and Politics*, ed. Brenda Swann and Francis Aprahamian (London: Verso, 1999), 78–100. Moholy-Nagy learned of Bernal around 1935–1937, when living in London. See Terence A. Senter, "Moholy-Nagy: 'The Transitional Years,'" In *Albers and Moholy-Nagy: From the Bauhaus to the New World*, ed. Achim Borchardt-Hume (London: Tate Publishing, 2006), 85–91; and Reinhold Martin, *The Organizational Complex: Architecture, Media, and Corporate Space* (Cambridge, MA: The MIT Press, 2003), 52.

46 John Desmond Bernal, "Architecture and Science," *Journal of the Royal Institute of British Architects* 44, no. 16 (June 26, 1937): 805–812. During the war Bernal participated in testing the resistance of bomb shelters with the engineers Ove Arup and Felix Samuely. See Ritchie Calder, "Bernal at War," in *J.D. Bernal: A Life in Science and Politics*, ed. Brenda Swann and Francis Aprahamian (London: Verso, 1999), 166–67; and Andrew Saint, *Towards a Social Architecture: The Role of School-Building in Post-war England* (New Haven: Yale University Press, 1987), 12.

47 "Glass in Wartime," *Architects' Journal* 92, no. 2395 (December 12, 1940): 471–486.

48 John Desmond Bernal, *The Social Function of Science* (London: Routledge, 1939), 350–351.

49 Bernal, *The Social Function of Science*, 350.

50 Moholy-Nagy, *Vision in Motion*, 253. The Haefeli, Moser & Steiger office did not exist in 1927 (it was founded in 1937). Moholy-Nagy may have suggested the gas curtain to Werner Moser, who submitted a proposal for a casino as part of a 1927 competition in Aarau, Switzerland, or to Rudolf Steiger, who designed a cinema with a mobile roof in Zurich in 1929. I thank Bruno Maurer and Sonja Hildebrand for this information. On Haefeli, Moser, and Steiger, see Sonja Hildebrand, et al., eds., *Haefeli, Moser, Steiger: die Architekten der Schweizer Moderne* (Zurich: gta Verlag, 2007). Nor can the existence of an air curtain designed for Arthur Korn be conclusively proved. A 1931 issue of *Bauwelt* mentions only "an (artificial) ventilation device." Ulf Dietrich, "Gummi Fabrik in Cöpenick: Korn und Weitzmann," *Die Bauwelt* 22, no. 15 (April 9 1931): 1–8. On the history of the air curtain, see Kim Förster, "Air Curtain," *Archplus* 191/192 (2009): 258.

51 Moholy-Nagy, *Vision in Motion*, 102–103.

52 Raymond McGrath et al., *Glass in Architecture and Decoration* (London: Architectural Press, 1961), 18.

53 McGrath et al., 58–68.

54 "Secondary School at Hunstanton, Norfolk," *Architects' Journal* 120, no. 3107 (September 16, 1954): 349.

55 For various examples, and more, see McGrath, *Glass in Architecture and Decoration*, 252–294.

56 D. Dex Harrison, "Window into Wall," *Architectural Review* 108, no. 644 (August 1950): 113–114.

57 Banham, *The Architecture of the Well-Tempered Environment*, 283.

58 Reyner Banham, "Criticism: History Faculty Cambridge," *Architectural Review* 146, no. 861 (November 1968): 329–341.

59 See Inner London Education Authority, *Pimlico School*, undated internal report; J. Hanson and R. Coltman: Pimlico School: Appraisal," *Architects' Journal* 153, no. 15 (April 14, 1971): 837. For further details see "Form in Pimlico," *Architectural Review* 101, no. 893 (July 1971): 16.

60 Advertisement for Heywood Williams Ltd., *Architectural Review* 150, no. 893 (July 1971): vii.

61 See F. R. S. Yorke, *The Modern House* (London: Architectural Press, 1934), 46–54.

62 Frederick Measham Lea, *Science and Building: A History of the Building Research Station* (London: HMSO, 1971), 21.

63 See "The Functions of the Wall," in Robert Fitzmaurice, *Principles of Modern Building, Walls, Partitions, and Chimneys*, vol. 1 (London: HMSO, 1938), 17–104.

64 Fitzmaurice, "The Functions of the Wall," 19.

65 This discussion is vivid within the architectural field. See Le Corbusier and Pierre Jeanneret, "Analyse des éléments fondamentaux du problème de la maison minimum," in *Die Wohnung für das Existenzminimum*, ed. Internationale Kongresse für Neues Bauen und Städtisches Hochbauamt Frankfurt a.M. (Frankfurt: Englert and Schlosser, 1930), 25; Le Corbusier, "Architecture d'époque machiniste," *Journal de psychologie normale et pathologique* 18 (1926): 303–350; and Siegfried Ebeling, *Der Raum als Membran* (Dessau: Dünnhaupt, 1926). On Ebeling, see Christoph Asendorf, "Bodies in Force Fields," in *From Energy to Information: Representation in Science and Technology, Art, and Literature*, ed. Bruce Clarke and Linda Dalrymple Henderson (Stanford: Stanford University Press, 2002), 201–203. On membrane architecture, see Georges Teyssot, "Architecture as Membrane," in *Explorations in Architecture: Teaching, Design, Research*, ed. Reto Geiser (Basel: Birkhäuser, 2008), 171–172.

66 Boris Jardine, "Science Fiction, Left Science and the Politics of Planning," in *A History of 1930s British Literature* ed. Benjamin Kohlmann and Matthew Taunton (Cambridge: Cambridge University Press, 2019), 299–300.

67 John Desmond Bernal, *The World, the Flesh and the Devil; An Enquiry into the Future of the Three Enemies of the Rational Soul* (London: Kegan Paul, Trench, Trubner, 1929), 23.

68 Bernal, *The World, the Flesh and the Devil*, 36.

69 Bernal, *The World, the Flesh and the Devil*, 56.

→ "Flats at Ham Common. Architects James Stirling and James Gowan," *Architectural Review*, 1958

Interior

Usually, James Stirling and James Gowan's flats at Ham Common in southwest London are judged in term of their particular "image." Built between 1957 and 1958, the project's mastery of late Corbusian plasticity, its use of raw materials and overall De Stijl-inspired geometry, made it, in the words of Reyner Banham, a perfect example of the architects' "dexterity with the niceties of style."[1] What has gone less acknowledged but remains equally significant to understanding the particularity of the architectural culture of the postwar period are the drawing techniques the architects chose to present their project. Beyond plans and photographs, the two most common representational forms to appear in architectural journals and newspapers at the time are represented in the layouts of Ham Common: two axonometric drawings and four sectional perspectives. One axonometric depicts the housing from above, allowing the distribution of the three buildings on the deep and narrow plot to be seen undistorted and at the same scale. The second axonometric combines a section with a view from above in order to show the relationship between the concrete and brick exterior, the interior spaces, and the more general massing of the volumes on the site. Of the four sectional perspectives that focus on the interior, three look down on the flats from just below the ceiling, illustrating the different apartment types and their distribution. Such a technique reveals the interplay between services, structural elements, and the spaces in-between. The final sectional perspective, drawn from an interior wall and at a larger scale, shows a similar relationship while also signifying the material completeness of a typical living room, from the brick fireplace and walls, to the slabs of concrete, the tiles on the floor, the wooden kitchen cupboards and the timber window frames.

These drawings stand out both for their precision—the viewpoint, the exacting scaling between them, the combination of axonometric and perspective—and for their early date. But even the most cursory of glances through the books and periodicals of the postwar years suggests that the techniques used for Ham Common were widespread. They were found in prospectuses and technical handbooks and used by corporate architects and the avant-garde alike, whether in detailed studies that looked at how to furnish a student dormitory, or more complex urban and regional projects. Even more remarkable is the variety in which these two representational techniques came to be used—from sectional perspectives taken either laterally or from above, to sectional axonometrics, seen from a frontal- or worm's-eye view, to sections that penetrate walls or membranes. There are composite views, including sections with vanishing points that vary from story to story, and sections combining orthographical elevations with perspectives or axonometrics. There are sections through single rooms, through apartment blocks, even through megastructures and entire urban environments. Some are didactic, offering construction details with annotations, while others are left as floating abstract objects. Some show the intermingling of materials while others reveal the unfolding of space. Yet, what all of these variations share is a common interest in an attempt to depict a new relationship between the living interior and its environment.

FLATS AT HAM COMMON

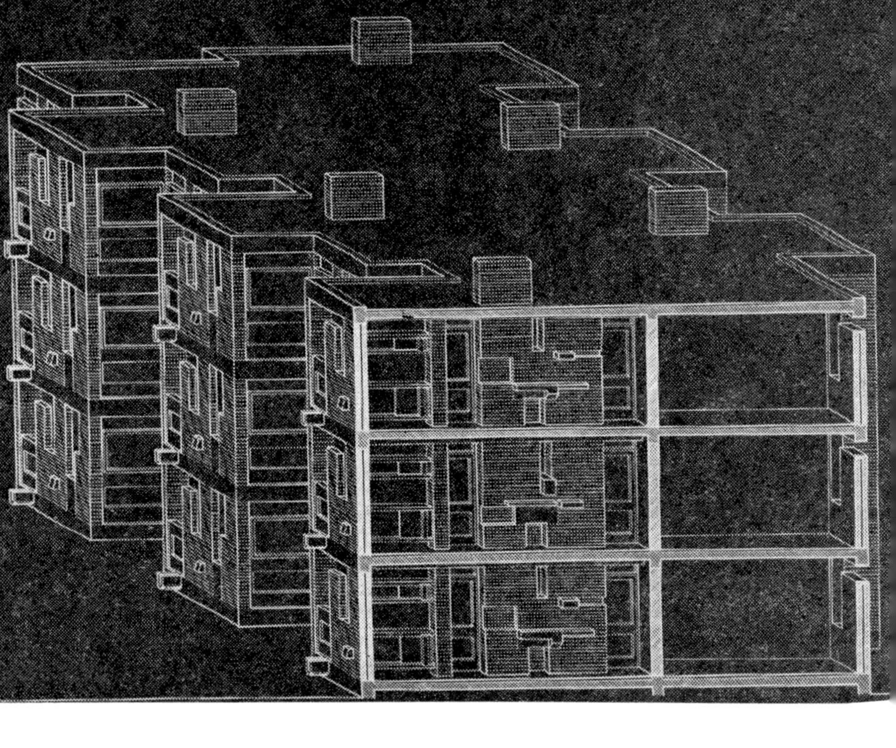

The structural and aesthetic elements of these flats, exemplified by the stair-well of one of the smaller blocks, opposite (above), are brick walls carrying bare concrete slabs, and white-painted wooden frames carrying large panes of glass. The resulting rich complexities of rough and smooth, solid and transparent, are enhanced—on the larger block—by a deeply indented façade (below) and —in both types of block—by fireplace units that bring exterior surfacing materials indoors.

FLATS AT HAM COMMON

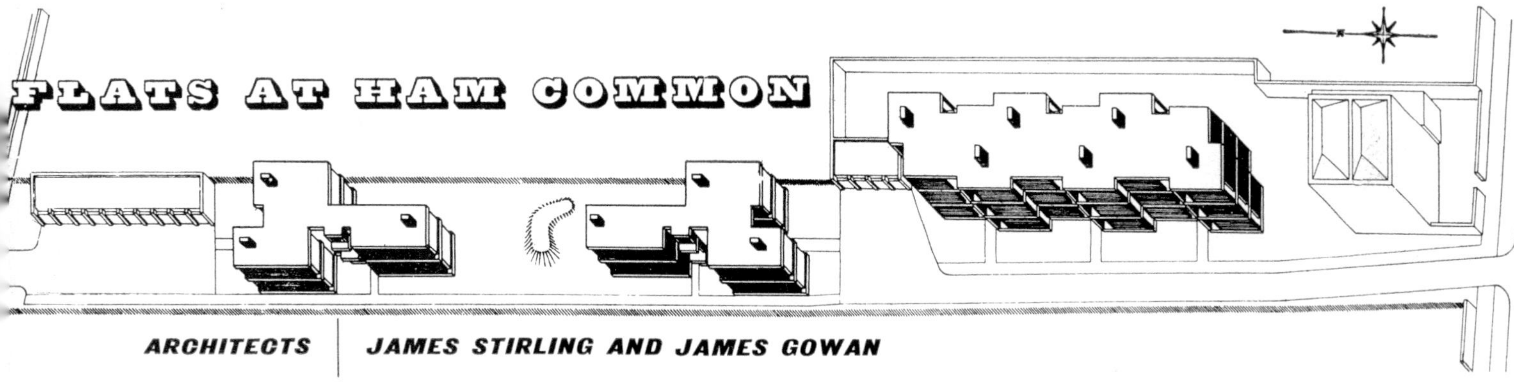

ARCHITECTS | JAMES STIRLING AND JAMES GOWAN

1, the three-storey block seen in its setting of established trees—as the site plan shows (above) the wall on the boundary of the site stands farther from the ground floor windows than might appear from this view.

Younger English architects' attitudes to what they call 'the white architecture of the Thirties' are ambivalent: on the one hand they respect and even envy the significance as revolutionary gestures of such buildings as Wells Coates's Lawn Road Flats, but on the other hand they are suspicious of the 'naive conviction that all buildings could be designed in "international style".' Most of them now conceive of the possibility of 'multiple aesthetics', or 'the style for the job', rather than a single dominant style to be applied to all classes of buildings.

It is in housing that this changed mind appears most clearly, and the REVIEW has already published such buildings as the Smithsons' Sugden House at Watford (September, 1957), and the houses in Hampstead by Howell and Amis (November, 1956), as well as an earlier house by Stirling and Gowan (April, 1958) in all of which it can be seen, in spite of divergent tendencies of personal style and professional philosophy. What emerges from all these examples, and even more forcefully in the flats illustrated on the following pages, is an attempt to face the economic realities of dwelling construction in England today, and to extract from them an architecture that is workable in plan and grouping, and an aesthetic that is affective, rather than merely sufferable. The result seems to open the prospect of a sophisticated vernacular—and if that appears to be a contradiction in terms, then it may well be that our terms are in need of revision, for a vernacular without affectations of primitive innocence is one of the possible lines of delivery from the present depressed state of housing design in England.

FLATS AT HAM COMMON

10, the living-dining room window of an upper flat in the north two-storey block, seen from the access gallery. The wooden transomes at top, bottom and hip level give a greater feeling of security than would total glazing, and create a deliberate wall/window ambiguity.
11, the detailing throughout emphasises the separate identity of parts, in this corner of the projecting stair-landing of a two-storey block, the side and front windows are distinguished by the extent to which they have, or have not, been taken up into the concrete above.
12, while in this detail the glazing of the main hall window, on the opposite side from the stairs, is isolated from

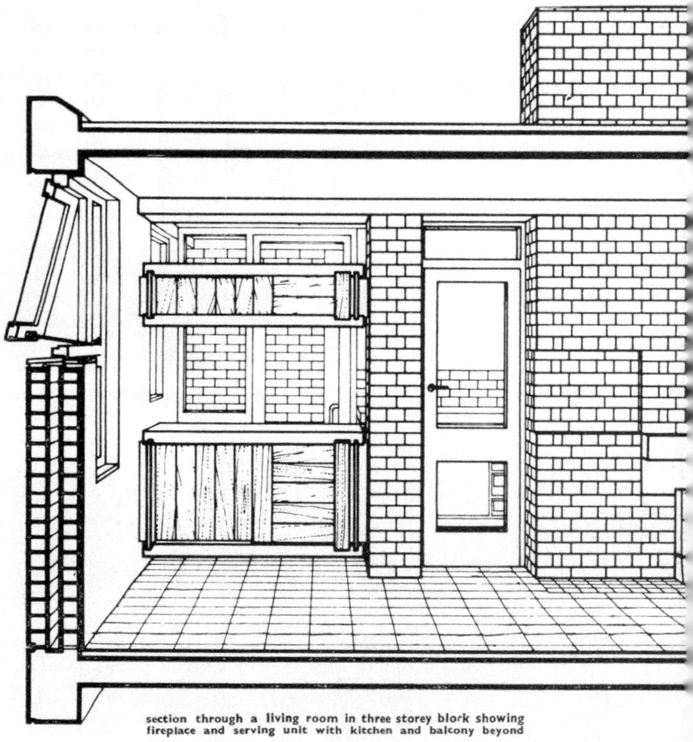

section through a living room in three storey block showing fireplace and serving unit with kitchen and balcony beyond

the return glazing of the windows of the flats by a vertical strip of glass an inch and a half wide.
13 and 14, the scale of the kitchen and servery details has been made to that of the exterior, using timber sections of a large size by fashionable standards, and massive teak draw-pulls.
15, the consonance of exterior and interior extends to materials as well—although most of the surfaces inside the rooms are plastered and painted white, the fire-place units are of the same brick as the main structure, and contain cast units, such as shelves, of precast concrete, similar to the ventilators and spouts on the outside.
16 and 17, in the entrance halls of the two-storey blocks, circulation at the upper level is by a concrete gallery carried clear of the brick-work on transverse beams, the landing slabs of the staircase are cantilevered from beams set in the length of the walls that flank the stairs, and the hand-rails and balustrades to the stairs are formed from overlapping triangular frames of steel tube.

10

11

12

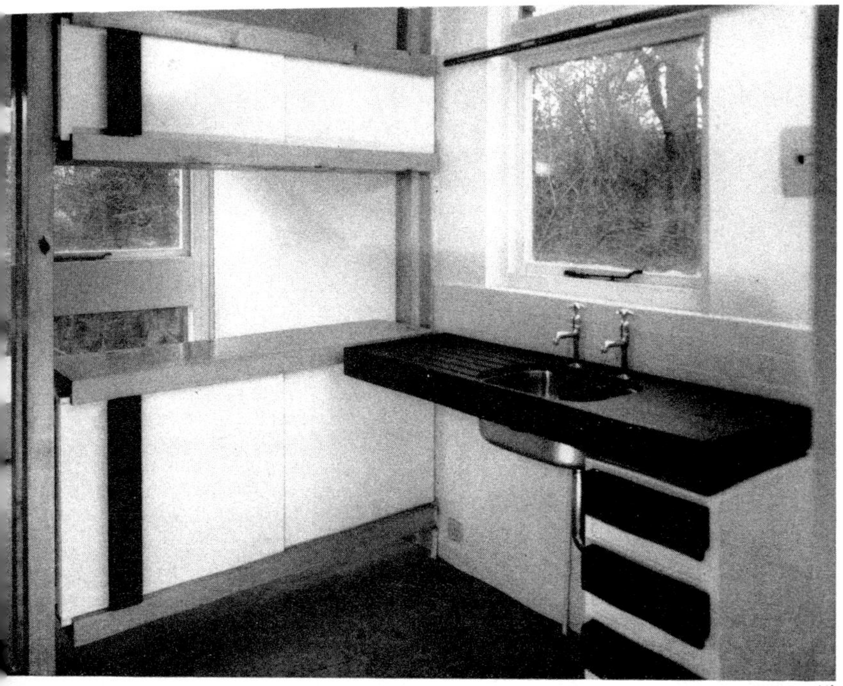

13

14

15

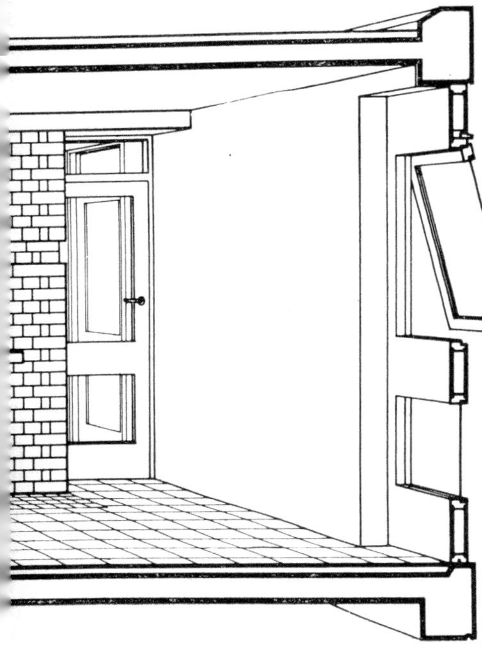

16

17

A section that was combined with a perspective or axonometric was just the latest development in the life of a drawing type that has preoccupied architects as far back as the middle ages and the first attempts to codify architectural representation[2]—or even to Vitruvius's sciographia and its later interpretation as section or perspective.[3] The variant that emerged after the Second World War came to challenge both the predominant orthographic drawing and, primarily, the ground plan favored by classical modernists. As early as 1944, Ernő Goldfinger was using cutaway axonometrics in a series of drawings for an Army Bureau of Current Affairs exhibition called "Planning Your Home."[4] But it was during the late 1950s when sectional perspectives and axonometrics found their most imaginative expression, through the work of Tecton, Denys Lasdun, Chamberlin, Powell & Bon, and, of course, Gowan and Stirling. The latter, with the help of Léon Krier, would combine them with spectacular Auguste Choisy-inspired worm's-eye views some years later. These drawing types achieved arguably their most prominent place in the history of western architecture when Paul Rudolph's monumental sectional perspective proposal for the Lower Manhattan Expressway appeared on the cover of Reyner Banham's *Megastructure: Urban Futures of the Recent Past* (1976). To the same extent that the book declared the end of its subject, the drawing itself marked the last time this drawing technique would assume such an important role as a representational device. As the idea of the "well-tempered environment" grew increasingly outdated, the drawing types that were ultimately meant to show the interior in its full depth lost their fascination as well their *raison d'être*.

While the twentieth-century life of the sectional perspective and axonometric was brief—debuting in the late 1940s to only then be classed as a historical timepiece by 1976, a document of a past future—these drawing types have been captivating architects again and again throughout history. As Jacques Guillerme and Hélène Vérin demonstrated in their study of early Renaissance depictions of antique Roman ruins and the cutaway drawings of the Pantheon, it is only the section that conveys a dimension of architecture which otherwise remains hidden to the eye, transforming the trace, or outline, into a *tracé*—a journey in the mind's eye.[5] Ruins revealed the building in section while the Pantheon, whose structure remained hidden, inspired the imagination. By the late Renaissance specific combinations of cutaway drawings and perspectives allowed the simultaneous depiction of different architectural elements and milieus within a single drawing, where inside and outside, facade and the interior could be perceived simultaneously.[6] In the eighteenth century a similar aim was pursued in the depiction of more complex buildings, such as theaters, where the sectional perspective enabled their organization to be economically drawn and easily understood in a glance.[7] This capacity to both portray complexity while clarifying it was what inspired Auguste Choisy in 1899 to use a worm's-eye sectional-axonometric technique that appears in *Histoire de l'Architecture*. It was, he recognized, the only representational form that concurrently described the relationship between plan, elevation, section, and the inner structure of a building at once.[8]

Choisy's work—especially his drawings of the Acropolis—was to be influential in the 1920s and 1930s (most notably in the work of Le Corbusier or Sergei M. Eisenstein), but it was only in the postwar period that his sectional axonometric found its worthy successors. Drawings made in the twentieth century, prior to the Second World War, favor either a pure axonometric or an orthogonal representational approach, with ground plans and flat sections showing the organization of a building. Wall thicknesses are often shaded in black, and only in a small number of cases is a wall situated behind the section plane included as an elevation—this, however, is merely to indicate the limit of the space, not reveal its depth. Material and structure play a subordinate role, and when those elements are included, they appear in isolation or as construction details. In contrast, the sections produced during the postwar years reveal the hidden dimensions of the building that other forms, such as the elevation or plan, fail to deliver (this is analogous to the drawings studied by Guillerme and Vérin). Therein lies their particularity.

These sectional drawings were not limited to the English scene. One can find similar early types from the same period for Le Corbusier's Maison Jaoul or his Unité d'habitation, for Aalto's Finnish Pavilion or his apartment houses, or for Paul Maymont's submarine proposals for the River Seine. Yet the sheer variety of sectional axonometrics and perspectives drawn by British practices, not least the fact that in most cases they are used specifically to depict the home, gives them a special significance and particular identity in the history of postwar architecture. The rise of these drawing types coincides with a major shift in housing policy—when the preference for flats introduced in the 1930s along with the Housing Act and the MARS Group's London Plan to rebuild the entire city, became over the course of the 1950s a reality.[9] While sectional perspectives or axonometrics were the unofficial presentation method for the radical proposals of the avant-garde, among them the capsule homes of Archigram, the Smithsons' "House of the Future" (1956) and the machines for living in François Dallegret's and Reyner Banham's "A Home Is Not a House" (1965), they were also put to more practical use to clarify and give character to the mass-housing projects that were swiftly rising in cities and new towns across Britain.

The reasons for using sectional perspectives and sectional axonometrics often overlap, but the latter are more likely to appear when it is necessary to convey a progression of time. A whole series of presentations, which crop up in architectural journals between 1940 and 1950, show an unfinished dimension similar to ruin-esque drawings made during the eighteenth century: breaking through a wall to show its construction, a bare structural frame yet to be filled, or a set of pieces that have to be fixed together. There is less of a temporal element attached to sectional perspectives, although some might record construction. Instead, these drawings are meant to emphasize the interplay between structure and space. For instance, in the case of Stirling and Gowan's sectional perspectives for the house on the Isle of Wight (1955–1958) as well as for the flats at Ham Common, the wall structures

← Paul Rudolph, Lower Manhattan Expressway, 1970, on the cover of Reyner Banham, *Megastructure: Urban Futures of the Recent Past*, 1976

↓ Julius Posener, "Choisy," *Architectural Review*, 1956

↑ Arthur Ling, district center at Coventry, 1957–1959

→ Warren Chalk, elevation and plan, Capsule Tower, 1964

are implied but not shown in any detail. The sections through the windows remain schematic, while the walls in the horizontal sections from above are completely dispensed of any material specification. The goal involved is not to show the material qualities of the building, but rather its spatial arrangement. This is demonstrated by the choice in the square-shaped drawing for the Isle of Wight house to set the vanishing point slightly off-center, so that the walls, which are conceived as simple slabs that define the space, can be understood at their full height. And while the plan remains "the same at whatever level it is taken," as James M. Richards commented in the *Architects' Journal*,[10] the deliberate placement of the viewpoint allows the relationship between floor plan, elevation, and structure to be fully understood.

This type of perspectival illustration, one which emphasizes spatial qualities, is applied in numerous interior studies of the period: in historical depictions—for instance, a representation of the traditional Japanese house and its plan layout using tatami mats appeared in the *Architects' Journal* in 1955;[11] in various presentations of interior fittings and fixtures, such as those for the newly refurbished *Architectural Review* offices (1959);[12] in comparative studies, including drawings for rooms in student halls of residence.[13] The technique was also applied to public spaces, as shown, revealingly, in an early detailed report on the "South Bank Exhibition" (1951), illustrated by Gordon Cullen and in which different spatial sequences are used to present the various pathways in, around, and through the complex.[14] Drawn in a sketchy, pictorial hand attributable to the townscape movement, these representations pre-empt a development in which the design objectives of the architect are no longer restricted to individual interior spaces or isolated urban areas, but instead encompass the entire built environment. Apartments, squares, shopping concourses, and parking garages are treated as the framework for an interiorized public realm which can be moved through as effortlessly as one's own home.

Paramount to the sectional perspective is the interior of the architectural object. In contrast to the axonometric, whose reversibility makes it difficult to give an impression of depth, the sectional perspective assists in resolving a central and enduring question of architectural representation: how to adequately render an interior. It can be shown either orthogonally as a true-to-scale record, with the background elevation set between the lateral wall-sections; or perspectivally, as a figurative depiction of the depth of a three-dimensional space.[15] Some drawings combine both techniques, as seen in the exemplary presentation of the Cooper Taber Seed Warehouse in Essex (1956) and even more in that of the duplexes on the Golden Lane Estate in London, both by Chamberlin, Powell & Bon (1962). The lower and upper maisonette of the Golden Lane flats are shown in perspective, each one from a single viewing point, allowing both spaces to be seen in their entire depth. Between them is the middle flat, presented orthogonally in section with an elevation of the back wall. These combined techniques allow the drawing to provide not just a spatial sense of the flats, but also a true-to-scale understanding of the interiors. To the extent that the differing viewpoints in this perspective emphasize the coherence of spatial layout and structure, the representational type underscores the autonomy of each living unit.

That is, while the sectional perspective focuses attention on the interior spaces of the individual apartments, it simultaneously divorces the interior from the context beyond the boundaries of the cone of vision. In a sectional perspective, the projection stops just before the world outside. This separation applies in equal measure to similar representations, whether of individual spaces, single buildings or megastructures. In Stirling and Gowan's house on the Isle of Wight, it is the garden that lies beyond the scope of the cone of vision; in Leslie Martin and Patrick Hodgkinson's Harvey Court in Cambridge (1962), it is the neighborhood; in Chamberlin, Powell & Bon's Barbican Center (1963–1976), it is the office buildings of the City of London.

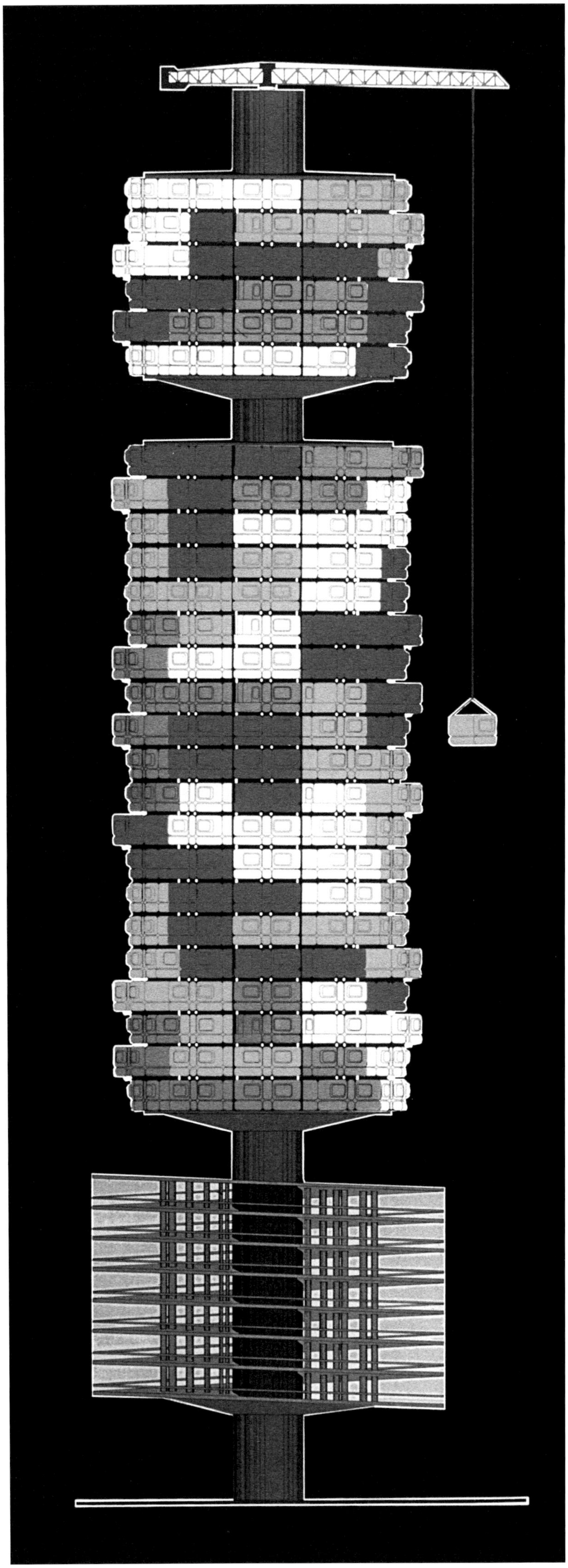

↓ James Gowan
and James Stirling,
sectional perspective,
House on the Isle of
Wight, 1955–1958

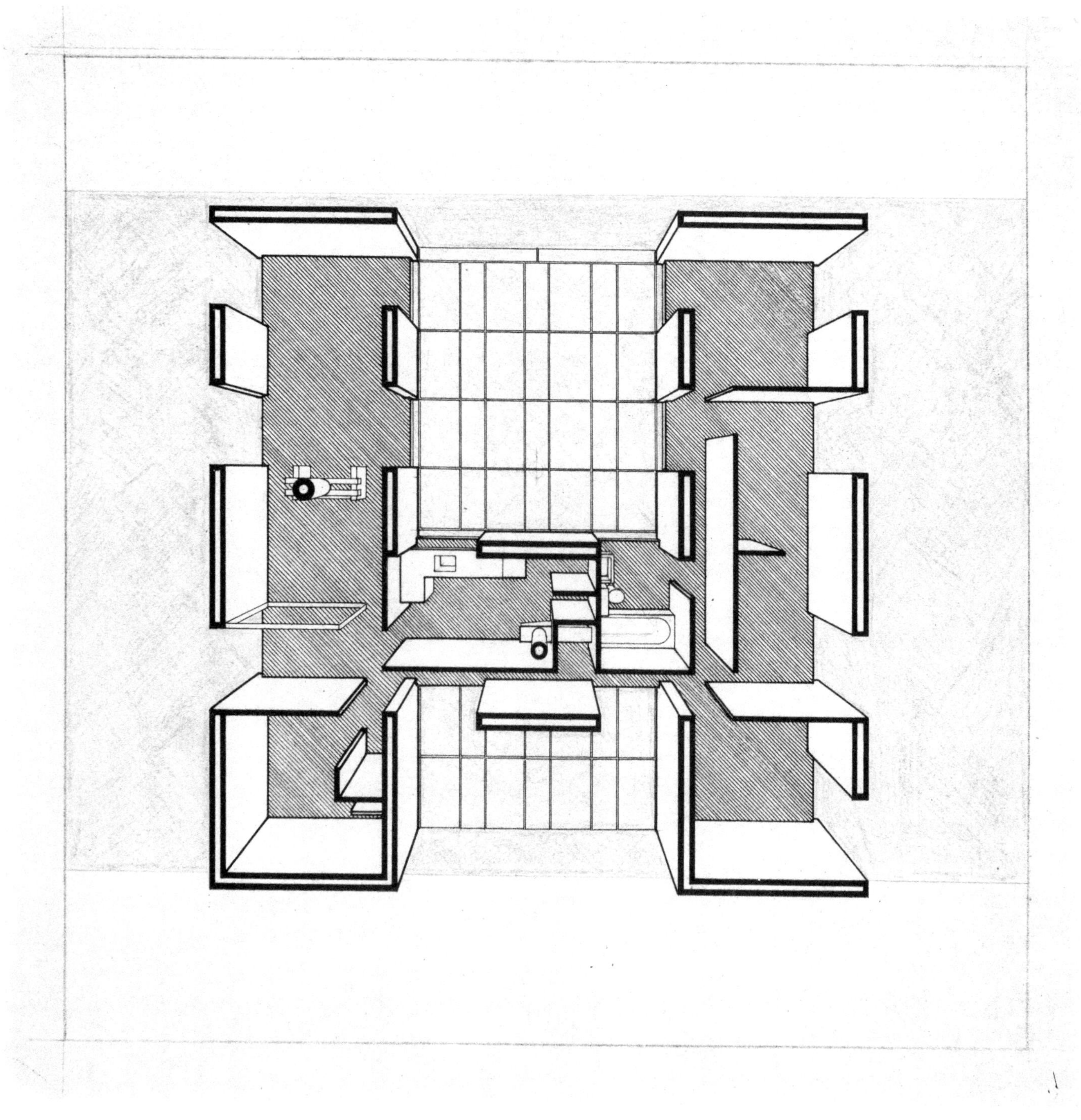

↓ "Planning on the Mat," *Architects' Journal*, 1955

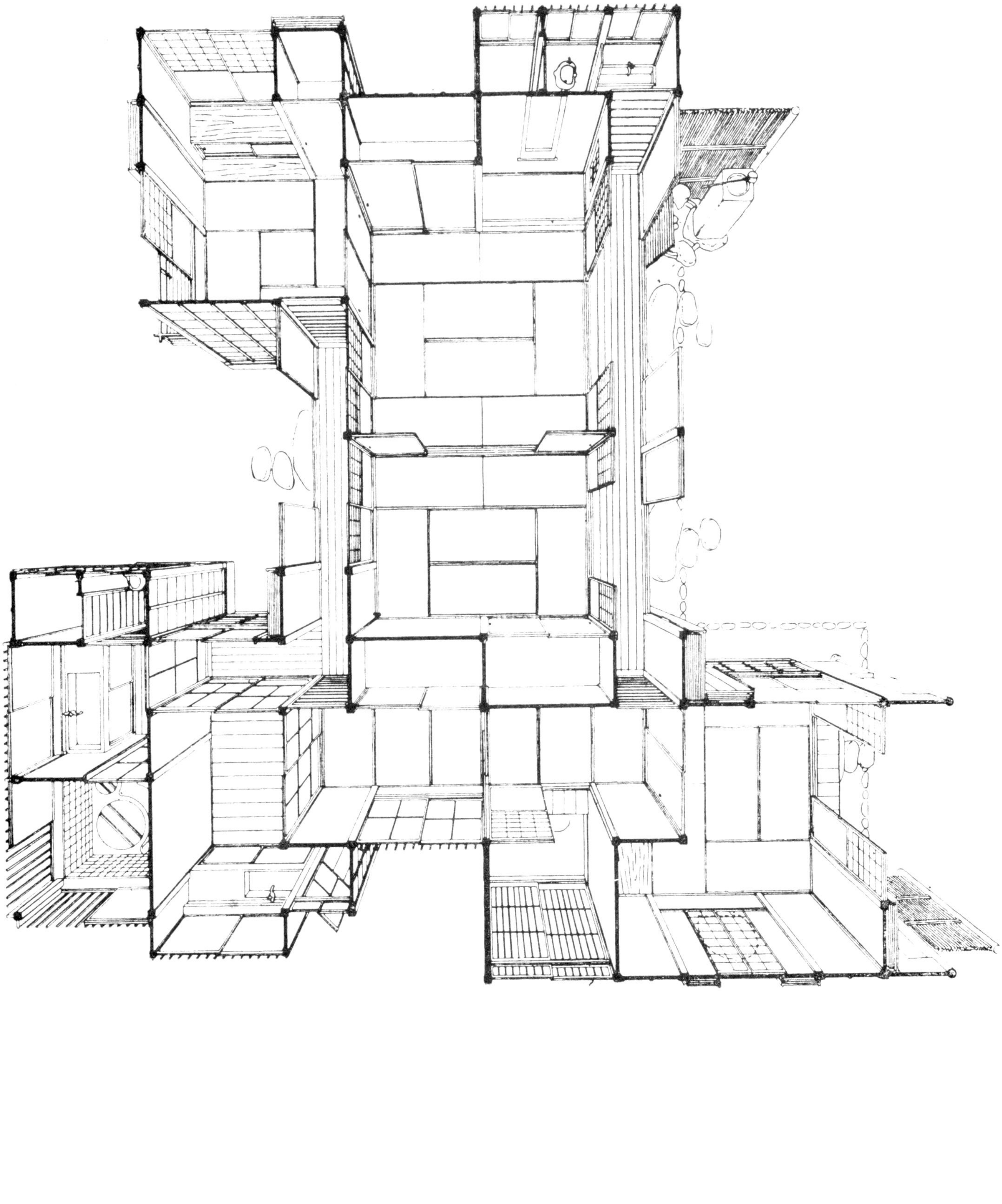

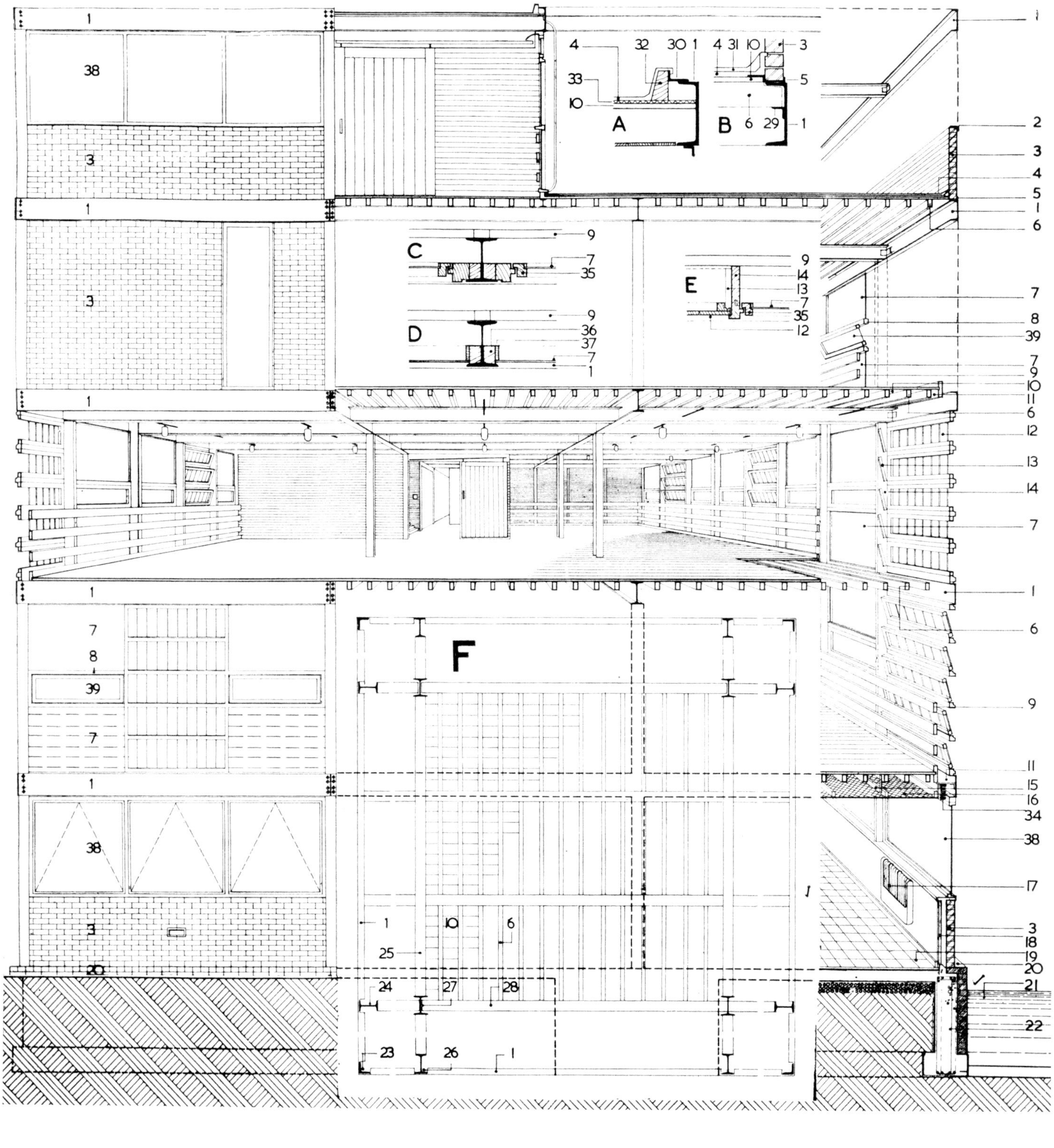

↓ Chamberlin, Powell & Bon, sectional perspective, Cooper Taber Factory, Essex, 1956

↓ Chamberlin, Powell and Bon, sectional perspective, Golden Lane Estate, London, 1952–1956

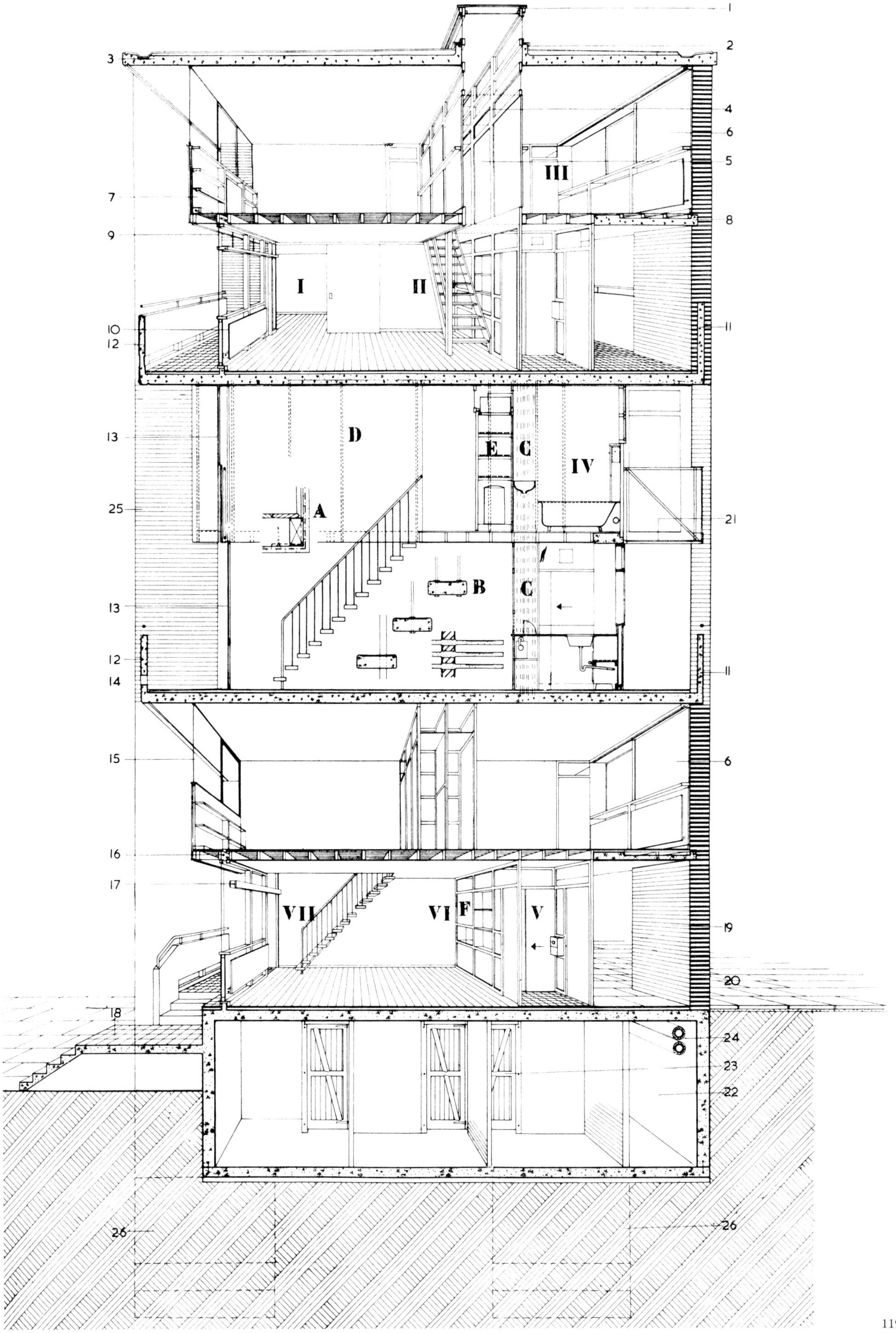

↑ Chamberlin, Powell & Bon, sectional perspective, Barbican Center, London, 1954–1979

Unlike the modernist plan and its nineteenth-century predecessors that were concerned with the proper distribution of the functions within the house, the postwar section shifts the focus towards the articulation of an individualized interior environment. This shift is evident in numerous avant-garde projects, perhaps most conspicuously in the two installations by Alison and Peter Smithson made in 1956: "Patio and Pavilion" for *This Is Tomorrow* and "The House of the Future" for the *Daily Mail Ideal Home Exhibition*. On the one hand is the perspective from above of the "Patio and Pavilion," produced in collaboration with Eduardo Paolozzi and Nigel Henderson. Around a three-walled shed runs a mirrored fence that isolates a "piece of the world" from its surroundings while monadically reflecting it in an endless series.[16] On the other hand is the model photograph of the "House of the Future," which similarly shows the inverted (and this time well-tempered) interior from a vertical bird's-eye perspective.[17] The image affords a volumetric understanding of how the space is interconnected and organized, and yet its tight cropping, with the walls of the structure partly running beyond the frame, separates the House of the Future from any present condition or context. This form of isolation—a social, technical and formal detachment that is conspicuously evident in the projects of the avant-garde—was fundamental to postwar architecture.

To precisely map out the organization of these increasingly complex interior layouts, the axonometric would prove again to be most suitable. More than any other representational form, axonometry is "a-topic," without place, as recognized by modernist painters, above all Kazimir Malevich. It is based on the infinite viewpoint of the beholder.[18] Within the postwar flat, where residential units constitute self-contained entities, the effect is a liberation of the housing unit from its context.[19] But at the same time that it isolates the individual unit, the technique also reveals the precise interplay of the rooms in a true-to-scale representation.[20] Its range is visible in the numerous apartments of large-scale flats—from Chamberlin, Powell & Bon's double split-level layouts at the Barbican, to the three-story flats in Neave Brown's Winscombe Street (1968) and later in his stepped two-story terraced flats at Alexandra Road Estate (1972–1978), the two-over-three section of Denys Lasdun's large apartments at 26 St. James's Place (1958–1960) or the units of different room size in Patrick Hodgkinson's Brunswick Center (1967–1972), tested for the first time in his influential fourth-year project at the AA for a social housing scheme in Lambeth (1953).[21] Typically represented in the same style, as simple black-line drawings on white background, no matter their status as council-subsidized or luxury projects, the variations of apartments alternate between split-level and maisonette types that explore the permeations of various living activities and their spatial articulation.[22] Such an approach sat in contrast to modernist textbooks which

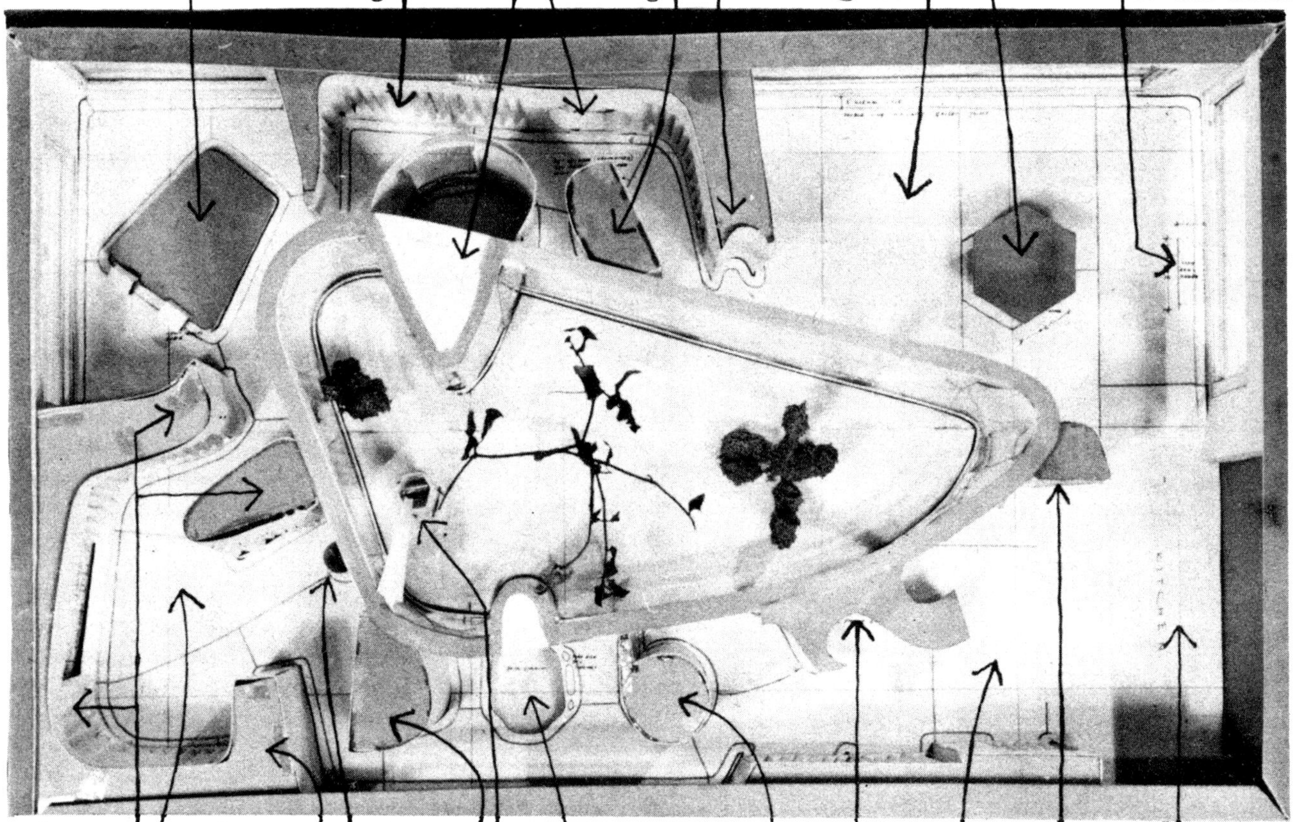

← Alison and Peter Smithson, bird's-eye perspective, Patio and Pavilion, 1956

↙ Alison and Peter Smithson, model photo from above, House of the Future, 1956

→ "Homes for Family Needs," *Homes for Today & Tomorrow,* 1961

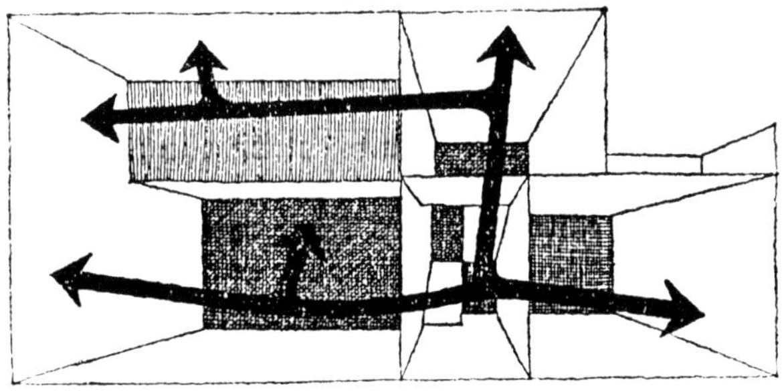

stipulated that the various functions of living be distinctly distributed in floor plans according to a minimum size and the right orientation.

After the Second World War focus shifted from the size of rooms to questions of "functional requirements" and "levels of performance." The authors of the 1961 report of the Ministry of Housing and Local Government *Homes for Today & Tomorrow* recommend, for instance, that the design of these new houses and flats should begin with "a clear recognition of" the activities that will take place within them, to better answer to "the conditions necessary for their pursuit in terms of space, atmosphere, efficiency, comfort, furniture and equipment."[23] Thus, what was once drawn as a standard flat becomes a "mixture of dwelling types;"[24] the anonymous or universal apartment takes on an identity as a "particular home."[25] And unlike orthogonal sections of apartment blocks that emphasize the monotonous mass of stacked units, a variegated section[26] accounts for quantity while making differences in the interior immediately evident. In this sense, Michael Webb's description of the house as the last refuge of individuality[27] is equally applicable to the design of large flats or tower blocks.

The isolation and accompanying individualization of the apartment, in both section and floor plan mirrors the sweeping transference of housing conceptions in the postwar era away from two-story terrace houses to the social and spatial implications of multi-story blocks of flats.[28] Sectional axonometrics, especially those of large-scale developments, visualize this shift from a "place where the family is likened to relatives, neighbors and friends"[29] to a "place where [the housewife] might speak to no one."[30] In other words, a transition from a "people-centered to a house-centered existence" takes place. These are the words used by the sociologists Michael Young and Peter Willmott whose famous study *Family and Kinship in East London* compared domestic life in the workers neighborhood of Bethnal Green, subject to slum clearance since the beginning of the century, with those of the families who had left for the newer, and more isolated, suburb of "Greenleigh cottage development" (in reality, the Debden Estate in Epping Forest, built in 1945 by the LCC).[31] Correspondingly, the recommendations issued by the Ministry of Housing in its 1961 *Homes for Today & Tomorrow* were that the single flats in multi-story blocks should be the equivalent of houses.[32]

While the translation of the typological model from the terrace house to an individual apartment as a formal exercise was stimulating the spatial imaginations of architects

↓ Denys Lasdun & Partners, exploded axonometric, St. James's Place, London, 1960

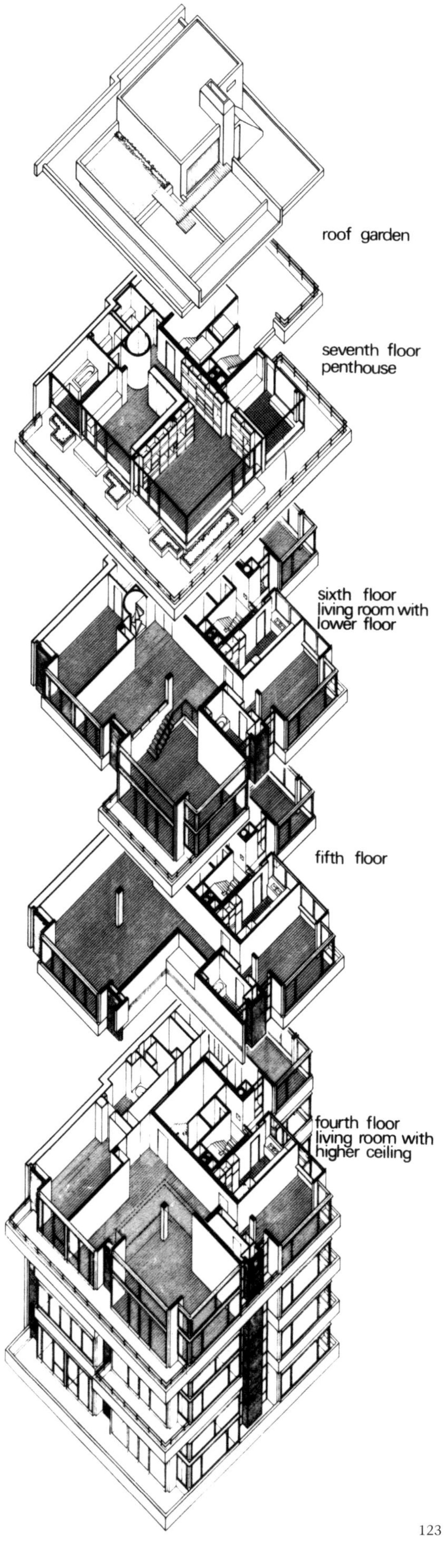

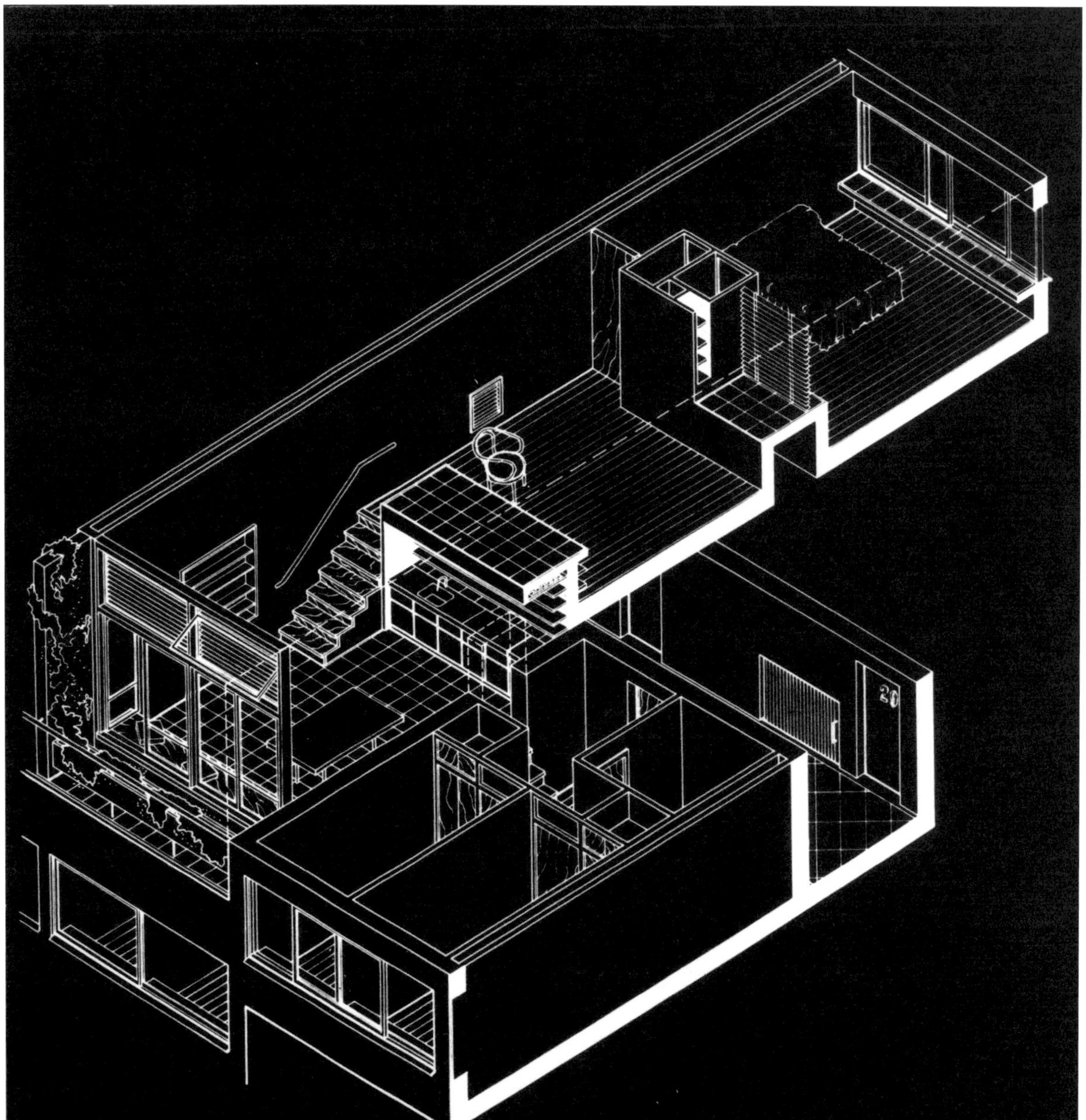

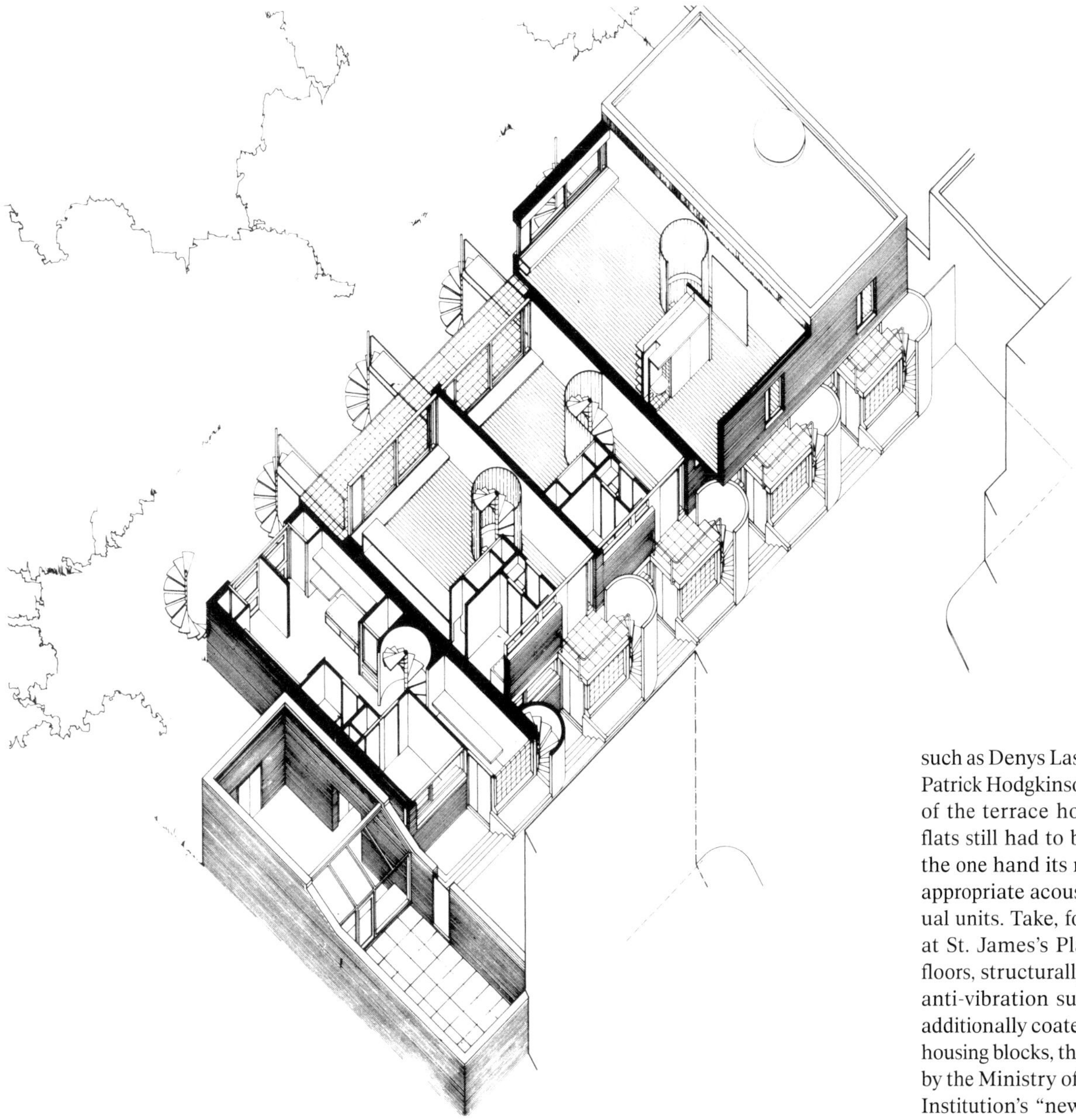

← Patrick Hodgkinson, axonometric section, AA School fourth-year student project for Lambeth Council, London, 1953

↑ Neave Brown, axonometric section, Winscombe Street, London, 1968

such as Denys Lasdun, Alison and Peter Smithson or, later, Patrick Hodgkinson, the transposition of the additive model of the terrace house to the superposition of individual flats still had to be technically resolved. It would find on the one hand its response in the growing endeavor for an appropriate acoustic and thermal isolation of the individual units. Take, for example, Lasdun's luxury apartments at St. James's Place, with their double-glazing, floating floors, structurally isolated bathrooms, lifts assembled on anti-vibration supports, and sound-absorbing air ducts additionally coated in felt;[33] or in the case of lower-income housing blocks, the corresponding recommendations issued by the Ministry of Housing to follow the British Standards Institution's "new Code of Practice on Sound Insulation and Noise Reduction" to "achieve reasonably satisfactory reduction of noises." This included the "tap-tap of stiletto heels, the noise of children running and jumping in the flat above, the sound of the vacuum-cleaner and of other pieces of electrical equipment, the radio or television program," and so on.[34]

But more equipment was required for the interior to be truly isolated, and these appliances gradually came to occupy a central position in the flat's layout. Herein lies another advantage of the axonometric drawings. In contrast to perspectives, in which all of the rooms outside the cone of vision are hidden, axonometric representations show not only living areas but also service spaces: bathrooms, kitchens, stairwells, corridors, and even built-in cupboards that became integrated into the walls. More than any other presentational form, these drawings reveal the close functional interplay between apparatuses, appliances, furnishings, and the flexible architectural elements that support daily life. What unfolds between the service areas and the soundproofed load-bearing cross-walls is an open apartment whose different spaces are distinguished by means of steps, variations in height or flexible walls—the promise of continually alterable interactions.

Along with this ability to emphasize spatial sequences another role of the sectional axonometric was to suggest what might take place in those interiors. This type of drawing matched an understanding of an apartment that was determined less through its form than through the performance of those who dwelled within it; a character revealed not through materials or tectonics but in the flexibility that its spaces allowed, even if only temporarily. In drawings of numerous apartments, white walls form the neutral

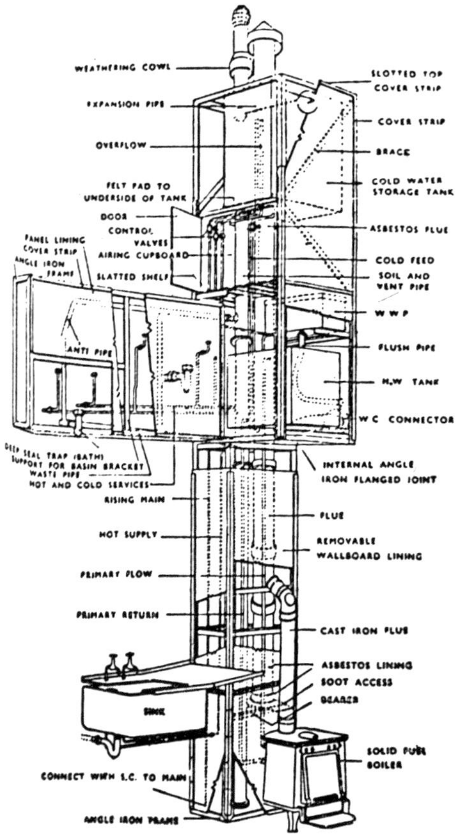

Denham plumbing unit, W. N. Froy

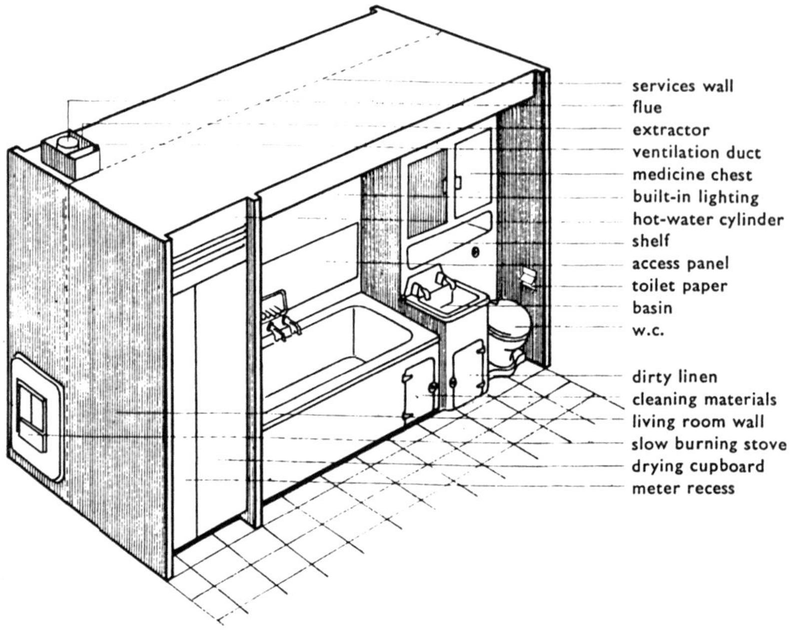

Arcon house plan and MoW mechanical core (FBW)

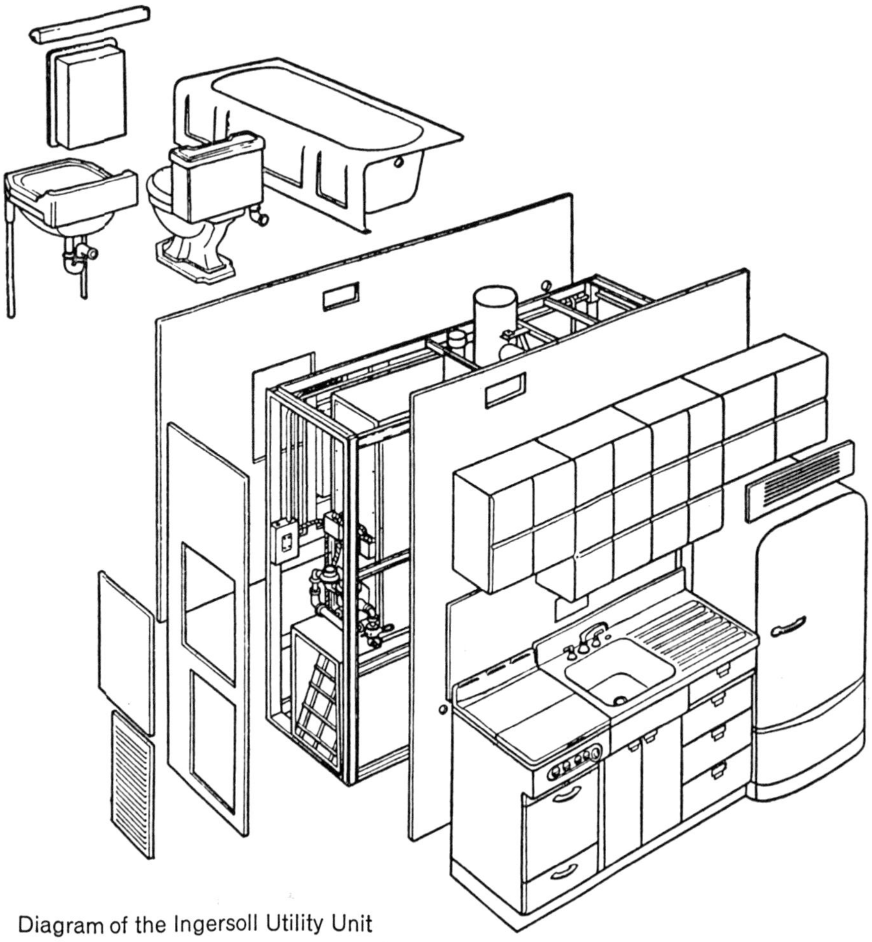
Diagram of the Ingersoll Utility Unit

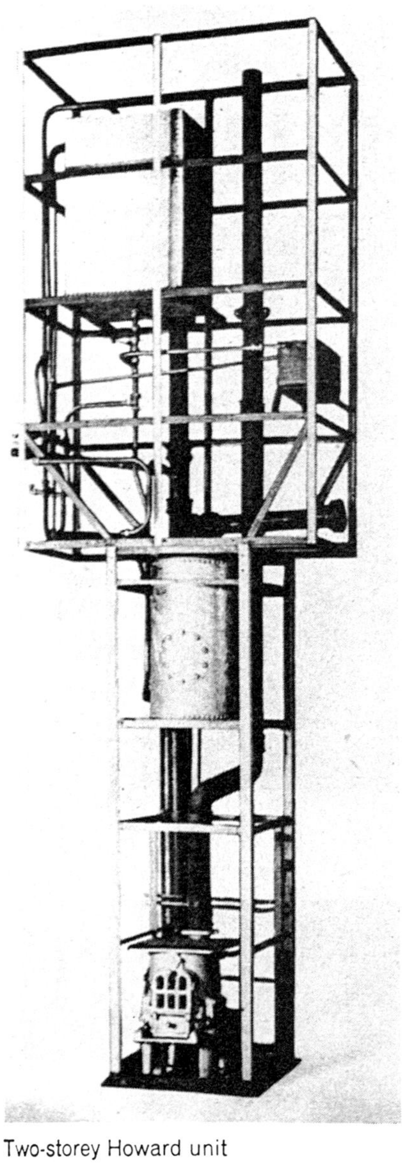
Two-storey Howard unit

← "Product Analysis 5," *Architectural Design*, 1966

↓ Denys Lasdun, exploded axonometric, Churchill College, Cambridge, 1971

background against which the paraphernalia of a nomadic tenant existence would be staged: lightweight, often stackable furniture, portable appliances, radios, televisions, and other "objects of desire" provided by a growing consumer society. What these axonometrics suggested was the real-life possibility of a radical idea. Even if the projects of the avant-garde were never implemented beyond exhibitions or the pages of magazines, the real postwar housing projects of Great Britain were articulating their most fundamental ambitions. Instead of the literal fusion of architecture, fittings, and machines with one another, as seen in the various capsules of the 1960s or the extension of the rationale of the compact kitchen as described by Sigfried Giedion to the entire flat, it was the extent to which apparatuses, appliances, furnishings, and flexible architectural elements transformed the interior world that made it into a totally controlled environment.

While the sectional perspectives and axonometrics of individual apartments that were published in journals such as *Architectural Design* and the *Architectural Review* were intended to address spatial questions, in more technical journals sectional or cutaway axonometrics were used to show the construction details that invisibly complicate and facilitate the forms of living sketched out above. Accompanied by elaborate captions and annotations, they illustrate the stages of the building process (from the structure to the facade, from the base to the apex), summarizing it either in a single drawing that reveals a sequence of steps or in a detailed true-to-scale drawing that presents the interplay between the individual constructive elements. The origins of these drawing types can be traced back to nineteenth-century engineering colleges where they were used to depict the assembly of scaffolds. By the early twentieth century, the technique was familiar to architects who were keen to introduce the spatial sensibility of an exterior construction to an inner tectonic world.[35] A prime example of this is a drawing by Tecton of the Rosebery Avenue building on the Spa Green Estate (1946–1950) in London.[36] As a sectional axonometric it shows the building process and constructional design, presenting the successive infilling of the reinforced concrete box-frame with walls, windows and balcony parapets from the ground floor upwards. But beyond its purely constructional qualities, the drawing demonstrates how a rationale of systems-building was increasingly defining postwar architecture. This approach would eventually lead to the dissolution of the traditional load-bearing, protective and insulating wall to give way to functionally independent layers of construction[37] whose performances could be illustrated and described in detail thanks to the chosen drawing technique,[38] from the cell of

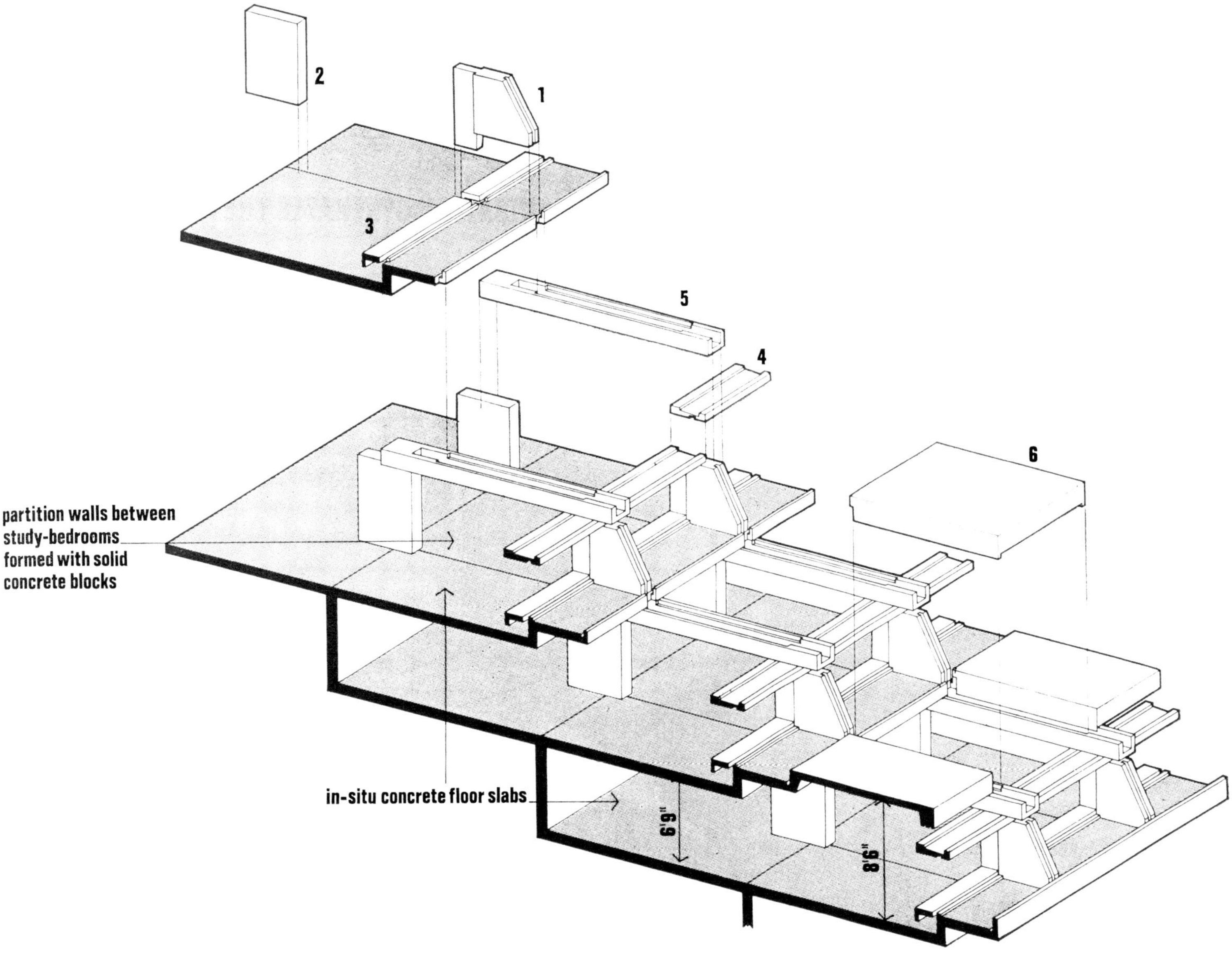

← Tecton Architects, axonometric section, Sadler House, Rosebery Avenue, Finsbury, London, 1946–1949

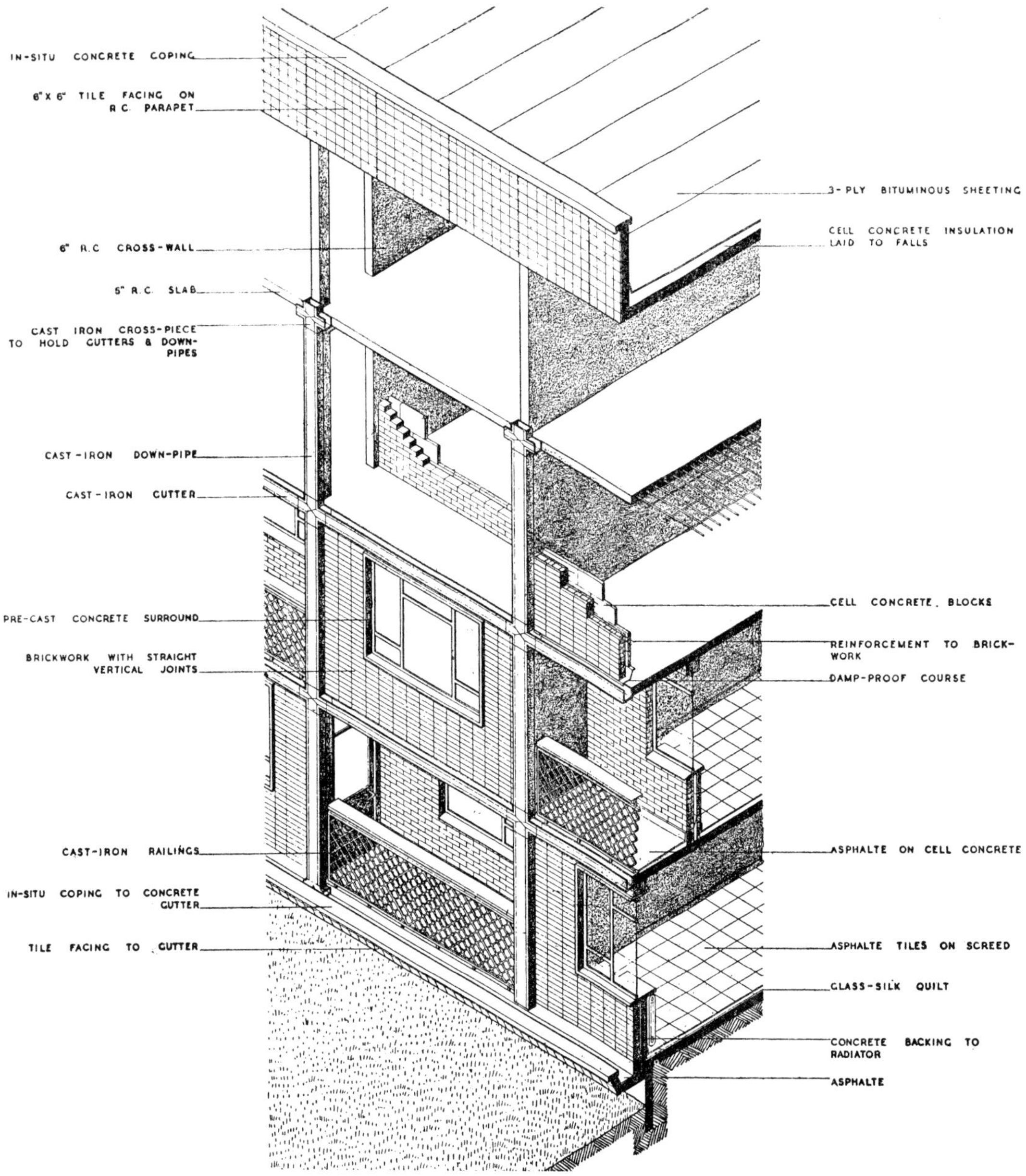

concrete blocks, to the water-resistant damp-proof course, to the two-inch air cavity and the non-load-bearing brick facade with its vertical mortar-joint pattern.[39]

In fact, what becomes even more evident in the sectional axonometric of the 1960s is its capacity to visualize the increasing mechanization of the building process and the growing significance of building with prefabricated elements. One example shows up in James Stirling's 1966 drawing of the crane assembling the concrete elements in the residential expansion for St Andrews University.[40] In another instance, this time for Denys Lasdun's 1970 presentation of the modular structure of the residential extension for Christ's College, Cambridge, a "blown-up" axonometric makes comprehensible the sequence of the individual and functionally distinct building elements: precast structural mullions,[41] precast window slabs, precast transoms, precast combined rainwater gutters and structural beams and precast roof units. Accompanied by captions and instructions, the heavily annotated drawings recall the instruction booklets of a building set—or, as Reyner Banham suggested in an essay on the drawings of James Stirling, military assembly manuals from the Second World War, which would have been impossible for their generation to miss and whose diagrams were "intended to make it possible to strip, reassemble and, above all, understand, sophisticated and enigmatic items of machinery."[42]

What these drawings, all of which investigate the construction, ultimately challenge is the idea of absolute insularity—the interior world of the bunker or the space capsule or the camper van that recent historiography has highlighted.[43] They illustrate the transformation of the articulation between interior and exterior from separate entities into one seamless realm that is defined by a series of greater or less opaque, translucent or permeable layers, as for instance in the case of the facade construction. This idea of relative transparency is made particularly explicit in a perspectival drawing of Golden Lane, published in 1956 in *Architectural Design*, in which the laws of perspective that would otherwise block out all points, surfaces and spaces beyond the gaze of the beholder are nullified.[44] In this

→ Tecton Architects, axonometric section, Tunbridge House, Rosebery Avenue, Finsbury, London, 1946–1950

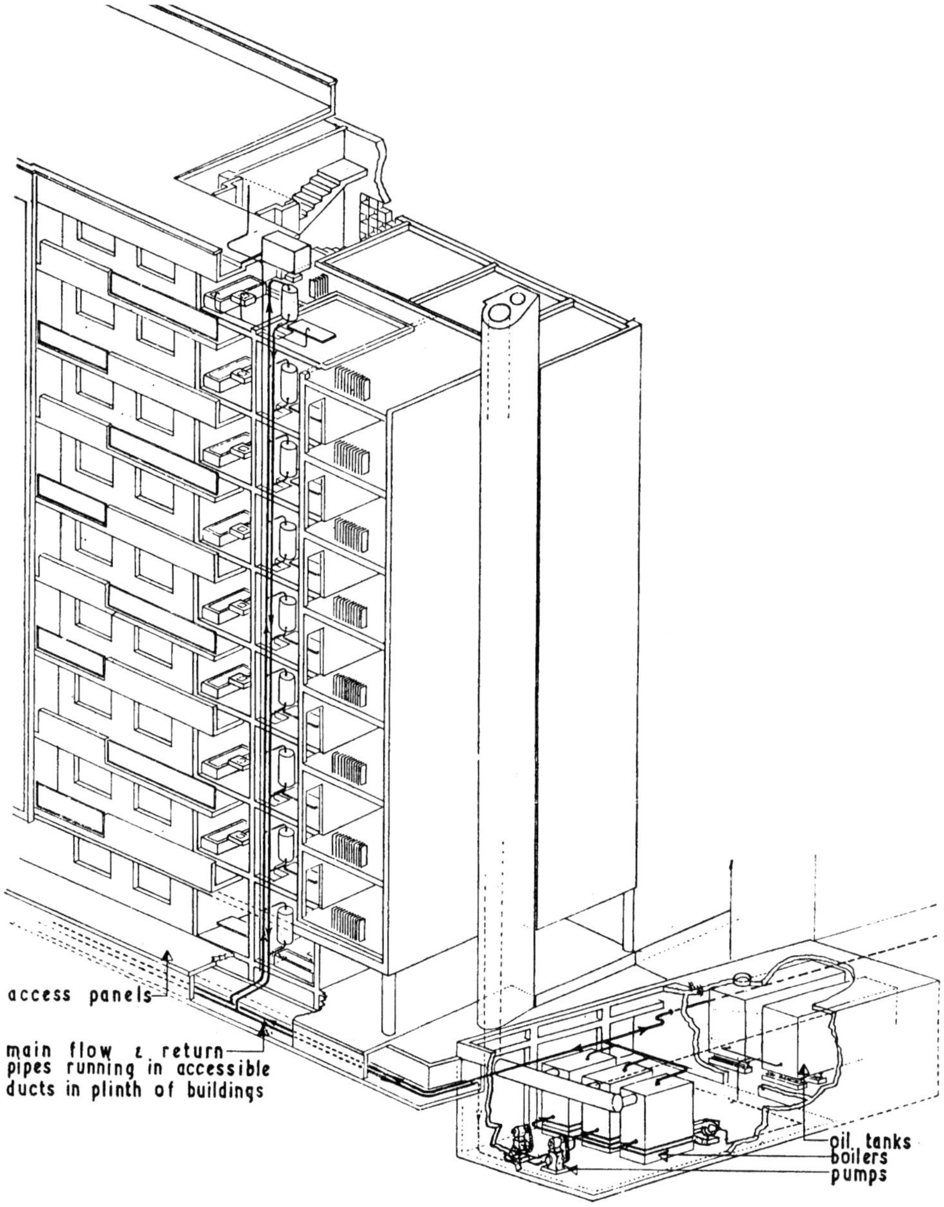

perspective, the individual apartments are not cut lengthwise but in cross-section. The massive ceilings and exterior walls still visually and acoustically divide the individual units from their joining neighbors in order to maintain their individuality, while the inner partitions of every unit are shown as transparent surfaces. However, the balcony parapets, the large two-story window front, various interior walls and the massive rear facade, represented as a series of transparent frames mutually related through their proportions, interpret the flat as a unified system of spatial layers, if not in terms of construction, then at least visually. Depending on the viewpoint the facade can be read as a "screen," "filter," or "skin," as Banham convincingly interpreted in his 1954 essay on Tecton's Hallfield Estate (1951–1958) in Bayswater, London.[45]

But the threshold between what is perceived as inside and outside, or as private and public does not stop with the construction. This is illustrated in yet another type of sectional drawing that emerged in architectural journals in the 1950s: the bird's-eye perspective or axonometric,

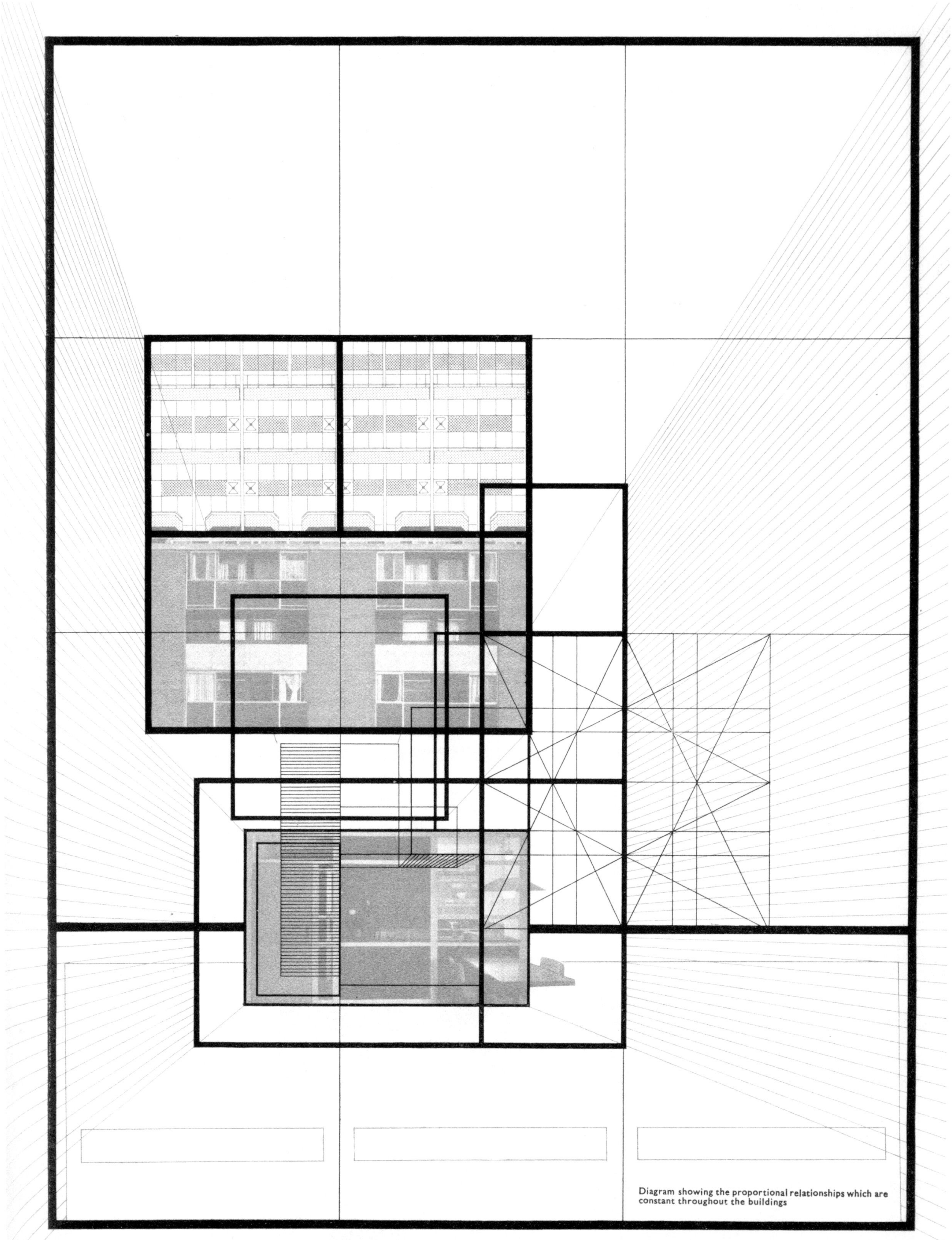

Diagram showing the proportional relationships which are constant throughout the buildings

← Chamberlin, Powell & Bon, perspective through a flat, Golden Lane Estate, London, 1952–1956

in which entire blocks of flats, including their infrastructure, are shown cut away at the center. This form adopts an additional property of axonometry that had been introduced by mechanical engineers in the nineteenth century and which found widespread use in professional manuals. In contrast to other forms of visual presentation, this convention allowed the functional correlation of the individual parts or their systems to be depicted. In architecture, this translated into the representation of the individual infrastructures, such as plumbing pipes, telephone lines, electricity cables, or entire systems connecting the individual apartments with municipal services and running through the different floors of the building (even its basement), connecting the secluded private flat to the public realm by a series of infrastructure—ducts, pipes, and other lines.

The examples of this breakthrough, by which the intimacy of the interior becomes interconnected with the whole city, are numerous in architectural journals of the time: the refuse-disposal system of Tecton's Spa Green Estate (1949), which links individual kitchens via a drain with an underground collection chamber that then runs to a collection tank in the central disposal station;[46] the heating system in the blocks of flats at Churchill Gardens in Pimlico by Powell and Moya (1962), whose central heat-accumulator supplies its 1,600 flats with warm water via a heat accumulator that is fed by an underground pipe running from the Battersea Power Station on the opposite bank of the Thames;[47] or, seen from the perspective of motorized transport, the covered street-level roads and carparks of the Barbican Center.[48] What is new is not the fact, that these buildings are connected to the network of the city (a network in London that was more than one hundred years old) but that these buildings and networks are no longer conceived of as separate entities.

More than other forms of representation, the perspective and axonometric section while addressing the interior, allowed the possibility to unlock the different spatial limits that were otherwise still constrained in the plans, sections, and even more in the slick axonometric drawings of the interwar moderns. They reflected a new form of articulation between the private and the public realm, whose relation could be precisely modulated. Unlike the modernist plan and its nineteenth-century predecessors that were concerned with the distribution of the functions within the house, these drawings shift the focus towards the articulation of individualized environment and the activities taking place within it. Revealing the transparency of the facades, the spatial articulations of the ground plans, and the infrastructural equipment of the buildings, they enabled architects and engineers to visualize the internal and external worlds of any part of architecture: from the inside of a room and the makeup of a wall, to the service networks that connected the individual home with subterranean power, refuse, and energy sources, and buildings with the city and its territory.

In these drawings, the more operative elements—understood both technically and socially—become a central characteristic of the building, pre-empting a growing equivalency between the idea of infrastructure and that of megastructure.[49] But with the critique of the all-encompassing (or even mega) structure in the 1970s, and its subsequent disappearance from architectural publishing in the following years, any apparent interest in the sectional axonometric and perspective drawing seemed to also find its end. Or at least it reached a provisional end, because the phenomena exposed there, especially the transformation of the home into a secluded interface of different networks, would in reality continue out of sight (and out of mind) of most practicing architects. In the process, the once fruitful relationship between architectural representation and building practice that had emerged in the postwar years—a relationship perhaps best symbolized in the perspectival and axonometric section—ultimately collapsed into its own heterogeneity.

1 Reyner Banham, *The New Brutalism: Ethic or Aesthetic?* (London: Architectural Press, 1966), 87.
2 James S. Ackerman, "Villard de Honnecourt's Drawings of Reims Cathedral: A Study in Architectural Representation," *Artibus et Historiae* 18, no. 35 (1997): 41–49.
3 Werner Oechslin, "'Sciographia,' die vierte Darstellungsform ('species dispositionis'): Daniele Barbaro, Andrea Palladio und die Kodifizierung der Architekturzeichnung," in *Daniele Barbaro 1514–1570: Vénetien, patricien, humaniste*, ed. Frédérique Lemerle et al. (Turnhout: Brepols, 2017), 199–220.
4 Thanks to Helen Thomas for this information.
5 Jacques Guillerme and Hélène Vérin, "The Archaeology of Section," *Perspecta* 25 (1989): 226–57.
6 Guillerme and Vérin, "The Archaeology of Section," 232.
7 Guillerme and Vérin, "The Archaeology of Section," 236.
8 See Auguste Choisy, "Note sur le mode de représentation des documents graphiques," in *Histoire de l'Architecture* (Paris: Librairie Baranger, 1929); significantly, this commentary is also found in Julius Posener, "Choisy: A Historical Assessment of Auguste Choisy's 'History of Architecture,'" *Architectural Review* 120, no. 747 (October 1956): 235.
9 John Robert Gold, *The Practice of Modernism: Modern Architects and Urban Transformation, 1954–1972* (London: Routledge, 2007), 169; John Robert Gold, *The Experience of Modernism: Modern Architects and the Future City, 1928–53* (London: Routledge, 1997), 151.
10 J. M. Richards, "Criticism: House Near Cowes, Isle of Wight, Designed by James Stirling and James Gowan," *Architects' Journal* 128, no. 3308 (July 24, 1958): 120.
11 "Planning on the Mat," *Architects' Journal* 122, no. 3154 (August 11, 1955): 174.
12 For example, as in the newly refurbished *Architectural Review* offices (1959) or the modernization of the Royal Air Force Club in London (1968). See "Offices in Queen Anne's Gate," *Architectural Review* 126, no. 751 (August/September 1959): 115; "Royal Air Force Club, Piccadilly, London," *Architectural Review* 143, no. 853 (March 1968): 219.
13 See H. Rothschild, "Study Bedrooms Compared," *Architectural Design* 36, no. 12 (December 1966): 213–15.
14 See for instance the drawing by Gordon Cullen of the South Bank Exhibition: "The Exhibition as Landscape," *Architectural Review* 110, no. 656 (August 1951): 80–106.
15 The term "sectional perspective" is taken from the title of an essay by Wolfgang Lotz, "Das Raumbild in der italienischen Architekturzeichnung der Renaissance," *Mitteilungen des Kunsthistorischen Institutes in Florenz* 7, no. 3/4 (October 1953): 193–226. English translation in Wolfgang Lotz, *Studies in Renaissance Architecture*, ed. James Ackerman et al., (Cambridge, MA: The MIT Press, 1977), 1–65.
16 Alison Smithson, Peter Smithson, et al., "Patio and Pavilion," in *This Is Tomorrow*, ed. Theo Crosby (London: Whitechapel Art Gallery, 1956).
17 "House of the Future: (1) Firing the Imagination and (2) Forward to Back-to-Back Housing: A Preview of the Smithsons' Ideal Home," *Architects' Journal* 123, no. 3183 (March 1, 1956): 232, 236–37. See further, Beatriz Colomina, "Unbreathed Air," *Grey Room* 15 (Spring 2004): 29–59, 47–49.
18 See Yves-Alain Bois, "Metamorphosen der Axonometrie / Metamorphosis of Axonometry," *Daidalos* 1 (1981): 57.
19 Georges Teyssot, *Die Krankheit des Domizils: Wohnen und Wohnbau 1800–1930* (Braunschweig: Vieweg, 1989), 121–122.
20 On axonometry as a representational form used to demonstrate functional relationships, see Bois, "Metamorphosis," 55.
21 Patrick Hodgkinson, "Foundling Conception. Notes by Patrick Hodgkinson on the Development of the Design of the Brunswick Centre," *Architectural Review* 152, no. 908 (October 1972): 216–218. See also: Thomas Weaver et al., "A Ship Called Patrick Hodgkinson," *AA Files* 73 (2016): 3–39, here 7, in a comment by John Miller on the Lambeth scheme, and 10–13, in an appraisal of the leading (hardly credited role) of Hodgkinson in Leslie Martin's office, especially the unbuilt St Pancras housing project (1957–1958).
22 "Flats in St. James's Place," *Architectural Design* 31, no. 11 (November 1961): 512.
23 "Summary of Main Conclusions and Recommendation," in *Homes for Today & Tomorrow*, ed. Ministry of Housing and Local Government (London: HMSO, 1961), 49. In the same book see also "New Patterns of Living," 2.
24 Robert Maxwell, "Housing, School and Community Centre, Alexandra Road, Camden, London," *Architectural Review* 166, no. 990 (August 1979): 87.
25 "Cluster Block, Claredale Street, Bethnal Green, London," *Architectural Design* 30, no. 6, (June 1960): 244–247.
26 For example, "Flats in St. James's Place, London," *Architectural Review* 130, no. 773 (July 1961): 20–28.
27 Michael Webb, *Architecture in Britain Today* (Feltham: Country Life, 1969), 113.
28 See the discussion on the Unité d'Habitation in "Le Corbusier's Unité d'Habitation," *Architectural Review* 109, no. 653 (May 1951): 292–300.
29 Michael Young and Peter Willmott, *Family and Kinship in East London* (London: Routledge and Kegan Paul, 1957), 154.
30 Young and Willmott, *Family and Kinship in East London*, 133.
31 Claire Langhamer, "Domestic Dreamworlds: Notions of Home in Post-1945 Europe," *Journal of Contemporary History* 40, no. 2 (April 2005): 341–362; 349.
32 *Homes for Today & Tomorrow* (ninth edition), ed. Ministry of Housing and Local Government (London: HMSO, 1975), 28.
33 "Flats in St. James's Place," *Architectural Design*, 511.
34 Ministry of Housing and Local Government, ed., *Homes for Today & Tomorrow*, 30–31.
35 Bois, "Metamorphosen der Axonometrie," 42.
36 "Housing Estate at Rosebery Avenue, Finsbury Borough Council," *Architects' Journal* 104, no. 2694, (September 12, 1946): 195.
37 See Banham's analysis of the Armée du Salut building in Reyner Banham, *The Architecture of the Well-Tempered Environment* (London: Architectural Press, 1969) 155–158.
38 Ministry of Technology, Building Research Station, ed., *Principles of Modern Building*, vol. 1 (London: HMSO, 1959); cited in Miles Glendinning and Stefan Muthesius, *Tower Block: Modern Public Housing in England, Scotland, Wales and Northern Ireland* (New Haven: Yale University Press, 1994), 73.
39 "Flats at Finsbury: Tecton Architects," *Architectural Review* 112, no. 670 (October 1952): 245–246.
40 See "James Stirling: Two New Projects," *Architectural Design* 36, no. 7 (July 1966): 330.
41 "Christ's Cascade," *Architectural Review* 150, no. 895 (September 1971): 139–140.
42 Reyner Banham, "Introduction," in *James Stirling: Exhibition, Royal Institute of British Architects, Heinz Gallery, 21 Portman Square, London, 24 April–21 June, 1974*, second ed., (London: RIBA Publications, 1976) 5–14.
43 Colomina, "Unbreathed Air."
44 "Golden Lane Housing, City of London," *Architectural Design* 26, no. 9 (September 1956): 296.
45 Reyner Banham, "Facade: Elevation Treatment of the Hallfield Estate Paddington," *Architectural Review*, 116, no. 695 (November 1954): 304.
46 "Flats in Rosebery Avenue, Finsbury," *Architectural Review* 109, no. 651 (March 1951): 148.
47 "Flats at Antrobus Street, Pimlico, London," *Architectural Review* 109, no. 650 (February 1951): 72.
48 "Detailed Proposal for the Barbican Redevelopment," *Architects' Journal* 129, no. 3353 (4 June 1959): 836.
49 Reyner Banham, *Megastructure: Urban Futures of the Recent Past* (London: Thames & Hudson, 1976), 21, 63, 157.

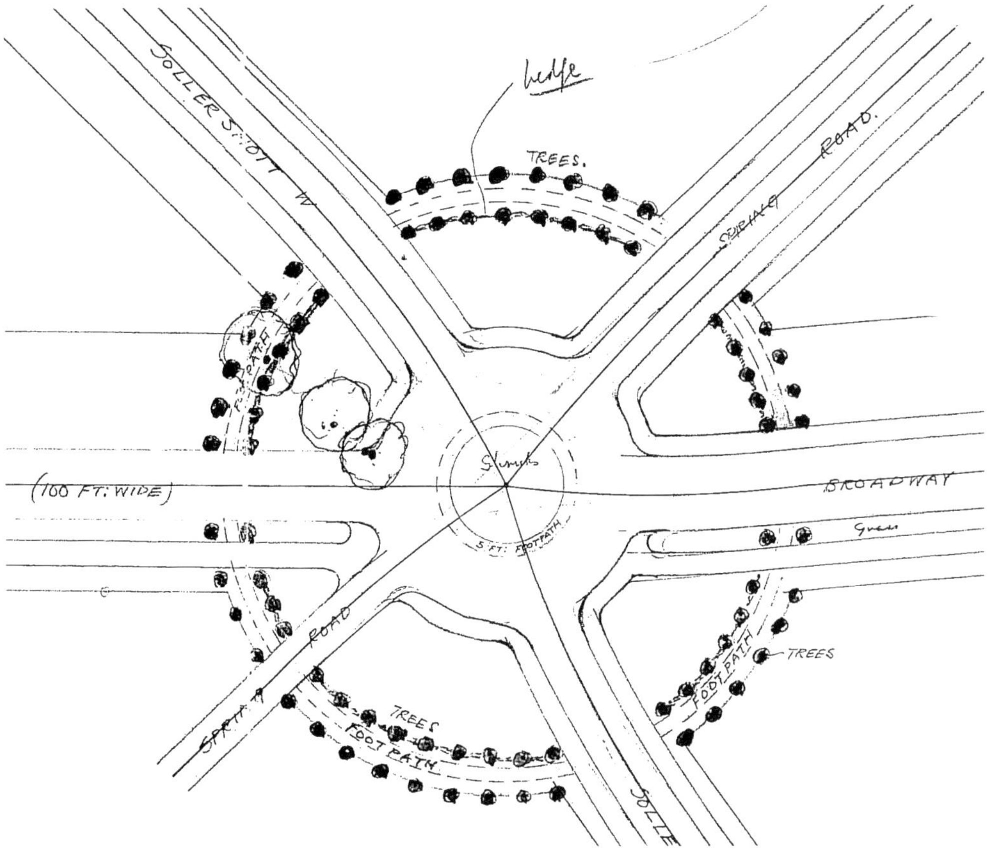

← Parker and Unwin, Plan of the suggested layout of Sollershott & Broadway Circus, Letchworth, 1908

Circles

→ “Royal Academy Plan for the Reconstruction of Central London,” drawing by A. C. Webb, *London Replanned*, 1942

When confronted with London and its reconstruction after the Blitz of 1940 and 1941, even Edwin Lutyens—an architect more acquainted with monumental urban gestures, such as great axes with their points of view that dominate his late architectural, landscape, and urban plans—would fall back on the circular figure. This is immediately evident in the booklet *London Replanned* of 1942, in which a large road firmly circumscribes the devastated city. Coauthored by Lutyens and the engineer Charles Bressey, *London Replanned* was elaborated by a committee of architects and experts at the Royal Academy to “draw attention to the advantages that may be obtained by replanning on imaginative lines.” The document accompanied a public exhibition of drawings and models at the Royal Academy.

At the core of the proposal was a large charcoal drawing that captured the committee’s ambitions in plan form. The bombed-out capital is envisioned as a thriving center marked by new tunnels, bridges, squares, and roundabouts, all of which are contained within the ring-road that takes in Hyde Park in the west, Vauxhall in the south, the City of London in the east, and in the north, King’s Cross and the edge of Regent’s Park. As the principal limit used by planners to frame the modern and ever-expanding city, the ring-road connects all major train stations around London’s central periphery, encircling—both spatially and metaphorically—the city center while everything that lies beyond the boundary fades away—that is, at least as far as the drawing is concerned. The formal quality of this *parti-pris* is enhanced by the representational technique: blocks are shaded in black and open spaces in white, resulting in an instantly legible, well established graphic that communicates the public throughfares within the built form of the city. These passages are in turn connected by a series of carefully redesigned squares, projected avenues, and bridges that extend across and around, up and down within the limits of the ring-road.

REGENT'S PARK
HYDE PARK
GREEN PARK
1
2
3
K
C
B
A
7
8
DRAWN BY A. E. WEBB.
1942

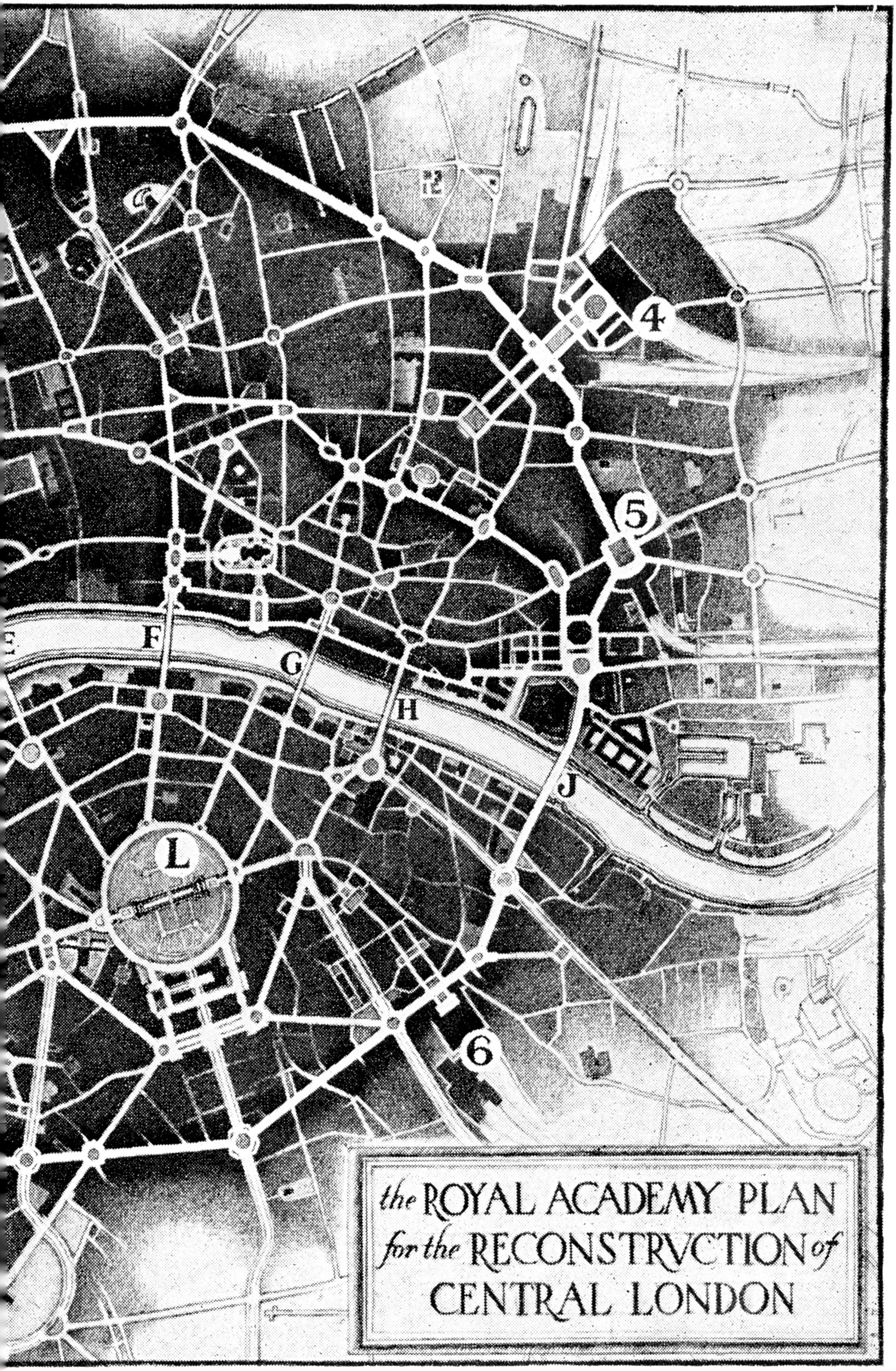
4
5
6
E
F
G
H
J
L
the ROYAL ACADEMY PLAN
for the RECONSTRUCTION of
CENTRAL LONDON

CHARING CROSS AND TRAFALGAR SQUARE

Charing Cross Station is removed and a road bridge provided, with suitable access to adjoining streets. In the Strand a large roundabout is formed between King William Street and the present Station, to distribute the traffic and as an architectural feature, with underground garages entered through archways.

Charing Cross Road is re-aligned in its lower length to bring the traffic to the roundabout and to overcome the congestion between St. Martin's Church and the National Gallery.

The Westminster City Hall is rebuilt approximately on its old site with improved road facilities.

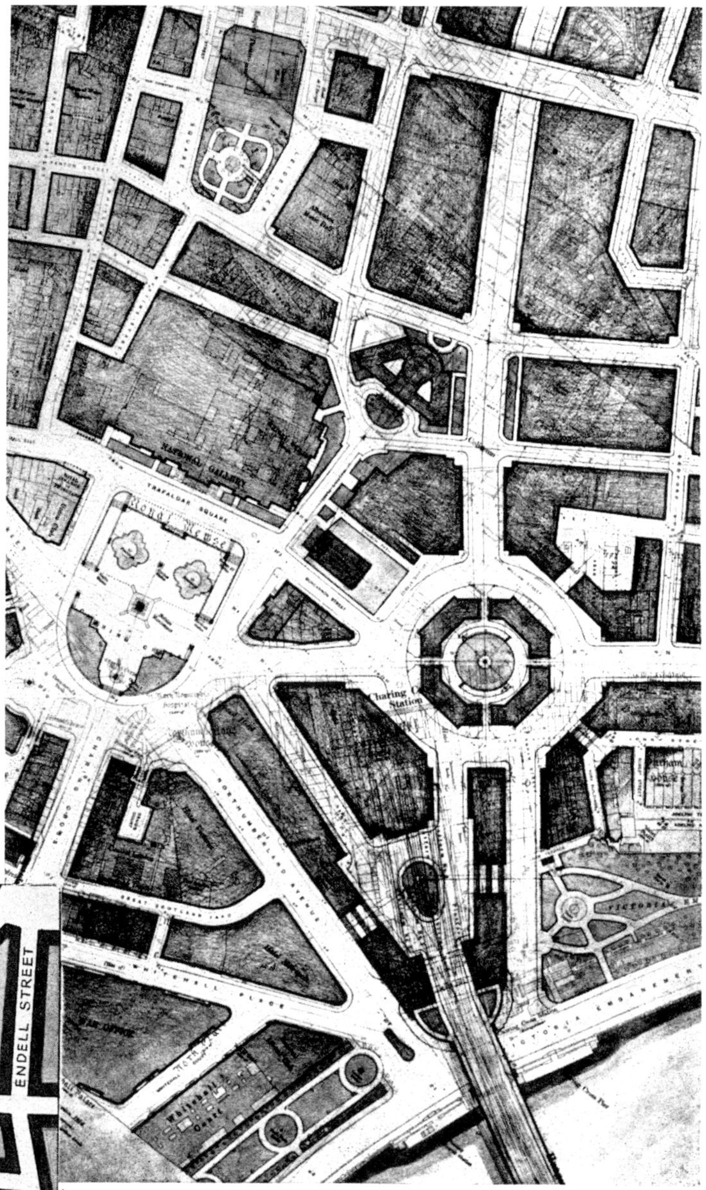

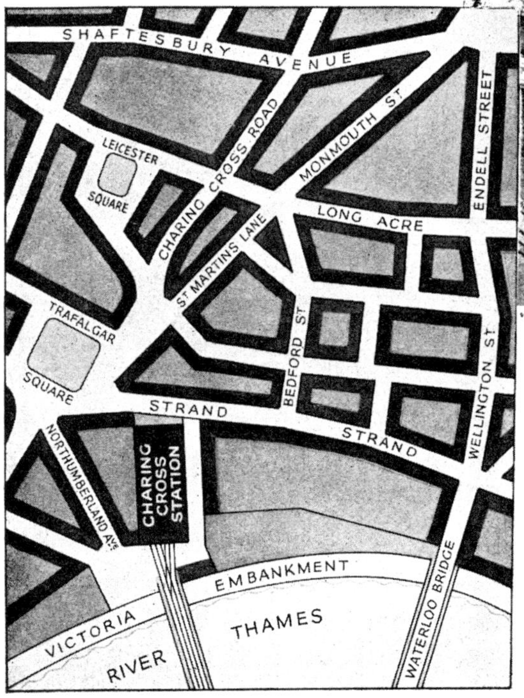

Trafalgar Square is enlarged on the South side, thus bringing the Nelson Column into the centre of the Square. Obstructions to the Admiralty Arch and Northumberland Avenue are removed, and the buildings brought into proper architectural relation to the Square.

To the North, the new Eastward extension of Piccadilly is seen carried over Charing Cross Road by a viaduct.

Inset : Present condition of the area.

↑ "Charing Cross and Trafalgar Square," *London Replanned*, 1942

A NEW PARK FOR SOUTH LONDON

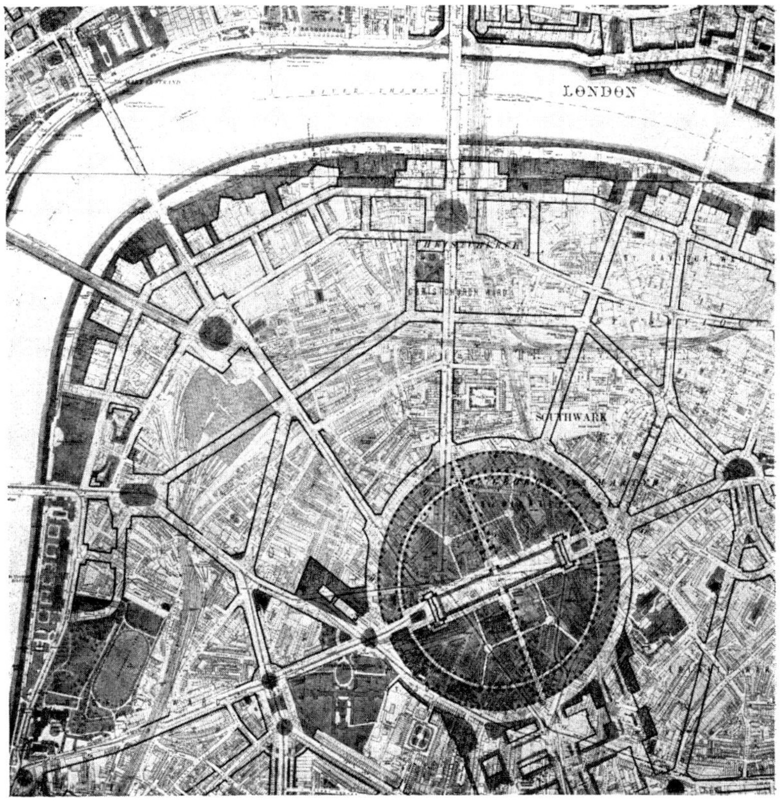

The Surrey bank of the River is developed with Embankment gardens and office buildings. At St. George's Circus, the geographical centre of London, a new Park is formed to provide circulation between all the bridge roads that radiate from this spot, and to give the much-needed open space to this crowded district. It is anticipated that the older portions of the district will be entirely rebuilt.

Below : Present condition of the area.

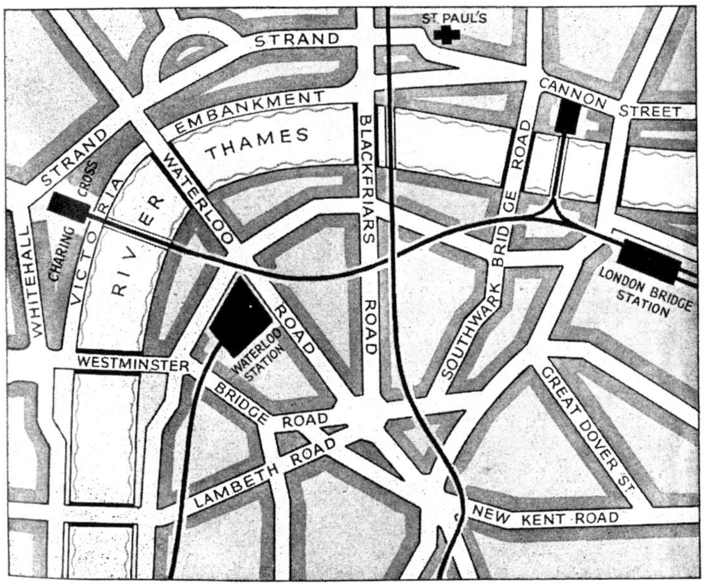

↑ "A New Park for South London," *London Replanned*, 1942

PICCADILLY CIRCUS AS IT MIGHT BE

Drawn by A. C. Webb.

The size of the Circus is doubled to meet the traffic requirements. This involves the removal of the London Pavilion and other buildings to a point in line with the Haymarket, from the centre of which a new terminal building is seen, and closing the South end of Shaftesbury Avenue and adjacent streets. A new main street continues Piccadilly Eastwards from the Circus, passing approximately along the line of Lisle Street to a new circus North-East of Covent Garden (see page 10).

North of the Circus an open space (or piazza) for pedestrians is formed, in front of a public building or possibly a theatre. The architecture reproduces that of Regent Street for the purpose of this drawing, but the whole question requires careful consideration at the appropriate time.

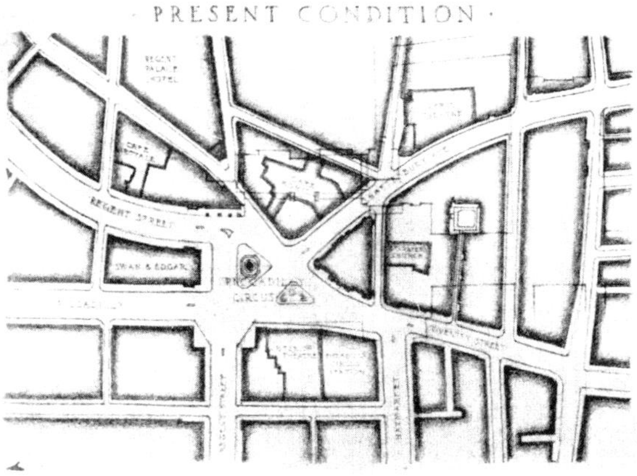

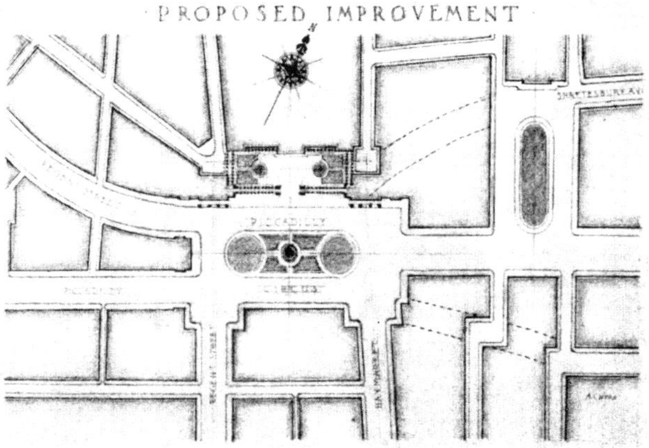

↑ "Piccadilly Circus as It Might Be," drawings by A. C. Webb, *London Replanned*, 1942

Drawn by A. C. Webb.

WATERLOO BRIDGE—STRAND JUNCTION

A large roundabout is formed on the Lyceum site connecting the Bridge on the South with the Strand, Aldwych, and the new northern approach (see page 10).

A suitable building is designed to close the vista from the bridge ; Savoy Chapel and churchyard are opened up so that they can be seen from the Strand.

↑ "Waterloo Bridge—Strand Junction," drawing by A. C. Webb, *London Replanned*, 1942

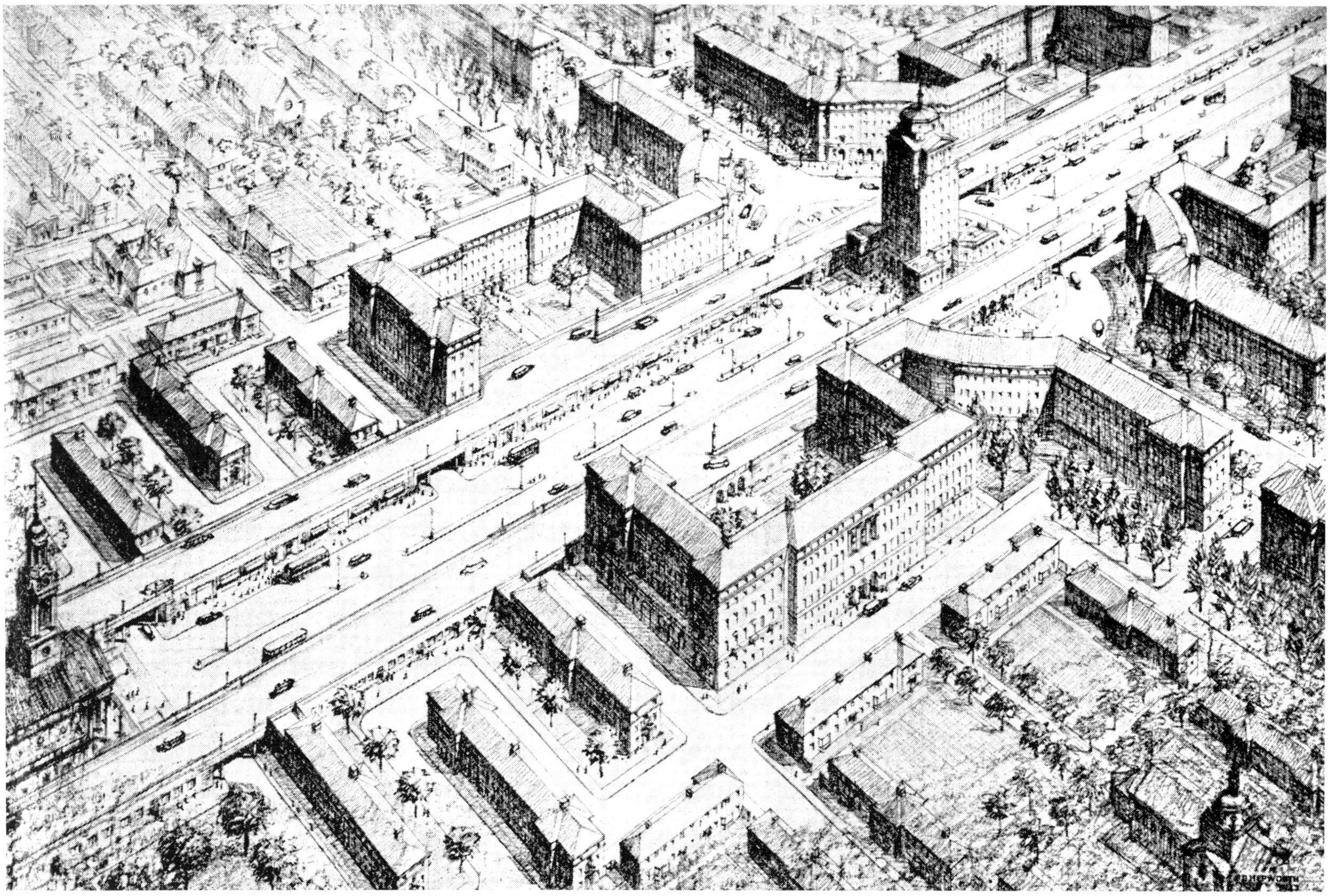

← "Arterial Traffic Route, Central Viaduct," drawing by P. D. Hepworth, *London Replanned*, 1942

Particular care was taken with "the building lines and the design of street junctions, roundabouts, and vistas" in the city center,[1] and committee correspondence indicates that every intervention called for a continuous negotiation between the requirements of modern urban design and those of historic preservation. As one committee member described: "The circus at the back of the Guildhall is badly blocked by a church, which I think someone should visit to ascertain its character and condition, or perhaps the Committee can find a solution without demolishing it."[2] Several squares and interchanges were also due to be embellished. For instance, Piccadilly Circus, which, since the late 1880s and the opening of Shaftesbury Avenue, had existed as more of an unhappy traffic junction at the end of Regent Street than a proper circular square (as proposed by John Nash in 1817), was doubled in size to form an elongated rectangular space. Meanwhile, George's Circus on the South Bank was converted into a circular park, its edges absorbing the irregular geometry of the adjoining streets. Squares also became the stages for London's principal monuments, buildings, and statues—Trafalgar Square, for example, was enlarged to locate Nelson's Column at its center. Additionally, the approach from Waterloo Bridge was enhanced with a "suitable building ... designed to close the vista"[3] at its south end, and the area around St Paul's incorporated a new western axis that drew on a scheme by Christopher Wren, while a lateral perspective opened up a view from the river.[4] And where flyovers were proposed for the flow of "arterial traffic," their undersides were designed to incorporate shops, while the access ramps were framed by monumental blocks. Rather than offering rough sketches of these additions, the detailed drawings in the report emphasized the relationship between the new thoroughfares and architecture, placing equal importance on both the volumetric quality of the urban space and the facades that close a vista or frame a new square or street.

According to the authors, the individual elements, streets, buildings, and blocks, as well as materials and colors had to contribute to the "unity and harmony" of the city while giving an order to the "existing chaos." To achieve this, *London Replanned* seemed to rely, as a reviewer in *Country Life* noted, more on the "extinct art of street planning and urban design"[5] than the contemporary planning ambitions of the modern avant-garde. Given the careful composition of its elements, the plan might seem closer to a forerunner proposed almost a two centuries earlier, John Gwynn's 1766 *London and Westminster Improved*, which straightened out the urban landscape, punctuating it with squares, widened streets, monumental buildings, and sharp boundaries (substantially informing the transformation of the City during the nineteenth century, leaving traces even in the 1943 LCC County of London Plan).[6] Lutyens himself would confirm *Country Life*'s assessment, albeit by citing a different, even earlier scheme. As far as he was concerned "the only predecessors of the present Royal Academy Plan"[7] were Christopher Wren's proposals for reconstruction following the Great Fire of London in 1666, which drew stately boulevards, elegant public buildings, and grand outdoor spaces over the fire-ravaged city.

Other than the MARS plan for London, which had radically proposed to level the capital with the exception of the historic center and port in favor of an exemplary modern city, since the start of the twentieth century, very few projects had so broadly reimagined London. Though there had been several designs for individual neighborhoods that aligned with Lutyens' understanding of urban design as civic art, such as those exhibited in the 1910 Town Planning Conference[8]—among them Norman Shaw's rearrangement of Piccadilly Circus, or Beresford Pite's design for a new approach to St Paul's Cathedral from the Thames, or Stanley Davenport Adshead's project that cleared the narrow streets in front of the British Museum to make way for a half-circle—these incidences of intervention took a localized approach to the urban form. By contrast, Lutyens' view was not only more spatially expansive but also temporally so, looking back across the centuries and forward by as many years. His summation in 1913 of the colossal Viceroy's House at New Delhi—"The Viceroy ... thinks only of what the place will look like in three years' time; three hundred is what I think of"—seems equally valid for his plan for London. And similarly, some of the main figures that emerge from the drawings of *London Replanned* were embedded almost as strata in Lutyens' classical repertoire. "The square, the rectangle, the circle occur everywhere in his work," wrote Pevsner in the *Architectural Review* in 1951, highlighting the circular room at court at Papillon Hall, remodeled by Lutyens in 1903.[9] For a man obsessed with geometrical figures and their potential for both clarity and delight, it was perhaps inevitable that squares, rectangles, and most especially circles would find their way beyond the walls of architecture and into the urban fabric of London.

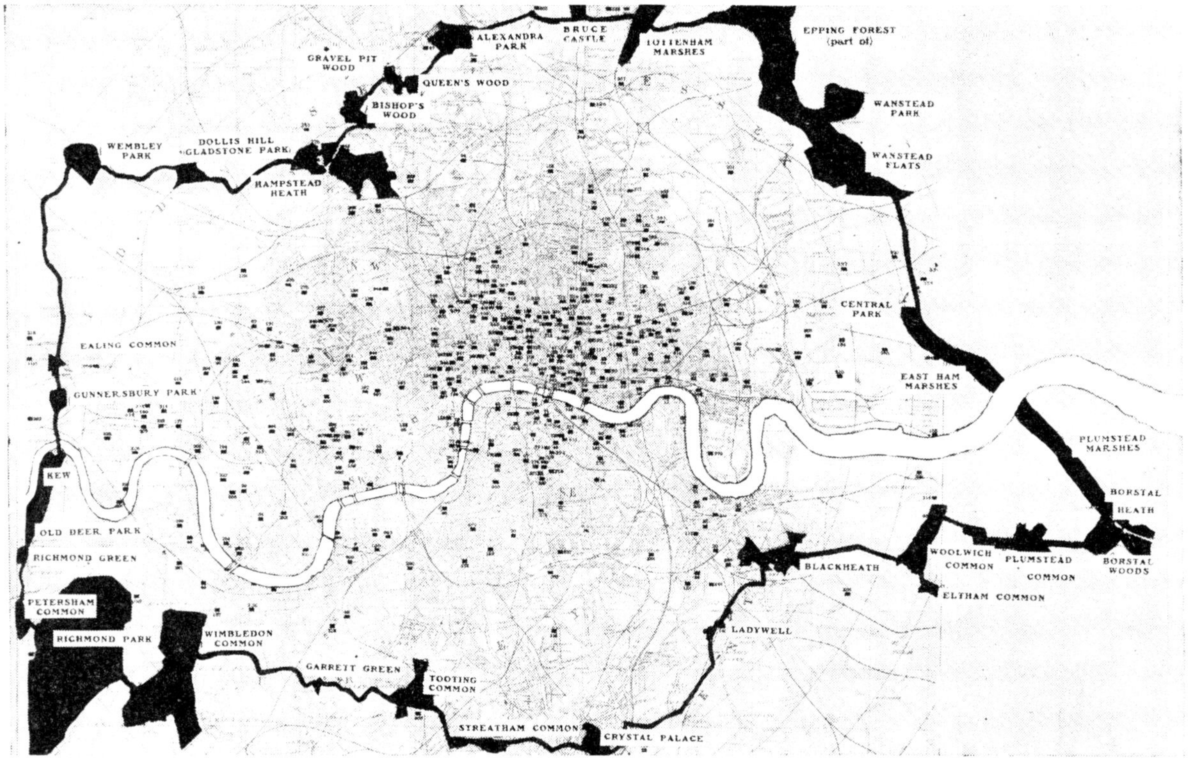

← William Bull, "A Green Girdle around London," *Illustrated London News*, 1901

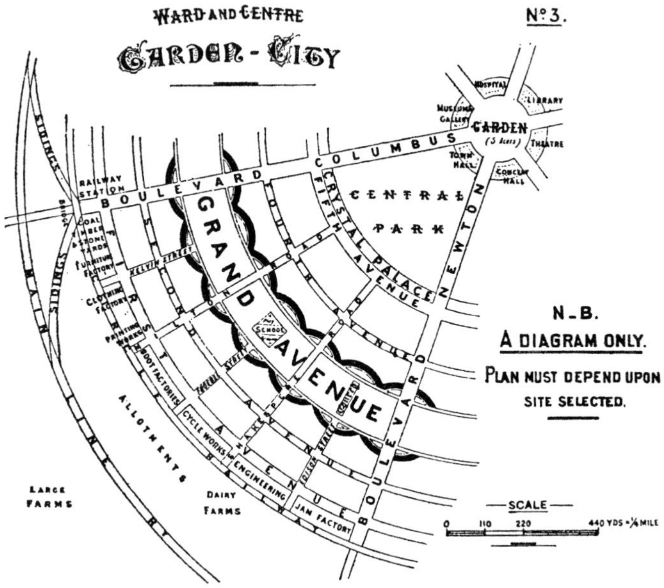

↓ Ebenezer Howard, "Ward and Centre Garden-City," *Garden Cities of To-Morrow*, 1902

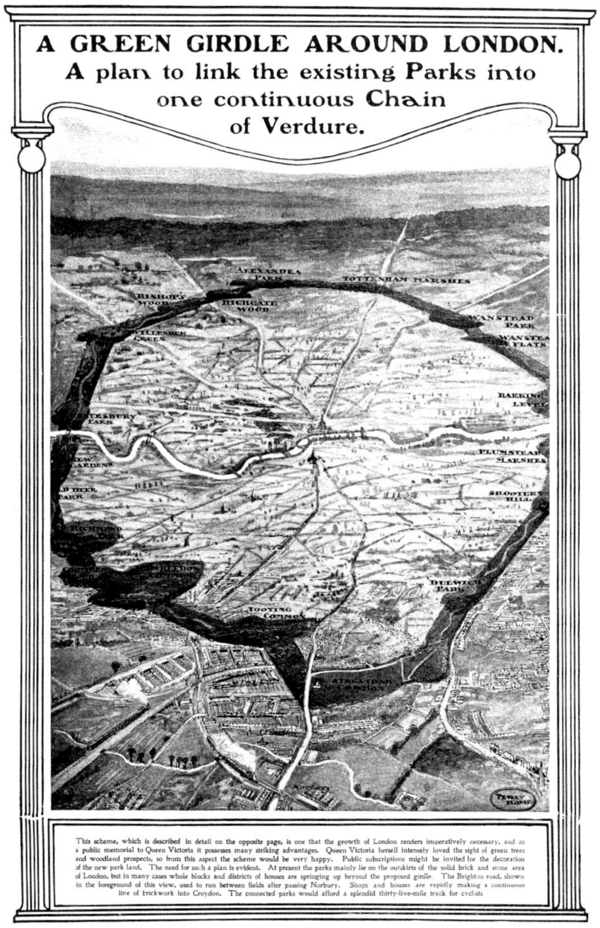

↑ Lord Meath, "The Green Girdles," *Illustrated London News*, 1901

↙ George L. Pepler, "Greater London," 1910

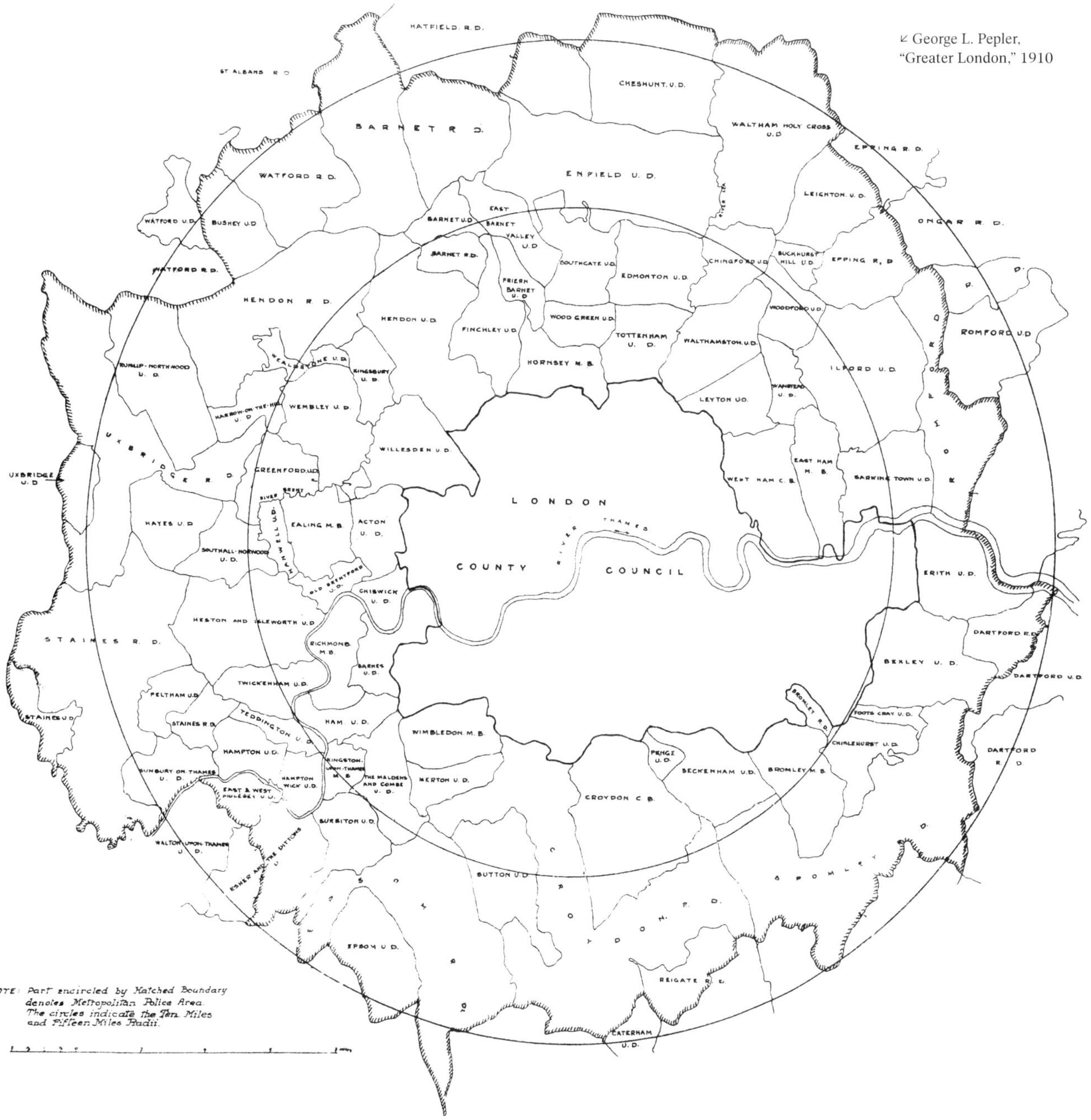

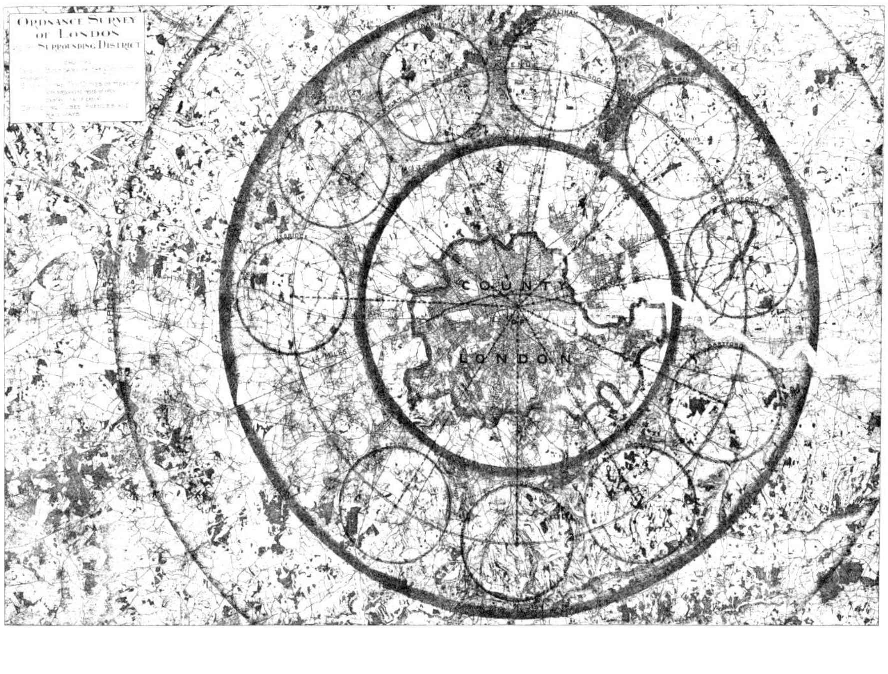

→ Arthur Crow, "Map of the Ten Cities of Health," 1910

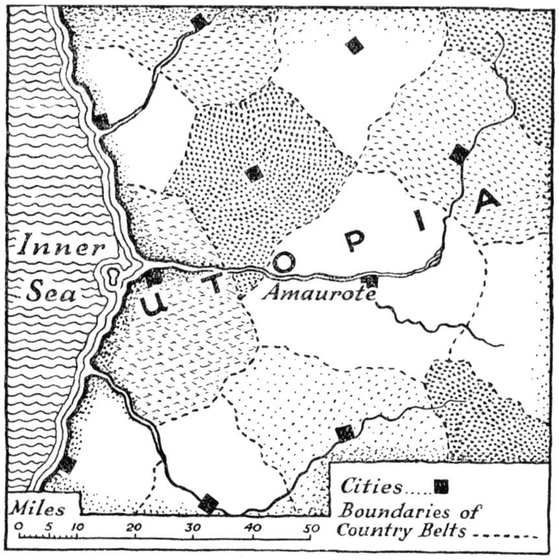

→ Frederic James Osborn, "Diagram of an Area of Sir Thomas More's Utopia," *Green-Belt Cities*, 1946

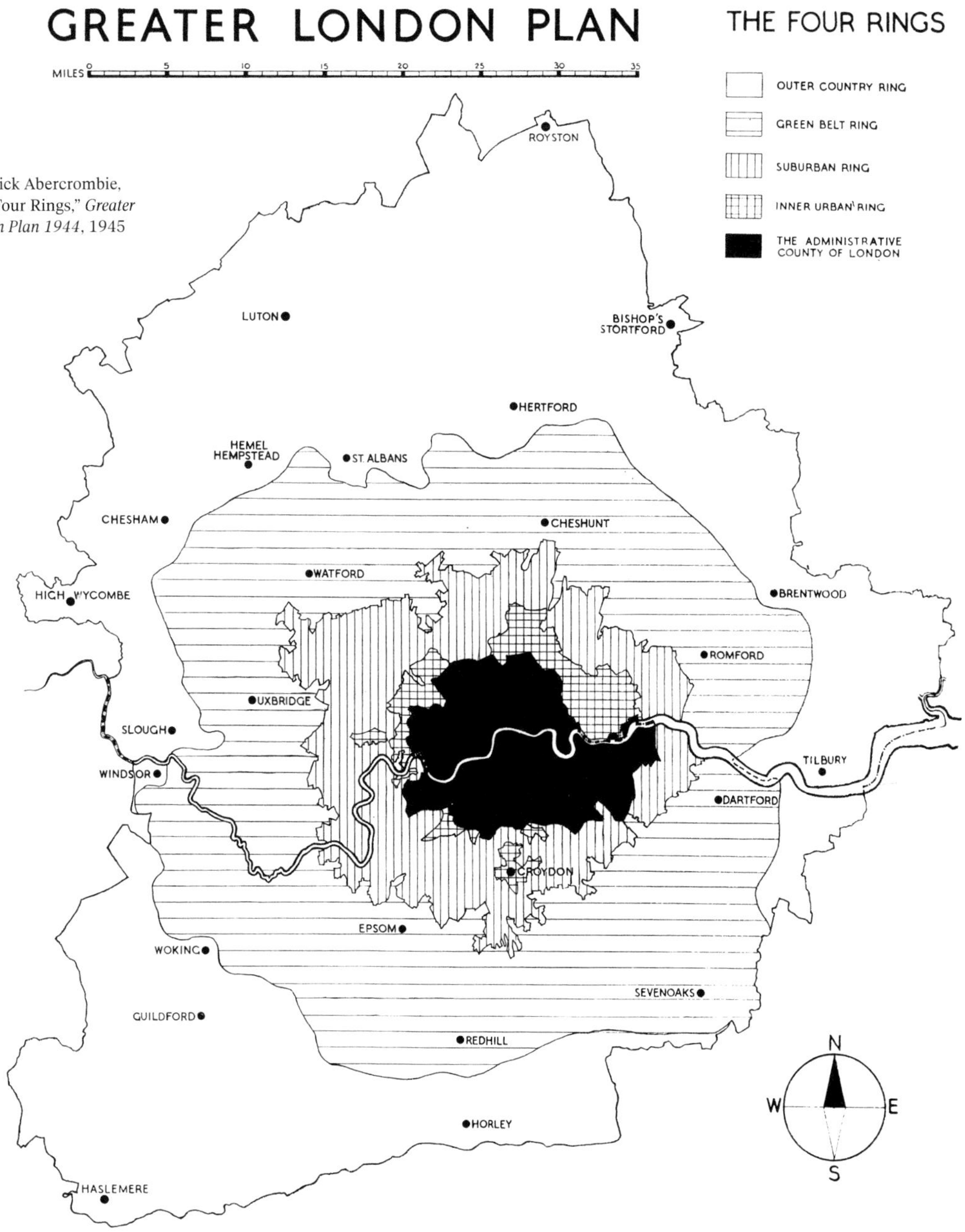

→ Patrick Abercrombie, "The Four Rings," *Greater London Plan 1944*, 1945

↓ “Road Pattern,” in
Design and Layout of Roads in Built-Up Areas, 1946

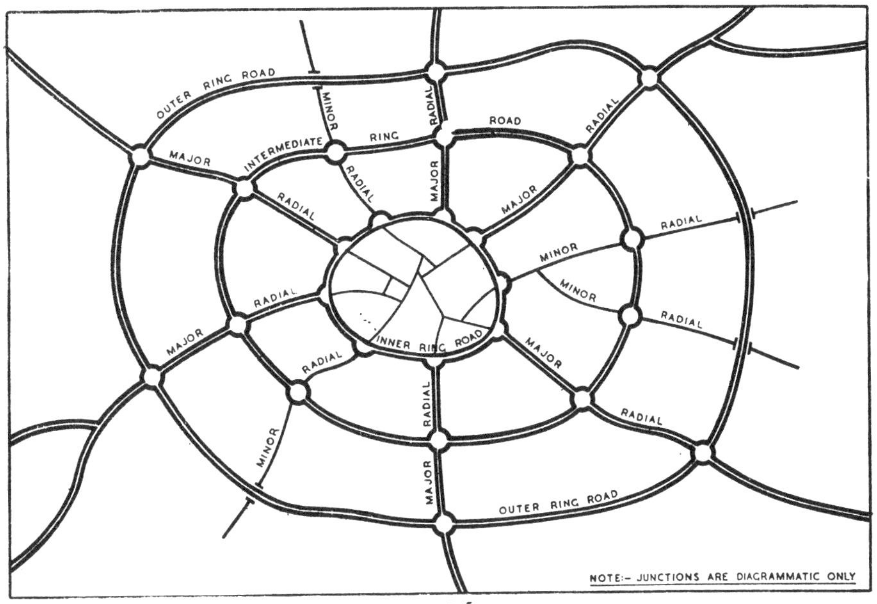

FIGURE 5

↓ H. Alker Tripp, “Lay-out for a New Town,” *Town Planning and Road Traffic*, 1946

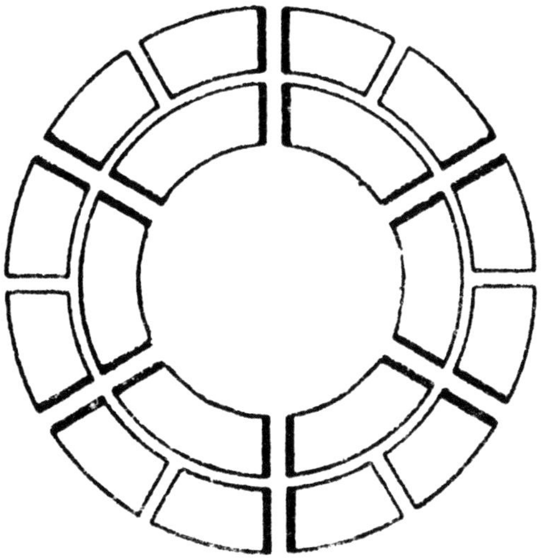

↓ “The Development Plan Green Belt 1954–8,” in Ministry of Housing and Development (ed.), *The Green Belts*, 1962

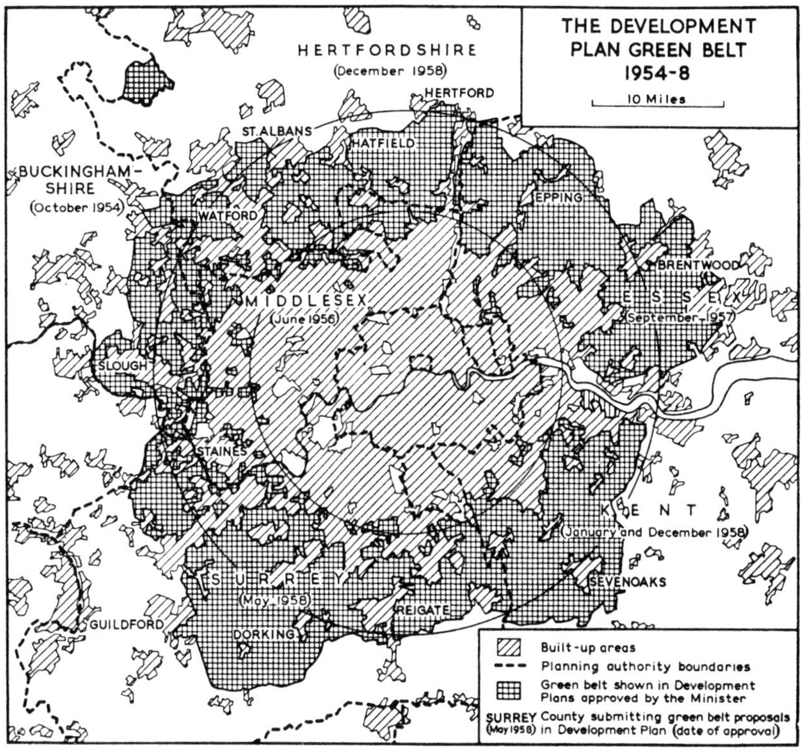

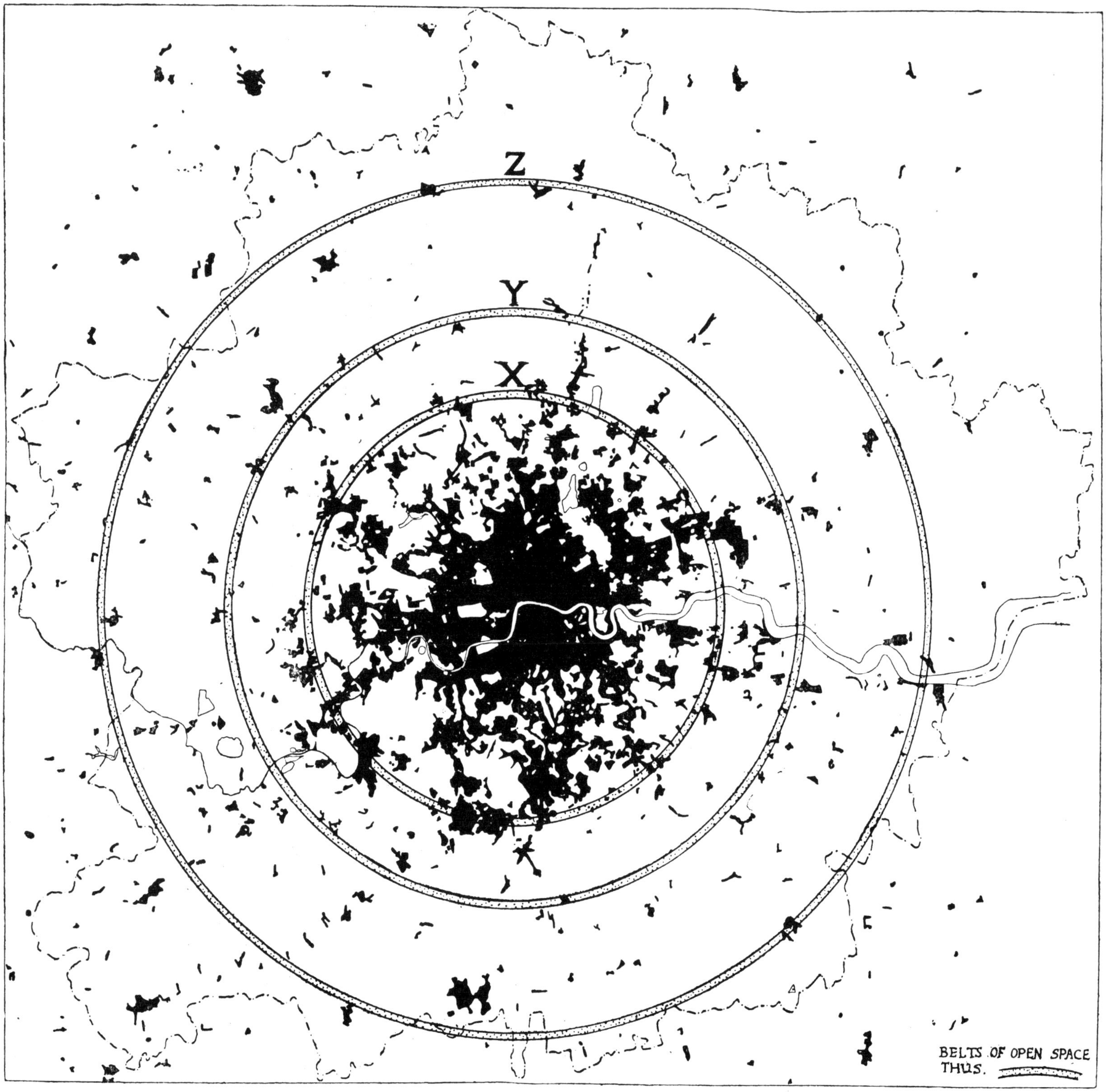
Z
Y
X
BELTS OF OPEN SPACE THUS.

← "Three imaginary belts of open space. Each one-half mile wide," *First Report of the Greater London Regional Planning Committee*, 1929

If for Lutyens, the idea of circumscribing the city of London was new, he was not alone in recognizing the essential qualities of the circle for the planning of the capital. Concentric schemes had been put forward since at least 1910, and similar proposals would later be offered, perhaps the best-known among them Patrick Abercrombie's Greater London Plan of 1944. In the postwar years, the figure that circumscribed the city and assured its circulation generally became the convention for London and other urban areas in Great Britain, be it in the reorganization of existing cities like Manchester or Birmingham, or in the planning of New Towns. To legitimate its significance, some traced its origins if not to the Old Testament then at least to the work of Thomas More, Robert Owen, or Ebenezer Howard.[10] Laying each of these plans on top of one another, a continuous genealogy emerges that understands the circular city as both a political (at least in its planning) and a formal entity separated from the countryside and with a clear hierarchy between the center and periphery. In Howard's scheme, *To-Morrow: A Peaceful Path to Real Reform* (1898), for instance, the city is clearly limited by an agricultural belt, with industry at its margins and a core formed by cultural institutions. Abercrombie's *Greater London Plan* follows a similar logic. The "Capital of the Empire," as he would call it,[11] with Westminster and the City in the center, is famously circumscribed by a series of rings that radiate outward, from the band that denotes the suburbs to the green belt and outer country ring.

Apart from the ring-road, however, Lutyens' *London Replanned* differs fundamentally from the concentric models: all recommendations within the academy proposal are limited to singular interventions, breaking through the congested city as a series of streets with well-designed roundabouts at their junctions. A closer look suggests that the aim of the report was in fact not to replan London, but to beautify a series of existing squares, junctions, and streets inside a city that, barring few exceptions, had never been planned— "to carve symmetry into the irregular face of London"[12] as John Summerson would put it, resulting in an urban plan with a series of visual "Doppelgängers."[13]

If much of the Royal Academy report was shaped by a certain stiff formalism, the basis of *London Replanned* derived from a highly technical one: the *Greater London Highway Development Survey* of 1937, written by Bressey with Lutyens acting as consultant (the authorial roles had been reversed on *London Replanned*). Composition was never a consideration for this earlier survey, which could be brought back to numerical data, as represented in four graphs at the end of the booklet. The first three graphs illustrated various increases over the last fifteen years: of motor vehicles in Greater London, the city's total population, and the number of vehicles per mile of road. A further graph aggregated this information to present a two hundred percent spike in vehicles between 1922 and 1936, compared with a five percent increase in population over the same period. Lutyens 1942 plan may have been playing to classical principles, but in the *Highway Development Survey* the car was the name of the game.

Despite their rather crude, hand-drawn presentation and limited informational value, these graphs stand for the popularity of data visualization in the 1930s, largely due to the increased influence of the social and technical sciences in urban planning over the last one hundred years. In nineteenth-century London, statistics had been one of the tools used to argue for urban reform. Edwin Chadwick's 1842 *Report on the Sanitary Condition of the Labouring Population of Great Britain* was the first to make visible the relationships between social status, sanitary conditions, mortality, and their distribution across the city. Chadwick was able to construct a close correlation between the working class and its environment while pointing to the necessity to engage and change it through concrete interventions such as the proper and adequate supply of resources within the city and the de-densification of new neighborhoods.[14] Building on these new forms of statistical knowledge, the social researcher Charles Booth, who had already contributed to the establishment of empirical urban research with his survey of London's working-class population, would later advocate for slum clearance by using data gained from poverty maps. From the late 1880s onward, similar statistics formed the core of innumerable traffic reports that recorded busy areas, traffic density, and the average speed of different vehicles, all with a shared goal to transform the city—thanks to and informed by the gathered data.[15]

One notable example of the impact of a statistical approach on the design of cities is a pair of reports published by the Greater London Regional Planning Committee between 1929 and 1933, overseen by Raymond Unwin. The documents address questions of "Open Spaces," "Ribbon Development," "Additional Town Planning Powers," and "Regional Planning Authority," as well the "actual processes of development."[16] The first report, from 1929, is still illustrated by perspectives and photographs, building on picturesque precedents and combining, in a surprising way, an English tradition as outlined in Humphry Repton's *Red Books* with that of modern German *Kulturarbeiten*, as fostered by architect and conservative preservationist Paul Schultze-Naumburg. This is best seen in the specific use of illustrations to make powerful oppositions—old versus new, good versus bad. Out of this didacticism came a visual method that saw success well into the Townscape Movement.

And yet what remains of a picturesque tradition is outnumbered by other illustrations comprising maps, urban diagrams—all colorful and masterfully rendered—of open and built spaces, or simple tables dealing with density, population increases or decreases per district, and movement between districts. While seemingly trivial at first sight, their impact is substantive. Graphically compelling and succinct in their representation of information, these forms of visualization have replaced more traditional spatial or formal representations: movement of inhabitants, circulation of traffic, the distribution and development of housing, industry, and land are abstracted from the fabric of the city. The chapter on road traffic, for instance, includes a detailed list of planned and proposed thoroughfares alongside a map of Greater London showing the various categories of intervention—from the widening of existing roads to the construction of new parkways—all represented by colored abstract lines. Here, the crooked streets of London have ceded to straightened roads, not only transcending the classical boundaries between city and countryside, but also introducing a shift from civic art to planning, from an understanding of urban design as a spatial and formal challenge to that of an organizational one.

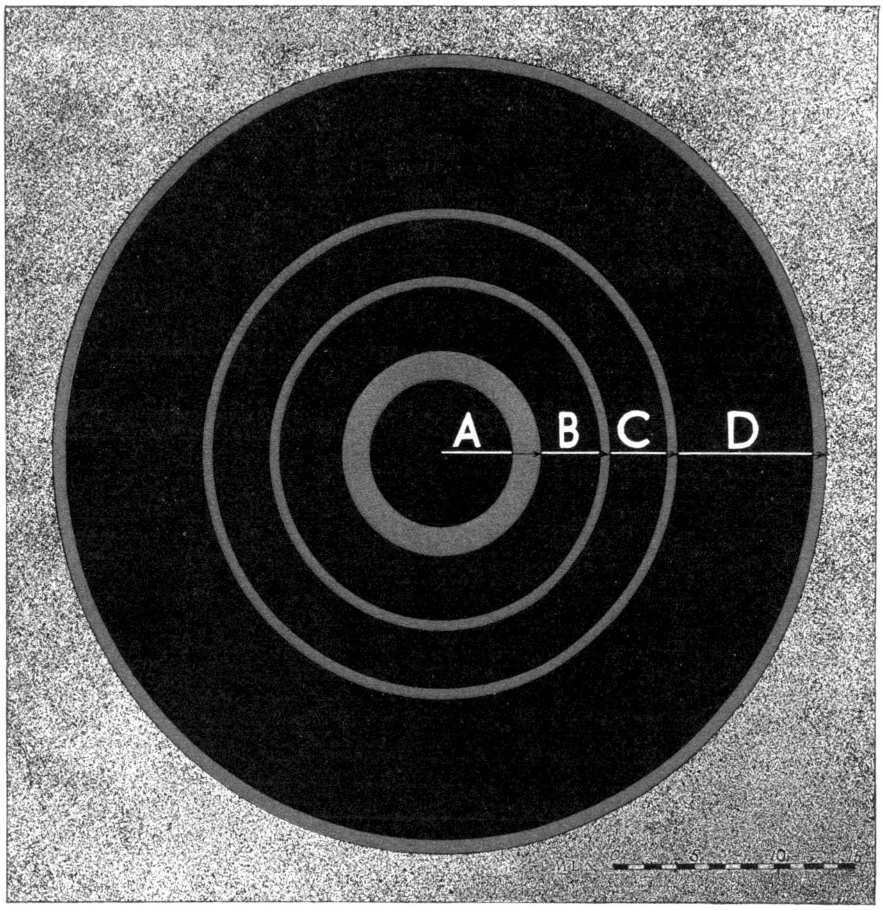

← "Diagram of Open Space," *First Report of the Greater London Regional Planning Committee*, 1929

↙ Diagrams of "Open Space Designed on a Background of Potential Building Land" (left) and "Building Areas Designed on a Background of Open Land" (right), *First Report of the Greater London Regional Planning Committee*, 1929

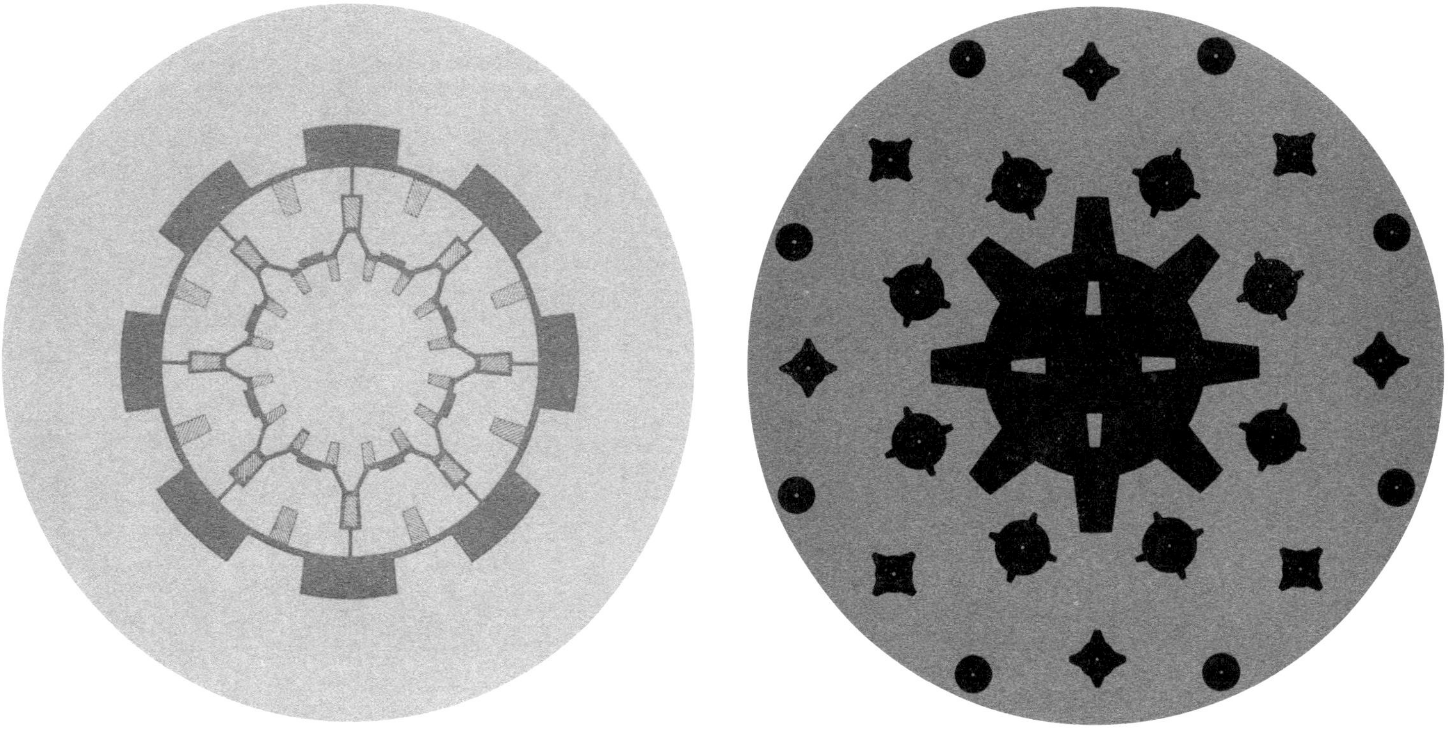

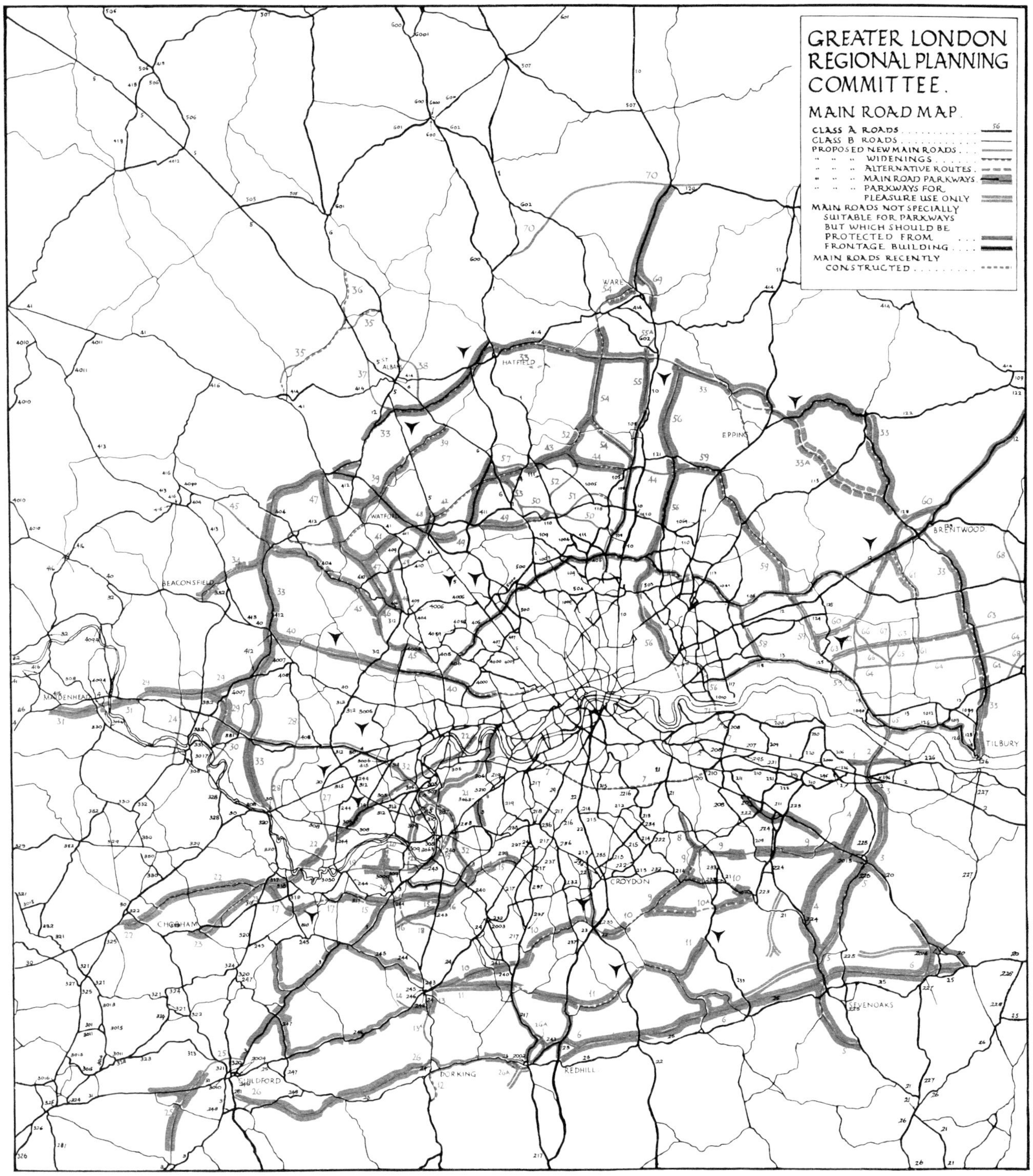

↑ “Map of the Greater London Region,” *Second Report of the Greater London Regional Planning Committee*, 1933

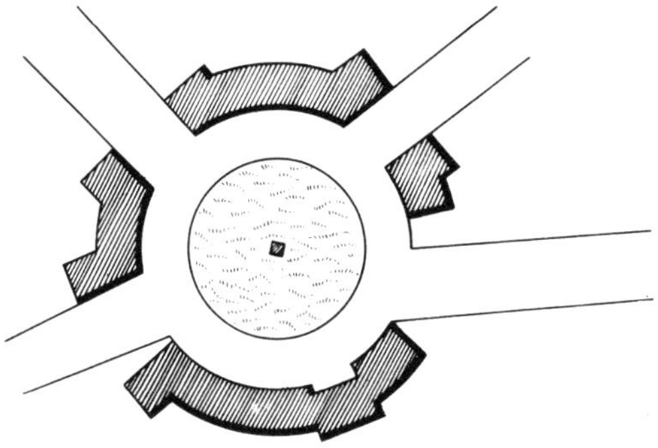

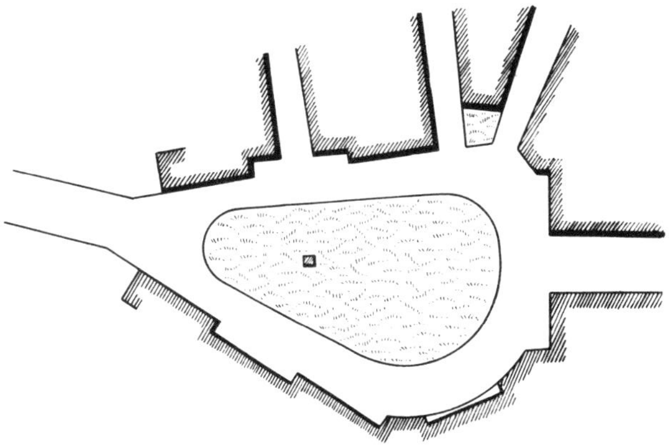

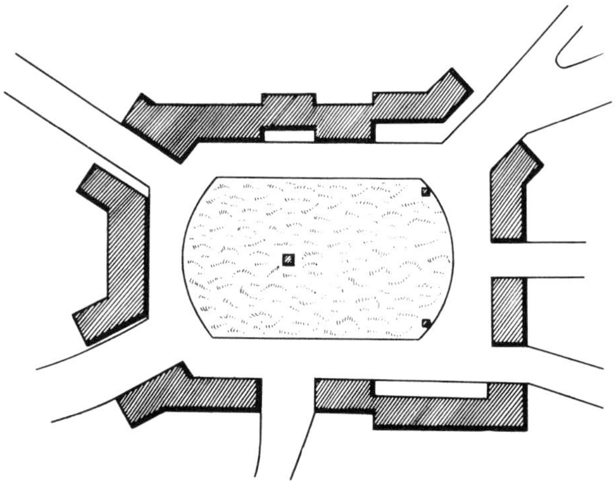

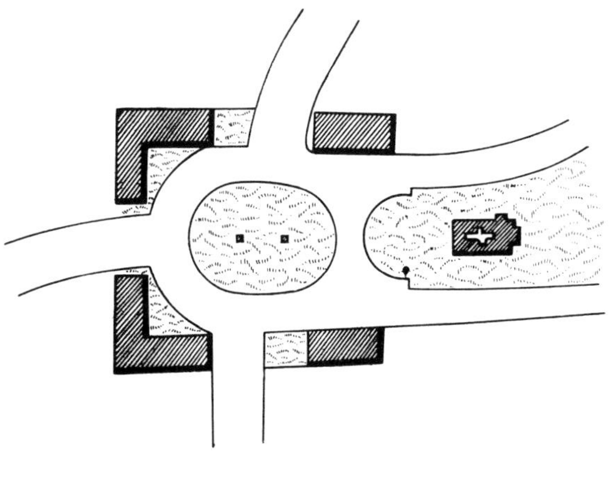

← Edwin Lutyens, "Typical Round-Abouts," in Charles H. Bressey, *Greater London Highway Development Survey*, 1938

Unwin's report is representative of its time, but had it been published earlier, it would have been deemed too radical. Take for instance and as a comparison, Ebenezer Howard's *To-Morrow: A Peaceful Path to Real Reform* from 1898 (reprinted in 1902 as *Garden Cities of To-Morrow*), often considered the first modern treatise on urban reform in Great Britain and lauded for its diagrammatic proposals for the city of the future. In one of the book's final chapters, Howard points to the migration of people, transportation issues, and the cost of land as both the root of London's poor housing situation as well as its remedy. Here, as with the later reports by Unwin and Lutyens, questions regarding the well-managed circulation of people, goods, water, railways, and capital are central to Howard's arguments. But when describing his own future city of about 30,000 inhabitants, he draws upon classical typologies,[17] borrowing their forms and names from sites in London, New York, and Chicago: Central Park, Fifth Avenue, Grand Avenue.[18] A Circle Line even runs around the edge of the city. Filling the physical area between these formal quotations are houses, public buildings, and factories, as well as parks, whose "observance of the street line or harmonious departure from it" are controlled by "municipal authorities." Along Grand Avenue, houses depart from the concentric line to form crescents, thus enlarging the already "splendid width" of the road.[19]

In *Town Planning in Practice* (1909), Unwin's main book on urban design, Howard is praised for precisely outlining the need for a clear hierarchy between "first making a plan" and then "securing the development of the town along the lines of this plan."[20] While acknowledging a variety of performance-based improvements, for Unwin and many of his contemporaries what was at stake was the "art" of town planning.[21] Indeed, the prewar period did not view requests for a "civic art" and an efficient city as contradictory; efficiency and representation were part of the same endeavor. Such an art, according to Unwin, had to consider certain practicalities—for example, the "supply of pure water," the "drainage and removal of waste," the "paving, lighting, and cleansing of streets," the restriction of "overcrowding," or the insurance of "minimum standard of air-space, light, and ventilation"—while also addressing the individuality of historical towns. "There are in each," wrote Unwin, "certain settled characteristics arising from the nature of the scenery, the colours of local building materials, the life of citizens, the character of the industries prevalent in the district, and numerous other circumstances, which taken all together, go to make up that flavour which gives to the town its individuality."[22] For Unwin, town planning was determined by a set of clear divisions: that of city and countryside; main city centers and those of districts, suburbs, parishes, and wards; buildings and public spaces; and, finally, divisions between main and residential roads (with the former further divided into pavements, roadways, riding tracks, tramways, etc). Every built example illustrated in the book follows these divisions—whether historical enclaves, like Hampstead, or more recent conurbations, such as Letchworth—and each is portrayed with black-and-white plans, perspective drawings, and photographs.

Unwin's approach was also the prevailing stance taken in the interwar period, spanning David Gilbred's *London of the Future* of 1921 to Lutyens' *London Replanned* of the early 1940s.[23] Even in Bressey's *Highway Development Survey*, which proposed specific interventions, the organizational requirements of a modern, motorized city are combined with the volumetric clarity of squares designed in the civic art tradition. An appendix of seven "typical roundabouts," all designed by Lutyens, concludes the study by illustrating Bressey's desire to address both the formal and organizational challenges posed by traffic junctions—what he identifies as the principal causes of "congestion," "obstruction," and "speed," all of which require particular care. For Bressey these are "prosceniums of the streets that converge upon them." Hence the necessity to design each roundabout "by a single mind."[24]

In the charcoal drawing that appears in *London Replanned* Lutyens represents the capital as an enclosed entity. However, Bressey's earlier report opens up London, towards the territory. Of particular interest is a map of inner London detailing a vast swathe of parks, buildings, unbuilt areas, and existing streets, while a number of recommended roads, tunnels, and viaducts are laid overtop. The principal interventions along the north-south axis facilitate connections across the river Thames via new tunnels and access roads to the existing bridges. Further proposals appear along the lateral axis on both sides of the river, with two new east-west connections, as well as improvements to central London's existing thoroughfares. Most of these interventions are pragmatic, operating within the existing urban layout and fabric to simply increase the traffic performance of Greater London. Yet they profoundly challenge the inherited logic of the city plan by superimposing onto the circular and concentric organization of the inner city a new, albeit irregular, grid-like network of streets extending into the surrounding territory and joined by more than one hundred roundabouts that would later find their way into Lutyens' interventions. The word "network" is not used by Bressey, but the proposed intervention, a net of roads, is precisely intended to evenly distribute the traffic—not around or within London, but over the city. This is all the more remarkable as models generally proposed by contemporaries and several followers still stick to the circular, concentric model, whether the aforementioned Abercrombie plans, or one of the Ministry of Transport's official postwar publications, including *Design and Layout of Roads in Built Areas*, or even Alison and Peter Smithson's *London Road Study*, hotly debated by the avant-garde in the last CIAM Congress in 1959.

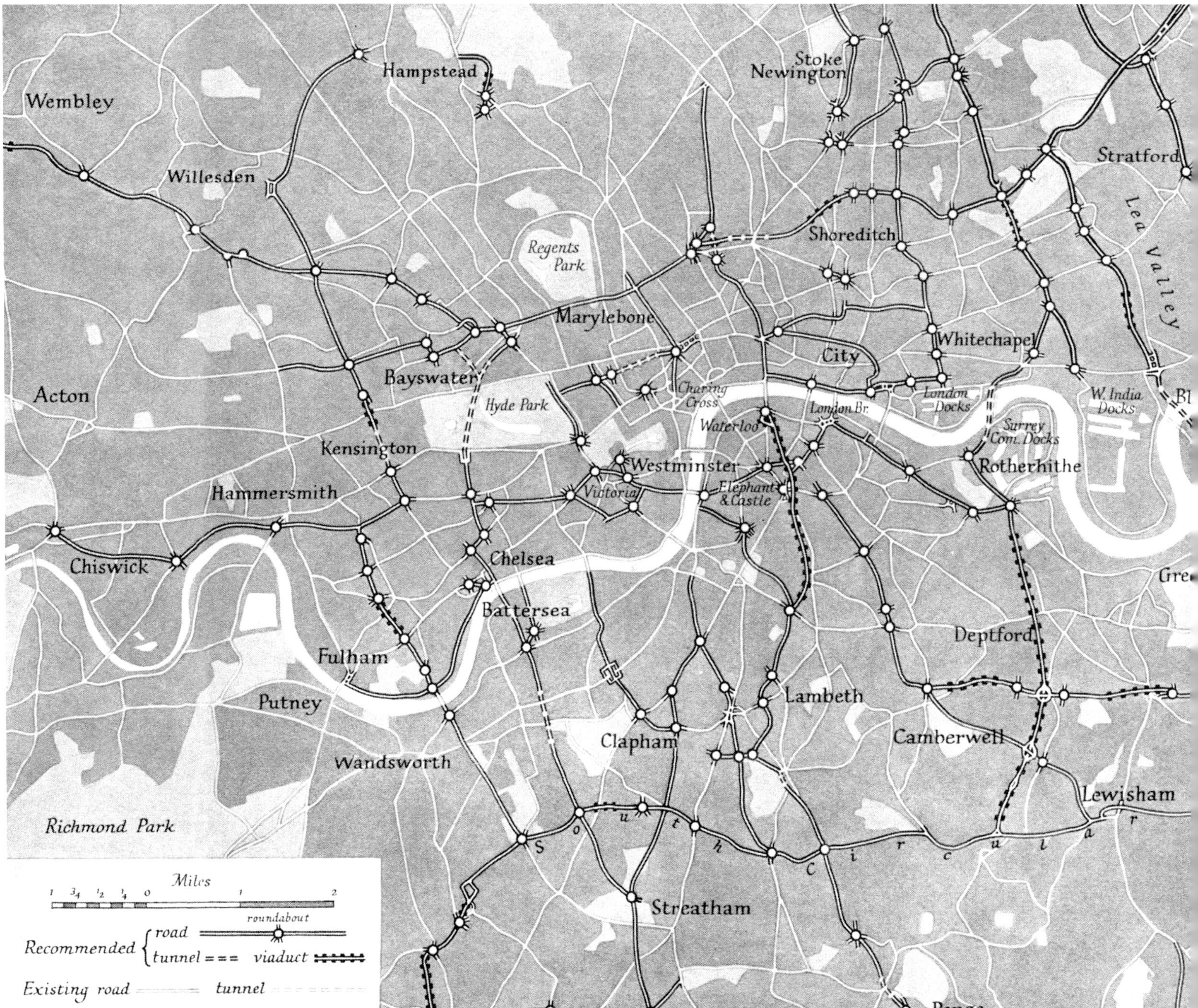
Hampstead
Wembley
Willesden
Stoke Newington
Stratford
Lea Valley
Regents Park
Shoreditch
Marylebone
Whitechapel
City
Bayswater
Acton
Hyde Park
Charing Cross
London Br.
London Docks
W. India Docks
Waterloo
Surrey
Rotherhithe
Kensington
Westminster
Hammersmith
Victoria
Elephant & Castle
Chiswick
Chelsea
Battersea
Deptford
Fulham
Lambeth
Putney
Clapham
Camberwell
Wandsworth
Lewisham
Richmond Park
South Circular
Streatham
Penge
Miles
roundabout
Recommended road
tunnel
viaduct
Existing road
tunnel

← Raymond Unwin and Barry Parker, Sollershott Circus, Letchworth, 1908

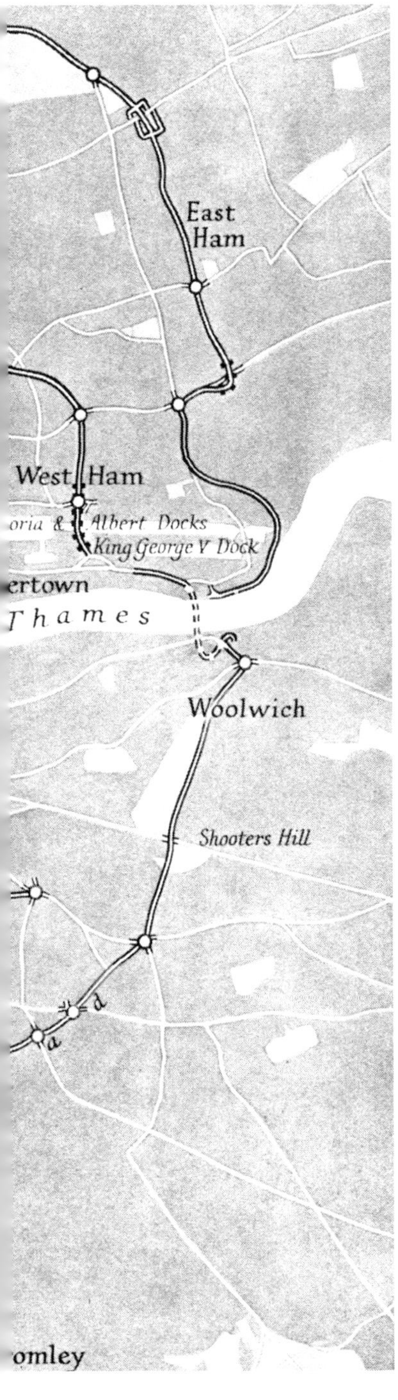

← Charles H. Bressey, inner London, "Greater London Highway Development Survey," 1939

↓ Inigo Triggs, “Plan Showing the Traffic Situation in London,” *Town Planning: Past, Present and Possible*, 1909

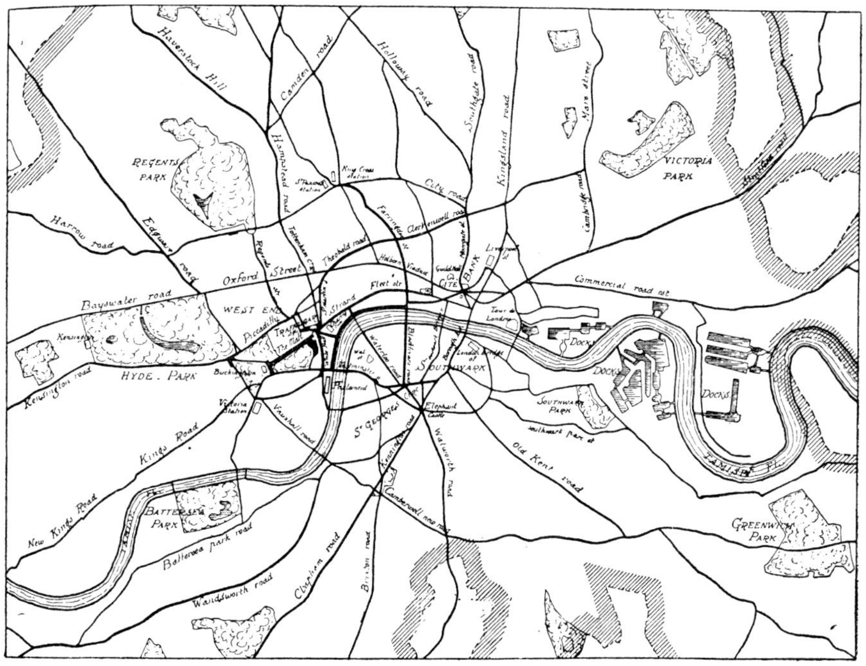

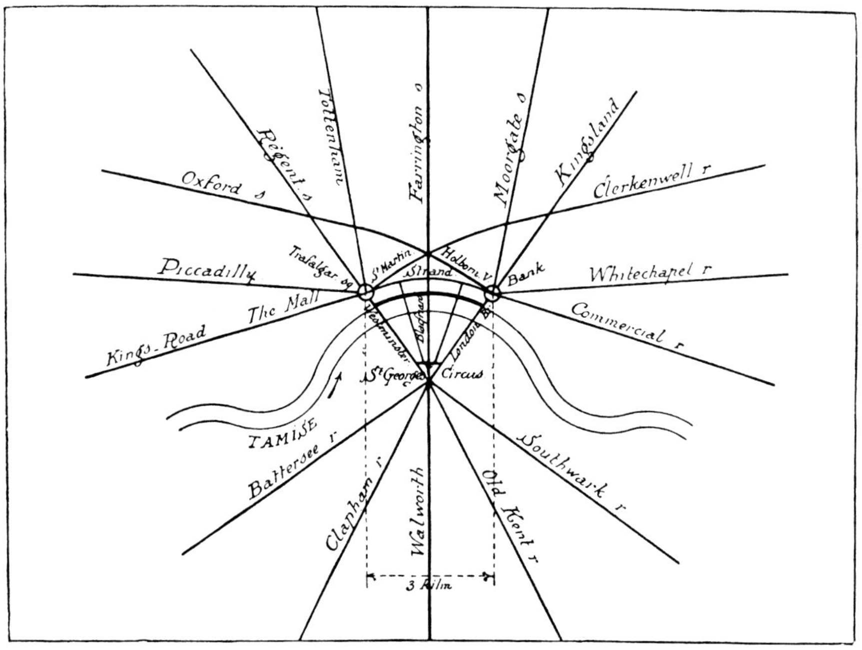

↑ Inigo Triggs, “Theoretical Plan of the Traffic Circulation of London,” *Town Planning: Past, Present and Possible*, 1909

↓ Walter Noble Twelvetrees, Piccadilly Circus, "London Street Traffic Regulation," 1907

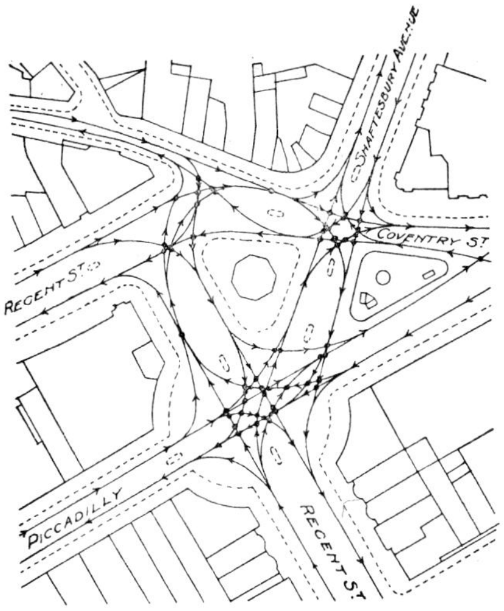

FIG. 9.—PICCADILLY CIRCUS.

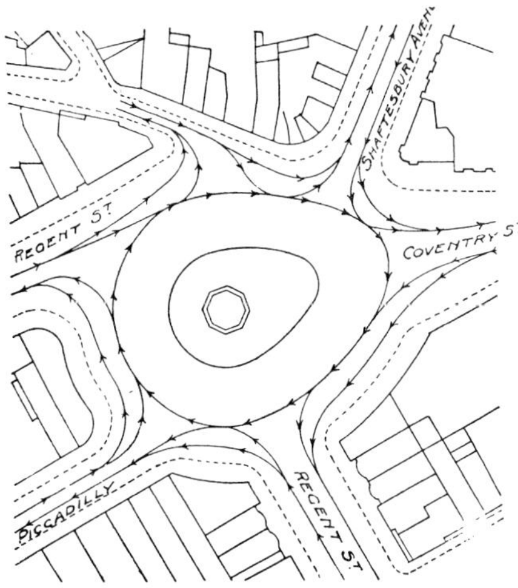

FIG. 10.—PICCADILLY CIRCUS WITH GYRATORY REGULATION.

↓ Walter Noble Twelvetrees, typical circus, "London Street Traffic Regulation," 1907

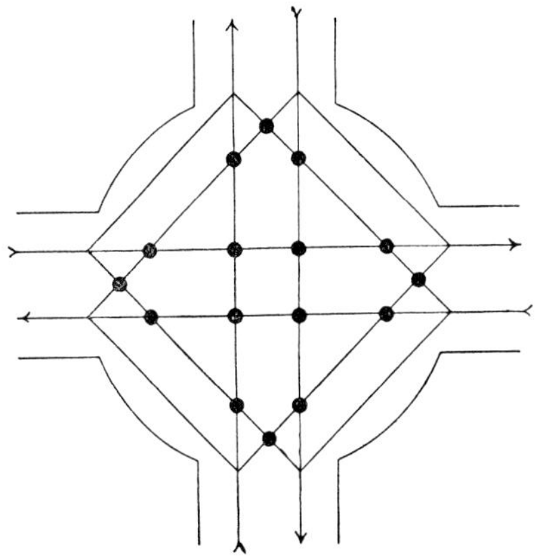

FIG. 1.—TYPICAL CIRCUS.

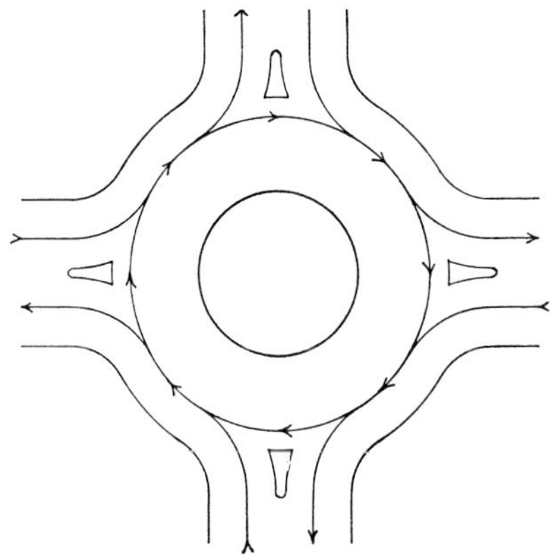

FIG. 2.—TYPICAL CIRCUS WITH GYRATORY REGULATION.

FIVE-BRANCH CROSSWAY

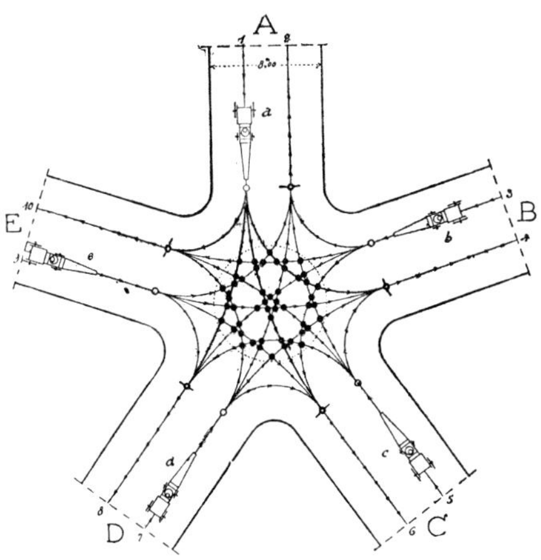

FIG. 46

○ 5 points of deviation from line of traffic
ϕ 5 points of junction with line of traffic
● 50 collision points

SIX-BRANCH CROSSWAY

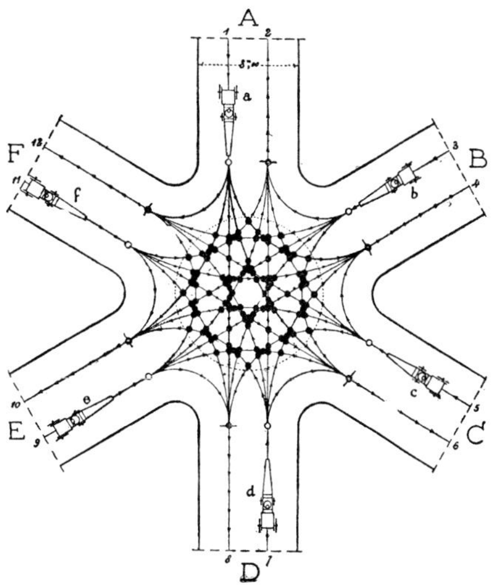

FIG. 47

○ 6 points of deviation from line of traffic
ϕ 6 points of junction with line of traffic
● 120 collision points

← Inigo Triggs, "Five and Six Branch Crossway," *Town Planning: Past, Present and Possible*, 1909

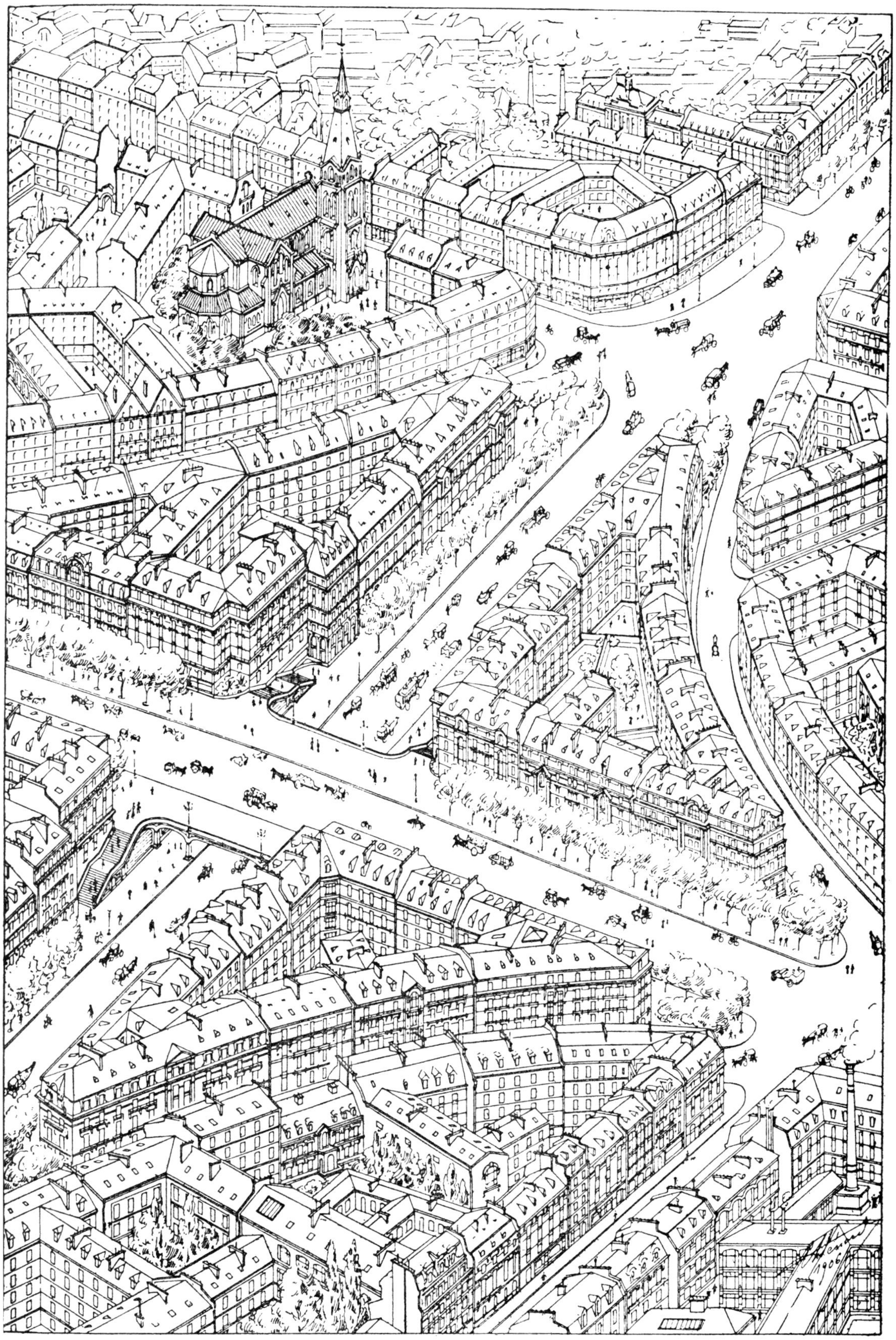

← Inigo Triggs, "Superimposed Thoroughfare after E. Hénard," *Town Planning: Past, Present and Possible*, 1909

As surprising as the attention paid by Bressey and Lutyens to roundabouts might seem, especially compared with plans drawn by their contemporaries, they were addressing precise needs that had long been considered by politicians, engineers, and architects alike. For example, a 1927 report published by the London and Home Counties Traffic Advisory Committee proposed roundabouts for the very places that were detailed ten years later in Bressey's report,[25] while in the previous year, a gyratory system was installed in Parliament Square (similar systems around the Victoria Memorial near Buckingham Palace, Hyde Park Corner, Trafalgar Square, and Marble Arch soon followed). Their function was to prevent traffic congestion at peak times by suppressing the number of cars crossing an intersection. (This was also the aim of a series of one-way streets introduced to manage traffic flow in the West End at Haymarket and Lower Regent Street between 10:30 and 11:30 p.m., the very time theaters were emptying.)[26] The first proposal for a modern roundabout to facilitate the flow of traffic in London was made in 1897 for Ludgate Circus. Ten years later, the engineer Walter Noble Twelvetrees placed roundabouts at eleven other locations across the city (one finds most of them, again, in Lutyens' map of 1942). In light of these precedents, the ingenuity of Bressey and Lutyens seems to derive less from the introduction of the roundabout to resolve a specific instance of circulation than from the decision to transfer that singular problem into a scheme that increases the flow of traffic across the entire city.

Bressey and Lutyens were of course not the first to broadly use this motif.[27] *Rond-points* had appeared in Paris since as far back as the seventeenth century. Initially a feature of forest and park design, they were installed by André Le Nôtre, gardener to Louis XIV, to give shape to what would become the grand avenue Champs-Élysées.[28] British relatives can be found in John Wood the Elder's design of the Circus at Bath (1754–1769) (whose inspiration was supposedly found in the circular, yet inverted shape of the Colosseum in Rome),[29] and in John Gwynn's 1766 improvement plans for London, which sought to clean up the city's haphazard streets, replacing them with straight, wide avenues as well as rectangular and circular garden squares. In Gwynn's proposal, however, the squares are situated outside principal routes[30] and are therefore not aimed at improving traffic flow. Instead, they participate in the "magnificence" of the city.[31] Three circular squares also appear in John Nash's 1811 scheme for Regent Street to facilitate circulation between Portland Place and Charing Cross: one for Oxford Circus, another at Piccadilly Circus, and a third at Regent's Park.[32]

Within the literature on architectural and urban design in Great Britain, the question of traffic in towns—and of the roundabout as a possible answer to its growing importance—was prominently discussed for the first time by Inigo Triggs in *Town Planning: Past, Present, Possible* of 1909. Among the books published on urban design around 1900, it is without doubt, one of the lesser known. Triggs, if mentioned at all, is better known for his historical studies on formal gardens.[33] One reason for his absence from British scholarship could be due to the reliance of *Town Planning* on existing contemporary theories in urban design, especially those of French engineer Eugène Hénard, whose conclusions on main routes and junctions in modern metropolises are closely followed by Triggs in his chapter on traffic. Triggs also reproduces Hénard's analysis of major European cities depicting Paris, Berlin, Moscow, and London as regular, often symmetric, figures developed out of the straight lines of their main thoroughfares. The plan of London and its narrow, twisting streets is transformed into a triangular scheme, with St George's Circus, Trafalgar Square, and Bank located as the junctions at each corner. Paris, by contrast, becomes an ellipse crisscrossed by a north-south and an east-west axis, while Berlin appears as an almost perfect circle of radials, and Moscow as a concentric city, partially interrupted by the Moskva. In line with his newly envisioned metropolises, Triggs offers several proposals to prevent any impediment, including the division of traffic by speed or the superimposition of one street over the other (as with the Holborn Viaduct), or—more easily implemented—the organization of traffic by way of a "gyratory system."[34] Such a solution could transform the "hopeless confusion" at any junction into a "gyratory procession, receiving and distributing traffic along tangential curves" and therefore "obviating all forms of conflict."[35] Triggs borrowed his urban examples not only from Hénard, but also Walter Noble Twelvetrees, the expert in "traffic regulation,"[36] whose roundabouts for Oxford Circus and Piccadilly Circus both turn out in *Town Planning*.[37]

For architects, planners, engineers, or urban historians in the second half of the nineteenth century and the first years of the twentieth, the challenges of urban design are first and foremost problems of circulation and the containment of "flow." Any kind of obstruction—congestion, accidents, or even riots—is to be avoided.[38] The necessary interventions not only concern the breakthrough of new roads but also the development of new systems for waste, sewage, or ventilation.[39] By the interwar period, however, the focus shifts from the simple provision of new circulation spaces to the flawless operation and regulation of those traffic flows.[40] When it came to the "street traffic flow," wrote the railway engineer Henry Watson in his 1933 book which devoted over four hundred pages to the subject, it was necessary to analyze the "behaviour of street traffic ... the causes that retard its circulation; the magnitude of their effect; and the means, that can be adopted to expedite movement."[41] Special attention is given to crossing and junctions. For Watson, these represented the biggest cause for delays in modern cities, and he concluded that in such instances, the roundabout was "supreme" for its "low cost, little delay, ability to pass heavy turning traffic, freedom from the danger of collisions, architectural opportunities and ease of supervision."[42] Perhaps unsurprisingly, and in contrast to the thoroughfares of Hénard and Triggs, Watson's "ideal city" featured no fewer than 250 roundabouts all dotted across the urban area and its surrounding territory.[43] Watson's city is a pure network represented by dotted, dashed, and straight lines illustrating the different traffic types and circular nodal points whose resulting shapes are determined by traffic types and its relation to the activities of the city. At the core of Watson's scheme is a rectangle that frames a central park. This is transected by local traffic. The park is surrounded by a larger, still rectangular, grid for slower traffic, which is in turn bordered by further parks, mainline train stations, and shopping or leisure areas. Three further rings and arterial roads distribute the traffic between the center and the outskirts of the city.

By comparison, the proposals by Bressey and Lutyens are less systematic than Watson's, focusing still on "through routes," roundabouts for junctions, and their formal expression, but the overall ambition of the plan as network seems to have gone unnoticed by their contemporaries who considered the schemes old fashioned. Maxwell Fry had ridiculed the proposal of "Sir Charles" as "clearing a way here, joining up this point and that" while describing the Academy plan of "Sir Edwin" as merely "dropping Georgian nosegays at focal points."[44] Lionel Brett had been more succinct in his summation, labeling the Academy plan simply as "new Haussmann."[45] And indeed, the plan did not respond to the formal ambitions that would be pursued, neither by the avant-garde nor by engineers. A good impression of the rather distant reception of Bressey's plan by contemporary architects and planners was given some years later by Colin Buchanan, the planner and academic who oversaw the influential study *Traffic in Town* of 1963 and who drily described the proposal as an "improvement of the 'through routes.'"[46] Even if some of those very routes would be realized in the postwar years, Buchanan's appraisal denied the plan any innovative value for modern traffic.[47]

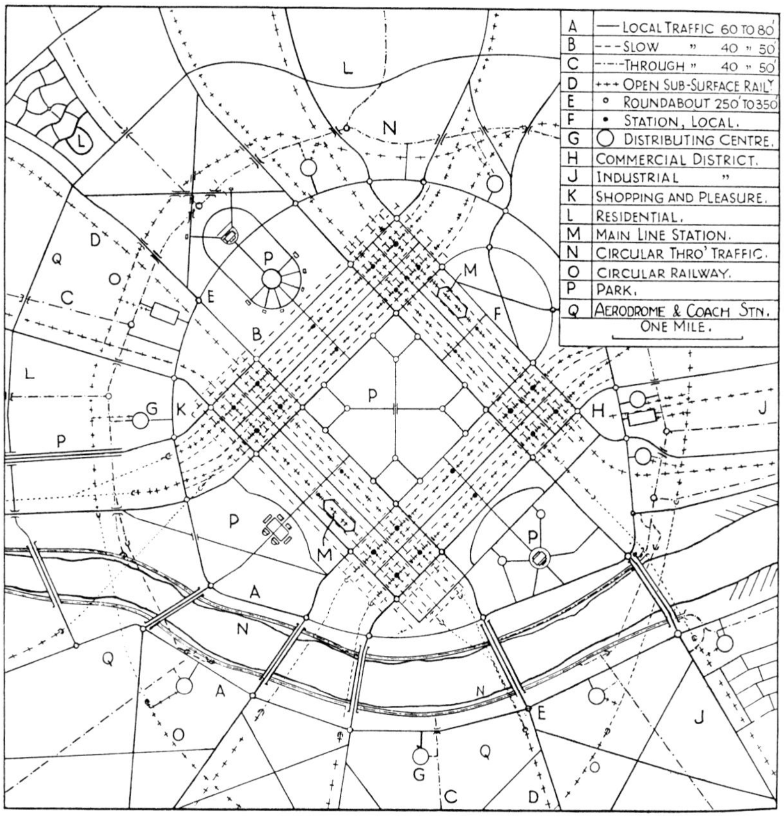
A — Local Traffic 60 to 80'
B --- Slow " 40 " 50'
C -·-·- Through " 40 " 50'
D +++ Open Sub-Surface Rail'y
E ∘ Roundabout 250' to 350'
F • Station, Local.
G ○ Distributing Centre.
H Commercial District.
J Industrial "
K Shopping and Pleasure.
L Residential.
M Main Line Station.
N Circular Thro' Traffic.
O Circular Railway.
P Park.
Q Aerodrome & Coach Stn.
One Mile.

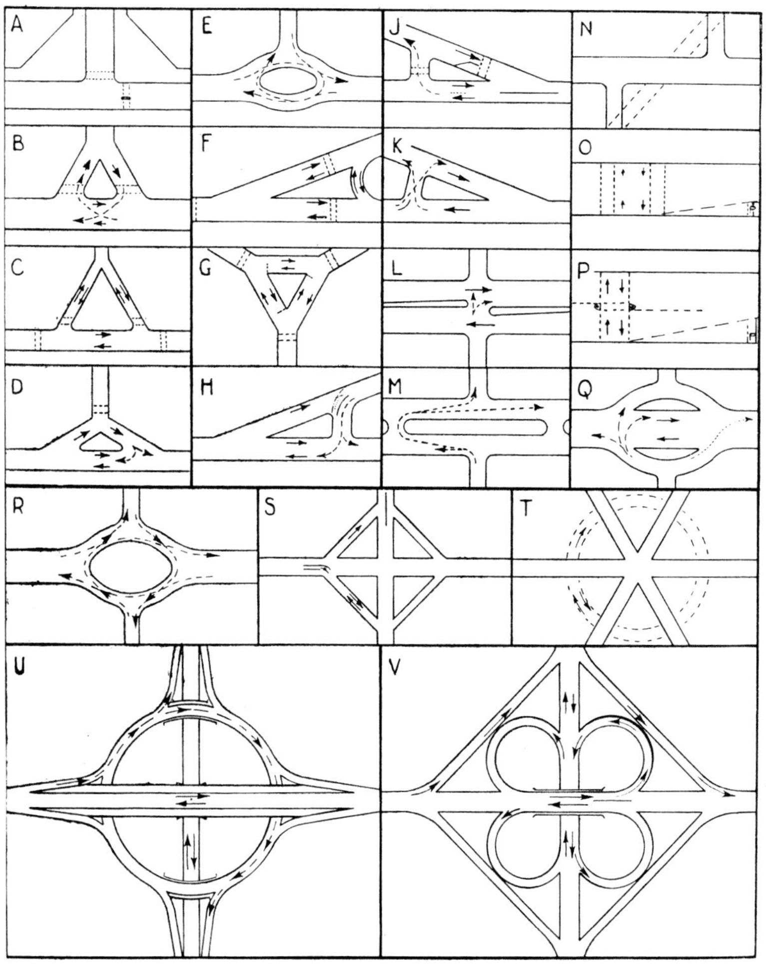
A
E
J
N
B
F
K
O
C
G
L
P
D
H
M
Q
R
S
T
U
V

← Henry Watson, "Ideal City," *Street Traffic Flow*, 1933

↙ Henry Watson, "Arrangement of Junctions and Crossings," *Street Traffic Flow*, 1933

In formal terms, Bressey's and Lutyens' proposals may have been less innovative than those that followed. What they did manifest, however, was the very idea of a network, as formulated by Watson, both in its technical dimension as a grid-like arrangement of roads linked together by traffic-nodes, as well as in its organic sense, as an overall system for traffic flows.[48] This idea sits at the core of British post-war planning, statistically corroborated and systematically elaborated in Buchanan's study two decades later.[49] The report looked at the long-term development and effects of motor traffic in Britain's urban areas and argued for town and road planners to work together. More surprising perhaps was the fact that despite presenting a number of detailed options for dealing with traffic in cities—from restricting it to completely rebuilding whole areas—the report made no definitive recommendations, but proposed alternatives:[50] "We have taken a bull into the china shop and to that old problem there are only two answers: shoot the bull, or, more creatively, build a new china shop specifically designed for bulls," wrote Buchanan.[51] For him, it was not a matter of choosing one option or the other, but using the information at hand to tame the traffic beast.

In a section titled "Practical Studies," Buchanan observed the effects of traffic in four different locations across the UK, including the small town of Newbury, the large town of Leeds, the historic city of Norwich, and an area of Central London. For the Central London study a quadrant southwest of Euston and Tottenham Court Road (essentially Fitzrovia) was analyzed. Buchanan carefully outlined the dimensions of the area, which he determined based on the activities taking place and the size of a basic unit of the road network laid out over the city. This led to a slightly distorted module of eight-lane primary roads, which covered the northern portion of the central area analyzed by Bressey in 1937. In Bressey's plan, roads, squares, bridges, and tunnels were simply inscribed within the existing urban tissue. The primary function of the network was to guarantee good circulation and to avoid accidents or delays. While Buchanan's grid might have followed the same geometrical order, at least in the explanatory schemes, what held it together was its organizational logic. Hence the need to determine the most efficient relation between the size of the required area, the capacity of the road (especially for accommodating junctions and ramps), and the amount of traffic.[52] The geometry of the network, writes Buchanan when explaining its advantage for urban planning, is justified because of its good distribution and the advantage of simple intersections.[53]

Even if Buchanan had dismissed the innovative value of Bressey's work, it was Bressey's study that first introduced two innovations into urban planning research, that would unfold in the Post War years: the first, a "Traffic Delay Observation," measured the speed and delays on different routes through central London and recommended the advantages of roundabouts to ease congestion; the second, an "Origin and Destination' Census," charted the courses of vehicles through the metropolis. Focusing on the Docklands area, Bressey recorded the destinations of individual transport drivers as well as their chosen routes, transforming the map of London into a register of vehicles and people in motion. By reducing the city to points of origin and terminus, Bressey replaced the more conventional space-time continuum that had once characterized the urban experience of the pedestrian or carriage-driver (represented by Lutyens in his large perspectives) with the duration (or delay) of travel between two separate addresses across the city, recorded as figures in a series of tables.[54]

In Bressey's scheme and more so in Lutyens' academy plan, the effect of the census was secondary to the issue of the overall design of the network. Of course, Lutyens had presented the city's new junctions and squares to be crossed by people and vehicles (cars, buses, and ships), but in the drawings they are merely symbols for traffic. Eighteen years later, however, both origin and destination were central to *Traffic in Towns*. As Buchanan writes, "every building in a town has become dependent for its continued functioning upon frequent servicing by motor vehicles,"[55] a condition that now necessitated the proper study and layout of journeys in and out of the city. In a series of diagrams overlaid onto different town plans, the journeys are represented as straight lines of different colors and thicknesses depending on their type and frequency of movement. Graphically, at least, the problem of traffic is reduced to that of a linear communication between "origin" and "destination." In a study of Leeds, for example, no fewer than four diagrams are deployed to show different journey types: a web-like network illustrates a worker's commute; a concentric network describes that of a shopping trip; bulk-transport is represented by a concentric network around three cores; and forecasting into the year 2010, industrial, commercial, and business journeys appear again as webs. Together these networks inform Buchanan's fittingly professorial proposal for a "theoretical network," comprising a ring-road around the town center with a two-tier hexagonal system to answer questions of density and desired movement. In the different diagrams, more than in the final proposal, traffic is recorded as (statistical) data moving from one point to the other. As a result, addresses—houses, shops, factories, or public buildings—become points of varying activity.

↓ Colin Buchanan, "Theoretical Arrangement of internal Distributors within the Primary Grid," *Traffic in Towns*, 1963

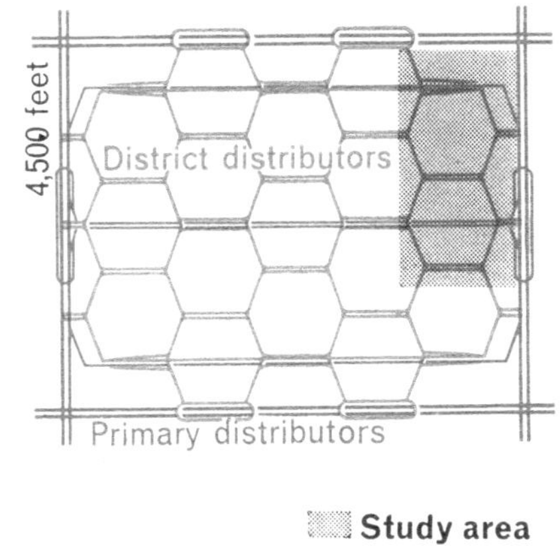

↓ Colin Buchanan, "Alternative Arrangements of the Primary Grid," *Traffic in Towns*, 1963

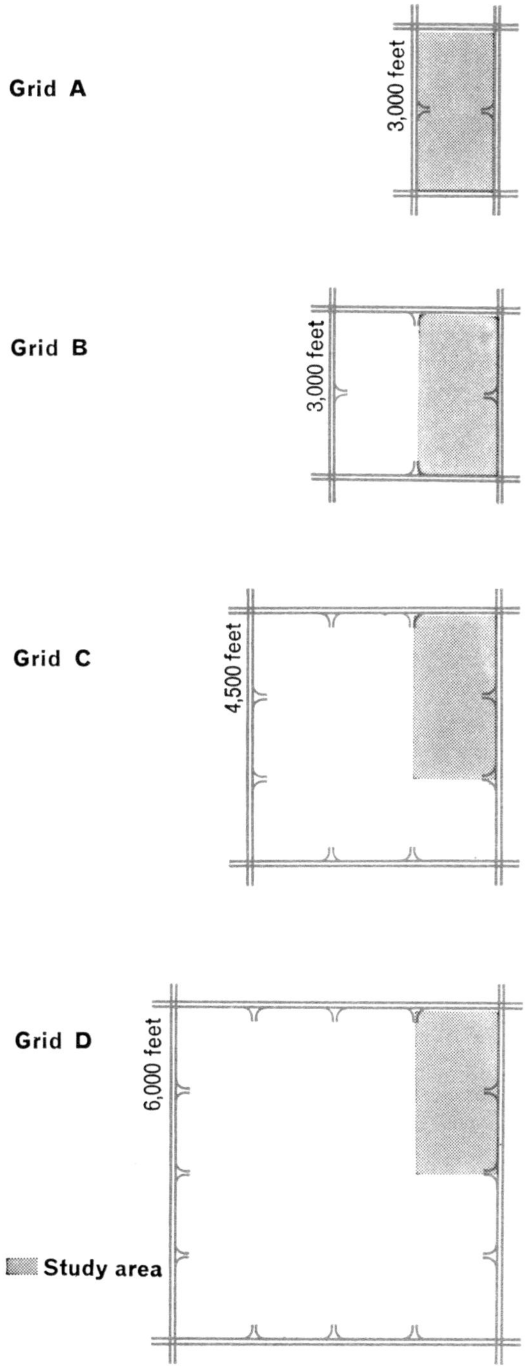

↓ Colin Buchanan, "The Assumed Relationship of the Study Area to Hypothetical Primary and Regional Networks," *Traffic in Towns*, 1963

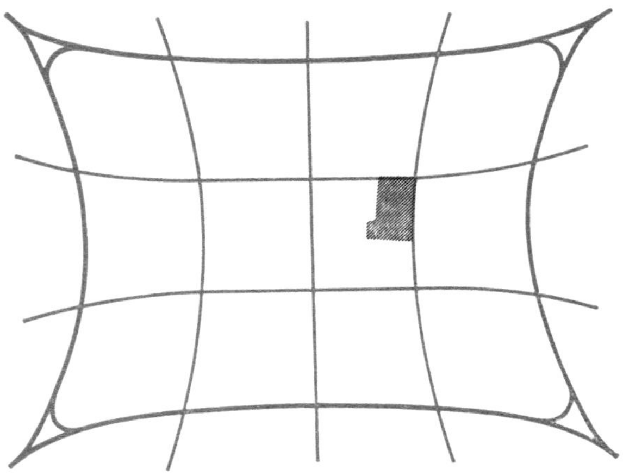

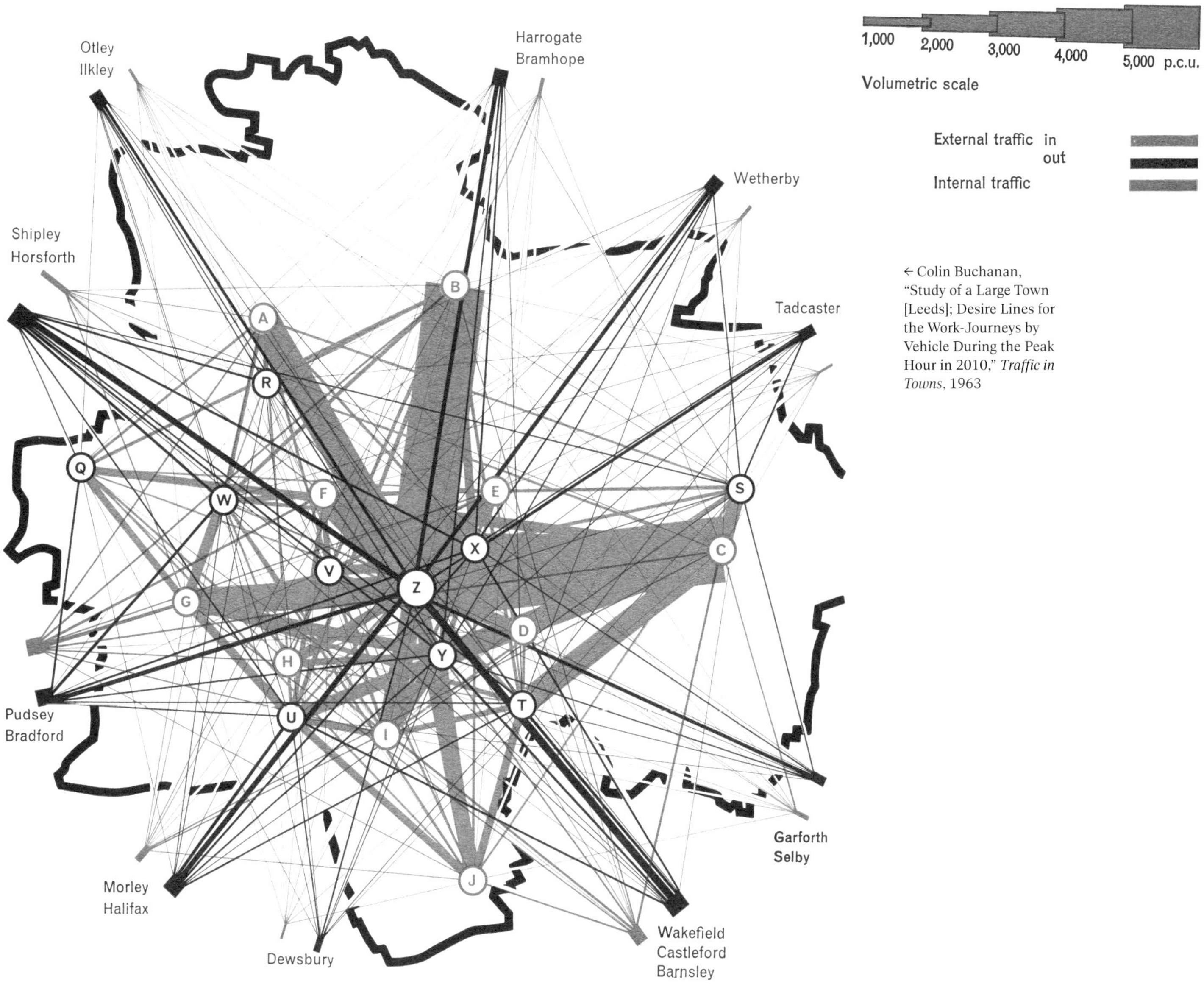

← Colin Buchanan, "Study of a Large Town [Leeds]; Desire Lines for the Work-Journeys by Vehicle During the Peak Hour in 2010," *Traffic in Towns*, 1963

↓ Colin Buchanan, "Study of a Large Town [Leeds]; Three Alternative Arrangements for the Treatment of Distributors within the Central Part of the City," *Traffic in Towns*, 1963

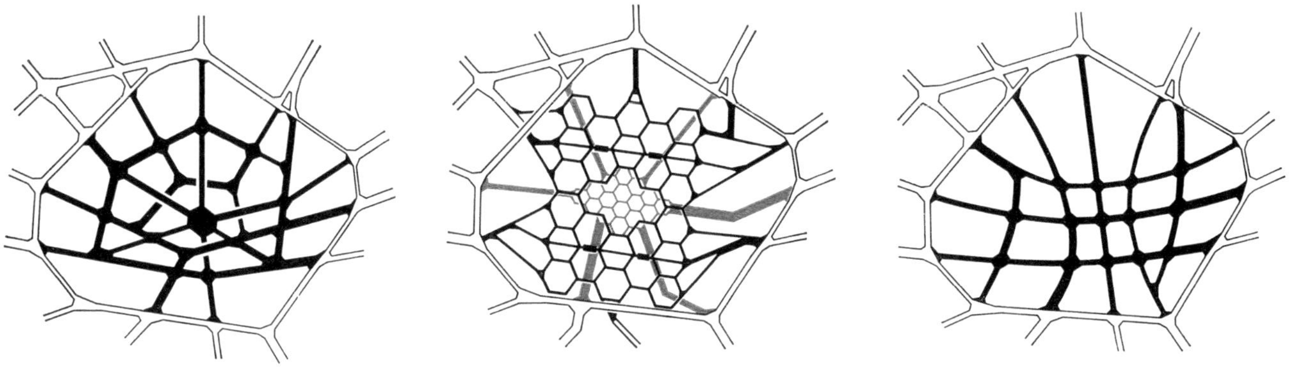

→ "Land-Use Budget," in Milton Keynes Development Corporation (ed.), *The Plan for Milton Keynes*, 1970

→ "Strategic Plan," in Milton Keynes Development Corporation (ed.), *The Plan for Milton Keynes*, 1970

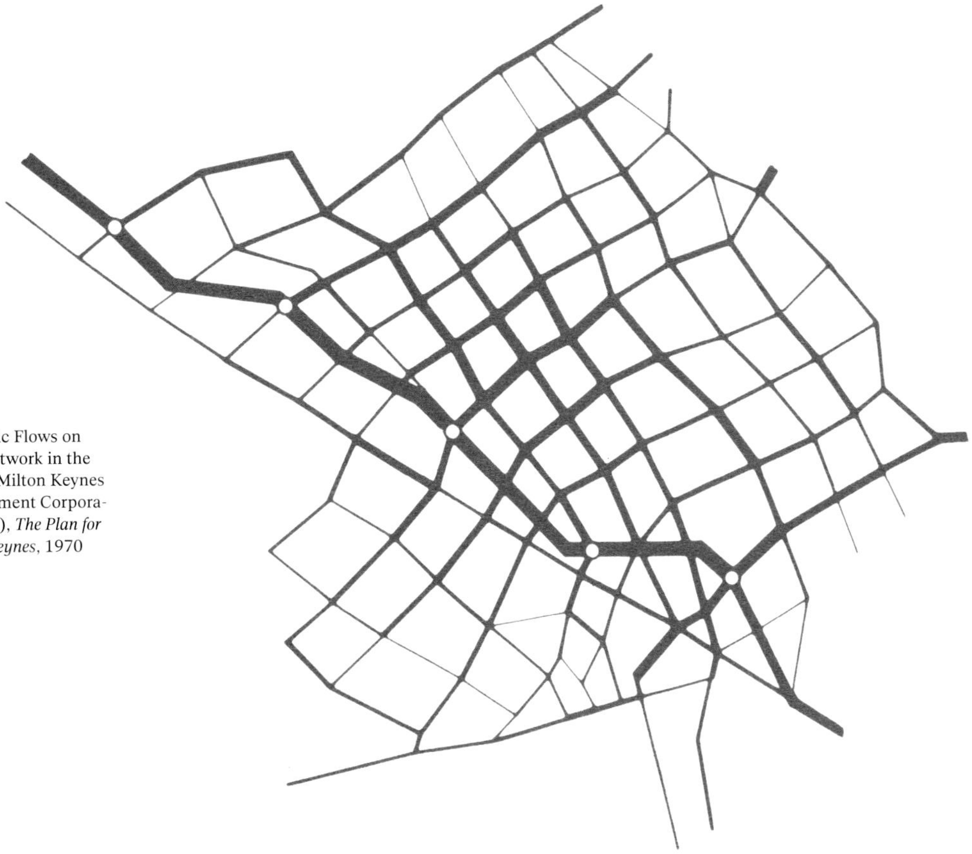

→ "Traffic Flows on Road Network in the 1990s," Milton Keynes Development Corporation (ed.), *The Plan for Milton Keynes*, 1970

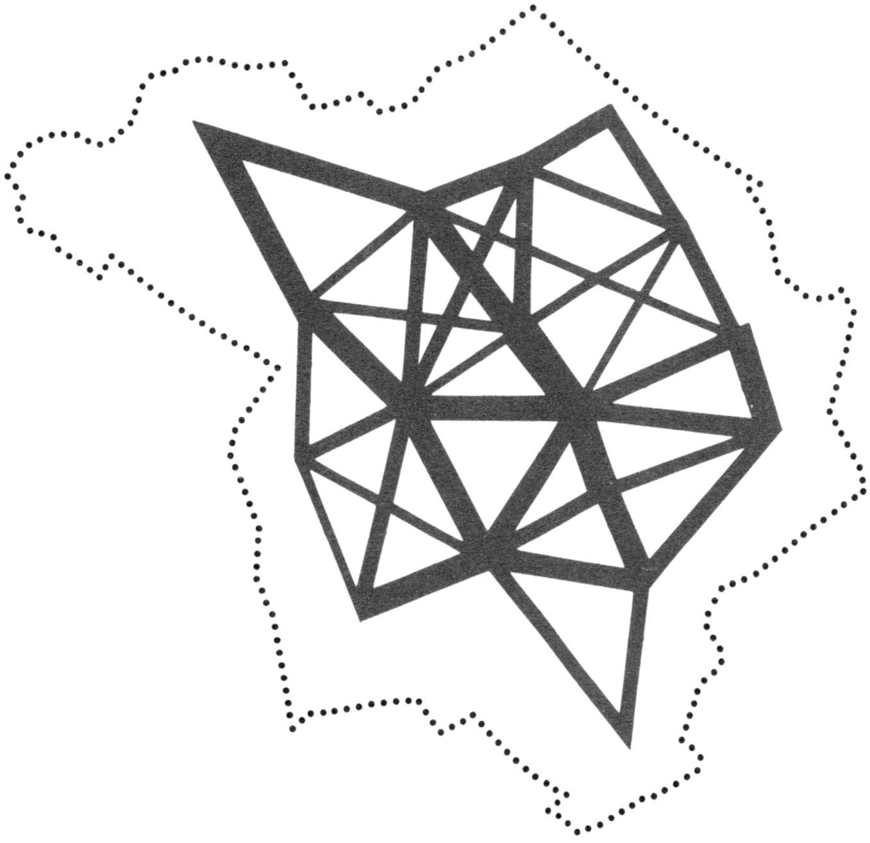

→ "Total Peak Hour Trip for Preferred Distribution of Employment Areas," in Milton Keynes Development Corporation (ed.), *The Plan for Milton Keynes*, 1970

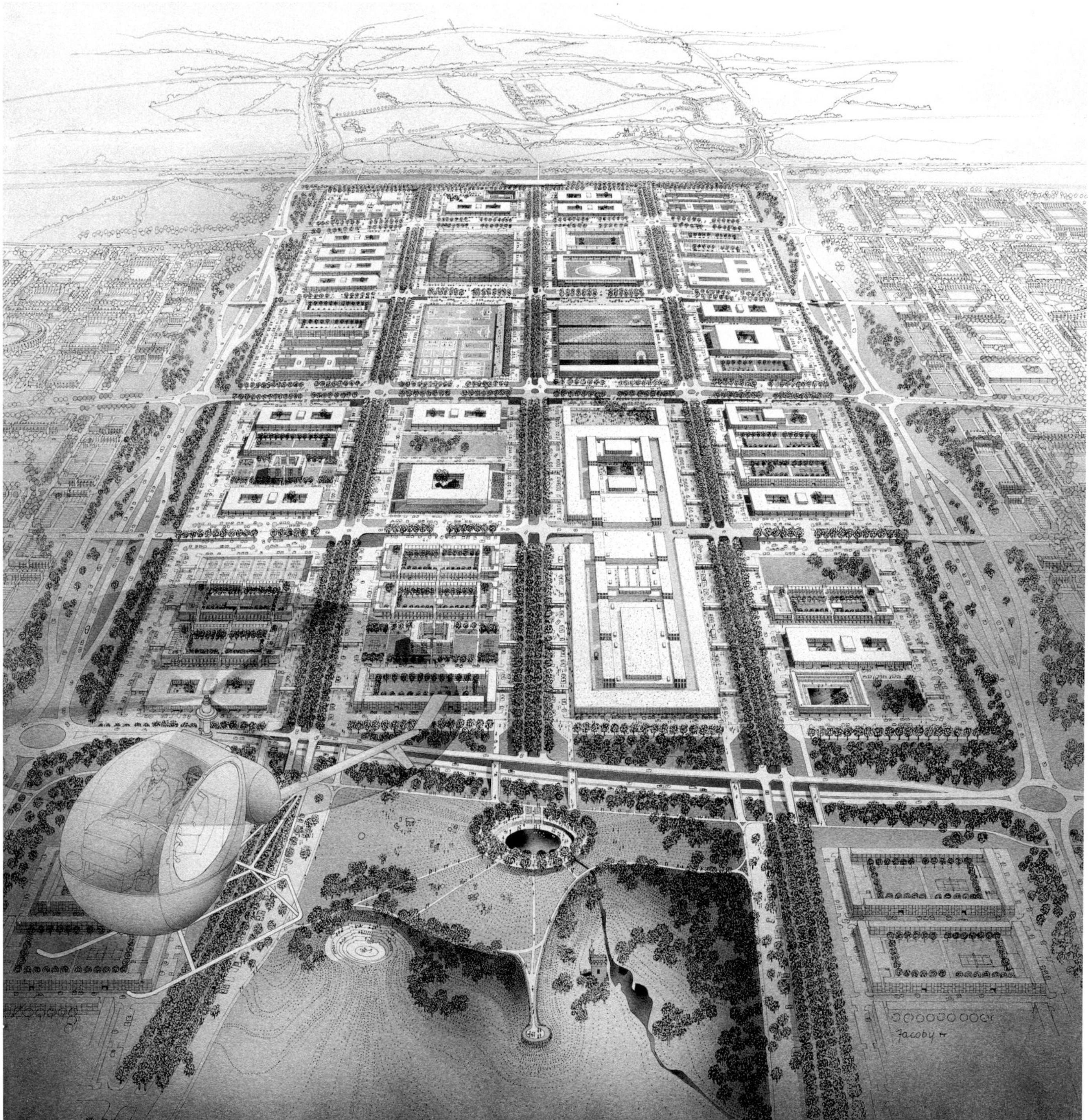
Jacoby

← Helmut Jacoby, Central Milton Keynes in 1990, 1974

How to understand the city-plan as a register was precisely the question that the interdisciplinary team led by the architect and planner Richard Llewelyn-Davies addressed only a few years later, first in the planning of the New Town of Washington in 1965,[56] and most prominently in the New Town of Milton Keynes, from 1967.[57] Two sketches best illustrate their intentions: in the strategic town plan of Milton Keynes, aimed at giving the "maximum opportunities and to increase choice,"[58] the different land uses are shown as dots or squares of different colors regularly dispersed over the site, so as to ensure their best access. Residential areas are evenly distributed, employment is dispersed in concentrated zones, the main town center is located at the junction of the two main roads. The ideal traffic pattern is represented in a web or "spider diagram" reflecting the "volume and direction of peak hour car travel" between employment areas and housing. That pattern would later be translated into a grid of main roads to assure a smooth and convenient distribution over the whole site, with local "activity centers" comprising shops, schools, bus stops, or pubs situated at the cross-points to the pedestrian routes. The grid system, write the plan's authors, "would combine good general accessibility for the dispersed land uses of the plan with a high degree of flexibility to adapt to growth and change."[59]

At Milton Keynes the grid, network, and register collapse. The new town is not only a geometrical layout (in the sense of a vertical projection of a real or imagined form of settlement), or a network (i.e., a diagram of traffic streams), but also a register, because Milton Keynes was not planned for existing inhabitants, but for a targeted population. The strategic plan, and indeed the realized town itself, presupposed the ability to attribute any spot on the ground to a (future) activity. In Milton Keynes in return, both vehicles and people represent data that, in the words of media historian Bernhard Siegert, are either stored under addresses that precede them, "logically and temporally," or defined by "addresses in advance."[60] Within this context the idea of an address implies either transportation routes and their nodes, which are likely to become congested in peak travel periods and are represented by the width of the spider diagram, or the activities described by the distribution of land uses illustrated as colorful dots and squares in the strategic plan.

It would be tempting to compare the grid of Milton Keynes to that of the MARS Plan of 1938[61] and to the great number of grid-like schemes that have shaped Britain's urban and landscape history, from its Roman origins and Wren's proposals for London, to the extension of Edinburgh and other cities. Both the MARS plan and the scheme for Milton Keynes break the well-known genealogy of circular models. They rely instead on the modern grid, a cultural technique that stands for a rational, even autonomous, approach to urban planning. Individually, however, the two grid-proposals represent their own specific understanding of urban organization as it evolved throughout the twentieth century: from a conception of the modern city as a well-defined entity, whose functions are individualized and precisely distributed in time and space (and circumscribed, as in Howard's *Garden Cities of To-Morrow* or in the MARS Plan, by a circular road and rail service for goods), to an understanding of the city as an environment conceived to accommodate the different activities of its users and to react to their changing needs through time. The MARS Plan consists of individual elements with clearly distinct functions:[62] factories, houses, places of leisure, and traffic infrastructures.[63] Milton Keynes, by contrast, despite all that it evidently borrows from the modernist city, consists of a system of activities linked together by an evenly distributing grid that no longer separates different functions in individual units, but connects them. Milton Keynes knows no function, only activities that, stimulated or not, are all smoothly connected by roundabouts.

Already in 1937 Bressey had been commissioned to improve "communication" by road. To achieve this, he secured "data" by traffic-census with the precise aim of opening up new and more "adequate communications."[64] Yet however radical the approach may have seemed, the proposed solutions remained conventional. Thirty years later, communication was central to the planning of Milton Keynes, with "easy movement, access and good communication" considered a primary goal.[65] But the issue was no longer a simple matter of facilitating transit "from home to certain defined locations." Instead, communication had to guarantee the "convenient movement in any direction across the whole town."[66] The very notion of communication as a physical and communal undertaking as defined throughout the nineteenth century and interwar period is, in Milton Keynes, challenged by novel technologies. The car allowed communication to occur with increasing independence of questions of distance or place, leading to a growing distinction between "accessibility" and "propinquity."[67] The result in the new town is the separation between roads and frontage that enables one to drive through the city and not realize it.[68] The main aim of the road is primarily to carry the traffic easily from "door to door,"[69] smoothly and without interruption through the numerous—today more than 130—roundabouts that eventually replaced the intended computer-phased traffic lights.[70] If the circle that defines London and those of other cities, like Birmingham or Manchester, represents the signs of a hierarchic relation between city and countryside, or in the case of the green belt, the expansion of the urban environment, at Milton Keynes, its role is reversed. The circle no longer circumscribes or circumvents any urban area but, rather, forms its very center, evenly distributing traffic throughout an ever-expanding environment.

1 Anonymous, "A Nobler City," in *London Replanned: The Royal Academy Planning Committee's Interim Report*, foreword by Edwin Lutyens and introduction by Charles Bressey (London: Country Life Limited, 1942), 16.

2 "Papers relating to the Royal Academy Planning Committee," 1941–1942, Royal Academy of Arts Archive, Sir Edwin Lutyens, PRA, papers, RAA/PRA/7/2, https://www.royalacademy.org.uk/art-artists/archive/papers-relating-to-the-royal-academy-planning-committee.

3 Anonymous, "Waterloo Bridge—Strand Junction," in *London Replanned: The Royal Academy Planning Committee's Interim Report*, foreword by Edwin Lutyens and introduction by Charles Bressey (London: Country Life Limited, 1942), 16.

4 See Christopher Hussey, "A Vision of the New London," *Country Life*, October 9, 1942, 692–696, here, 692, 695.

5 Hussey, "A Vision of the New London," 696.

6 John Summerson: *Georgian London* (London: Barrie & Jenkins, 1988), 97–99.

7 *London Replanned*, 5.

8 Gordon Emanuel Cherry, *Town Planning in Britain Since 1900: The Rise and Fall of the Planning Ideal* (Oxford: Blackwell Publishers, 1996), 39–40.

9 Nikolaus Pevsner, "Building with Wit: The Architecture of Sir Edwin Lutyens," *Architectural Review* 109, no. 652, April 1951, 216–225, here 220.

10 David Thomas, "London's Green Belt: The Evolution of an Idea," *Ekistiks 17*, no. 100 (March 1964): 177–181, here 177. See also: Frederic James Osborn, *Green-Belt Cities: The British Contribution* (London: Faber & Faber, 1946).

11 Patrick Abercrombie, *Greater London Plan 1944* (London: His Majesty's Stationery Office, 1945), 20.

12 John Summerson: "The Royal Academy Committee's Plan for London: London Hereafter," *The Architect and Building News* 172, October 30, 1942, 77–78, here 77. First published in the *Listener*, October 22, 1942, 532–533

13 Summerson, "The Royal Academy Committee's Plan for London."

14 Christa Kamleithner, *Ströme und Zonen: Eine Genealogie der "funktionalen Stadt"* (Basel: Birkhäuser, 2020), 66–67.

15 David John Rooney, *The Traffic Problem: Geographies, Politics, and Technologies of Congestion in Twentieth-Century London* (PhD diss., University of London, 2016), 36–37.

16 Banister Fletcher, "Report of the Committee," in *Second Report of the Greater London Regional Planning Committee* (London: Knapp, Drewett & Sons, 1933), 7–11, here 8.

17 Howard was influenced by Edward Bellamy's science-fiction novel, *Looking Backward*, whose main character time travels from late-1900s Boston to the same city of the twenty-first century where he encounters familiar monuments and buildings of the past.

18 See Peter Hall, Dennis Hardy, and Colin Ward, "The Town-Country Magnet," in Ebenezer Howard, *To-Morrow: A Peaceful Path to Real Reform* [original edition with commentary by Peter Hall, Dennis Hardy, and Colin Ward] (London: Routledge, 2003), 39.

19 Ebenezer Howard, *To-Morrow: A Peaceful Path to Real Reform* (1898), 12–19

20 Raymond Unwin, *Town Planning in Practice: An Introduction to the Art of Designing Cities and Suburbs* (London: Fisher, 1909), 3.

21 Unwin, *Town Planning in Practice*, 3–4.

22 Unwin, *Town Planning in Practice*, 16.

23 David Gilbert, "London of the Future: The Metropolis Reimagined after the Great War," *Journal of British Studies* 43, no. 1 (2004): 91–119, here 106–107.

24 Edwin Lutyens, quoted in Charles H. Bressey, *Highway Development Survey 1937 (Greater London)* (London: His Majesty's Stationery Office, 1938), 34.

25 *Second Report of the London and Home Counties Traffic Advisory Committee* (London: HSOM 1927).

26 *Second Report of the London and Home Counties Traffic Advisory Committee* (London: HSOM 1927), 29–33, quoted in Kenneth Todd, "A History of Roundabouts in Britain," *Transportation Quarterly* 45, no. 1 (January 1991): 143–155, here 145–146.

27 In engineering literature, the roundabout is first mentioned, retroactively around 1914. C. J. D. Laurence, "Roundabouts—Evolution, Revolution and the Future," *The Highway Engineer* 27, no. 5 (May 1980): 2–10, here 2–3.

28 John Summerson, *Architecture in Britain: 1530 to 1830* (Harmondsworth: Penguin, 1969 [1953]), 232.

29 John Joseph Bishop, *The Role of the Circus and Crescent in 18th and 19th Century British Town Planning* (PhD diss., Boston University, 1962), 24.

30 Éric Alonzo, *Du rond-point au giratoire* (Marseille: Parenthèses, 2005), 43–44.

31 John Gwynn, *London and Westminster Improved, Illustrated by Plans: To which is prefixed, a Discourse on publick Magnificence with Observations on the State of Arts and Artists in this Kingdom, Wherein the Study of the Polite Arts is recommended as necessary to a liberal Education: Concluded by some Proposals relative to Places not laid down in the Plans* (London, 1766), 1–21.

32 John Summerson, "The New Street," in *The Life and Work of John Nash, Architect* (London: George Allen and Unwin, 1980), 75–89. See also Geoffrey Tyack, "Reshaping the West End," in *John Nash, Architect of the Picturesque*, ed. Geoffrey Tyack (Swindon: English Heritage, 2013), 101–124, here 103–107.

33 See Mrs. W. de l'Hôpital, "Harry Inigo Triggs [Obituary]," in: *RIBA Journal* 30, no. 13 (12 May 1923): 431.

34 H. Inigo Triggs, *Town Planning: Past, Present and Possible* (London: Methuen, 1909), 152

35 Triggs, *Town Planning*, 156–157.

36 Walter Noble Twelvetrees, "London Street Traffic Regulation," *Transactions: Civil and Mechanical Engineers Society* (1907): 1–24.

37 Triggs cited examples from Twelvetrees, "London Street Traffic Regulation," 1–24.

38 Triggs, *Town Planning*, 285.

39 Moritz Gleich, "Liquid Crowds: Regulatory Discourse and the Architecture of People Flows in the Nineteenth Century," *Greyroom* 67 (2017): 44–63, here 49.

40 On the society of control, see Frédéric Gros, *Le Principe Sécurité* (Paris: Éditions Gallimard, 2012), 173–218.

41 Henry Watson, *Street Traffic Flow* (London: Chapman and Hall, 1933), 1.

42 Watson, *Street Traffic Flow*, 334.

43 Watson, *Street Traffic Flow*, 337–338.

44 Maxwell Fry, *Fine Buildings* (London: Faber & Faber, 1944), 111.

45 Lionel Brett, "The new Hausmann" *Architectural Review* 93, no. 553 (January 1943): 23-26.

46 Colin D. Buchanan: "The Road Traffic Problem in Great Britain," *Town Planning Review Quarterly* 26 (January 1956): 215–237, here 225.

47 Buchanan, "The Road Traffic Problem in Great Britain."

48 On networks, see Alexander R. Galloway, "Networks," in *Critical Terms for Media Studies*, ed. W. J. Thomas Mitchell (Chicago: University of Chicago Press, 2010), 280–296, here 286.

49 Colin D. Buchanan, *Traffic in Towns: A Study of the Long-Term Problems of Traffic in Urban Areas: Reports of the Steering Group and Working Group Appointed by the Minister of Transport* (London: Her Majesty's Stationery Office, 1963), 1. On the Buchanan report, see Simon Gunn, "The Buchanan Report, Environment, and the Problem of Traffic in 1960s Britain," *Twentieth Century British History* 22, no. 4 (2011): 521–542.

50 Colin D. Buchanan, "Urban planning: 'Only way to avoid future chaos,'" quoted in Otto Saumarez Smith, *Boom Cities: Architect-Planners and the Politics of Radical Urban Renewal in 1960s Britain* (Oxford: Oxford University Press, 2019), footnote 13.

51 Colin Buchanan quoted in Otto Saumarez Smith, *Boom Cities: Architect Planners and the Politics of Radical Urban Renewal in 1960s Britain* (Oxford: Oxford University Press, 2019): 17

52 Buchanan, *Traffic in Towns*, 132.

53 Buchanan, *Traffic in Towns*, 43.

54 See Wolfgang Schivelbusch, *The Railway Journey: The Industrialization of Time and Space in the Nineteenth Century* (Berkeley: University of California Press, 1986) 33–44.

55 Buchanan, *Traffic in Towns*, 35.

56 On New Washington, see *Washington New Town: Master Plan and Report* (Washington: Washington Development Corporation, 1966).

57 On the history of Milton Keynes, see Mark Clapson, *A Social History of Milton Keynes: Middle England/Edge City* (London: Frank Cass, 2004). Note the reference to the importance of the city for contemporary literature. For more on the plan of Milton Keynes, see Mark Clapson, "The Plan for Milton Keynes: The Garden City Heritage and the New Towns programme," in *The Plan for Milton Keynes* (London: Routledge, 2013), 1–26. On the American influences on British urbanism and on Milton Keynes in particular, see Mark Clapson, *Anglo-American Crossroads: Urban Planning and Research in Britain, 1940–2010* (London: Bloomsbury, 2013), esp. 79–98. A lively account of the voices involved in the planning of Milton Keynes is given in Mark Clapson et al., eds., *The Best Laid Plans: Milton Keynes Since 1967* (Luton: University of Luton Press 1998). On the broader socio-political context, see Guy Ortolano, *Thatcher's Progress: From Social Democracy to Market Liberalism through an English New Town* (New York: Cambridge University Press, 2019). On the representation of Milton Keynes in the media, see Lauren *Pikó, Milton Keynes in British Culture: Imagining England (London: Routledge, 2019).*

58 Milton Keynes Development Corporation, ed., *The Plan for Milton Keynes*, vol. 1 (Wavendon: *Milton Keynes Development Corporation*, 1970), 23.

59 Milton Keynes Development Corporation, ed., *The Plan for Milton Keynes*, vol. 2. (Wavendon: *Milton Keynes Development Corporation*, 1970), 284.

60 Bernhard Siegert, "(Not) in Place: The Grid, or, Cultural Techniques of Ruling Spaces," in *Cultural Techniques: Grids, Filters, Doors, and Other Articulations of the Real* (New York: Fordham University Press, 2015), 107–108.

61 On the MARS Group, see John Gold, "The MARS Plans for London, 1933–1942: Plurality and Experimentation in the City Plans of the Early British Modern Movement," *Town Planning Review* 66, no. 3 (July 1995): 243–267; and John Gold: "'A Very Serious Responsibility'? The MARS Group, Internationality and Relations with CIAM, 1933–39," *Architectural History* 56 (2013): 249–275, here 261–268.

62 Cf. Gilles Deleuze, "Postcript à une société de contrôle," *L'autre journal* 1 (May 1990).

63 Fry, *Fine Buildings*, 106–114. See also Arthur Korn and Felix J. Samuely, "A Master Plan for London: Based on Research carried out by the Town Planning Committee of the M.A.R.S. Group," *The Architectural Review* 91, no. 546, 1942, 143–150; Arthur Korn, Maxwell Fry, and Dennis Sharp, "The M.A.R.S. Plan for London," *Perspecta* 13/14 (1971): 163–173.

64 Bressey, *Highway Development Survey 1937 (Greater London)*, 5–6.

65 Richard Llewelyn-Davies, "Changing Goals in Design: The Milton Keynes Example," in *New Towns: The British Experience*, ed. Hazel Evans (London: Knight for the Town and Country Association, 1972), 102–116, here 105–106.

66 Llewelyn-Davies, "Changing Goals in Design."

67 John Durham Peters, *Speaking into the Air: A History of the Idea of Communication* (Chicago: University of Chicago Press, 2000), 5. This is also the argument that Melvin Webber, who was part of the Consultant Team in Milton Keynes, developed most prominently in his essay "The Urban Place and the Nonplace Urban Realm," in *Explorations into Urban Structure*, ed. Melvin Webber et al. (Philadelphia: University of Pennsylvania Press, 1964), 79–153.

68 Lee Shoshak, "The Witness Seminar," in *The Best Laid Plans: Milton Keynes Since 1967*, ed. Mark Clapson et al. (Luton: University of Luton Press, 1998), 28.

69 Llewelyn-Davies, "Changing Goals in Design: The Milton Keynes Example," 102–116, here 113.

70 See David Lock, "The Witness Seminar," in *The Best Laid Plans: Milton Keynes Since 1967*, ed. Mark Clapson et al. (Luton: University of Luton Press, 1998), 28. See also Michael Edwards, "City Design: What Went Wrong at Milton Keynes," *Journal of Urban Design* 6, no. 1 (2001): 87–96. Edwards was a member of the initial design team and systematically lists the differences between the plan and its realization.

→ Reyner Banham, "The New Brutalism," *Architectural Review*, 1955

In the chapel of Notre Dame du Haut *at Ronchamp, Le Corbusier is generally felt to have achieved one of the most personal and surprising buildings of his career. In the first flurry of excitement at its unexpected forms, consternation has been expressed at the way a master of logical structure has set his great curving roof apparently afloat above the apexes of the massive and perforated walls—the narrow glazed gap between roof and walls can be seen in the exterior views opposite. Maturer consideration will be able to evaluate how far the success of the plastic effect justifies such anti-structural usages and, as a step toward such evaluation, James Stirling will contribute an appreciation of* Notre Dame du Haut *in the new year.*

Reyner Banham

THE NEW BRUTALISM

'L'Architecture, c'est, avec des matières bruts, établir des rapports émouvants.' Le Corbusier: *Vers une Architecture.*

Introduce an observer into any field of forces, influences or communications and that field becomes distorted. It is common opinion that *Das Kapital* has played old harry with capitalism, so that Marxists can hardly recognize it when they see it, and the wide-spread diffusion of Freud's ideas has wrought such havoc with clinical psychology that any intelligent patient can make a nervous wreck of his analyst. What has been the influence of contemporary architectural historians on the history of contemporary architecture?

They have created the idea of a Modern Movement—this was known even before Basil Taylor took up arms against false historicism—and beyond that they have offered a rough classification of the 'isms' which are the thumb-print of Modernity into two main types: One, like *Cubism*, is a label, a recognition tag, applied by critics and historians to a body of work which appears to have certain consistent principles running through it, whatever the relationship of the artists; the other, like *Futurism*, is a banner, a slogan, a policy consciously adopted by a group of artists, whatever the apparent similarity or dissimilarity of their products. And it is entirely characteristic of the New Brutalism—our first native art-movement since the New Art-History arrived here—that it should confound these categories and belong to both at once.

Is Art-History to blame for this? Not in any obvious way, but in practically every other way. One cannot begin to study the New Brutalism without realizing how deeply the New Art-History has bitten into progressive English architectural thought, into teaching methods, into the common language of communication between architects and between architectural critics. What is interesting about R. Furneaux Jordan's parthian

Robin Boyd

THE SAD END OF NEW BRUTALISM

The Second World War, which should have made the world safe for that one great architecture, true to the twentieth century, only made it cosy for the pragmatic development and commercial exploitation of the ideas for which two generations of pioneers had fought. In many parts of the world after 1945 various regional, related offspring of the central movement went through a similar life-cycle, though not quite simultaneously. Scattered pockets of believers engaged in brief and not very violent skirmishes with public taste to establish or re-establish the tenets of modern architecture. Impatience for a quick decision led to some concessions being made, both consciously and unconsciously. Then the believers were joined by many others and in no time formal recognition was gained. Almost immediately an unexpected wave of popularity carried modern architecture to heights of worldly success undreamed of in pre-war Europe.

However, it was no longer the same thing. The purity was gone. The principles were one by one set aside and practice quickly declined into relative decadence of various kinds: in the USA to an effete arcaded prettiness, in Scandinavia and England to picturesque cottage-mongering, in many other places to tasteless featuristic ornamentation. Success spoiled modern architecture. But not completely. Even in the darkest hours the spirit of the real architecture, true to its new social attitudes and new technological methods, never really died. It was kept alive in the side channels away from the mainstream, in earnest talk and little publications, and in drawings for competitions or other dream projects that would never be built.

In this sort of night studio life the spirit flickered on. A fairly inevitable reaction to the weakness of all the watering-down set in, and the true spirit flared up again. The different blazes which ignited around the world about the same time—it was the middle of the 1950's—showed rather different sparks and colours. Yet, unalike as they looked, they were strongly linked by motive. Kenzo Tange reacting against modern *shibui*, Paul Rudolph or Louis Kahn reacting against the growth of which Yamasaki is the blossom, the Smithsons reacting against early Roehampton, and other links of the chain-reaction in many places, all produced works which had in common at least one thing: the quality of aggressive candour.

It was no coincidence, of course, that this was precisely the quality with which Le Corbusier, just a decade earlier, had reacted against the most tiresomely elegant of all European cultures. All these architects wanted to emphasize, with the assurance of mass, their new stand against compromise and any kind of pandering to popular aesthetic conventions. Le Corbusier took obvious pleasure in rubbing the smug taste of Parisians with rough, raw concrete and pouring pots of his hideous off-primary paints into the wounds. Not really sadistically; only to make absolutely certain that everyone got his message.

The exciting story of this revival of the rebellious spirit of early modern architecture may either be taken chronologically, or dissected by regions or personalities or visual sub-fashions, or sub-divided into personal intellectual theories. Whichever standpoint is taken, the same people, events and buildings inevitably will be cited again and again to show a different aspect of the development. If for instance one wants to make the point that regionalism lingers on despite the levelling influences of this century, then quite a number of interesting observations can be made about the points where British, Continental, Japanese and American works, all in this same genre, depart from one another. Or if one cares to take a stand on the most thoroughly discussed and documented of the theories associated with this return to strength, then those same buildings may suddenly seem all of a kind. All will look to be New Brutalist.

Dr. Reyner Banham, taking a steady central position on this stand in his book,* sees evidence of the English section of this movement radiating influence out to at least three corners of the earth. Not that his is a boisterous book, bragging about the extent of the influence of the peculiarly English thing called New Brutalism; on the contrary, in the end it leaves behind a wistful, almost haunting sense of sadness. Nevertheless, Dr. Banham wanted, as well as to tell a chapter of recent history, to establish a point without which the chapter might seem unworthy of a full-dress book. The point was, of course, that the impact of this one regional phenomenon was world-wide. That he submits his case with skill goes without saying, and if it was an impossible task it was still well worth the try. For the New Brutalism was certainly the most articulate of all the attempts to re-establish the original integrity and strength of modern architecture that occurred after the soft decade following the war. Yet it cannot be inflated more than that.

**The New Brutalism* By Reyner Banham. London. 1966: The Architectural Press. 80s

← Robin Boyd, "The Sad End of New Brutalism," *Architectural Review*, 1967

Accidens

The architectural debate of the immediate postwar era began with a series of competing claims for a "New Humanism," a "New Empiricism," a "New Palladianism," and even, as an antithesis, a "New Brutalism."[1] This rush for innovation, at least rhetorically, is by no means limited to the period, if only for the fact that modernism has often been synonymous with the "new": new ways of living, new ways of building, new materials, new construction methods, new processes; and moreover new vocabularies and new ways of writing, or new optics and new ways of seeing. Even human beings, from the new protagonists—"pioneers" of the 1930s or postwar "visionaries"—to the actual inhabitants of architecture (the standardized modern man, or the individualized personality of postmodernism), have constantly been cast and recast anew. Newness is the path *vers une architecture*, regardless of whether one calls this path new or not.

The interwar protagonists, following in the footsteps of their predecessors—most notably Otto Wagner and Hermann Muthesius—set the tone for this paradigm. If in the late 1920s modern architecture was proclaimed the "new building style," and in the 1930s its pioneers, from William Morris to Walter Gropius, were canonized in a first appraisal,[2] by 1941 it was already being hailed as a "new tradition."[3] In short, if by around 1930 "contemporary," "new" and "modern" were used interchangeably,[4] then in just one decade this collusion was given a historical legitimacy, which would carry on beyond the Second World War.

But if "new" is imperative to progress, then "old" must be eclipsed. From its very beginnings, the modern was wedded to the idea of the "old": Neue Sachlichkeit replaces Expressionism; the Movimento Rationale replaces the Novecento. New Brutalism can only exist in opposition to a rehashed and trivial Corbusian modernism; and postmodernism displaces the International Style before deconstructivism finally propels it into ultimate obscurity. Whereas the interwar modernists demonstratively abolished the old, the postwar architects and historians meticulously dismantled the modernists' convictions. And even when newness was reversed—when parts of the old became new again, as in the various proposals of postwar publishing—the argument remained unchanged: whatever the architecture of the immediate past, raze it, burn it, or, as Charles Jencks would have it in *Postmodern Architecture*, just blow it up.

These instances have already been acknowledged in great detail, not least as a typical, almost ironic, trope of the avant-garde whose very identity implies progression.[5] However, what has been surprisingly neglected is the question of what it would mean to examine the modern less as a series of ruptures but in all of its subsequent iterations and derivations; not simply as rhetorical exercises (such as Giedion's supposition that the Eiffel Tower was the immediate precursor to the Van Nelle Factory), but as real, physical phenomena (as illustrated in an issue of the *Architectural Review* of 1959, in an apposition linked by arrows of La Villa Savoye labeled "then" and "now"); not as postulates for a new style or approach, but in terms of specific functions and performance. Crucially, what could be discovered by homing in on the moment when the new gets old, when the materials start to fail, when infrastructure no longer

↓ Eiffel Tower and Van Nelle Factory, in Sigfried Giedion, *Bauen in Frankreich*, 1928

→ Ian Nairn, "Counter-Attack," drawing by Gordon Cullen, *Architectural Review*, 1956

Abb. 58. HÄNGENDE STIEGEN im Innern des EIFFELTURMS

(Verbindung vom Erdgeschoß zur ersten Plattform.)
Man sieht neben den Stiegen die Fahrbahn des Aufzuges. Bis zu formalen Details wie den horizontalen Geländern der luftigen Stiegen, findet das heutige Wollen seine Vorgängerschaft. Vgl. Abb. 62.

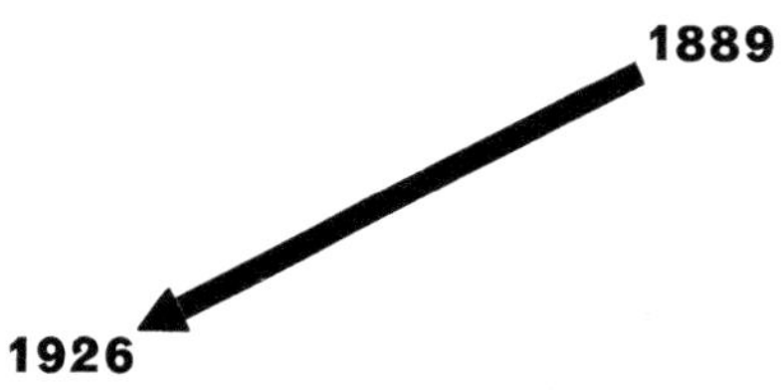

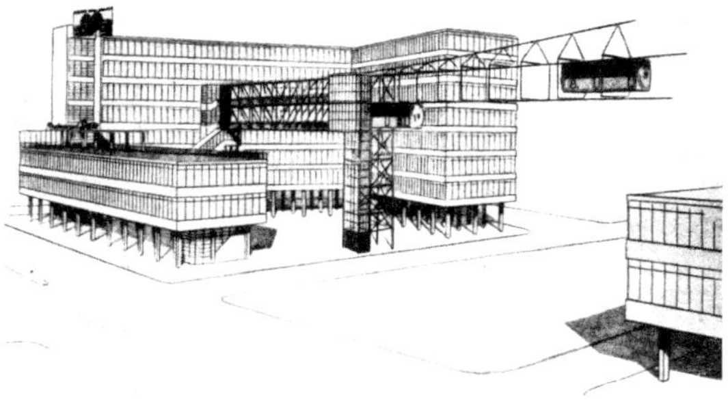

Abb.59. MART STAM: ÜBERBAUUNG DES ROKIN DAM AMSTERDAM 1926

Erst jetzt erfahren die Keime, die in Bauten wie dem Eiffelturm liegen, ihre eigentliche Auswertung. Nicht nur in der Verbindung und Durchdringung eines Baus mit schwebenden Verkehrsmitteln oder freihängenden Stationen liegt das sinnverwandte mit einem Bau wie dem Eiffelturm; wie dort wird man zu der Feststellung veranlaßt: DIE ARCHITEKTUR HAT KEINE STARREN GRENZEN MEHR.

how the sequence works: two scenes rescued from subtopia and restored to town and country.

TOWN | **COUNTRY**

rock-bottom subtopia

The two views below, although imaginary, are all too familiar. Wildernesses that in 1956 pass for town and country. How did they get like this? How can they be reclaimed? The TECHNIQUE of reclaiming the wilderness and creating true urbanity and rurality is demonstrated in the following sequence of drawings.

1 restore the unities

The first principle is respect for the category. Ask the question: What am I dealing with? Wild, country, arcadia, town or metropolis? Having decided, stick to the category and augment its proper character. Town: remove suburban rockery roundabout and hoarding decoration; respect architectural integrity in shopfronts. Country: informal road and footpath are adequate: replace suburban rockery and planting by mixed hedge, remove urban advertising.

(over) *(over)*

← "The last second," in *Der gefährliche Augenblick* [The dangerous moment], 1931

↙ "The fateful spark," in *Der gefährliche Augenblick* [The dangerous moment], 1931

→ "The collapse of the tower," in *Der gefährliche Augenblick* [The dangerous moment], 1931

↓ "The sinking of the Vestris," in *Der gefährliche Augenblick* [The dangerous moment], 1931

runs and when construction no longer meets its required demands. To put it another way, what if, in looking at the history of modern architecture, the emphasis was placed less on the arrival of innovations than on their degradation. The building would then no longer be a vehicle for rhetoric or a symbol of newness but, more practically, it would become an object that weathers and wears. In short, by looking both at *what* happens (in Latin, *accidens*)[6] and *when* things happen accidently, modernism would have to be recast not only as a succession of innovations but also as a historiography of breakages, destructions, abandonments, and failures, shading light into the neglected side of architectural modernism through innumerous incidents, that paved its parkour.[7]

Failure is wedded to the modern endeavor, its progress and its technical inventions. Unlike the natural catastrophes that defined the pre-industrial age, which came without warning or explanation, the accident is not an exception. It heralds the "perilous moment" that Ernst Jünger associated with the turn of the twentieth century, whose spectacular accidents—the sinking of the Titanic, the explosion of the Zeppelin, the oil explosion in Santa Fe or the burning down of the Church Tower of the Michaeliskirche in Hamburg—are more memorable than the inventions that prompted them. As Paul Virilio has similarly written, technologies rush on ahead of their users who have a lag of several years of being suspicious or skeptical before adopting them. Above all, technologies outpace their inventors,[8] taking the form of improbable confluences, erroneous assumptions, and epistemological limitations.[9]

↑ Train wreck at Montparnasse Station, Place de Rennes side (now Place du 18 Juin 1940), Paris, 1895

While etymologically, architecture can be considered a technical object, its existence is more paradoxical than that of other technical objects. Very few structures are so profoundly ingrained in our lives than those produced by architecture—the partitions that shield us from prying eyes, the cold, or noise; walls and supports that guarantee sturdiness; windows that allow us to interact with the outside; various technical fixtures that ensure comfort. But as physically present as many of these elements, infrastructures, and appliances are, they remain largely invisible to the user. It is only when the system breaks down, when the cable or the pipe falters, when the promised comfort fails to materialize that we become conscious of it. At this point architecture shifts from its role as a backdrop to an object of general concern.[10]

Le Corbusier's Villa Savoye is a particularly good example for illustrating this paradox. Celebrated by its contemporaries as a breakthrough in modern history, within a few years it had become "bad ruins," as Nikolaus Pevsner wrote in the *Architectural Review*, two decades after the villa's completion.[11] The "Five Points of Modern Architecture," which had been quickly adopted as key characteristics of modern architecture—as for instance in F. R. S. Yorke's *Modern House* (1934)[12]—were the very reasons for its endangerment: there was the noise of the rain on the skylight in the bathroom, which due to the open plan penetrated through to the bedroom; the lack of rigidity in the framework of the free facades, which required reinforcement and the seepage of rainwater into the son's bedroom, into the guestroom and even into the bathroom via the roof terrace: "It is raining in the hall, it's raining on the ramp and the wall of the garage is absolutely soaked ... it's still raining in my bathroom, which floods when it rains," wrote a desperate Madame Savoye to Le Corbusier only a few years after the completion.[13]

Failure is therefore also invariably a disclosure. It is only the occurrence of the accident that enables the invention to be understood and, simultaneously, its technical system to be disclosed. Viewed from this perspective it is a knowledge gain.[14] It is therefore somewhat surprising that in the history of modern architecture, the documentation of failure has been of little interest to modern historians. Sigfried Giedion, while fascinated by new technologies, largely avoids the topic, with the exception of some short remarks on the unexpected phantasmagorical dimension associated with upholstered furniture, or the dysfunctionalities of the mechanized household.[15] Reyner Banham, while celebrating the industrial age as the era of invention, also named it the "dark satanic century" due to the pollution caused by those very inventions. Even in the 1950s and 60s, as postwar architecture was experiencing rapid deterioration in Britain, members of the Independent Group and their followers explained its decline not in terms of failure but as part of an "aesthetic of change" or "expendability."[16] More technically Richard Llewelyn-Davies' Joint Unit for Planning Research identified some years later "structural degeneration" and "functional obsolescence" as two categories of "aging."[17]

While the theoretical and practical contributions to architecture of postwar Britain, especially of those of the protagonists of New Brutalism, are largely recognized, hardly any of the buildings produced by the internationally celebrated avant-garde have escaped, at the very least, the threat of demolition. The scope of reasons for this is broad: from the failing of a single technical object, like the air conditioning, to that of a whole social system. A good example is the Hunstanton School (1954), the debut project of Alison and Peter Smithson, applauded as revolutionary and praised by Banham for its "clear exhibition of structure," its "valuation of materials 'as found,'" and its "memorability as image."[18] But "clear exhibition of structure" could also be read as one of the main reasons for the substantial thermal bridges caused by the steel, glass, and brick architecture. By the same measure, the "valuation

↓ Villa Savoye, in Nikolaus Pevsner, "Time and Le Corbusier," *Architectural Review*, 1959

→ James Gowan and James Stirling, Leicester Engineering Building, Leicester, 1957–1963

↘ James Gowan and James Stirling, Leicester Engineering Building, Leicester, 2016

of materials 'as found,'" could be singled out as the culprit behind the reverberating effect of the brickwork in the hall. And the extreme heat and cold ultimately caused by the single glazing on the south side of the building could prompt one to question the enduring quality of its image.[19] Another example, Stirling and Gowan's Engineering Building at the University of Leicester (1963), was hailed as a "world-class building," one of the few produced in postwar England or for that matter at all,[20] "far ahead of its technological performance."[21] While its innovations rushed on ahead of critics attached to their own formal canon, such as Pevsner, who cited a series of infringements of the rules set by the building's modernist predecessors (projects he cherished), the object also outpaced its inventors: on the very first night it opened, the workshop suffered "leaks, draughts, and extremes of hot and cold" caused by the "flimsy aluminum stick system" holding "two thin sheets of float glass, separated by a fiber-glass matt." This was not rectified until fifty years later.[22]

Add to the list John Bancroft's Pimlico School in London (1970), distinguished by its innovative in-house installations. The environment was so well-tempered that when the air conditioner was vandalized in the school's first term, cooling the building became impossible given its extensive glazing.[23] As with all technical objects in which discrete parts coalesce to form a coerced whole, the failure of a single component sufficiently paralyzed the entire system. Lauded as a "historical monument of the future" on completion, the commendation took on new meaning when, forty years later, the building was finally demolished.[24]

These examples, in which the rhetoric of the new is describing innovation while also standing for the physical building's demise, can be extended almost indefinitely. At the same time, the potential failures of this period are so numerous and varied that it is almost impossible to formulate a meaningful hypothesis on the overall significance of the failure in architecture. The most obvious way to tackle these failures would be to categorize them by type. Thus, within the category of faulty design, which can be traced to a single element, one finds the single-glazing, lack of sun screens, and open joinings in Hunstanton; the leaking roof of the Engineering Building at Leicester; or accidents where external forces have resulted in the collapse of a building or building parts, such as the 1968 fall of the corner of the Ronan Point Council Estate in Newham, two months after the project was completed. Another category might potentially summarize the flaws of the in-house technical installations where the roots of the failure lie less in an isolated element than in the different parameters that must be factored into the built equation, such as heating, ventilation, glazing, alignment, or, eventually, the number of visitors or machines. Here, in addition to Bancroft's school, is James Stirling's History Faculty Library in Cambridge (1968), whose large, glazed reading room became a hothouse in summer, made even hotter due to

the large ventilator that remained permanently off because it proved too noisy.[25] That the sweltering conditions were the result of faulty pre-planning, which forced the building to be swiveled ninety degrees southeast, also places it in a third category, which covers parameters such as the legal or economic circumstances that directly influence a building and its planning.

Often negligence, errors, or accidents are so complex and numerous that they compound one another, prompting a fourth category. In this case the technical failures appear to be subsidiary to external factors, even if time and again technical shortcomings are part of the equation.[26] The failure of the Southgate Estate (1967–76) for the new town of Runcorn (Stirling again), was not only due to technical or architectural factors, such as poor access to transport infrastructure, physical construction weaknesses in pre-fabricated elements, high heating costs, and typological deficiencies (such as the open-air galleries conceived as public access routes or the undefined open spaces between the block rows). The harsh economic climate played its part, as the onset of the recession drove the middle classes away from the region.[27] But also take into account the failures arising in the planning process—as in the case of Alexandra Road Estate (1978)—in which differing factors such as rising labor costs, alterations in the program during the course of construction, legal uncertainties, administrative hurdles, inflation, or an unstable building ground (the result of incorrectly determined premises) caused substantial financial obstacles and time delays.[28]

That such a prescient observation can also be wrong, or at least dependent on the social context, reveals the complexity of failure in architecture, and its ability to transform. While Runcorn was demolished fifteen years after its completion, in the same amount of years Alexandra Road was the first twentieth-century housing project to be listed as a British monument.[29] So was, a few years later, Park Hill Estate (1957–61) as the then largest listed estate in Europe.

↖ Jack Lynn and Ivor Smith for the Sheffield City Council, Park Hill Estate, Sheffield, 1957–1961

↑ Jack Lynn and Ivor Smith for the Sheffield City Council, Park Hill Estate, Sheffield, 2007

To be sure, compared to other highly complex technical objects that can result in catastrophic consequences, the failures of these projects are simultaneously more complex, yet less stark,[30] even if, as in the different housing projects, this failure applies to an entire system in both its architectural and political dimensions.[31]

At first glance these various categories seem distinct (what does single-glazing have to do with the placement of an apartment block?). However, they inform one another. Depending on the perspective, a project like Hunstanton, could be understood in practical terms as one single, containable failure—glazing, for example. Yet, at the same time the failure can also be rationalized as the result of a collection of underlying technical, political, and economic conditions that stretch back to the state of glass production in the late 1940s, the scarcity of steel in Britain, the war-time economy, notions of comfort, and the development of steel-window frames to accommodate new aesthetic concepts. Such is the slipperiness of failure and its capacity, depending on what is at stake (or who is looking for someone to blame), to absorb one or many reasons for its appearance.

Housing projects (like Southgate), in turn, are subject to a logic similar to the technical detail, which is closely tied to precise expectation concerning performance in terms of measurable costs, construction time, social well-being or energy. This calculable rationality,[32] which applies equally to the individual object and the system, is mirrored in the respective manuals of the postwar period (from the technical guidelines issued by the Building Research Station and other firms, to the reports from the Ministry of Housing), in regulations and laws, and in diverse statistics. The material published was regularly updated to reflect prior practice, new findings, or shifting socio-cultural premises, trying to weed out the uncertainties both of experience and assumption. In turn, standards were never fixed for long, as the ever-changing present was constantly forced into the immediate past in order to respond to various shortcomings and new demands. This paradigm was outlined in an astonishingly clear-sighted essay of 1967 concerning the ostensible failings of social housing, whose authors hypothesized that more slums would probably be built in the following five years than in the preceding twenty.[33] As much a criticism of the official prognoses as the technical flaws, the statement—similar to accident research—pre-empts the risk of failure. While precisely trying to prevent—or to at least protect from—failures and errors, these diverse forms of institutionalization, illustrate the intricate relationship in architecture between real and metaphorical precision.

This endeavor to objectify the means and instruments of architectural design and to make it seemingly more plannable can be traced in postwar modernism at various levels: from the level of urban planning in the division of the city (be it by function, by traffic categories, or on social criteria); to the level of the house (first, with the precise calculation of the room sizes and lighting, later with the determination of the patterns of life); to the level of the object with the introduction of various apparatuses, machines and infrastructures that could be assigned a specific task, and finally to the level of materials, whose performance could be continually quantified and reassessed, by institutions like the Building Research Station, or by an array of experts: construction engineers, buildings physicists, traffic engineers or cyberneticists among others.

Looking again at Hunstanton, the thin roof-girders, calculated by the young engineer Ronald Jenkins from Ove Arup's office, were based on the so-called plastic theory, which had first been introduced in the faculty of engineering at Cambridge University in 1946 and taken up in the English Building Code only a few years later in 1948.[34] A similar kind of contact-tracing extends to Stirling's library at Cambridge, where Heppenstall, the heating and ventilation engineer, took on the precarious brief to plan the ultimately dysfunctional ventilation system. This, along with the vinyl-coated glazing, the exact placement of the heating elements in the floor and wall panels, and the over-dimensional ventilator strove to create a wholly climate-controlled environment as expressed in the complex's pyramid-formed glazed roof. Finally, the cluster concept of urban sociology, which postulated a relationship between urban and social form (and in this case even social class) found both name and form in Denys Lasdun's Cluster Block comprising four wings, each made up of stacked terraced-type housing, with "streets in the air."[35]

What the rise and acceptance of all these diverse forms of specialization foreshadow is a situation where the rationalism of enlightened modernism is abandoned in favor of an instrumental, reactive, calculable, and, above all, easily administrable performance. Banham would aptly demonstrate its architectural consequences with the example of the failed and refurbished facade of the Armée du Salut building, showing how the technological advancements of Le Corbusier's *machine à habiter* (that is precisely what he called it) dissected the traditional supporting, protective, isolating walls to reveal individual, distinct, functional components: the glass wall against the rain, the *brise-soleil* for the sunshine, the *mur neutralisant* for the climate, or the sound-proofed wall against noise. Yet while le Corbusier linked the "machine" to a singular object—the chair as *machine à s'assoir*; the house as *machine à habiter*; the plane as *machine à voler*; the temple as *machine à émotion*—by the late 1960s this notion would encompass a whole technical ensemble of the building and its environment.[36]

But beyond the increasing numbers of specialists and functionally individualized elements and the ever-more calculable performance that determines the operational character of architecture is one final dimension. As early as 1934, Lewis Mumford, writing in *Technics and Civilization*, located the social role of technology by distinguishing between machines as concrete technical objects (this implicitly included architecture) and "the machine," which he saw as the total technological complex of both a society and an epoch, and what he considered to be the prerequisite for the former.[37] Mumford inverts the rule of architecture as a machinic object whose functions can be ascribed, isolated and identified. It is in fact "the machine" that creates the preconditions, because the machine is social before it becomes technological—or architectural.[38]

Here, the limit between technical failure and the trespassing of normative margins of failure collapse. The accident is not related solely to a single technical object, whose failure can be easily inferred, but to something more abstract: to the array of new professional expertise (such as statistics, material-science, or sociology), new processes (such as pre-fabrication) and new actors (such as mechanical engineers or urban sociologists), that all inform the matter of architecture (since ever considered the source of errors).[39] These factors, while redefining its norms, operate within and outside of the object of architecture, incrementally reorganizing and redesignating the profession. They would far more profoundly transform the discipline and the role of the architect than any formal invention, whether called "New Objectivity," "New Empiricism," "New Brutalism," or otherwise.

← James Stirling and Partners, Southgate Housing, Runcorn, 1967–1976

↓ James Stirling and Partners, Southgate Housing, Runcorn, 1991

1 Joan Ockman, "New Empiricism and the New Humanism," *Design Book Review* 41/42 (Winter/Spring 2000): 18–21.

2 Nikolaus Pevsner, *Pioneers of the Modern Movement: From William Morris to Walter Gropius* (London: Faber & Faber, 1936).

3 Sigfried Giedion, *Space, Time and Architecture: The Growth of a New Tradition* (Cambridge, MA: Harvard University Press, 1941).

4 A good example for this interchangeability are the different titles used in the English and German editions of Bruno Tauts study of contemporary architecture: Bruno Taut, *Modern Architecture* (London: The Studio, 1929), respectively: *Die neue Baukunst in Europa und Amerika* (Stuttgart: Hoffmann, 1929).

5 See for instance the special issue "Das Neue/What's New," *Daidalos* 52, no. 15 (June 1994) and more recently Daniel Abramson, *Obsolescence* (Chicago: University of Chicago Press, 2016)

6 Paul Virilio, *Ce qui arrive* (Arles: Actes Sud, 2002), 23–24.

7 The role of the incidental accident in architecture and landscape has been beautifully layed out in Edward Eigen, *On Accident: Episodes in Architecture and Landscape* (Cambridge, MA: The MIT Press, 2018): here especially 1–9.

8 Peter Glasner, "Entgleisungen im deutschen Kaiserreich: 'Das Eisenbahnunglück' von Thomas Mann," in *Die Unordnung Der Dinge: Eine Wissens—Und Mediengeschichte Des Unfalls*, ed. Christian Kassung (Bielefeld: Transcript Verlag, 2009), 187.

9 John Downer, "On Ignorance and Apocalypse: A Brief Introduction to 'Epistemic Accidents,'" in *Safety Science Research: Evolution, Challenges and New Directions*, ed. Jean-Christophe Le Coze (Milton: CRC Press LLC, 2019): 75–85, here 83.

10 Bruno Latour, "Why Has Critique Run out of Steam? From Matters of Fact to Matters of Concern," *Critical Inquiry* 30, no. 2 (Winter 2004): 225–248.

11 Nikolaus Pevsner, "Time and Le Corbusier," *Architectural Review* 125, no. 747 (March 1959): 159–65.

12 F. R. S. Yorke, *The Modern House* (London: Architectural Press, 1934), 40–41, 52–53.

13 Jacques Sbriglio, *Le Corbusier: La Villa Savoye* (Basel: Birkhäuser, 2015), 110–112. Quotation: letter from Eugénie Savoye to Le Corbusier, September 7, 1936, Fondation Le Corbusier, Paris, H112157.

14 Virilio, *Ce qui arrive*, 23–24.

15 Sigfried Giedion, *Mechanization Takes Command: A Contribution to Anonymous History* (New York: Oxford University Press, 1948), 481–507.

16 Alison and Peter Smithson, "The Aesthetics of Change," *Architects' Yearbook* 8 (November 1957): 14–22; Reyner Banham, "Vehicles of Desire," *Art* 1 (September 1, 1955): 3. See also Daniel Abramson, *Obsolescence*, 67.

17 Peter Gowan, "Studies in the Growth, Change, and Ageing of Building," *The Transactions of the Bartlett Society* 1 (1962): 67–72.

18 Reyner Banham, "The New Brutalism," *Architectural Review* 118, no. 708 (December 1955): 361.

19 Steve Parnell, "The Smithsons," *Architectural Review* 231, no. 1380 (February 2012): 102–103.

20 Ellis Woodman, "Functionalism is not Enough: Leicester Engineering Department and the Question of Style," *OASE* 74 (2007): 88.

21 Stephen Cousins, "Precision Engineered," *RIBA Journal* 123, no. 11 (November 2016): 42.

22 Cousin, "Precision Engineered," 42.

23 Richard Padovan, "Comprehensive School, Pimlico, London Borough of Westminster," *Architectural Review* 150, no. 893 (July 1971): 17.

24 "The Westminster Tradition," *Architects' Journal* 152, no. 43 (8 October 1970): 992.

25 William Fawcett, "Understanding the History Faculty, Cambridge," in *Jim Stirling and the Red Trilogy: Three Radical Buildings*, ed. Alan Berman (London: Frances Lincoln, 2010): 48–50.

26 For instance, the poorly isolated prefabricated panels in Runcorn, or the badly functioning heating in Alexandra Road that would kick on in the middle of a heat wave. See Mark Swenarton, "Politics versus Architecture: The Alexandra Road Public Enquiry of 1978–1981," *Planning Perspectives* 29, no. 4 (2014): 440. (Or the glazing of the veranda sections in the Brunswick Center.)

27 "Runcorn New Town: Demontage einer Utopie," *Bauwelt* 82, no. 15 (May 1991): 764–765.

28 Swenarton, "Politics versus Architecture," 425.

29 Swenarton, "Politics versus Architecture," 425.

30 See Charles Perrow, *Normal Accidents: Living with High-Risk Technologies* (Princeton: Princeton University Press, 1999), 232.

31 These complex interrelations between material and political failure have been lucidly analysed already thirty years ago by Katharine G. Bristol, "The Pruitt-Igoe Myth," *Journal of Architectural Education* 44, no. 3 (1991): 163–171.

32 Daniela Fabricius, "Calculation and Risk: The Rational Turn in West German Architecture 1965–1985," PhD diss., (Princeton University, 2017), 32.

33 Nicholas Taylor, "The Failure of 'Housing'," *Architectural Review* 142, no. 849 (November 1967): 341.

34 Anthony Vidler, "Another Brick in the Wall," *October* 136 (Spring 2011): 117.

35 See William J. R. Curtis, *Denys Lasdun: Architecture, City, Landscape* (London: Phaidon, 1994), 51–52.

36 Le Corbusier, *Vers une architecture* (Paris: Crès, 1923 [1924]), 73, 200, 85, 173.

37 Lewis Mumford, *Technics and Civilization* (London: Routledge, 1934), 12.

38 Gilles Deleuze, *Foucault* (Paris: Les Éditions de Minuit, 2004 [1986]), 47.

39 Francesca Hughes, *The Architecture of Error: Matter, Measure, and the Misadventures of Precision* (Cambridge, MA: The MIT Press, 2014).

↙ Alison Smithson, detail from table of contents, *AS in DS*: 1983

Coda

In 1983 Alison and Peter Smithson concluded their long-term studies on mobility with the publication of *AS in DS: An Eye on the Road*. The travelogue, compiled roughly between 1972 and 1973, documents their numerous journeys up and down the A303, from their home-office in South Kensington to the Upper Lawn Pavilion at Fonthill Abbey, their holiday retreat in southwest England, as well as other trips to Cambridge and Oxford, where both architects were engaged in various teaching and research projects.[1] The *AS* in the title refers to Alison Smithson, who penned and illustrated the diary entries that make up the book; *DS* is a nod to the extremely popular model of Citroën driven by the Smithsons on these journeys—the couple owned four different models in succession, from the early 1960s to the 1980s.[2]

Manufactured from 1955 to 1975,[3] the Citroën DS was created by the Italian automobile designer Flaminio Bertoni with André Lefebvre, whose background was in aerospace engineering.[4] The car immediately captivated the public with its string of technical refinements including wide, curved windscreens, front-wheel drive, improved road grip, broad axles, hydro-pneumatic suspension, and servo-steering of the major functions.[5] Ads and brochures promised "comfort such as you have never seen before," "a home on wheels," "a theatre box" on the road, and its aerodynamic form was lauded as the epitome of modern ease. Liveability, in all senses, was the driving force behind the DS,[6] which went as far as being a lifesaving device during an assassination attempt on then-President Charles de Gaulle. Even with its tires blown out by bullets, the hydro-pneumatic suspension system leveled the car, allowing a safe getaway. Indeed, it was much more than a means of traveling. Pronounced *dé-esse*—homophonous for goddess—the DS, as Roland Barthes would articulate in 1957, as both image and object, represented a consummate collective accomplishment of its day.[7]

This was also the thrust of the arguments advanced by the Smithsons in their book. As Peter Smithson writes in the introduction, the travel diary was to be read as a modern-day "sensibility primer." Citing the ability of Jane Austen's short stories to "[add] her generation's perception of distance and time" to the eighteenth-century understanding of the English landscape by way of warfare, maritime movement, and the use of trunk roads, the Smithsons' travelogue demonstrates "the evolving sensibility of a passenger in a car to the post-industrial landscape."[8] To capture this new sensibility, the DS served as the framing device for the entire project. Thus, the shape of the book is the plan of the car. Opening the book is like opening the door (or rather the roof) and sinking into the driver's seat, as the world seen from this "private room on wheels" comes into view: alongside technical drawings of the car itself and Alison Smithson's freehand sketches, presumably made as a passenger, are maps, children's drawings that include a meandering board game "to do with the car," panoramic photographs, and snapshots arranged in time-based sequences. In the case of the photographs, the DS is always in sight—with the edges of the dashboard and car roof framing the landscape. In other instances, the view changes, becoming less first-person and more omniscient, with the car shown in its completeness parked on the shoulder of a motorway, or in front of the house in Fonthill, or near a poppy field, or in front of a hilly landscape. Sometimes the trunk opens to reveal a road-side picnic, or the door is left ajar as the driver or passenger (the photographer) stretches their legs.

If the accompanying illustrations present the objects encountered or referred to along these journeys (the road, the pitstops, the scenery), then the six chapters that make up the book present the thoughts that emerge in the minds of the passengers. Smithson's diary entries—a mix of shorthand, key words, and fleeting impressions—are organised around the question of mobility ("A New Kind of Freedom Offered by the Car"); established and novel modes of perception ("The Inherited Sensibility" and "The New Sensibility Resulting from the Moving View of Landscape," respectively); the proposal for a new semiology of motion ("The Graphics of Movement"); the domesticity of the car ("The Private Room on Wheels"); and improvements in road-building ("Change").[9] They are sometimes accompanied by geographical markers or notes regarding time of day ("night" or "evening," in the case of nocturnal journeys) or season. While in the context of the travelogue the primary focus is the road seen from the Citroën DS, the broader ambition is to survey contemporary life from the motorist's point of view.

As personal and incidental as these ideas first appear, they are consistent with the Smithsons' lifelong project to assess the impact of motorization on architecture and urban development, an endeavor they pursued in numerous publications, from their early essays on mobile and non-mobile forms of dwelling, to their studies on the reorganization of city centers in Britain. The immediate rapport that is supposedly established between a society's modes of transport and its urbanism, or between specific means of movement and forms of perception, was a recurring theme in the earlier writings of Peter Smithson: from his studies of the layout of buildings and cities in ancient Greece, characterized by their common lack of spatial planning,[10] to his analysis of the city of Bath whose architecture he claimed was a reflection of past "technologies,"[11] to his publication on Euston Station, a witness to the bygone "Railway Age" beginning with the opening of the Liverpool & Manchester Line in 1830 and which left its mark on the English landscape and the country's social structures.

The travelogue reflects this line of thought. The diary entries comprising the first chapter, "The Inherited Sensibility," paint the landscape as a traditional and picturesque sequence of stills. A "Rembrandt light-rayed sky" gives way to "fields with the pre-ripening bloom Monet saw," before a "day's-end Courbet sky of light" and a "threatening sky of a type favoured for Victorian seascapes." Colors are shades of "Millet-green," and a "delicious blue-green, such as portrayed by the Île-de-France painters." Whooshing by the passenger is an image true to the English tradition, bringing "to mind picturesque landscape drawings of travel in rain in Swiss Alps."[12] How forms of perception and architecture mutually influence one another is noted in this context too, as Alison Smithson describes the effect of depth conjured by the rounded arches of old bridges as a formal expression in the tradition of "Renaissance perspectivists."[13] Images are selected accordingly. The route is illustrated by two historical maps—one sixteenth- and one nineteenth-century—that portray the area around Fonthill not with geographical accuracy but through narrative elements such as abstract hedgerows, forests, rivers, and mountains. Drawing on this method of representation, the sketches in this chapter depict country roads as they were when traveled by horse and carriage. Crucially, though, it is not the DS that transports the reader along this first "inherited" scenic byway, but the heroic American military jeep, an homage to the first machine age, a car owned by the Smithsons when they were working on their Hunstanton School. The focus, then, with regard to modes of representation, forms of perception, and means of transport, is set squarely on the past—not a specific moment, but a collective, layered, and eclectic vision that has led the passengers to the present moment.[14]

This portrait of a past sensibility, however arbitrary its inclusions and omissions might seem (note, for example, the absence of the railway and its panoramic gaze), provides the set-up for the next chapter, "The New Sensibility."

↗ Alison Smithson, "Eye on the Road," *AS in DS*, 1983

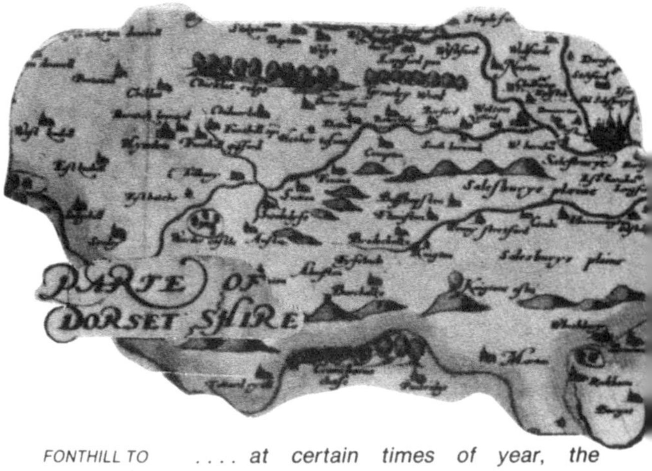

FONTHILL TO LONDON

. . . . at certain times of year, the countryside looks at its best when thoroughly wet; the colours all distil out and are water-clear; become in tone more vital than themselves in nature: as are the green plants just under the water-surface at Fontaine de Vacleuse . . . . the washed and made misty wet-laden grey-sky can be looked at as soothing in its quality . . . .

the light lasts in such a rain-washed atmosphere . . . . the dome of the sky shows the surrounding horizon clearly . . . . sheep standing in three's . . . .

cow tracks show what a wet winter's travel would have been covering this route in Beckford's time; today sitting warmly, looking forward; different from sitting beside a coachman where eyes, face, clothes would be movement-ravaged, if not torn at by weather; sheltered in a coach meant looking sideways and half the seats faced the way traversed: no conditioned heating; on a horse gave height to viewing and the possibility to stop at individual-will and look at a view longer, but could mean half-closed eyes, face turned away from the prevailing weather; in wind little or no spontaneous conversation with fellow travellers; yet in decent weather, more widespread possibilities of conversation with travellers going the other way and people met with by chance . . . .

car travels at speed in fitful, winter-tea-time traffic . . . .

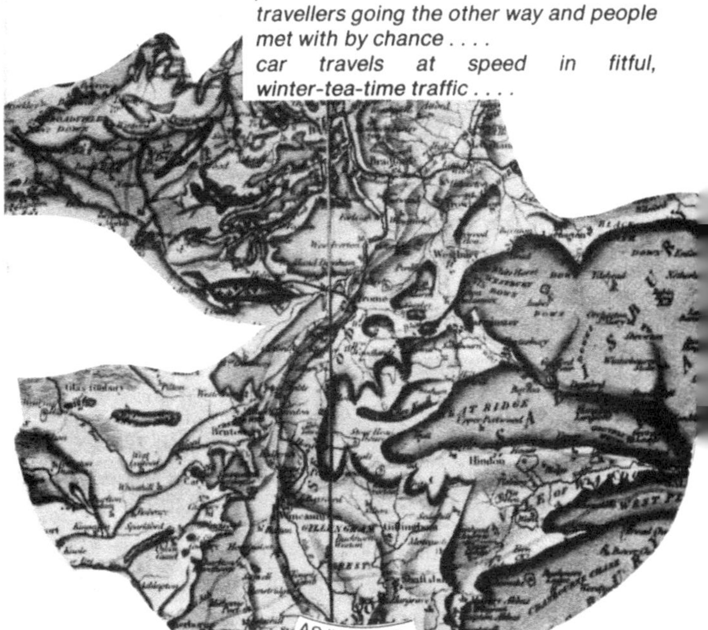

↗ Alison Smithson, "The Inherited Sensibility: The way we have been brought up to see," *AS in DS*, 1983

.... wind blowing the young wheat into the semblance of a surface of a lake, ripples across and across each rectangle without causing an overspill at the far edge ....
road passes under a slew bridge: compressed brick lines in an arching/slewing movement on a curve so precisely aim their lines these would be connected to a vanishing-point .... such visible play of geometries introduce into the bloodstream that stirring excitement described by the Surveyors to the Railways: 'the brick arches twisted their way into position': the connection of this particular heightened sensibility extends back to the Renaissance perspectivists ....

LONDON TO FONTHILL: Basingstoke old road

.... rays of golden light – a Rembrandt light-rayed sky – beams shine down from behind a skyplate of charcoal shaded clouds, on to a sooty wood ....

FONTHILL TO LONDON: Andover bypass

.... sun raying down from clouds; very Dutch looking altogether this area .... day lifting slowly .... trees – particularly birch – hang limp .... the road surface being eaten up by the car is damp .... grass banks marred with the dried remnants of the year ....
honey coloured clouds edge openings in the grey and reveal very high blue patches .... a few heaps of yellow tinted cumulus over to the east .... fumes caught in a breath of wind while speeding in damp air are reminiscent of the jeep on a German road throughout storm-ridden, wild autumn ....

LONDON TO CAMBRIDGE

a sunny patch ahead ....
a train sound .... instinctively first look at some smoke .... only then realise a train pulled by a diesel will be sliding along elsewhere ....
into the sunshine at last .... road dry

AS IN DS: 37

↗ Alison Smithson, "The Private Room on Wheels," *AS in DS*, 1983

SPECT 6: CHANGE

s something of a stocktaking ten years after e first writing of THE EYE ON THE ROAD: A ARY OF A PASSENGER'S VIEW OF CAR OVEMENT, this selected text covers the provement of roads in the decade neteen-seventy to nineteen-eighty.
e know we need to mutate places by building wards an image of towns-in-the-landscape at will satisfy the new sensibilities and allow eedom from pressures of all kinds.

BLACKBUSH

. . pines rest very easily on the mind: a erson does not even have to think about e problems of agriculture . . . .
credibly mild weather means the yellow elms is wonderfully perpetuated . . . .
olly and such shiny evergreens glisten arkly in the rain until obliterated from ght by the rain becoming a downpour . .
orse in bloom has furry cases against the ain . . . .
e car slides endlessly forward, past ecimen trees of the English landscape, e car movement allows the viewing of ach specimen in three-quarters round: if ot a mite more . . . .
dd thickets, perhaps allotment-land tended for poor cottagers to gather ggots in – certainly that sort of eak-trees of ages-past – seen in in-and-sack-cloth-weather . . . .
isty sky touches the ground now and en as the contours rise . . . .
n the tarmacadam the steely glint varies road-tilt alters towards the sky-glare . . and the road angle alters wildly, anging continually in passing the car rough the countryside under the sky . .
e car moves forever forwards, chasing me tail-lights . . . . some, but fewer, eadlights approach, and pass . . grass bright-wet . . . . hedgerows ternately line the way . . . . either make e car's progression an avenue way . . or slip in a glimpse of a ploughed ece of topography . . . .

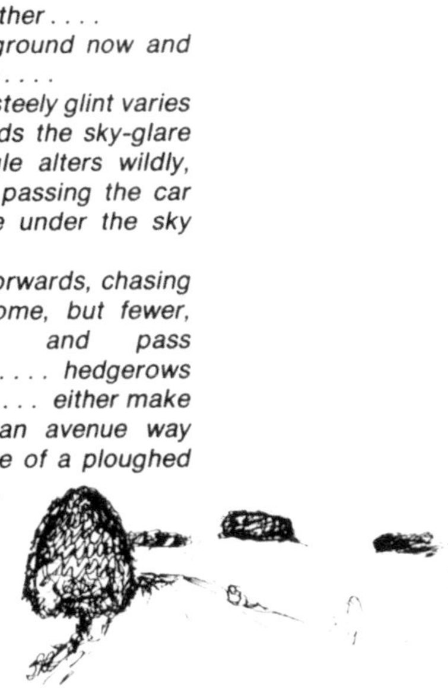

AS IN DS 131

Now the slow, contemplative gaze gives way to events that rush past one another. The ungainly tank-like American jeep has been traded in for the taut DS that now races down the motorway. The car, writes Smithson, "runs within a trapezium shaped frame: out-riding concrete kerb-faces white, the under-belting tarmac textured, fore-road ever seen in perspective." The static nineteenth-century is now a twentieth-century motion picture whose frames "[dip] further into the landscape, the effect of the long descent ... flattening to the surroundings; gradually expanding the dimensions of the hollow entered until at a certain moment, field hedgerows rise up and, shouldering leafy branches, blot out the bowl that recently was the surrounding landscape. Then, quite suddenly, the road is topping the next rise of the Plain, the car launched again into a topography that rises and falls."[15]

The frames rush by and the viewer-driver becomes aware of another cinematic quality, as movement and lighting take on a more intense and expressive character. "The sun position swings round crazily" on the journey to Oxford, so "the visors, moved not two miles/minutes ago, [must be] again adjusted as the sun now on the right."[16] Then, on a night drive from Cambridge to London, it is the moon that "slides out of the frame of the windscreen, far to the left," compelling Smithson "to further and further turn to see the moon's face over [my] her left shoulder."[17] Rain and sun, winter and summer, day and night chase each other in quick succession. The result is a breathless documentation of countless car journeys: London to Fonthill, Bullington Cross to Stonehenge, Fonthill back to London, Fonthill to Southampton or to Oxford, from Harrow to Kensington. These in turn conjure other voyages, such as a ferry crossing in Djerba. But even as Alison Smithson observes the world from her window, even as her thoughts take her to other places altogether, the car and its driver are bound to a strip of asphalt, excluded from the incessantly opening landscape. The relationship of the viewer to her environment is indirect, consisting of a rapid succession of visual sequences that are always mediated by the car: a ground that is navigated by a steering wheel, bumps that are dampened by tires and suspension, views that are experienced through the windscreen. From the car, the traditional landscape image with its depth-of-field is seen only when looking straight ahead. At the same time, a variety of new scenes are reflected via the rear-view, wing, or cosmetic mirrors that offer focused but distorted images not unlike the dark surface of a Claude glass.[18] And through the windows, even the most familiar stretch of road constantly changes depending on the weather—or how clean or dirty the glass is.

What unfolds, both outside and inside the car, is a landscape of decorative panels, Smithson later writes: a sequence of flat, abstract planes composed of tree girths and misty shadows, the contours of which become successively distinct as they drive deeper into the very rear of the stage-set, so to speak.[19] The gaze is kinetic: "cars—as if on slides—go off to the left between folds, to reappear, to pass over this car moving forward."[20] When she trails a truck laden with bales of hay, "all movement is slow motion."[21] As in the cinema, the onlooker finds herself in a seat that faces forwards, allowing her to survey the landscape while enjoying the shelter of the "glass windowed box."[22] But also—as in the cinema—the onlooker is not free. The spectrum of her gaze is relatively fixed, permitting at best an angle of twenty-five degrees to the left or the right, as Smithson discovers when she measures the width of the image framed by the curved windscreen (the gaze, as for English drivers, is directed more to the left, she notes).[23] Thus the car constitutes a closed sphere. The external environment it navigates can be surveyed only with the help of artificial viewing aids and apparatuses, such as rear-view and wing mirrors, headlights, indicators, or—even beyond the car—streetlights. In this sense, its interior may be described as a fully controlled and controllable environment completely independent of its surroundings. This was especially the case for the DS, thanks to its extraordinary level of comfort and ease of handling, which made it a "cell of perfected technology"[24] to be driven in any weather and at any time: "Sealed in a glass box on wheels, we ... do not sense the air outside, smell something only after it has passed through the ventilation system, ... read the weather through the glass of the windscreen or the side windows, feel the sun through this glass."[25] The motor drowns out the sound of the wind and the rain is merely a patter on the chassis of the car.

Yet the car is far more than a "glass-viewing-box-on-wheels." Instead, Alison Smithson ascertains, it comprises the "Private Room on Wheels." A room for enjoying a "picnic in armchair comfort, looking at a view we choose"[26] as well as a fast drive through the velvety black night. It is a place for love ("love in a box"), for playfulness, for sketching, and for work. It is a room with carpet and a radio where one can even read *The Times*.[27] It is a place in which "the delicate balance ... between togetherness/apartness" can be satisfied, a place for family and for pets. When stopped, it is even "a house on wheels."[28] When the car qualifies as housing of sorts—inasmuch as it enables its passenger to move from one controlled or controllable sphere to another—the distinction between a house, a home, and a mobile home, as coined some years earlier by Reyner Banham in a "A Home Is Not a House,"[29] becomes obsolete. While the Smithsons never voice so radical a proposal in *AS in DS*, the travelogue reflects a paradigm shift in architecture and urban planning that the couple had already posited far more emphatically. In their essay "Caravan—Embryo Appliance House?" of 1959, the caravan is identified as a symbol or, rather, a harbinger of the mobile society, and one that is well-placed, in their view, to challenge the small brick house with its expensive supply systems and tiny garden. Likewise, in their 1960 essay "Fix: Permanence and Transience," they point out that architecture has relinquished its constancy in favor of infrastructure and would therefore be subject to an "aesthetics of change."[30] Against the backdrop of these demands, the entries made in the diary, to the effect that the car is a house on wheels, or that the environment—including the city—can no longer be grasped in all its detail but only in the abstract terms of profiles and planes, fit seamlessly into the repeatedly formulated aspirations and endeavors to instate an architecture that can give expression to calls for "transformation, growth, flow and life."[31]

This new perception of a built environment is no longer understood in terms of its elevation but rather as a system of infrastructure, and the gaze that originated within the car is not only shaped by the frames of the windows, or the speed of the vehicle, but by the line of the road itself and its various interpretations as bridge, tunnel, curve, intersection, and roundabout. In turn, that road acquires a dual function as not only a traffic artery but, in the driver's unerring gaze, a monument, a topographical landmark, and the symbol par excellence of the Car Age, the characteristics of which are no longer the winding paths, but the A-road and the motorway, no longer the horse and carriage but the Citroën's horsepower, no longer the static gaze of the traveler on foot but that of the person at the wheel comfortably taking measure of speed, space, and time—all while completely ensconced in a well-tempered shell that is both everywhere and nowhere.[32] Yet unlike the outward-looking gaze, that characterizes the road views of the Townscape movement, as well as contemporary studies by the Smithsons' student Denise Scott Brown in Las Vegas,[33] or by Reyner Banham on Los Angeles[34]—all of which looked to the car as a tool for visualizing the urban environment (the road, the highway, the storefronts, the city)—the Smithsons' gaze is bi-directional, cast both on the road and on what develops within the tight frame of the box on wheels. It takes in scenes from that safe, domestic world of newspapers, radio, and children's games, as well as the rapid, changing world that is reflected in the mirror. Here, neither road nor car exists without the other, and the passenger navigates both, covering vast distances while doing the crossword, racing down the motorway, and daydreaming simultaneously. In the windshield of the car, speed, space, and time collapse, inside and outside, here and there, everywhere and nowhere.

1 According to Alison Smithson, "the idea to write this diary took hold ... on a stretch of road" between Cheltenham and Worcester. Alison Smithson, *AS in DS: An Eye on the Road* (Delft: Delft University Press, 1983), 15, 89. The publication came about in 1981–1982, during the Smithsons' guest professorship at the Technical University of Delft, which they had been invited to take up at the initiative of Otto Das and Izak Salomons following the death of Jaap Bakema. As Das kindly revealed in conversation (January 22, 2008), the booklet—and not least its contours in the shape of a DS—could be published thanks to the support of Citroën Netherlands.

2 The Smithsons owned four different models of Citroën: until 1965 an ID model' from 1966 until the early 70s a DS; until 1981 a DS Safari; and from 1981 the CX-Reflex. Alison Smithson, *AS in DS*, 157–163.

3 On the general history of the DS, cf., among others: Olivier de Serres, *Le grand livre Citroën: tous les modèles* (Paris: EPA Éditions, 1988); René Bellu, *Toutes les Citroën: des origines à nos jours* (Paris: Delville, 1979); Jacques Borgé and Nicolas Viasnoff, *L'Album de la DS* (Paris: EPA Éditions, 1992); Daniel Puiboube, *Das grosse Citroën-DS-Buch* (Königswinter: Heel, 2002). On the DS as an industrial product, cf.: "Mostra dell 'Industrial Design,'" in *Undicesima Triennale*, ed. Agnoldomenico Pica (Milan: Arti Grafiche Crespi, 1957), cv, cvii, 143–144; *Modellfall Citroën: Produktgestaltung und Werbung* [exhibition at Kunstgewerbemuseum Zurich, February 18 to April 9, 1967] (Zurich: Kunstgewerbemuseum, 1967). The latest analysis of the DS, especially its formal genealogy, is: Christian Sumi: *The Goddess—La Déesse: Investigations on the Legendary Citroën DS* (Zurich: Lars Müller Publishers, 2020).

4 Christian Sumi, "The Car: Citroën DS," in Alison Smithson, *AS in DS: An Eye on the Road* (Baden: Lars Müller, 2001), appendix.

5 Wolfgang Schmittel, *Design, Concept, Realisation: Braun, Citroën, Miller, Olivetti, Sony, Swissair* (Zurich: ABC, 1975), 60.

6 Cf. the advertising brochures in: Alison Smithson, *AS in DS*, 13; and Walter Zeichner, *Citroën ID/DS, 1955–76. Eine Dokumentation* (Stuttgart: Schrader, 2002), 10–83, here, 25, 43, 40.

7 Roland Barthes, "La nouvelle Citroën," in *Mythologies* (Paris: Éditions du Seuil 1957),169–171.

8 Peter Smithson, "AS in DS. An Eye on the Road: A Sensibility Primer," in Alison Smithson, *AS in DS: An Eye on the Road* (Delft: Delft University Press, 1983), 1; and William Cobbett, "Rural Rides," cited in Alison Smithson, *AS in DS*, 153–155.

9 Including in the publication are a brief introduction by Peter Smithson, a preface by the editor Otto Das, as well as an unpublished introduction from 1972, followed by some of William Cobbett's diary entries.

10 Peter Smithson, "Theories Concerning the Layout of Classical Greek buildings," *Architectural Association Journal* 74, no. 829 (1959): 194–209.

11 Alison and Peter Smithson, *Without Rhetoric. An Architectural Aesthetic 1955–1972* (Cambridge, MA: The MIT Press 1974), 66.

12 Alison Smithson, *AS in DS*, 45.

13 Alison Smithson, *AS in DS*, 34, 38–39.

14 Cf. here the special "Outrage" issue of the *Architectural Review* edited by Ian Nairn and illustrated by Gordon Cullen: *Architectural Review* 117, no. 702 (1955). Under the title "Route Block" (393–438) a mix of historical and contemporary maps, photos of the road (and taken on the road), and sketches is already in evidence. In a 1981 conversation with Michiel Polak and Karin Theunissen, Peter Smithson mentioned the influence of the writings of John Brinckerhoff Jackson: "He does what we try to do on England. He tries to observe American landscape as it is." As shared by Otto Das with the author (the unpublished interview took place in London in autumn 1981).

15 Alison Smithson, *AS in DS*, 47.

16 Alison Smithson, *AS in DS*, 64.

17 Alison Smithson, *AS in DS*, 65.

18 Alison Smithson, *AS in DS*, 111.

19 Alison Smithson, *AS in DS*, 71, 76, 78.

20 Alison Smithson, *AS in DS*, 76.

21 Alison Smithson, *AS in DS*, 55.

22 Alison Smithson, *AS in DS*, 16, 84.

23 Alison Smithson, *AS in DS*, 16.

24 Alison Smithson, *AS in DS*, 111.

25 Alison Smithson, *AS in DS*, 17.

26 Alison Smithson, *AS in DS*, 111.

27 Alison Smithson, *AS in DS*, 144, 141.

28 Alison Smithson, *AS in DS*, 53.

29 Reyner Banham and François Dallegret, "A Home Is Not a House," *Art in America* 2 (1965): 70–79.

30 Alison and Peter Smithson, "Caravan—Embryo Appliance House," *Architectural Design* 29, no. 9 (1959): 248; Alison and Peter Smithson, "Fix: Permanence and Transience," *Architectural Review* 128, no. 766 (1960): 437–439.

31 Alison and Peter Smithson, "Cluster City," *Architectural Review* 122, no. 730 (1957): 333.

32 Comprehensive literature on the architectonic design of roads and motorways came out of this era. See Donald Appleyard, Kevin Lynch, and John R. Myer, *The View from the Road* (Cambridge, MA: The MIT Press, 1964); Christopher Tunnard and Boris Pushkarev, *Man-Made America: Chaos or Control? An Inquiry into Selected Problems of Design in the Urbanized Landscape* (New Haven: Yale University Press, 1963); Lawrence Halprin, *Freeways* (New York: Reinhold, 1966).

33 See Robert Venturi, Denise Scott Brown, and Steven Izenour, *Learning from Las Vegas* (Cambridge, MA: The MIT Press, 1972). See also, among others, Stanislaus von Moos and Martino Stierli, eds., *Eyes that Saw: Architecture after Las Vegas* (New Haven: Yale School of Architecture, 2020). On the complicated relation between the Smithsons and Scott Brown, see: Denise Scott Brown, "Learning from Brutalism," in *The Independent Group: Postwar Britain and the Aesthetics of Plenty*, ed. Jacquelynn Baas et al. (Cambridge, MA: The MIT Press, 1990), 203–206.

34 See Reyner Banham, "Ecology IV: Autopia," in *Los Angeles: The Architecture of Four Ecologies* (London: Penguin, 1971), 213–222; *Reyner Banham Loves Los Angeles*, directed by Julian Cooper (BBC, 1972). On Banham and the perception of Los Angeles through and in movement, see Ed Dimendberg, "The Kinetic Icon: Reyner Banham on Los Angeles as Mobile Metropolis," *Urban History* 33, no. 1, special Issue "Urban Icons" (May 2006): 106–125; as well as: Tony Vidler lauds Banham for destabilizing the codes of architectural history (and one should add history of urban design). See Tony Vidler, "Introduction," in Reyner Banham, *Los Angeles: The Architecture of Four Ecologies* (Berkeley: University of California Press, 2009): xxxiii–xlix.

Index

Acknowledgments

The publication of this book was made possible thanks to the astonishing perseverance and immense generosity of Thomas Weaver, the incisive but always benevolent editing of Sarah Handelman, and the clarity and brilliance of Rosa Nussbaum's graphic design. Additional thanks to the archivists at the RIBA, Tate Britain, and more especially at the CCA Montreal, GSD Harvard, and ETH Zürich. Much of the work on this book hugely benefitted from the advice of colleagues at conferences and lectures as well as from the intellectual environment at ETH Zurich, and especially in that most favorable one at the gta institute. As many of the essays contained within this book were first developed through discussions at home, it seems only right to dedicate the book to Carlotta Darò.

Image credits

pp9, 14 (middle left, middle right, bottom), 15 (bottom left, top left), 18, 37, 38, 39, 98 (top), 114, 120–121, 122 (bottom), 127, 128, 167, 168, 175: © EMAP. p11: © Sainsbury Archive. p12: © Daily Mail Archive. p13 (top): Tate, London © Trustees of the Paolozzi Foundation / 2023, ProLitteris, Zurich. p13 (bottom): Tate, London © R. Hamilton. All Rights Reserved, 2023 ProLitteris, Zurich. p14 (top left): © Royal Society of Arts. pp14 (top right), 162, 163: Crown Copyright: Open Government License. p15 (bottom right): © Routledge. pp20, 30, 31: © Nigel Henderson Estate. pp22, 23, 32: © Lucy Bullivant / Dargan Bullivant Estate. p27 (right): © Stanley Meltzoff / Scientific American, Inc. p29 (top): © Tate Museum / ICA / ProLitteris. p33 (bottom left and right): © 2022, ProLitteris, Zurich. pp35, 50, 51, 52, 53, 56–57: James Stirling / Michael Wilford fonds, CCA, Montreal © CCA. p40: © Wilhelm Ernst & Sohn Verlag für Architektur und technische Wissenschaften GmbH & Co. KG. p42 (top): © Weitzman School of Design. p42 (bottom): © gta Archive, ETH Zurich. pp55, 60, 122 (top): © Courtesy the Frances Loeb Library. Harvard University Graduate School of Design, Alison and Peter Smithson Estate. p54: © ELSEVIER. p58: © London: Batsford. p59: © Nuffield Trust. p64: © Ludwig Museum, Köln. p65: © Gordon Cullen Estate/University of Westminster Archive. p67: © Sigfried Giedion Estate, gta archive, ETH Zurich. p70: © Courtesy of HES (William Burn Collection). p71: © The Hunterian, University of Glasgow. p72 (top): © Sir John Soane's Museum, London. p72–73 (bottom): © Scone Palace Archives. p80: © PROLITTERIS / François Dallegret. pp83, 84, 101, 177 (top): © RIBA PIX / Photo John Donat. p86: © 2022, ProLitteris, Zurich. p87 (top): © Succession Picasso / 2022, ProLitteris, Zurich. pp90, 91 (top): © RIBA PIX / Photo Dell & Wainwright. p91 (bottom): © EMAP / Photo Dell & Wainright. p92: © Reproduced with permission of the Licensor through PLSclear. p93: © Courtesy the Society of Glass Technology. p94: © Photo Stewart Bale. p96: © Photo Edward Rinker, 1944. p97: © L. F. Ehrke and Dr. C. M. Slack, 1941. p98 (bottom): © Photo Jan Versnel. p99: © J. W. Kitchenham. p102: © RIBA PIX / Photo Henk Snoek. p103: © The Journal of the Institution of Heating and Ventilating Engineers. p105: © Phillips Auctioneers LLC. pp108–109, 110–111: © EMAP / CCA. p115: © Archigram 1964. p116: © Courtesy Drawing Matter Collections / Estate of the Architect. pp118, 119: © AD / WILEY. p123 (left): © Gordon Cullen Estate. p123 (right): © RIBA PIX / Lasdun & Partners. pp124, 125: © Courtesy Private Collection. p126: © Borg-Warner Corporation / EMAP. pp129, 130: © WILEY. pp133, 153: © First Garden City Heritage Museum. pp134–140: © RIBA Collections courtesy Country Life / Future Publishing Ltd. p142 (top and bottom right): © Illustrated London News Ltd / Mary Evans. p143: © RIBA Collections. p145 (bottom left): © Liverpool University Press. pp146, 148, 149: © London Metropolitan Archives. pp150, 152: © The National Archives. p158: © Nature portfolio. p164: © Buckinghamshire Archives, Collections. p171: © Gordon Cullen Estate / University of Westminster Archive. p177 (bottom): © Peter Bale. p178: © Architectural Review—Reyner Banham. p179: © Photo Laurent Stalder. p180: James Stirling / Michael Wilford fonds, CCA, Montréal © CCA / Richard Einzig / Arcaid Images. p181: © Joe Blundell (YouTube). pp183–187: © Smithson Family Collection.

On Arrows: Essays in British Architecture and Its Environments
Laurent Stalder

© 2025 Massachusetts Institute of Technology

All rights reserved. No part of this book may be used to train artificial intelligence systems or reproduced in any form by any electronic or mechanical means (including photocopying, recording, or information storage and retrieval) without permission in writing from the publisher.

The MIT Press would like to thank the anonymous peer reviewers who provided comments on drafts of this book. The generous work of academic experts is essential for establishing the authority and quality of our publications. We acknowledge with gratitude the contributions of these otherwise uncredited readers.

Graphic design by Studio Christopher Victor
Typeset in Aktuell by Thomas Thiemich
Printed and bound in China

Library of Congress Cataloging-in-Publication Data

Names: Stalder, Laurent, author.
Title: On arrows : essays in British architecture and its environments / Laurent Stalder.
Description: Cambridge, Massachusetts : The MIT Press, [2024] | Includes bibliographical references and index.
Identifiers: LCCN 2023050675 | ISBN 9780262548991 (paperback)
Subjects: LCSH: Architecture and society—Great Britain—History—20th century. | Architecture and society—Great Britain—History—21st century. | Arrow (Symbol)
Classification: LCC NA2543.S6 S655 2024 | DDC 720.941/0904—dc23/eng/20240103
LC record available at https://lccn.loc.gov/2023050675

10 9 8 7 6 5 4 3 2 1